D1286409

PRIVATE WEALTH AND PUBLIC LIFE

PRIVATE WEALTH & PUBLIC LIFE

Foundation Philanthropy

AND THE

Reshaping of American Social Policy

FROM THE

Progressive Era

TO THE

New Deal

JUDITH SEALANDER

THE JOHNS HOPKINS UNIVERSITY PRESS
Baltimore & London

© 1997 The Johns Hopkins University Press
All rights reserved. Published 1997
Printed in the United States of America on acid-free paper
06 05 04 03 02 01 00 99 98 97   5 4 3 2 1

The Johns Hopkins University Press
2715 North Charles Street
Baltimore, Maryland 21218-4319
The Johns Hopkins Press Ltd., London

Library of Congress Cataloging-in-Publication Data will be found at the end of this book.
A catalog record for this book is available from the British Library.

ISBN 0-8018-5460-1

For Jerry Friedman
who has returned immediacy to my life
and who daily gives it meaning

CONTENTS

ACKNOWLEDGMENTS

Has the tradition of crediting words of inspiration so faded that even historians neglect it? In hope of its revival, let me begin this pleasant duty of thanks by repeating a quotation found in the University of Chicago Archives, one that has long occupied a prominent place on my study's bulletin board and to which I look often for comfort and chronological perspective. In the summer of 1926, after a long weekend spent reviewing grant requests from university professors, University of Chicago political scientist and Rockefeller philanthropies consultant Charles Merriam jotted a few "private impressions," including this one: "The mouths of the *ever hungry* Historians water as they envisage Basic Materials and Centers of Documentation at every filling station and A and P. No more flimsy paper. Amen."

Having begun with a prayer, let me continue with anthems of praise. I began this book in earnest in 1990, as scholar in residence at the Rockefeller Archive Center in Tarrytown, New York, by far the most important archive available to any serious student of the history of American philanthropy. Those who have never enjoyed a few days, much less uninterrupted months, of research time at the RAC should know that the archive provides a perfect setting in which to work. Where else can one sit in a comfortable reading room (at least, Tom Rosenbaum and I always thought the temperature was right), surrounded by expertly organized manuscript materials, delivered with daunting efficiency by a thoroughly professional and wonderful archival staff? Where else can a researcher take a few minutes' break to stand at tall Palladian windows from which views of sweeping lawns stretching down to the Hudson beckon? Where else do the archivists keep a pot of coffee and endless cans of cookies and celebrate any conceivable occasion with lavish cake festivals? I can only be grateful that I chose to walk to and fro from my lodgings and had to climb a steep hill every morning before arriving to work. Everyone at the Rockefeller Archive Center, ably directed by Darwin Stapleton, deserves much credit for making my stay so memorable and my research so productive. However, among archivists, Tom Rosenbaum and Melissa Smith stand out as ideal practitioners of their profession.

Skilled professionals at many other archives and libraries also provided much appreciated help, especially those who patiently answered my queries at the University of Chicago Archives, the Butler Library, Columbia University, and the Social Welfare Archives at the University of Minnesota. Shannon Wilson, head archivist at Berea College, Berea, Kentucky, was an especially gracious host and guide. The staff at Jerome Library, Bowling Green State University, has faithfully processed my unending requests for interlibrary loans.

A grant from the Center for the Study of Philanthropy, Indiana University, made a summerlong research trip to Chicago possible in 1993. Several smaller grants from university and departmental sources at my own institution, Bowling Green State University, helped in many ways to speed this book's completion.

If I owe thanks to librarians, archivists, and grant-givers, so too do I to colleagues and friends. Chief among the latter are two I have the privilege of claiming as mentors. The unfortunates who have never studied with him usually discount my descriptions of Willard Gatewood as an academic's fantasy. But he is indeed who I say he is. A master teacher and a wonderful scholar, Willard is also a man of immense charm and warmth. I have never met anyone else who can so perfectly mix trenchant criticism with extravagant encouragement. For twenty-five years, I have rarely sent anything into print without first seeking Willard Gatewood's approval.

Ellis Hawley, too, is a scholar's paragon, as his legions of fanatically devoted former students will tell anyone at any opportunity. I never spent one day in any classroom at any university where Ellis ever taught. Instead, I claimed my share of the time he spends, red pen in hand, carefully improving every sentence he reads as a petitioner, seeking adoption. Therefore, I am even more grateful. Both Ellis and Willard read drafts of every chapter of this book, to the finished manuscript's immense benefit.

Guy Alchon has encouraged this project since its inception; his enthusiasm and good advice have been invaluable.

Dan Nelson also read the entire manuscript. Dan has a knack, with a few carefully placed comments, of pinpointing an argument's weakness. Even more important, he has the ability, invariably, of suggesting improvement. Steve Turner read chapters 1 through 4, saving me embarrassment by noting several chronological errors. Are there many others in America who can cite correctly (and without checking) the founding date for the journal *Social Forces?* I am in awe, especially since Steve keeps such an impressive store of knowledge right at hand while teaching in South Florida. What prevents him from succumbing to the temptations of the local popular culture, piercing his nose and navel, and lounging in the sun? I have probably been living in northern Ohio too long? Of course, I should mention that Don Fisher too remains remarkably productive, not only as an important scholar of philanthropy but as a conference organizer without peer. He and Terry Richardson kindly invited me in April 1995 to a Colloquium on Social Science and Rockefeller Philanthropy at the University of British Columbia which proved invaluable as I finished a final draft of this book. Don manages all this while teaching at a unversity located right above a local nudist beach, where I discovered that given the distinctly non–Floridian climate, most habitués wear a couple of vests and woolly sweaters to offset the chill incurred by their wearing absolutely nothing else. Up here in northern Ohio, we keep our down parkas close at hand and suffer no such distractions to tempt our full concentration on the life of the mind.

Jacqueline Wehmueller, Senior Acquisitions Editor at the Johns Hopkins University Press, possesses a keen editorial eye, an inquiring mind that appreciates things slant, and a complete set of red glass crab plates. Moreover, this brief litany only begins to describe her virtues. David Anderson's copyediting is both skillful and graceful. I owe him many thanks.

My colleagues in the History Department at Bowling Green State University deserve my collective thanks, since they all make me happy to come to work. I am the lucky member of a department where fights are fair, help is generously offered, and genuine respect and good feeling abound. Don Nieman's comments helped me redirect the argument in chapter 2, so he deserves special thanks, as do Ed Danziger and Gary Hess, who have ably coordinated the department's Policy History program and have helped me tap its Academic Challenge grant when I needed money to travel to do research. Lisa Heineman's extremely intelligent reading of chapter 4 convinced me to rewrite its conclusion.

Finally, my greatest debt is due another historian, who read every draft of every chapter of this book. His editorial skills and imaginative suggestions improved each one. But in this he was not unique, rather, one of several colleagues who gave me important criticism. However, only this historian also makes my life a joyous cacophony; only he sends coded love letters; only he dances while the breakfast toasts. I shake my head in delight at my good fortune and dedicate this book to my husband, Jerry Friedman.

Private Wealth and Public Life

FOUNDATION PHILANTHROPY AND PUBLIC POLICY MAKING IN THE EARLY-TWENTIETH-CENTURY UNITED STATES

During the first three decades of the twentieth century, profound change wrenched the United States from its nineteenth-century moorings. Few of its major institutions remained unaltered. New ones emerged. One, the incorporated philanthropic foundation, transformed long-standing traditions of charity among the very rich. The rapid ascent of the United States to the first ranks among world economic powers spurred its creation.

Between 1880 and 1912 the United States catapulted to the status of a major power. Its transportation systems, industrial capacity, and its population grew enormously. The wealth that such expansion produced, however, was by no means shared equally among the country's citizens. By the beginning of the twentieth century, only 8 percent of America's families controlled more than three-quarters of the nation's real and movable property.[1] Such a concentration of money and power challenged a welter of traditional assumptions about opportunity for the poor and responsibility for the wealthy.

The vast majority of rich people continued to behave as they always had, giving little or nothing away to anyone not a member of their families. That behavior echoed the actions of the privileged in most societies throughout history. Only a minority has ever really accepted the biblical injunctions to charity. In the late-nineteenth- and early-twentieth-century United States, moreover, most members of this minority did as had the philanthropic rich for centuries. They personally distributed funds for causes they deemed worthy. They built schools and hospitals. They endowed symphonies. They aided artists.

Only a few owners of vast new fortunes began to rethink the vehicles through which they would distribute charity. They created philanthropic foundations: new institutions structured on a corporate model with boards of trustees, annual reports, staffs of professional managers, and government-issued charters. A tiny percentage among the already small minority of the wealthy who created foundations began to re-imagine the purposes of charity itself. They intended the moneys distributed through their institutions to serve public-policy-making purposes. In effect, their organized charitable giving would grant them access to influence in the arenas of government at local, state, and federal levels and a role in the public decision-making process.

This book attempts to assess the general impact on domestic public policy of this latter type of foundation activity. It will focus on the years between 1903, marked by the formal establishment of the Rockefeller-funded General Education Board, and 1932, the year President Herbert Hoover suffered a stunning electoral defeat that spurred major change in federal government, and, concomitantly, a different role for policy-making philanthropy. It examines foundation influence on public policy making in three areas: education, social welfare, and public health.

The period between 1903 and 1932 forms a definable epoch in the history of American foundations. Many statements made about these early-twentieth-century institutions would not be true if extended to the 1940s or the 1990s. However, one would. Overwhelmingly, their influence has been misunderstood. As Alan Pifer, longtime president of the Carnegie Corporation noted in 1984, virtually everyone commenting on the subject has ascribed to foundations powers "quite out of proportion to reality."[2] Consistently some analysts have seen them as the driving force behind revolutions in human betterment. Others, in direct contrast, have viewed them as evil threats to democracy: the sinister creations of the very rich. Both interpretations have always been grossly overdrawn.

To attempt yet another evaluation and to attempt to get it right is a daunting prospect. At the very least it demands definitions of the hurdles the topic of organized philanthropy imposes. It requires explanations of how such barriers can be leaped. This chapter seeks to provide both, through discussions of the premises upon which *Private Wealth and Public Life* rests.

Premise One: Until very recently, restricted access to records has severely limited scholarship about foundation philanthropy.

Before 1955, foundations, like most other private corporations, regarded their records as their property alone. Most scholars seeking access to foundation archives met rebuff, though information about foundations reached the public through their annual reports and books on the subject, most of which were the creation either of sworn defenders or bitter enemies of foundations. Memoirs, histories, and autobiographies produced by insiders, usually foundation officers fully familiar with their subjects, provided interesting information.[3] Sometimes the sheer amount of information published was exhausting, if not exhaustive. For example, John Glenn, Lilian Brandt, and F. Emerson Andrews, all members of the Russell Sage Foundation's executive staff, produced a two-volume history of the institution that provided a year-by-year summary of its activities and totaled nearly seven hundred pages, including dozens of bibliographies and appendixes, not to mention lists of all grants made by dollar amount between 1907 and 1946.[4]

Such accounts, not surprisingly, were portraits without warts. Benefactors, as well as their foundation employees, were invariably hard-working visionaries. Olivia Sage was "serene, intelligent, a presence of dignity and graciousness."[5] John D. Rockefeller Sr. used almost none of his immense fortune for his own family's comfort. Rather, "all of it, always and only, was used in the public interest."[6] George Vincent, president of the Rockefeller Foundation in the decade after World War I, was a "genial and alert eagle, attentive, spirited and eager."[7]

Embarrassing information about their subjects did not appear in these texts. For instance, Raymond Fosdick, another president of the Rockefeller Foundation and the court chronicler of the Rockefeller family and its institutions, knew that John D. Rockefeller Jr. suffered a nervous breakdown in 1904. The mental collapse was so severe that Junior felt unable to do any work for almost a year and instead retreated to a small village in the south of France to recover. No mention of what might have been an emotional turning point in the life of the Rockefeller heir appeared in Fosdick's biography.[8]

Policies and programs promoted by foundations were easily summarized. Behind them lay a "vision of release from ancient evils": hunger, ignorance, crime.[9] For many years, John D. Rockefeller Sr.'s principal advisor on philanthropic giving was a former Baptist minister, Frederick Gates. Other insiders may have written more prosaically, without the quality of Victorian sermon that imbued all of Gates's writing.[10] Nonetheless, most would echo Gates's assessment that foundation work was God's work: "Do not smile if I say that I often think [of the work of the Rockefeller Institute] as a sort of Theological Seminary. . . . If that Being has any favorites on this little planet, I must believe that those favorites are made up of that ever enlarging group of men and women who are . . . studying Him and His ways with men. That is the work of the Institute. In these sacred rooms He is whispering His secrets."[11]

Not all agreed that God looked with special delight on the labors of foundation members. Some believed they did the work of the devil. If one body of literature about foundations characterized them as on a level just below the angels, quite another saw them as opening the doors to hell. Before 1955, friends of foundations had access to their documents. Enemies did not. That fact did not prevent critics from attacking foundations as another institutional protection for "the Empire of Organized Wealth."[12] Supposed foundation benevolence, they argued, masked the fright of rich men, determined to maintain an economic and social structure weighted in their favor. Had they been constrained by laws that required fair wages and working conditions and imposed tighter government regulation on business, the men who endowed foundations would never have amassed their immense fortunes in the first place. Foundation programs were crumbs, thrown to distract recipients from necessary social reform. They existed as "premiums for insurance against social interference."[13]

Foundations, as private institutions whose records and agendas remained beyond public control, in fact posed immense potential danger to future public policy. What would have happened, angrily demanded one critic in 1910, had an institution like the proposed Rockefeller Foundation existed prior to the Civil War? What if it had championed the maintenance of slavery? Remember, the editorialist warned, Congress and the Supreme Court spent the years just before war's outbreak enacting and upholding fugitive slave laws. A proslavery foundation with tens of millions to spend might have exercised a major influence.[14]

Some opponents saw no need to detail dangerous hypothetical influence. Real threats already existed, especially when foundations sought to control American education. In a just society, the people themselves would have enough money to fund their own children's schools. They would have no need to accept the "sinister" charity of great foundations. What appeared to be support for improved public schools was in reality something else indeed. Foundations wanted to "limit the opportunities of the children of workers by establishing class schools like those of Germany."[15]

Any outsider wishing to learn more about foundations had only this Manichean body of literature until the mid-1950s. In 1955 the Ford Foundation made the first of a series of grants to encourage serious, independent investigation of the role of philanthropy in American society. Under Ford sponsorship, historians Merle Curti, Roderick Nash, and Daniel Fox produced pioneering volumes about philanthropy's impact on higher education and on art museums. By the mid-1970s, several other foundations, notably the Carnegie Foundation, had begun to encourage selected scholars to use their archives.[16]

What had prompted the change in foundation attitude? The most plausible explanation gives credit to the increasingly long arm of the Internal Revenue Service, although other governmental bodies had long since probed foundation activities. Descriptions of the activities of the presidentially appointed U.S. Commission on Industrial Relations appeared as front-page news throughout 1915. Traveling the country, members of the commission examined many hundreds of witnesses from miners to factory workers to the kings of American industry. John D. Rockefeller Jr., J. P. Morgan Jr., and Andrew Carnegie all answered summonses to testify. In effect the commission's meetings became a yearlong forum on the problems of American society. Were foundations, several commissioners questioned, one more part of the network of corporate trusts that endangered democracy?[17] So, prior to 1950, foundations had, on occasion, felt the intense heat of public scrutiny.

However, such investigation occurred within entirely different legal and governmental contexts. In 1915 the Sixteenth Amendment was still a fresh addition to the Constitution. Ratified in 1913, it allowed the federal government to tax income. Nonetheless, custom duties remained the primary source of federal revenues until 1932. Income taxes for even the spectacularly wealthy remained minuscule. Percentage rates actually fell during the 1920s. Most Americans paid no income tax at all. Moreover, federal revenue acts continued the nineteenth-century tradition of providing specific tax exemption to charitable, religious, and educational organizations. Only with the Tax Act of 1935 did the federal government begin to make significant use of its Sixteenth Amendment rights. Indeed, World War II spurred the real tax revolution that affected most Americans. Before then, only the very rich paid any federal income tax.

The Tax Act of 1935, however, set in motion a process of inexorable federal extension of taxation privileges, over both individuals and institutions. In 1950 Congress began extensive debates about the historic tax exemptions of American charitable institutions. Four years later, the federal tax code for the first time explicitly defined "charitable" organizations and forbade such institutions from participating in any way in political campaigns. The Tax Reform Act of 1969 elaborated the rules under which an institution could be defined as charitable, with rights to tax exemption. The federal government now had the right to limit cash contributions to foundations and to restrict deductions for gifts in trust. In short, it had the right to demand that charitable organizations open their books.[18]

Confronted with a different public climate, foundation officials worried. A widely reprinted essay by Alan Pifer summarized their attitude: "The Non-Governmental Organization" was "at Bay."[19] In order to survive, foundations had to become more skilled at convincing the American public of their utility. They could no longer afford to be perceived as secretive.[20] In 1974 the Rockefeller Archive Center, the largest and by far the most important archival institution holding foundation records, opened its doors to the public. By 1985 eleven other major foundations had established archives open to scholars or had deposited the bulk of their historical records in an archive.[21] For the first time, tens of thousands of cubic feet of documents about charitable foundations were readily available to scholars. By the mid-1980s the first body of literature about foundations produced by independent scholars began to appear.

Premise Two: This scholarship largely lacks chronological and comparative context.

Professors Barry Karl and Stanley Katz have published a series of thought-provoking articles that explore connections between philanthropy, public policy planning, and changes in American government during the early twentieth century.[22] To date, however, they have not produced a full-length monograph, nor have they investigated the influence of philanthropy on the public sphere below the national level. Aside from Karl and Katz, most scholars have produced case studies, either of particular foundations, like Ellen Lagemann's studies of the Carnegie Corporation and the Carnegie Foundation for the Advancement of Teaching, or particular projects, such as Steven Wheatley's analysis of the Rockefeller Foundation's support for medical education or John McClymer's investigation of the Russell Sage Foundation's Pittsburgh Survey.[23]

Much of this work provides valuable information and insight. What it lacks, however, is comparative context: a clear sense of the world in which the foundations and their creators operated, of the worldview out of which their programs grew, and, most important, of the collective impact of policy changes they sponsored. Moreover, it lacks chronological context. Most students of American philanthropy have analyzed the period after 1930, not before. Even those whose work includes analysis of foundation activities before the advent of the New Deal frequently betray a lack of familiarity with their early-twentieth-century history.

Barry Karl and Stanley Katz, for instance, have argued that congressional rejection in 1913 of John D. Rockefeller Sr.'s efforts to obtain a federal charter for the Rockefeller Foundation led him to "scrupulously avoid any interaction with the federal government."[24] In fact, as late as 1929, the Rockefeller Foundation funded a presidentially appointed national commission to predict future social trends. The chapters in this book provide numerous other examples that illustrate the ways the actual activities of early-twentieth-century foundations confound easy generalization.

Historians are scarce among analysts of philanthropy, multiplying the problems of chronological context so evident in the literature. A well-read scholar playing "What's my occupation?" might well answer "sociologist" when given the clue: "I'm seriously interested in organized private philanthropy." The answer "political scientist" would be equally logical. "Historian" would not, since members of that profession remain in a numerical minority among scholars of the subject.

Sociologists and political scientists often search for models, central tendencies, or types that help to explain the structures of organizations and groups. Foundations, for such scholars, exist as elements in a construction of society or government.[25] Jennifer Wolch's division of the voluntary sector into "eight ideal typical output types" illustrates this effort to fit foundations as pieces in solved puzzles of human organization. Wolch, like most of her social scientist colleagues, bases her analysis on published information about late-twentieth-century foundations.[26] Foundations, examined in this manner, can become abstract systems of organization, disconnected from time or place.

But the role played by philanthropists as policy makers in the years between 1903 and 1932 must be framed by historical awareness. The absence of serious attention to chronological context can distort subjects, sometimes unrecognizably. The times were different. The foundations were different. The public-policy-making process was different, but this has not been sufficiently recognized. Despite the relative openness of at least the most important foundations since 1974, and the much greater availability of primary documents upon which to base analyses, a strange parallel exists between the first body of independent scholarly literature about foundations and its antecedents.

> *Premise Three: Most scholarship about private philanthropy's public-policy-making influence still exaggerates its power, for good or for all.*

In an odd way, current scholarship about American foundations and the policy-making process echoes the old debate. A depiction of foundations as beneficent institutions with a mission to improve humankind challenges its polar opposite: a view of foundations as sinister, shadowy powers out to subvert democracy. One group of scholars, led by sociologist Martin Bulmer, argues that the history of charitable foundations shows them to be disinterested forces for good. The foundations did not promote policies for commercial or political ends, and the major ones assiduously avoided politically controversial topics. Although their trustees were most certainly members of the country's elite, they exercised token influence, since the foundation staffs set the policy agendas, and, in doing so, followed contemporaneous trends in the hard and social sciences.[27]

In striking contrast, another group of scholars, also led by a sociologist, Donald Fisher, views foundations as representations of "the interests of the ruling class."[28] These scholars argue that philanthropies promoted a kind of "cultural imperialism," especially in the early twentieth century when they were unregulated concentrations of money and power.[29] Any imperial system benefits most those who control it. Naturally, the foundations, as creations of the nation's richest families, sought to maintain the existing order. That task, however, proved much more complicated than it would have been in earlier centuries. Control of society required control not just of the production of oil or steel. It also required control of the production of knowledge, and foundations represented an effective vehicle for exercising ideological and intellectual "hegemony" over American society.[30]

The writings of Karl Marx influenced many of the critics of the incorporated foundations who wrote in the early decades of the twentieth century. The ideas of another Marxist, the Italian Antonio Gramsci, profoundly shaped the work of those whose scholarly analyses of foundations and policy making have filled the pages of leading journals like *Sociology* or *Minerva* in the years since 1980. For Marx, the ruling class dominated through force or threat of force. For Gramsci, the ruling class achieved domination as well, but through the use of far more sophisticated techniques. It had managed to convince the rest of society that it deserved "hegemony": that, in fact, its members belonged to a superior elite. Indeed, subordinate groups come to accept the views of the ruling elite as common sense, part of the given fabric of society, something unremarkable, not to be debated.[31]

As "hegemonic" leaders, foundation "experts" promoted the new field of psychology, for instance, because it "scientifically" proved that people were basically different, not equal. Theories of innate individual difference, once accepted, convinced governments at all levels to promote different kinds of social policies. As imperialists in search of a new slogan that would persuade the colonials to accept their dreary lot, foundation philanthropists substituted ideas of individual difference for the Protestant work ethic. In so doing, they helped to "legitimate industrial capitalism and made the American class system, unequal reward structure, and deadening workplace more palatable."[32] After all, confronted by "scientific" evidence of their weaker intelligence or inferior moral sense, the lower orders had no choice.

Gramsci exaggerated the influence exercised by upper classes, but the most interesting question is not "Is Gramsci right?" It is Why has the debate about the policy-making role of early-twentieth-century foundations remained so static? A better interpretation of policy formation and early-twentieth-century foundations requires a deeper understanding of both the opportunities and the limitations facing foundations during the decades before the New Deal, and it requires a clearer definition of terms.

Premise Four: The world of charitable foundations interested in public policy formation from 1903 to 1932 was very small and tightly knit. It by no means included all foundations.

In the 1980s the Yale University Program on Non-Profit Organizations and the Council on Foundations sponsored a series of investigations that sought to draw a portrait of America's philanthropic wealthy. By 1990 a group of seven social scientists had produced two volumes of conclusions. Who were the donors to foundations? Most important, they were a minority among the rich. America's wealthy enjoyed a widespread reputation for generosity they had not really earned. A tiny group of multimillionaires contributed most of the money given to all charitable causes in America in the late twentieth century, and even among members of this elite group, most clung to their assets until the last minute, making bequests only when they reached their deathbeds. Significantly, had they given similar amounts in increments throughout their lifetimes, these philanthropists would have enjoyed generous savings in both income and estate taxes. Sociologist Eugene Steuerle summarized, "The American rich hold on to wealth they will most likely never consume, and they pay a greater price for it."[33]

Of the more than twenty-two thousand independent charitable foundations that existed in the United States in 1990, only a handful, fewer than forty, had assets of more than $100 million. Fewer than thirty-five hundred had assets of $1 million. The vast majority of American charitable foundations had small budgets and limited objectives. Typically most contributed to time-honored good causes near the donor's hometown: benefiting local schools, hospitals, or cultural institutions. Almost all simply acted as organizational buffers that freed their patrons from person-to-person involvement, while enabling them otherwise to act in traditional ways.[34] Only a tiny fraction of contemporary foundations, some two dozen of the largest, sought to grapple with large problems. Only these few engaged in activities that could in any way be defined as involved with policy formation. If the world of private foundations with policy-making goals was still relatively small in the late twentieth century, it was minuscule in the decades between 1903 and 1932.

The numbers of the very rich in early-twentieth-century America grew with amazing speed, however. The industrial boom in the post–Civil War Midwest and North elevated the economy to international importance. It also created many new millionaires. Their numbers surged from fewer than one hundred in 1880 to more than forty thousand in 1916. Twenty of these individuals were millionaires many times over. Andrew Carnegie, at the time he sold his steel interests in 1901, controlled assets worth more than $350 million and was America's wealthiest man until John D. Rockefeller Sr. succeeded him. By the time of his death in 1906, Russell Sage had made a fortune of at least $65 million in lumber, railroads, and banking. Stephen Harkness, one of the original investors in Rockefeller's Standard Oil Company, left no will but probably a fortune in excess of $100 million. John D. Rockefeller Sr. himself became the nation's first billionaire in 1910 when the dissolution of Standard Oil greatly increased the value of his stock. And a billion dollars in 1910 was worth at least twenty times the real money value of an equivalent sum in 1995.[35]

These new rich were free to use their fortunes largely as they pleased. Neither local, state, nor federal governments extracted much money from them, which meant that fear of high taxes could not have motivated the wealthy to become philanthropists. Furthermore, charitable deductions in the years before 1932 were limited for individuals and nonexistent for corporations. In 1917 Congress passed legislation allowing persons donating to religious, educational, or charitable causes to deduct a maximum of 15 percent of adjusted gross income before paying any income tax. In addition, throughout the first three decades of the twentieth century corporations had a legal obligation to make profits for their shareholders, not to engage in good works. Courts took the view that "Charity has no business to sit at a board of directors." Throughout the 1910s and 1920s revenue bills containing provisions allowing corporations to deduct the costs of philanthropy from taxable income repeatedly failed in Congress, reinforcing the common law dictum that corporations could not be givers of charity.[36]

Personal or corporate tax advantage, then, did not spur those who created philanthropic foundations in the early twentieth century. A need for better organization did. Most of the charitable rich in the nineteenth and early twentieth centuries continued directly to practice "noblesse oblige." However, a few foundations did exist. Philadelphia vice reformers probably created the first when they incorporated the Magdalen Society, a home for reformed prostitutes in 1800. The society, like all subsequent foundations, was a legally incorporated private entity, with a charter from a government, but it remained a legal oddity until the twentieth century.[37]

By 1926, when the Russell Sage Foundation commissioned a survey of the field, there were 150 philanthropic foundations, but all they had in common was their legal status and an obligation to handle and disperse money. One-third of these organizations were community trusts, organized to enable groups within a particular city to coordinate local aid for the poor, the sick, or the arts. All but a handful of the remaining one hundred aided a specific group deemed worthy.[38]

In 1928 the trustees of the Julius Rosenwald Fund met to discuss its future. To prepare, they circulated a confidential document assessing the forty largest American foundations. Together, these forty controlled capital funds aggregating nearly a billion dollars. Significantly, however, to make the Rosenwald Fund's list a foundation need control only $20,000. The American Scandinavian Foundation, for instance, administered an endowment of that amount, devoting it to the travel costs of Scandinavian teachers who wished to visit the United States. Moreover, as this annotated roster of even the forty largest foundations made clear, most still acted as traditional charities, albeit with a new legal structure shielding donor from direct contact with recipient. The Engineering Foundation supported scientific publication in the profession. The Juilliard Foundation gave money to music students, while the

Presser Foundation maintained homes for retired music teachers. Amount of endowment did not determine breadth. One of the largest American foundations established before 1930 was the Hershey Fund, begun in 1909 with a capital endowment of more than $40 million, all of which had to be spent exclusively on the care of white orphan boys from Pennsylvania. Only six creators of foundations established institutions with broader purpose and more sophisticated, policy-shaping goals: Andrew Carnegie, John D. Rockefeller Sr., John D. Rockefeller Jr., Edward Harkness, Olivia Sage, and Julius Rosenwald.

In their complexity and wealth the philanthropic structures created by Carnegie and Rockefeller dwarfed those of the other three. By the time of his death in 1919, Andrew Carnegie had given most of his estimated $350 million fortune to a network of Carnegie philanthropies—most significantly, the Carnegie Foundation for the Advancement of Teaching, the Carnegie Corporation, the Carnegie Institution of Washington, and the Carnegie Hero Fund.

John D. Rockefeller Sr. did not die until 1937, at the grand old age of 98. By 1928, both he and his heir, John D. Rockefeller Jr., had contributed at least $600 million to a group of seven independent and incorporated philanthropies. The Rockefeller Institute for Medical Research began its work in 1901. The General Education Board, the second Rockefeller philanthropy, filed articles of incorporation in 1903. The Rockefeller Sanitary Commission, begun to fight hookworm disease in 1909, took a new name in 1913: the International Health Board. In that same year, John D. Rockefeller Jr. created the Bureau of Social Hygiene, and both Rockefellers Senior and Junior oversaw the incorporation of the Rockefeller Foundation. Senior launched the Laura Spelman Rockefeller Memorial in 1918 as a tribute to his late wife. Finally, the Rockefellers authorized the establishment in 1923 of the International Education Board since the charter of the General Education Board forbade it to work overseas. Only in 1929 did most of these formerly entirely separate Rockefeller philanthropies unite under the organizational umbrella of a differently conceived Rockefeller Foundation.[39]

Technically Anna Harkness, widow of Standard Oil founding partner Stephen Harkness, created the Commonwealth Fund in 1918 with an endowment of some $16 million. By that year, she had been a widow for a full three decades, but it would be more accurate to see the Commonwealth Fund as the creation of Anna Harkness's son, Edward, only fourteen at the time of his father's death in 1888.

The Russell Sage Foundation, incorporated in 1907 with an initial

John D. Rockefeller Jr. and John D. Rockefeller Sr. as they appeared at the Park Avenue Baptist Church where they witnessed the inauguration of Dr. Harry Emerson Fosdick as pastor of the church on 31 May 1925. Photograph probably by International Newsreel Photo, Rockefeller Family Photograph Collection. Courtesy of the Rockefeller Archive Center.

capital investment of $10 million, was Olivia Sage's own idea. Although already seventy-eight years old at the time of Russell Sage's death in 1906, Olivia Sage shaped the foundation that would be the major organization used to disperse the fortune she had inherited. She presided at the first formal meeting of the Russell Sage Foundation's Board of Trustees and announced that she was eighty years old, but "had just begun to live." Olivia Sage did continue to live, exuberantly, for another twelve years. One has to wonder, however, whether the widow of Russell Sage, an infamous miser who loathed charity in any form, performed an act of devotion to his memory by vehemently rejecting a proposal to name her foundation the Margaret Olivia Sage Foundation?

Finally, Julius Rosenwald, the multimillionaire who created the Sears-Roebuck retailing empire, established the Julius Rosenwald Fund with a capital fund of $10 million in 1917.[40]

What distinguished this group of foundations from all the others? It was not so much form as intent. All creators of foundations, as wealthy persons well known to be contributors to worthy causes, found themselves overwhelmed by personal appeals for assistance. All began to approach what they saw as the duty of charity with dread, facing literally tens of thousands of pleas for help. Olivia Sage was quite typical in her discovery that giving money away could be a daunting, bewildering task. Within six months of her announcement in 1906 that she wished to give much of her husband's fortune away, she had received over twenty thousand letters asking for money.[41] All foundation patrons decided that, even with the help of family members and advisors, they had great difficulty deciding which requests for charity were the most deserving. All saw in the entity of a legally incorporated foundation a tangible framework for giving. That framework followed a basic pattern: a principal sum, to remain intact in perpetuity or for a specified number of years, placed in the hands of a small body of trustees, organized as a corporation, empowered to use the income to accomplish a written purpose. The difference for the very few foundations with a role to play in shaping public policy lay in their interpretation of purpose.

The stated goals of the few policy-making foundations examined in this volume were quite general and eschewed single forms of benevolence. Rather than aid to white orphan boys or elderly violinists, these foundations explicitly eschewed grants to individuals. Moreover, they rarely granted moneys for emergencies or relief work. Instead, each stated a desire to "improve mankind." These well-defined policies reflected a common underlying assumption: that society's problems could be prevented, not simply ameliorated. It was more important to find ways to curb crime than to give aid to the victims of thieves or murderers. A cure for a disease was a better goal than another hospital for those already sick. Seeds that enlarged crop yield were more valuable than soup kitchens.

A buoyantly optimistic faith that major social problems, like ignorance, poverty, and crime, could be solved characterized these foundations. So did a belief that private foundations could play a role in stimulating better decisions in a public arena. Robert DeForest, the lawyer who acted as Olivia Sage's most trusted advisor and fellow foundation trustee, summarized both beliefs. A foundation "should take up the larger and more difficult problems, and it should take them up so far as possible in such a manner as to secure cooperation." To achieve the highest level of public good, that cooperation often should include alliance with government. Foundations, in fact, were uniquely positioned to lead the way to better public policy. By way of illustration DeForest suggested that a foundation might study the need for recreation and playgrounds, even establish model playgrounds in New York City, then expect the city eventually to take over their maintenance.[42]

The key to their success in playing a role in engineering a better society was for foundations to stay flexible. Edwin Embree, president of the Rosenwald Fund, urged during a trustees' meeting that "while driving steadily and powerfully toward a few definite ends, we should . . . proceed on the basis of enlightened opportunism."[43] Mary Richmond, the Baltimore social worker who came to head the Russell Sage Foundation's Department of Charity Organization, reflected such sentiments when she wrote that "the making of things public or keeping them private has never seemed to us as important an end as the development of high standards of service, whether public or private."[44]

Frederick Gates went even further. The best public policies blurred the lines between private wealth and public life. Describing the Rockefeller Sanitary Commission's efforts in the South to prevent hookworm and other infectious diseases he wrote approvingly, "The hookworm work is done in every state . . . under the guise of the state health boards, while it is in fact minutely directed and paid for by the Rockefeller Commission."[45]

However, foundations should be careful to be a "stimulus," not a "crutch." They should not do for government agencies what those agencies should be ready to do for themselves. The foundations, rather, should help promote the kind of social climate in which the public would demand that its governments be ready. "No organization," a Rosenwald Fund memorandum argued, "is in a better position than a foundation to engage in social experimentation. We are not looking for credit, so we can afford an occasional failure. Since we are not dependent upon a large constituency for our funds or our position, we can afford to take criticism. The possibility of criticism makes it almost impossible for a government bureau . . . to do any courageous experimenting."[46]

The following chapters will analyze the successes and failures of some of the "experiments" conducted by four major groups of philanthropies, those created by John D. Rockefeller Sr. and his son, John D. Rockefeller Jr., Olivia Sage, Edward Harkness, and Julius Rosenwald. It will examine their impact on the creation of public policy. However, the following chapters will devote little attention to the work of the several charitable organizations created by Andrew Carnegie. That demands explanation.

Premise Five: Scholars have overestimated the importance of the Carnegie philanthropies on public policy making before 1932.

Why have scholars overestimated the importance of the Carnegie philanthropies on public policy making before 1932? The vast size of the Carnegie philanthropic enterprises, far larger than any save those of the Rockefellers, provides one answer. Logically, benevolent entities with hundreds of millions to spend would have a major impact, especially if they claimed broad, very ambitious objectives. The Carnegie Corporation's stated purpose, for instance, was to "promote the advancement of knowledge." Similarly, the Carnegie Foundation for the Advancement of Teaching received a congressional charter that stated it was to "do and perform all things necessary to encourage . . . the cause of higher education." After 1960 the Carnegie institutions led most other major philanthropies in allowing scholars to review their archives. Alan Pifer invited Columbia University professor Ellen Lagemann to write two books about the Carnegie philanthropies and guaranteed funding for her research.[47] However, one ironic result of the greater access provided first by Carnegie officials has been a conflation of the history of Carnegie philanthropies before 1930 and after.

While the Carnegie Corporation helped to found the Washington-based Institute for Government Research (IGR) in 1915 and a sister organization, the Institute of Economics, in 1922, it mandated that both be explicitly nonpartisan collectors of data, not allies with government entities in the creation of public policy. Neither institute exercised much influence. Both issued a steady stream of reports urging that the national budget-making process be transferred from Congress to the hands of newly created councils of independent economists in the Department of the Treasury—to absolutely no effect. In 1927 with the Carnegie Corporation's blessing and financial support, the Brookings Institution succeeded the IGR, but like its predecessor, Brookings was slow to embrace any other role than that of supposedly neutral investigator. Only in the 1950s did Brookings officials seek to establish close ties with government. Beginning in 1955, with the appointment of John Gardner as its new president, the Carnegie Corporation did likewise.[48] By 1990, together with the Rockefeller Foundation and the newcomer Ford Foundation, established in 1936, the corporation was one of a triad of major foundations with significant public-policy-making influence.

However, the Carnegie philanthropies were different entities before 1930, and they were different in part because of the roles played by Andrew Carnegie himself. In 1889 Carnegie, then a fifty-four-year-old multimillionaire, published an essay, "Wealth," in the popular magazine the *North American Review*. Within two months, dozens of other periodicals reprinted the essay, often erroneously calling it "The Gospel of Wealth," after an English reader had identified Carnegie's idea as the "gospel" of wealth, as opposed to the gospel of Christianity. Within six months it had made its writer internationally recognized as a philosopher, not just as a fabulously rich steel baron.[49] Yet, the fact that Carnegie's essay quickly became famous did not make it the seminal document in the creation of a new kind of "scientific giving" in America, as some scholars have claimed.[50] In truth, the other philanthropists whose work this book examines rarely consulted Andrew Carnegie. Occasionally, but always in secret, they mocked him.

For one thing, Carnegie advised donors to give all their wealth away within their own lifetimes. Indeed, in his opinion, those among the very wealthy who chose to let their relatives inherit great riches thwarted the rise of the most fit to leadership. Each generation should create its own great fortunes from scratch for a true meritocracy to exist. This was a view that Carnegie's fellow philanthropists, even if they worried about the bad influence of inherited wealth, did not support. The fact that the Scot had no children of his own led others, at least privately, to speculate about the purity of his motives. John D. Rockefeller Sr. reflected such an attitude in a confidential letter to his son. "I must carefully consider not to give away everything to the public and fail to give to my own family and friends," he wrote.[51] Senior listened to his own advice. He donated over $540 million to philanthropy, but he also left at least $500 million to members of his family, primarily to his only son.[52] Not a single other major philanthropist of the early twentieth century followed Carnegie's advice that wealth was a "curse," and that heirs should receive nothing.

Second, Carnegie's "Wealth" espoused an extreme version of Social Darwinism, a version out of keeping with the religious beliefs of most of his peers. The millionaire, the product of a fierce struggle for domination, was society's fittest. He owed his success to himself, or at least to his genes, not to God. This latter idea would have struck most of Carnegie's fellow philanthropists as skirting the edge of blasphemy. They at least paid lip service to divine benevolence as the source of their good fortune.

Finally, the advice given in "Wealth" was not particularly new. In fact, Carnegie's idea exemplified traditional distributive charity, rather than "scientific philanthropy." Carnegie ended his famous essay by describing seven projects that illustrated the very best ways a millionaire could disperse his wealth: (1) founding a university, (2) building libraries, (3) building or contributing to hospitals, (4) building public parks, (5) building concert halls, (6) building public baths, and (7) contributing to nondenominational community churches.[53]

In theory, Carnegie established boards of trustees and delegated authority. In practice, he interfered constantly. The Carnegie Corporation, the largest of the Carnegie philanthropies, established in 1911, spent great amounts of its funds building the libraries and purchasing the pipe organs Andrew Carnegie loved. The Carnegie Foundation for the Advancement of Teaching devoted a very significant percentage of its resources to pensions for retired professors. The aptly named Hero Fund awarded prizes to those whom Andrew Carnegie found admirable. The pensions rescued thousands of deserving academics from penury in old age, and the libraries opened the world of books to many more. Nonetheless, these programs, while worthwhile, did not exemplify a new kind of philanthropic activity. Even Ellen Lagemann admits that, impeded by Carnegie, "the full extent of the Corporation's potential to influence public policy was obscured."[54]

Carnegie died in 1919, but his legacy remained strong. His personal commitments of money left the Carnegie Corporation heavily encumbered, and, for many years, with little actual money to spend. Additionally his influence was apparent in the rise of the two men who dominated the affairs of the Carnegie philanthropies between 1920 and 1930. One, Henry Pritchett, was Carnegie's personal choice to head his first philanthropy, the Carnegie Foundation for the Advancement of Teaching.

An astronomer and former president of the Massachusetts Institute of

Technology, Pritchett ran the foundation for a quarter of a century, from its creation in 1905 to his retirement in 1930, and used it to promote his visions of a properly and hierarchically ordered world. A rigid man, delighted at his invitation to become a founding member of Washington's elite Cosmos Club, he once remarked that "I have a notion that when all go to Heaven—and of course all members of the Cosmos Club will be there—we shall find Heaven made up of little clubs of good fellows."[55]

Pritchett, overwhelmingly, was interested in using the resources of the foundation to help organize the activities of other such influential, but private, "clubs of good fellows." When it became clear, for example, that even selectively given pensions could not guarantee a secure old age for most deserving college professors, the Carnegie Foundation established the Teachers' Insurance and Annuity Association of America. In the years between 1910 and 1930, it also sponsored surveys of the medical, legal, and engineering professions, which included medical reformer Abraham Flexner's famous report on the state of medical education. The surveys helped to encourage leaders in these fields to adopt standardized courses of training, with an emphasis on academic work at institutions accredited by the professions, but in all cases they affected small constituencies. Only the Flexner report generated any attention outside a limited circle of professionals concerned with issues of training, and by 1913 Abraham Flexner had accepted a staff position with the General Education Board and left the Carnegie Foundation.[56]

Pritchett's approach to the proper role to be played by government or members of the general public in making decisions about professional training and education was simple: They had no role to play. In that sense, Pritchett accurately reflected the message in "Wealth." Actions taken for the public good did not require public acceptance or even cooperation with public institutions. Indeed, Pritchett remained a fierce opponent of any foundation involvement with government agencies in any form.[57]

The other dominant figure after Carnegie's death, Frederick Paul Keppel, an expansively friendly New Yorker, left Columbia University to become president of the Carnegie Corporation in 1923 and would continue in that position until 1942. Keppel presented a striking contrast in personality to Henry Pritchett, but under his presidency, the activities of the Carnegie Corporation paralleled those of the foundation. Both promoted the "best."

The foundation, under Pritchett, urged more rigorous education for the tiny number of Americans who studied in the nation's most prestigious colleges. Influential professional leaders, especially in the fields of medicine and engineering, listened, and the foundation, at least, had an impact in the shaping of professional training for these elites. For its part, the corporation, in a disorganized series of programs directed by "hunch, coincidence, and opportunity" rather than "clear, consistently applied, 'scientific' goals," attempted to show the general American public "the best."[58] The "best" books would be reprinted and made available to libraries. Museums could use the services of corporation-supplied arts scholars—who could train their visitors how to appreciate "the best" paintings. Corporation-sponsored workshops and institutes would bring together the "best" minds of law, economics, and other spheres to discuss their fields. The public could read condensed versions of these deliberations in the newspapers, courtesy of Carnegie Corporation–supplied transcripts. Free lectures by the age's "best" minds, including historian Allan Nevins and sociologist Robert Lynd, would elevate average working-class Americans. They would be liberated from "materialism, from bad taste in living, in music, in drama, in recreation, and, most of all, from the utter drabness of unfulfilled lives."[59]

The lower orders, however, went on living in bad taste and utter drabness. At least, they stayed away from the Carnegie-sponsored associations, lectures, and workshops. There is no evidence that they followed the literary suggestions made by Carnegie experts and no evidence that they saw Rembrandt with new eyes. The people who composed the sparse audiences for these corporation-funded efforts to elevate American culture were members of the same aspiring middle class that supported the Chautauqua movement. If the Carnegie Corporation practiced cultural imperialism, most of the colonials practiced passive rebellion.

His own contemporaries can be forgiven for the attention lavished on Carnegie as a founder of "new" philanthropy. Scholars cannot. Early-twentieth-century journalists found "Merry Andrew" wonderful copy. He, in turn, happily gave interviews—on any and all subjects.[60]

If Andrew Carnegie was "merry," John D. Rockefeller Sr. seemed perpetually dour. His son loyally insisted that Senior took great joy in life and in an unpublished memoir recalled his father laughing and lunging through doorways in fierce games of blindman's bluff. The man Junior saw—one capable, when in his seventies, of challenging his grandchildren to midnight bicycle races—was certainly never on public view.[61] Generally speaking, Rockefeller Sr. avoided the press, and reporters, lacking any accurate information, made up "interviews," often suppressed under threat of lawsuit. According to these putative heart-to-hearts, Rockefeller Sr. drank only milk, ate only roast chicken, and loved South American orchids and kept them in a colossal greenhouse measuring over four acres in diameter.[62] Newspaper accounts of Rockefeller's personality were just as fanciful as the often-reprinted descriptions of his vast, but mythical, orchid greenhouse. No one, however, ever called Senior "Merry John."

But John D. Rockefeller Sr., not the more publicly accessible Andrew Carnegie, outlined the principles of "scientific giving" that underpinned the activities of the foundations this volume examines. The press delighted in describing a race between the nation's two richest men to create philanthropies. In truth, there was no such contest. Carnegie and Rockefeller Sr. maintained cordial, but cool, relations. Despite the private opposition of Rockefeller's chief advisor for philanthropy, Frederick Gates, the Rockefeller-funded General Education Board asked Carnegie to be a trustee in 1908. Carnegie accepted and continued to serve on the Board of the GEB until his death in 1919.[63] However, through the 1910s and 1920s, the most significant connection between the Rockefeller and Carnegie philanthropies was the human chain formed by disgruntled staff members of Carnegie institutions fleeing the former to take Rockefeller employment.

Such a change of employers promised the chance to practice "wholesale," not "retail," philanthropy. That phrase, for Frederick Gates, summarized the differences between the philanthropic giving of his boss and that of Andrew Carnegie. Gates's autobiography, *Chapters in My Life,* not "Wealth," provides the credo of the new "scientific philanthropy."[64]

Contemporary critics of the Carnegie programs often assessed them more accurately, and far more harshly, than have scholars. Frederick Gates barely bothered to conceal his contempt, at least in the lengthy confidential memoranda he sent to Rockefeller Sr. In 1906, for instance, he urged that Rockefeller moneys be spent for research, ideas, or endowments. They should not be used for buildings. The actual building housing an enterprise was, in fact, usually easy to secure. "The building bears the name of the donor and furnishes a splendid family memorial." "Sentimental" people, "especially ladies," loved to build libraries, with their "alcoves, their special sets of books, their special funds."[65]

Not content to portray Andrew Carnegie as a sentimental lady, Gates went further. He made it angrily clear in 1910 that if it was bad enough to have the former a member of the Board of Trustees of the General Education Board, it would be entirely too much to include Henry Pritchett, then a nominee, as well. As he always did when writing privately, Gates called the

Carnegie Foundation for the Advancement of Teaching, the "Carnegie Pension Fund." Carnegie, he wrote, had the perfect right to establish such a fund. Pritchett, as Carnegie's employee, had a duty to administer it. Could there be a policy purpose behind it, Gates wondered? "By pensioning off inefficient college teachers so that their places may be supplied with younger and better instructors the founder may hope," Gates wrote, "to bring an abler class of young men into college teaching . . . and increase the efficiency of college teaching." In that hope, if such a vision even existed, the irascible Gates continued, Carnegie was, of course, "erroneous."[66]

By the time he wrote these words in 1910, Frederick Gates had long since abandoned his work as a prominent Baptist fundraiser to work full time for a prominent fellow Baptist, John D. Rockefeller Sr. Senior, like many others among the rich men who created foundations, had begun to feel "hounded—almost like a wild animal" by the crush of pleas for aid.[67] He wanted, as did many of his peers, the protection a foundation could provide. The philanthropic institutions created by Gates did that too, but Gates sought to reorganize not just the vehicles, but the purposes of giving. Only "wholesale" giving could achieve serious social change. Major foundations should never deal in "retail": in the minutia of gifts to specific groups and individuals or the small details of particular projects. Rather, they should deal in "ideas, not projects." Moreover, those ideas should be "big ideas."

In effect, Gates intended all Rockefeller foundations to act as public policy makers.[68] They should not act alone, but rather in concert with all other necessary decision-making elements in society, including, of course, government, at many levels. "Matters directly affecting the machinery of government [should] be approached with caution for reasons of expediency. [But] . . . the problems of child life, of leisure time and recreation, vocational problems, problems affecting the immigrant, the aged, the poor . . . [among many others] . . . afford opportunities for correlated effort."[69] Gates found an eager collaborator in Rockefeller Sr., a fearsomely efficient, coolly organized builder of systems, a man who wanted his charitable giving to parallel the structures he created for his many business enterprises.[70]

Premise Six: Self-confident, self-proclaimed "Progressives" populated the highly interconnected early-twentieth-century world of policy-making foundations.

In contrast to the Carnegie philanthropies, the small number of foundations examined in the following chapters formed a kind of interlocking directorate for private policy making. A review of their archives reveals a complex structure of connections between the Commonwealth Fund, the Rosenwald Fund, the Russell Sage Foundation, and four of the seven much larger and much richer Rockefeller philanthropies.

All seven of the Rockefeller philanthropies created before 1932 were interested in policy making, but only four, the General Education Board, the International Health Board, the Laura Spelman Rockefeller Memorial, and the Bureau of Social Hygiene, sought a role in domestic public policy making. The Rockefeller Foundation, although chartered in 1913, did not assume its all-important role as the organization that coordinated most Rockefeller-sponsored philanthropic activities until a major internal reorganization of 1928–29 merged most Rockefeller projects. Before that date, the Rockefeller Foundation focused on efforts to support medical and scientific research and gave most of its aid to private institutions. The International Education Board, unlike the International Health Board, truly deserved its name. It provided an organizational vehicle for Rockefeller involvement in shaping the educational policies of other countries and thus does not fit within this book's structure. Neither does the Rockefeller Institute for Medical Research. Most of the latter foundation's partners were private organizations. In common with the Rockefeller Foundation, the institute primarily helped to shape the research agendas and policies of private hospitals and universities.

Of the four Rockefeller philanthropies with places at the domestic public-policy-making table, the General Education Board was, by far, the largest. With a mission to improve American education, public and private, its endowment, by 1930, exceeded $129,000,000. The Spelman Memorial received a gift of $74,000,000 from Rockefeller Sr. and used it to promote social science methodologies as policy tools, especially in the areas of child welfare, race relations, and public recreation.

The two remaining Rockefeller philanthropies this book examines were much smaller. Rockefeller Sr. pledged $1 million to establish the Rockefeller Sanitary Commission. As the International Health Board, the renamed foundation received slight increases in its endowment. However, it did not assume the status of a major Rockefeller philanthropy until its re-creation yet again as a division within the Rockefeller Foundation. Only then, as the International Health Division, did the institution begin significant public health activities abroad. Before 1929 the International Health Board did most of its work at home, though many East Coast philanthropists probably continued to see the region where its efforts centered, the American South, as a foreign country. Before the reorganizations of 1928–29, the chief public ally of the International Health Board was not another country's government but American county public health departments.

Finally, the Bureau of Social Hygiene operated between 1913 and 1933 and received a little over $5 million in gifts from John D. Rockefeller Jr. Over two decades it promoted policies to curb vice and teach sex education. Technically, it was not a foundation, since it had no endowment, instead receiving an annual budget from Junior. Nonetheless, in every other way it served as one. It provided an organizational vehicle for Junior's efforts to promote new public health policies. It had a government charter, a paid staff, and a board of trustees. While recognizing its lack of a capital fund, this volume will treat the Bureau of Social Hygiene as a foundation.

After 1932 the Commonwealth Fund directed its philanthropic giving almost exclusively to medical research. However, in its first decade, the organization's officers involved the philanthropy in a wider variety of issues, many of which touched public policy making, such as juvenile delinquency and legal reform.

Julius Rosenwald never intended his foundation to exist in perpetuity. Rather he stipulated that it complete its work in one generation, spending both interest and capital. Throughout its almost thirty-year history, from 1917 to 1948, the Rosenwald Fund's chief concern was race relations.

The charter document of the Russell Sage Foundation declared that the new philanthropy "sought the improvement of social and living conditions in the United States." To fulfill that mandate, the Foundation concentrated, as did the Spelman Memorial, on efforts to apply the insights of social science to social policy, especially in the areas of child welfare, industrial relations, housing, and city planning.[71]

In the first three decades of the twentieth century these seven policy-making foundations had a combined endowment of approximately $245 million. This immense sum, by contemporary standards, dwarfed moneys available to many of the public agencies with which these institutions dealt. Moreover, they frequently enhanced the value of their combined financial strength by coordinating efforts. Since a significant number of their staff members and trustees served more than one of these foundations, sequentially or simultaneously, such cooperation was logical.

For instance, Beardsley Ruml, head of the Spelman Memorial, accepted a seat on the Board of Trustees of the Rosenwald Fund, while Edwin Embree left his position as a vice president of the Rockefeller Foundation to assume the presidency of the Rosenwald Fund. Julius Rosenwald himself served as a longtime trustee for Rockefeller philanthropies.[72] Employees of the Commonwealth Fund and the Russell Sage Foundation served as trustees of John D. Rockefeller Jr.'s Board of Social Hygiene.[73]

Trustees and staff members of other foundations might know one another, especially before 1930, when at least half of all creators of foundations maintained a residence in New York City and enjoyed common circles of acquaintance. The trustees and staff members of the policy-making foundations also enjoyed each other's company socially. They too came from a largely East Coast, Ivy League–educated elite. However, only this latter group attempted to coordinate philanthropic efforts. In 1921, for example, when the General Education Board contemplated improving public school curriculums subject-by-subject, its staff deferred to the Commonwealth Fund. Rather than "encroach" on each other, the two foundations devised a coordinated survey and shared results.[74]

The communication between these foundations involved even the most delicate of matters, ones that required the skills of diplomats. Between 1914 and 1919, the Rockefeller interests suffered intense negative publicity because of the deaths and bloody violence that accompanied suppression of strikes at its Colorado mines. During those same years Mary Van Kleeck of the Russell Sage Foundation supervised a series of investigations of industrial conditions in Colorado. By 1920 she had concluded that the Rockefeller proposal of "Representation Plans" or company unions would not bring industrial peace, even though the United Mine Workers were "no more democratic than the Rockefeller Plan." John Glenn, director of the Russell Sage Foundation, saw "no reason" why the Sage study should not be forwarded to Rockefeller Senior and Junior. "Before sending it," however, he wanted to "cut out questionings of their moral right to do certain things, because [that] will put the Rs on the defensive."[75] If there were occasional moments, such as this, of awkward communication between members of these philanthropies, in general, they agreed, rather than disagreed. They shared a worldview that mirrored the salient features of contemporary Progressivism.

First and foremost, such policy-making philanthropy sought to help government as it grappled with the difficult problems of a society and economy experiencing rapid change. As Raymond Fosdick noted, "The machinery of our environment is increasing in complexity, but the tools of control remain largely the same. . . . Government is getting out of the hands of the people, not in the sense that anybody is taking it away from them, but in the sense that with the rapid extension of its technical aspects, it is becoming more and more difficult to comprehend and control."[76] Government alone did not command the resources to find the "tools of control," but society could not afford to wait patiently. It could not afford public policies derived from insufficient information and crafted only by the whim of politics. It faced great peril, in fact, if it continued to be saddled with such a public-policy-making process at a time when everything was being "speeded up infinitely." Writing in 1922, Fosdick warned that, even as he put words to paper, scientists were working to unleash the "incomparably abundant" power of the atom. When they did so, and "conceivably it might be tomorrow [that] one hundred and fifty tons of dynamite—enough to blow the city of Boston into oblivion—can be compressed to a pound weight and held in the hand!"[77]

These kinds of technological advancements, inconceivable to a previous generation, could be socially as well as literally explosive. Only a well-ordered, peaceful society could cope with such changes, and only fools believed such a society could be achieved through market forces alone. Public policy that allowed untrammeled free competition prophesied not order and control—but a "heap of human maggots," wrote Frederick Gates. Gates, as a boy in Kansas, had lived through grasshopper plagues where the country was "as barren of any green thing as Sahara, and the grasshoppers were starving. If you watched them closely, you could see one jerk a leg off another and eat it up. The competitive system is a sort of human cannibalism. . . . Is that system, or is it heap?"[78]

The rapid pace of social change demanded cooperative efforts to achieve better systems of social organization, especially in government. Great peril, perhaps even doom, faced the country if its leaders, including its private citizens with great wealth, did not face up to their charge. The latter, in fact, exercised more power than did most in America. "Few crowned kings," Gates argued, "have ever been able to exercise the power that twelve or fifteen uncrowned men actually do exercise every day, as they surround the table of the Board of Directors of the United States Steel Corporation."[79] Hence, their power and their money obligated the extremely rich to cooperate with public officials.

Not only was the logic of scientific philanthropy suffused with a sense of the dangers facing the United States, it was also distinguished, as was progressive reform, by an exuberant faith that improvement was possible. Mary Richmond decried the "false spirit of the age: the tendency of the human mind to be overwhelmed by the phenomena of the time." She underlined thickly the following sentence in a letter to John Glenn: "Men come to think that it is their business to explain, rather than to control, the forces of the hour." Nothing could be further from the truth. Rather, they needed to search for "explanation that leads to the control that this country sorely needs."[80] The resources of private foundations could help find such "explanation." In fact, foundations were the best agencies for "finding out what ought to be done, and for getting government and communities to do the things that ought to be done."[81]

Premise Seven: Early-twentieth-century scientific philanthropy was personal, not corporate, philanthropy.

Viewing these attempts to do "what ought to be done" both contemporary and scholarly critics have judged early-twentieth-century philanthropy to be a tool of the trusts. Such an argument, however, conflates early- and late-twentieth-century chronology and misunderstands early-twentieth-century America's corporations, philanthropic foundations, and even its structures of government.

The philanthropic foundations whose activities provide the grist for this study were personal, not corporate, organizations. That fact needs emphasis, since critics both inside and out of academe have used the term "corporate" in confusing ways. Neither state nor national legislatures had devised clear rules about when government agencies could and could not accept help from outside experts. They certainly had not forbidden private payments to state agencies for specific tasks—such as the supervision of a survey. Not until the New Deal did Congress require the president to pay all experts within all federal agencies with government money, a precedent that was only gradually, and incompletely, followed on the state and local level.[82] The appearance in a government agency of a person whose salary came from funds provided by private philanthropy did not, then, necessarily signal the presence of a conspiratorial "shadow government," though, as the following chapters illustrate, it sometimes prompted fierce debate. Whether controversial or not, the practice certainly indicated the unclear lines between public and private that characterized a society in rapid transition.

Anyone seeking to understand public policy making in the early twentieth century must be aware—acutely aware—of the speed with which social change occurred in the absence of very clear divisions between public and private spheres. Andrew Carnegie was astonished when Congress refused his offer to include former presidents of the United States as a special category within his pension systems.[83] Julius Rosenwald did provide pensions to retiring Illinois judges and was genuinely flabbergasted when this action prompted some in the Chicago press to charge him with efforts to corrupt public officials.[84]

If philanthropists frequently merged public and private, they also often collapsed distinctions between charity and business. John D. Rockefeller Sr. saw no problem with assigning Frederick Gates supervision of his philanthropic interests, as well as control of several of his ancillary companies. Some weeks found Gates immersed in the affairs of the General Education Board. Others saw him engaged in complex deal making as he sold Rockefeller shares of the American Smelting and Refining Company to the Guggenheims or reorganized the Lake Superior Consolidated Iron Mines to be sold at profit to U.S. Steel.[85] In 1915 John D. Rockefeller Jr. was both president of the Rockefeller Foundation and a member of the Board of Directors of Colorado Fuel and Iron Company, infamous since 1914 because of its bloody wars with striking miners. The younger Rockefeller was honestly puzzled when Samuel Gompers said that the dual affiliation prevented him from conducting objective investigations into the causes of industrial violence.[86]

The careers of those who shaped the course of scientific philanthropy emphasize the fact that they worked during years when professions themselves were in formation. Doors to what by the late twentieth century would seem remarkable occupational flexibility remained open. The only formal training Frederick Gates ever received was for the ministry. Who would have expected the graduate of a small Baptist seminary to manage the multimillion dollar corporate reorganizations of the Rockefeller mining interests, while simultaneously supervising the disbursement of hundreds of millions of dollars in philanthropic giving? Beardsley Ruml, one of a first generation of American-trained psychologists, with a Ph.D. from the University of Chicago, headed the Rockefeller Spelman Memorial. After his departure, he became a university dean, then a corporate executive, then a banker, ending his career as chairman of the Federal Reserve Bank of New York.[87] Leonard Ayres, director of the Russell Sage Foundation's statistical surveys, entered the world of incorporated philanthropy after careers as a professional cyclist, a taxidermist, and a theatrical stagehand. He had no formal training whatsoever in statistics. Indeed, his schooling at Boston University had emphasized the traditional course of study available at most nineteenth-century American colleges: Latin and Greek. Ayres was such a poor scholar that he barely squeaked through with a degree.[88]

Leonard Ayres had many counterparts in government and business, but Mary Richmond and Mary Van Kleeck, who like Ayres headed departments at the Russell Sage Foundation, did not. If there was one notable difference between the worlds of incorporated philanthropy and those of government and business, it was the presence in philanthropy of more women in positions of influence. Not until the New Deal did women in significant numbers begin to receive appointments to leadership positions in the federal government. Within state and local government, as well as in business, those in control remained white and male for decades to come.[89] The overwhelming majority of foundation officers were also white males. However, especially during the first three decades of the twentieth century, a group of able, highly educated women helped shape policy at a few major foundations.

Several of John D. Rockefeller Jr.'s key advisors, most important the sociologist Katharine Bement Davis, were women. However, the influence of women was most significant at the Russell Sage Foundation. At the insistence of Olivia Sage, the division between men and women on the Foundation's first board of trustees was almost equal: four women and five men. One of those trustees, Louisa Schuyler, founder of the State Charities Aid Association of New York, wrote approvingly, "I like the plan of having men and women working together on the same board. I have always worked so, all my life, and it works well." Women headed two of Russell Sage's original eight departments, and dozens of others received appointments to act as field investigators, writers, and editors. Yet, interestingly, rather than providing a model for other institutions, the Russell Sage Foundation over time offered fewer opportunities for women, rather than more. By 1930, a profile of its trustees and staff more closely paralleled that of other major philanthropies. As the original trustees died or retired, men replaced women. By 1930 an expanded board of twelve members was nearly all male. By 1938 all Russell Sage trustees were men.[90]

The personalities of board and staff members of the few foundations interested in public policy making have appeared in sketch form here. In the following chapters, clearer portraits of many will emerge. Suffice it to emphasize here that members of incorporated philanthropy were not "corporate types" or "bureaucratic types" as those stereotypes have come to be understood in the late twentieth century. These phrases reflect popular images of the late, not the early, twentieth century. However, foundation officials were not "Third Sector" types, either. In such a fluid professional world, the few hundred people who ran foundations saw themselves in more general terms, as reformers of society, not as members of a new profession.

Early-twentieth-century philanthropists were seekers of system, not entrenched defenders of system. They certainly did not wear gray flannel suits—though few matched in personal flamboyance Beardsley Ruml, who favored pink corduroy trousers and embroidered cossack blouses. Frederick Gates usually dressed in black. With a tangled mane of pure white hair flowing down his back and arms wildly gesticulating, he needed nothing else to command attention.

Neither their dress nor their style was "corporate."[91] If the leaders of scientific philanthropy typified anything it was the relentless optimism that characterized Progressivism—an optimism born of faith that solutions could be found to the most intractable social problems. They did not yet have a blueprint for the well-ordered society, but they were convinced such a blueprint could be drawn. With furious energy they sought to find the tools to do so.

Frederick Gates counseled those around him to "work rapidly, continuously, and at a *hot* pace. If the work flags, you are done. Never allow the least relaxation of the nervous tension in *yourself,* in your friends, or in the public until the work is done. . . . Bring every ounce of vital energy, every moment of waking time to bear. Regard every suggestion involving delay as *treason* and *death.*"[92] His friends worried that the schedule Beardsley Ruml followed suggested "a very real temptation to overstep the bounds of long-distance efficiency."[93] Wallace Buttrick of Rockefeller's General Education Board wrote of a trip to survey educational conditions in the South in 1902: "The day was boiling hot; the road was dusty, but we managed to have a good time, even though we fasted from 7am to 9pm, a few unripe peaches and a glass of uncertain buttermilk excepted."[94]

If foundation officers did not always secure good food, they were rarely without visions of grand possibilities. In 1952 a much older Beardsley Ruml complained that "foundations today seem to lack the boldness, imagination, and sense of scale of their founders. . . . Today [the foundations] spend so much time on so many good, but essentially tactical, objectives. Where are the single purpose contributions of foundations in the old amounts of five, ten, or even twenty or more million dollars?"[95]

Alan Gregg echoed Ruml's concerns. Writing in 1949, as head of the Rockefeller Foundation's Medical Sciences Division, he worried that foundations had become timid—burdened by a "chronic fear of being put upon . . . burdened by fear masquerading as caution." Tightly phrased policy had become a substitute for ambitious plans. Foundation officers were "neurotically suspicious" of giving offense or provoking controversy.[96] Whatever their failings, the first generation of officers of these same foundations were rarely guilty of too much timidity. However, their self-confidence did not guarantee success. The public-policy-making process was a more complicated one than they realized. They were to discover, as have many since, that it almost always includes unanticipated consequences.

Premise Eight: A few national philanthropic foundations spurred, but did not control, the emergence of a different American state, with a significantly expanded social-policy-making role.

Both critics and defenders of early-twentieth-century foundations have paid too much attention to stated goals—too little to results. The following chapters seek to examine both. They do not attempt to provide a comprehensive history of the foundations already named, but rather seek to analyze the impact of private wealth on public life through analysis of foundation-sponsored attempts to change policy in the areas of public education, social welfare, and public health.

A few early-twentieth-century leaders of foundations realized the immensity of the task. Historian Max Farrand, first director of the Commonwealth Fund, knew that money spent to support changed social policies would likely prompt more controversy than money spent for projects generally perceived to be pure science. "The problems [of American society] are neither so definite nor so concrete as problems of hookworm, chemical dyes, the milk supply. . . . But they are real problems." Effective policies had to "proceed from the *general consciousness of the American people.*" Here, Farrand's characteristic optimism reappeared: "And this consciousness is, in part, at least, *to be created.*"[97] Farrand was right. A climate of support for different social policies could, in part, be created. However, he should have stressed the words "in part" not the phrase "to be created." Private wealth did create significant changes in public life, but public life, including the machinery of government at all levels, proved difficult to control in its totality.

A few foundation officers warned that the effort would often be very difficult. In 1913 Harry Pratt Judson, president of the University of Chicago and trustee to the newly established Rockefeller Foundation, composed a long, thoughtful memorandum on foundations and the public-policy-making process. All plans to improve the welfare of humankind, he wrote, fell in one of two categories. They either accorded with human desire or they did not. People desired good health, long life, and escape from death. They wanted more money. If they were ignorant, it was usually from inertia or lack of opportunity, rather than active opposition to education. If people understood education as a vehicle through which to better themselves economically or viewed public recreation as a means to good health, then they would support policies promoting them.

However, some policies, also for the good of human civilization, would naturally meet opposition. They confronted contrary human desires. Policies seeking, for instance, to ban alcohol, prostitution, or drugs fell into this second category. Foundations should not expect much success. "That they can be to some extent lessened by the police power is admitted. But they cannot be eliminated by any process short of an entire change in human nature, involving a widespread self-control which at this writing seems unthinkable."[98]

Abraham Flexner noted that policies promoting higher standards of training and better salaries for public school teachers were good ones. However, foundation surveys illustrating the woeful state of pay for teaching were just a start in a chain of events necessary for implementation of any truly effective policy change. Foundations could pay salaries at model schools. They could provide examples to follow. In the end, however, improvements in education depended on public support. People had to be willing to pay higher taxes. Foundations could point the way, but they "could not work a revolution."[99]

Charles Merriam, University of Chicago political scientist and frequent advisor to Rockefeller philanthropies, knew that providing facts and models might not be enough to change policy. Indeed, he argued that "policies are often determined on purely subjective grounds. . . . More scientific knowledge about the tariff would change very little the demands of regional groups with regard to it. Science, it must be admitted, is in such cases very limited in its influence on policies."[100]

These men were right, but predictably, they saw much of their advice ignored. However, their contemporary analyses of the power of foundations to influence policy were more prescient than many offered decades later in scholarly assessments of the same topic. The immense financial resources concentrated in a few foundations could give these institutions a role to play in policy making, especially at a time when public agencies did not have comparable funds to spend, but the funds they controlled often "exceed[ed] their stock of ideas, the capacity of their personnel, and the possibility of obtaining corresponding outside support."[101]

Men like Judson or Flexner realized the limitations binding the power of foundations. What they rarely discussed were the equally troublesome structures of government with which any foundation wishing to influence public policy had to deal. In fact, most "scientific" philanthropists were remarkably bad politicians. Many, perhaps most, persisted in making largely artificial distinctions between "politics" and "government," sure that if only public life could be freed from the snares of politics, then good government and good public policy would blossom. Even though they rarely had much faith in the members of the public they wished to elevate, leaders of foundations suffered genuine confusion when critics grouped them with politicians as corrupt, antidemocratic influences.

Jerome Greene, secretary of the Rockefeller Foundation, did not intend the story he related in an "eyes-only" letter to fellow trustee Colonel Arthur Woods as a cautionary parable about private wealth and public life. Nonetheless, it serves that purpose. Dr. Winthrop Talbot, an unemployed linguist, was a "crank," someone who caused Greene to "gasp when I get word that he wants to see me." Yet, in spite of this, Greene concluded that the out-of-work professor had a splendid plan to teach foreigners to read and write English. "Personally," Greene confided to Woods, "I think that he has something far too good to be allowed to come to nothing just because he is so incompetent to push the thing adequately himself."[102] With Greene's encouragement, the Spelman Memorial granted Talbot five thousand dollars, for a secretarial staff, typesetting, design, and printing for a series of primers about teaching English to non-native speakers. By supporting Talbot, the Spelman Memorial had provided a resource intended for public adult education. However, the primer, available to state departments of education at cost, got no takers. The teachers who reviewed it gave it low marks for organization and refused to use it. In the end, even Greene had to admit failure. He sadly concluded that the money spent on Talbot had gone to waste but could not "get any satisfaction out of saying that it serves him right."[103] Greene did not say, but could have, that such were the frequently tangled final outcomes when private money sought to influence public life.

Each of the following chapters will explore those results. Some examine the activities of just one foundation from within the network of philanthropies created by the General Education Board, the International Health Board, the Spelman Memorial, the Bureau of Social Hygiene, the Sage Foundation, and the Rosenwald and Commonwealth Funds. Others examine the work done in concert by several of these foundations. Some will provide examples of striking foundation success in shaping public social policy. Others will illustrate ambiguous results or outright failures.

Moreover, this book seeks to broaden scholarly discussion of the public-policy-making process itself. Foundation philanthropy's legacy for domestic social policy raises a point that should be emphasized. The gap between policy on paper and policy in practice is often wide, even yawning. In the best of circumstances, policies rarely produce their expected goals. Good intentions are usually utterly insufficient to produce good outcomes. "Good outcomes" itself is a heavily value-laden phrase that demands dissection. A few national foundations, headed by sincere individuals clearly motivated to improve society and "benefit mankind," sometimes influenced results that they would never have consciously promoted.

This book's case studies begin with a subject that greatly interested organized scientific philanthropy: educational policy. Like most Progressives, foundation leaders saw education as a crucial key to social advancement. Therefore, when they identified a "crisis" in rural America, they experimented with new kinds of education policies in an effort "to save our country people."[104]

FOUNDATIONS, THE "RURAL CRISIS," AND THE BIRTH OF PUBLICLY FUNDED VOCATIONAL EDUCATION

A very real problem preoccupied America's leadership class in the early twentieth century. While the nation's cities and factories flourished, its farms languished. The country's rural areas were in "crisis." "Country people" were inefficient and unhealthy, out of touch with "modern life," and "solid progress" depended on the success of efforts to "obliterate the differences" that made city life more appealing than the farm.[1] The "rural crisis" was not a chimera. Indeed, throughout the industrialized West at the turn of the century, agriculture experienced far sharper cycles of boom and bust than did any other economic sector. The high tariff walls that nation after nation built in futile efforts to protect its farm products contributed to the climate of superheated competition and ultranationalism that ultimately exploded as World War I. Despite its deeply important role as an American cultural symbol, the family farm was doomed. Agriculture's revival in the decades after the Great Depression in the United States was a rebirth in which the farm emerged as factory, the highly efficient creation of consolidated, commercialized, indeed "industrialized" agriculture. The traditional family farm still existed, but ever more marginally.

However, even in the late twentieth century policy makers loved to make speeches praising this now all but nonexistent institution. Not surprisingly, between 1900 and 1930, when small farms were still common, America's leaders quite naturally tried to save them. The alliance examined here between private philanthropy, public land-grant universities, and government agencies at federal, state, and local levels emphasized "practical" programs of vocational education—meant to improve family farmers' productivity and physical health, as well as to remedy inequities perpetuated by racism and ethnic prejudice.

This ambitious agenda was, in part, the creation of men who had engineered revolutions in industrial productivity but remained oddly blind to the fact that those very innovations had blurred the clear distinctions they continued to see between farm and factory. John D. Rockefeller Sr., for instance, had eliminated forever the possibility that small-scale regional producers of kerosene or gasoline could thrive. The idea of a Mom and Pop "oil store" was, of course, laughable as early as 1900. Nonetheless, Rockefeller, in common with government and academic leaders, felt that the small farm was essential to American culture and American economic health. With a clear vision of the inevitability of agri-business consolidation, policy makers might have urged policies that relocated and retrained rural people. Instead, with no direction from their leaders, country people eventually voted with their feet, filling America's cities with the nation's formerly rural poor. In many ways the early twentieth century's rural crisis, unsolved, became its urban nightmare as the century neared its end.

Therefore, the innovative education policies examined here demand attention. From their very inception, they fecklessly challenged demographic inevitability. In 1900 some 60 percent of the American population lived in rural areas, with a little less than 40 percent actually employed as farmers. By 1920, fewer than one in four Americans earned a living in agriculture. By 1932 and the onset of the Great Depression, only 18 percent of Americans actually tilled the soil, while only a third lived in areas the Census Bureau considered rural. That dramatic contraction provided evidence not of the great differences between industrialized and rural America. Just the opposite: It reflected the fact that, using the tools of industrialization, far fewer farmers could produce a great deal more.

The basic problems of rural Americans did not stem from inefficiency. Hard times on the America farm in the late nineteenth century paralleled years of unprecedented increases in American agricultural output. Equipped with implements created by industry, farmers dramatically boosted their productivity. The steel plow, the tractor, and other machines helped the average farmer to increase yield per acre. However, between the Civil War and the 1890s, that increased production, combined with unrestrained expansion into new western territories, resulted in severe imbalances between supply and demand in a number of agricultural sectors. American farmers who sold their produce, hogs, or cattle locally and regionally never suffered as much as did their fellows. Indeed some prospered. However, many farmers, particularly those whose crops entered international markets, "overproduced." They were too efficient, at least in terms of the capacities of existing economic structures. In the late nineteenth century, for instance, wheat crops thrived, but wheat farmers went bankrupt.

Indeed, problems of productivity and inefficiency still widely plagued only one major agricultural area in the country. Southern farmers, by far the nation's poorest, lacked the tools and skills of their counterparts in other parts of the country. Although tenancy was a fact of rural life everywhere, southerners were more likely than their counterparts in other regions to work land owned by someone else. Foundation officials saw more clearly than did many of their public colleagues that the "rural crisis" was in important ways a "southern crisis." They wisely located all of the vocational education programs examined here in the South. Still, such education, even in the South, was no panacea, especially if its creators did not want those they trained to leave isolated, nonindustrial areas and therefore provided education to be understood only within the context of rural life and only for the vocation of farming.

During the same years that American leaders endlessly debated the malaise of country life, country life actually experienced one of the "booms" or periods of improvement that have characterized agricultural cycles since industrialization. The decades that spanned the Spanish-American and First World Wars saw steadily rising real money prices for all farm commodities. Some historians have credited the improvement in America's farm economy to increases in the nation's gold supply. Others have stressed the appreciation of land values that occurred as frontiers closed and vast amounts of good, cheap land ceased to be available. Most persuasively, some see the period as one of unique equilibrium between supply and demand. For more than two decades, an expanded domestic market was able to absorb farming's "overproduction." Only after 1920 would American agriculture again slip into economic doldrums.[2]

The worries of the nation's early-twentieth-century leaders about "our country people" did not, then, provide an accurate bellwether of agricultural economics. Instead, they reflected the thinking of policy makers utterly unable to do what was necessary: abandon the symbol of family farming as central to American life. The vocational policies crafted by a public-private alliance of philanthropy and government sought to safeguard that ideal.

They did not do so but should not suffer a full burden of blame. Philanthropists affiliated with Rockefeller entities, the Russell Sage Foundation, and the Julius Rosenwald Fund wanted to protect the American family farm by making rural life more prosperous, healthier, and, most controversially, more equitable. Nowhere did these goals win universal acceptance. Indeed, foundation-sponsored efforts to use vocational education to promote justice for African Americans and other mistreated minorities failed in the face of near-total local opposition. Even had the policies considered here been completely adopted, they would have faced a high hurdle: a historic trend toward increasing urbanization that has marked all twentieth-century industrialized societies. Farm policy in the West shared one constant. A welter of different approaches to the problems of rural areas had the same outcome: Difficult-to-assimilate country people fled to cities unprepared for their arrival.

Nonetheless, these early-twentieth-century American efforts to use vocational education to confront the "rural crisis" need scrutiny. They did not achieve their broadest goal, but they did permanently redefine expectations and definitions of public education in the United States. Spurred by concern about the lack of opportunity America's rural people suffered, foundation officials saw a unique chance to engage in an "experiment in [education and] Government."[3] This chapter focuses on three significant aspects of that effort. First, it examines the progress of the "farm demonstration" from an idea sponsored by the General Education Board to federally mandated "vocational extension education." Second, it analyzes the results of a cooperative effort between the Rockefeller Sanitary Commission/International Health Board and county health departments to educate rural people about communicable disease. Finally, it explores the roles played by the Russell Sage Foundation and the Rosenwald Fund as advocates of an expansion of public education to neglected rural minorities.

SCHOLARS, FOUNDATIONS, AND EDUCATIONAL POLICY

The tiny minority of foundations with expressed interests in policy making accepted the progressive view that education was a crucial tool of social reform. They worked to create elite private universities, to establish uniform codes or standards for education within the professions, especially within medicine and engineering, or to elevate standards for testing and teacher certification. Many of these efforts at policy making focused on private, not public, institutions.

When philanthropy did work to change the public school, scholars have usually concluded, as does historian William Link, that foundation leaders were quintessential "modernizers" who disdained participatory democracy. The average voter was to play no real role, except as grateful beneficiary of a more orderly and efficient society. Foundation agendas for education emphasized "maintenance of dominant class relationships . . . and did not conceive of public education as a vehicle for ending social, racial, and gender inequalities."[4]

The enthusiasm with which early-twentieth-century reformers, including members of policy-making foundations, greeted plans for education cannot easily be exaggerated. Their faith in the possibilities of engineering change within individuals and societies was fervent. Mary Van Kleeck, Director of the Russell Sage Foundation's Department of Industrial Studies, epitomized that kind of optimism and faith in education in a 1919 private memorandum. "The world," she exclaimed, "*can* be controlled, if we release intellect!"[5]

This zealous desire to "release intellect" rarely consulted the intellects of the people to be so released. Indeed, most people had to be "taught to want." Rural people, for example, had to learn that better opportunities for their children were possible. They had to be "taught . . . to be willing to dig the potatoes by themselves for six days—instead of keeping the children out of school and finishing the job in two days."[6] It was elite concern, not grassroots agitation, that spurred the foundation efforts chronicled here.

However, the picture heretofore drawn of foundation efforts to change American educational policy is excessively simplified. Like most Progressives, the leaders of the small number of policy-making philanthropies considered here talked incessantly about efficiency and scientific process. This was a part of their rhetoric, and if one relies on it alone, they emerge from private record into scholarly print as steely-eyed bureaucratic modernizers. But, in fact, most were hopeless romantics, convinced in the abstract about the infinite possibilities of humankind, while in the concrete they found themselves disappointed with the very people they idealized as perfectible. In fact, most better fit the stereotype of the missionary on a crusade. They wanted order and efficiency, but they also craved social justice.

It was a later generation of scholars, not their authors, who found hypocrisy in the constant references in foundation publications to the need for a new spirit of sacrifice and service in public life. Foundation policies often failed, but not because their creators secretly wished only to maintain the status quo. Many did set their plans within the context of a religious duty to implement society's "revival."[7] Nor did policy-making philanthropists deviously engineer the structures of society to their own benefit. In reality, they often misunderstood those structures, for during years of immense social and economic transformation, their vision frequently fogged. Essential to remember is the fact that publicly sponsored vocational education was a foundation innovation meant to save the family farm, not a policy advocated to promote the rapid spread of large-scale, high-profit commercial agriculture. As architects of projects to save small farms, foundation officials did not just make cloudy judgments about the future of American agriculture; they were blind.

Moreover, a minuscule number of policy-making philanthropists honestly did experience personal epiphany as they sought to educate and elevate their less fortunate fellow citizens. They, unlike the vast majority of their peers, advocated dramatic public policy changes in hopes of ending racial or social inequality. Julius Rosenwald wanted governments to spend exactly the same amount of money in their school budgets on all children, regardless of race.

John Campbell of the Russell Sage Foundation traveled to Appalachia in 1909 as a self-described "physician" seeking to instruct his "patients."[8] By the time he died suddenly in 1919 he regarded the poor white southern highlanders he had come to "uplift and train" as "comrades," not inferiors; he believed himself their student, with much to learn.[9] Campbell was an extraordinary individual. Most foundation figures did not make his intellectual journey. Most could not begin to understand why, by the end of his brief life, he refused to indulge their requests for stories told in full dialect about "quaint" mountaineers. Few became real democrats.

Most, however, confronted the democratic process. If the portrait drawn of the people who led foundations has been largely a caricature—so too has been the portrayal of the workings of the American polity. The example offered here of rural education policy underscores the complexity of the American public-policy-making process. Foundations, with vast sums of money at their command and a commitment to certain kinds of change, often could exercise significant influence and sometimes get their ideas embraced by the public sphere. But foundations formed only one group of players in a system characterized by pluralism, not monopoly, of power. In an arena that demanded negotiation, confrontation, and compromise, they sometimes won, sometimes lost. A foundation initiative could become publicly funded policy. A foundation initiative could, and was, just as likely to be thwarted.

Edwin Embree spent a long career as a central figure in two major "policy-making" foundations. In 1930, after years as a vice president of the Rockefeller Foundation, when he left to become president of the Rosenwald Fund, he reflected on "The Business of Giving Away Money." Embree, always insightful and usually candid, once again got it right: Foundation officers and trustees were more likely to suffer "timidity and lack of vision" than achieve true "subversion of democracy. . . . They have neither money enough nor brains enough to do it if they wished."[10]

THE COUNTRY LIFE COMMISSION

What a few exceptional foundations staffed by a closely connected network of self-described reformers did have money and brains enough to do was to win a place for private citizens at public-policy-making discussions. In the early twentieth century, many of those discussions concerned "country life." Theodore Roosevelt's Country Life Commission epitomized their nature.

In August 1908, with expenses provided by the Russell Sage Foundation and therefore, as he saw it, no need to go to Congress for funds, Roosevelt appointed a group of "experts" on the problems of rural life: journalists, foundation trustees, Department of Agriculture officials, university presidents. Their recommendations were to be delivered in written form to the White House no later than January 1909. Roosevelt, not surprisingly, chose some two dozen men who mirrored his own image: endlessly energetic, confident, self-proclaimed Progressives. He also quickly endorsed the group's plan to spend the five months allotted it in virtually nonstop travel. Touring the country in a special train, the Country Life Commission held thirty public hearings and over 250 meetings with farmers assembled in county courthouses and district schoolrooms. By Christmas 1908 the commission train had been through thirty-six of the forty-eight states. If Roosevelt had sent his emissaries off for a five-month ocean voyage he could not have created an environment more conducive to the development of alliances. Night after night commission members sipped sherry and dissected the day's events in the train's club car. Morning after morning, they shared coffee before detraining to meet the crowds assembled to meet them. The lasting personal connections formed between commission members proved its most significant legacy. This common past association linked many of those men who worked for the next two decades within government and within foundations to promote the cause of rural education.

The commission's actual report soon disappeared from sight. Congress, angry that Roosevelt had not sought its approval before appointing his investigative body, refused the $25,000 needed to print and distribute it. For decades it remained an uncirculated, typed manuscript, rediscovered and finally published only in the 1940s. The loss was not great. *The Report of the Country Life Commission* was a vaguely worded homily praising the curative power of education to correct the problems of farm America.

Roosevelt never campaigned to revive the commission. Its recommendations did not enter his speeches. Indeed, Roosevelt's purpose in creating the commission was primarily political. A ready supply of foundation money allowed Roosevelt to avoid hostile congressional debate about the necessity of financing a Commission on Country Life, and this allowed him, only days after the Democrats once again nominated that famous friend of the farmer, William Jennings Bryan, in August 1908, to achieve a clever political counterthrust. During the months just before the presidential election of 1908, a highly visible group of investigators received thousands of columns of press coverage as they toured the country—a perfect expression of Republican concern for rural areas. Roosevelt's chosen successor, William Howard Taft, not Bryan, next occupied the White House.[11]

If Roosevelt used the commission to frame the Republican Party as friend of the farmer, members of that body also found it useful as a bully pulpit, though their agenda differed. Simply put, the nation needed to promote an expanded public role for innovative education—education that took place both within and without schoolroom walls—education that reached adults as well as children. The need for experiment was, most critically, a southern one, and innovative educational programs should begin there. Between 1909 and 1930, the three foundation-supported educational campaigns examined here championed this approach. In various ways each provided chances for members and staff of the Country Life Commission to reunite.

Foundation officials continued to see the commission as a model to imitate: a perfect illustration of useful policy interaction between private and public spheres. Wickliffe Rose, dean of a small college in Nashville, Tennessee, was a very busy man in 1909. First he advised the Country Life Commission, then accepted an invitation to move to New York to help develop new Rockefeller philanthropic programs. Years later, in 1913, he still idealized the commission as the perfect vehicle for promoting change in public policy: "Let work be tried and started at no expense to the Government. Let it be privately financed—provided the President were willing to endorse it, thus giving it the sanction and moral power of the Government. That is the way President Roosevelt set his Country Life Commission going. They served without pay and their expenses were met from a private source.

The Commission undoubtedly gained in influence and in freedom by serving without compensation."[12]

Rose's views accurately reflected those of most of his colleagues at other philanthropies interested in influencing policy. They confirm Edwin Embree's judgments and demonstrate naiveté about the complexities of the American political process, not a sinister ability to subvert it. Had the Republican Party not faced William Jennings Bryan in a presidential election year, would the sitting president have so eagerly endorsed the Country Life Commission? If it were truly "free" of political influence, would not the commission have concentrated its investigations in the South, the one region most bypassed by progress? Would its members still have barnstormed the entire nation nonstop, greeting the press for photographs at every depot? What Rose and his fellows had "brains and money" enough to do was to promote new policies. As the following three examples illustrate, sometimes their suggestions gained acceptance. Others met rebuff.

THE FARM DEMONSTRATIONS

The General Education Board–sponsored farm demonstrations sought, above all, to improve agricultural productivity. Experts at the GEB warned that rural Americans, especially in the South, would continue to fall farther and farther behind their urban counterparts unless they could improve their productivity. Statistical facts alone would not soon dislodge the conviction shared by many foundation leaders that the nation's progress depended on agricultural productivity.

In 1930 Rockefeller Foundation trustees and staff met in Princeton, New Jersey, to assess the past thirty years of the foundation's efforts and to chart courses for the future. The contributors to the two days of discussion were uniformly well educated and well read: prominent businessmen, former university scholars, doctors, and attorneys. Yet, in a year when only 18 percent of the national population remained gainfully employed in farming, no one challenged Frederick Russell, the physician who headed the Foundation's Division of Public Health, when he said that "ours is a rural civilization, and notwithstanding our rapid commercial and industrial development, the great majority of our people must continue for generations to come to live under rural conditions."[13] Like "small taxes gradually increased over long years" the inefficiency of this majority would imperceptibly, but inexorably, drain national vitality. It was crucial that America's policy makers realize that "our more important vital losses, like our financial losses, are in driblets, pennies, nickels, dimes, and an occasional quarter—in little drafts, long continued."[14]

A revitalized and publicly supported program of education would not only reduce such losses but would also provide new hope to all America. At no time did the four foundations considered here attempt to work alone. "Revitalization of rural America" was "a work of such magnitude that it could be undertaken only with Government support." In fact, as Frederick Russell explained, "Year by year it became clearer that Government, both central and local, was the agency to which we had to look for cooperation and for eventually maintaining and carrying on the work. The first great principle that clearly emerged was that of Government cooperation."[15] The "farm demonstrations" sponsored by the General Education Board illustrate both the significant long-range influence exercised by private wealth over public educational policy and, in a quite dramatic fashion, the restraints placed by a pluralist political system on foundation power.

In 1901 John D. Rockefeller established his first major foundation, the Rockefeller Institute for Medical Research. In 1903 his second, the General Education Board, received a charter of incorporation from Congress. As originally conceived by Frederick Gates, in his customary role as chief advisor to John D. Rockefeller Sr. and, in this case, Rockefeller Jr., the GEB was to be a national clearinghouse for all philanthropic spending on education.[16]

Within three years of its creation the GEB had crafted an identity as a Rockefeller agency, with a focus, if not an exclusive focus, on the educational problems of rural America. If the nation's farmers were in trouble, those farming in the South faced disaster. Wallace Buttrick, a fellow former Baptist minister whom Gates had successfully persuaded in 1902 to accept employment as the GEB's general secretary, reminisced in his unpublished autobiography that initially the officers of the General Education Board had imagined that the problems of rural education centered around the schoolhouse: "We thought that a teacher with a schoolhouse constituted a school, and that if we could only multiply schoolhouses and schools . . . the problem of education would be solved."[17]

Within a few years, they decided they were wrong. What impoverished southern farmers needed first was not schoolhouses, but money. If they had more money they could build their own schoolhouses by supporting higher levels of state taxation to support education. They could get that money if they became more productive through an embrace of more efficient techniques of farming. The GEB's long-term goal was a higher level of taxation

Officers of the General Education Board at the Hotel Samoset, Rockland, Maine, on 8–10 July 1915. *Left to right, from the bottom row:* Edwin A. Alderman, Frederick T. Gates, Charles W. Eliot, Harry Pratt Judson, Wallace Buttrick, Wickliffe Rose, Hollis B. Frissell, John D. Rockefeller Jr., E. C. Sage, Albert Shaw, Abraham Flexner, George E. Vincent, Anson Phelps Stokes, Starr J. Murphy, and Jerome D. Greene. R. F. Portraits. Courtesy of the Rockefeller Archive Center.

by state and local governments to support public education. To achieve that objective, it championed scientific agriculture as a technique that would earn farmers the extra money necessary to gain their support for additional taxation. The long-term goal obviously required government cooperation; less obviously, so did the short-term one.

In its campaign to educate rural Americans, especially rural southerners, about scientific agriculture, the GEB embraced the farm demonstration system pioneered by Seaman Knapp, special agent for the U.S. Department of Agriculture. Its quiet alliance with the Department of Agriculture between 1906 and 1914 to fund an expanded farm demonstration program led to a new role for the federal government as a sponsor of vocational and agricultural "extension" education. It also prompted an ugly congressional battle and a public repudiation of the General Education Board.

In 1906, to help them in their search for a way to spread the gospel of scientific agriculture, Gates and Buttrick solicited the advice of members of the network of journalists, professors, and agricultural reformers who comprised the loose alliance some had begun to call the Country Life Movement. Among the most vocal proponents of scientific agriculture were the heads of state land-grant agricultural colleges. One, Liberty Hyde Bailey, Director of the Agricultural College of Cornell University, would eventually chair the Country Life Commission. Another, David Houston, the president of Texas A&M and a future Secretary of Agriculture, already knew Wallace Buttrick. Buttrick, a large, genial man with a genius for telling stories and acquiring lifelong friendships, trusted Houston and traveled to Texas to consult with him about the board's decision to promote scientific agriculture. Houston delightedly introduced Buttrick to another of his guests, Seaman Knapp. After a two-day visit that assumed the form of an informal tutorial conducted by Knapp, Buttrick rushed back to New York, convinced that Knapp's "farm demonstration" system provided the key to increasing agricultural income.[18]

At the time of his momentous weekend with Buttrick, Seaman Knapp was seventy-three years old. Since 1879, when he took a newly created position at Iowa State Agricultural College in Ames as Professor of Experimental Agriculture, he had been a tireless advocate of the techniques he introduced to his students as "scientific agriculture." The scientific farmer had to think of himself as the manager of a business. To succeed he had to employ new knowledge—about soil drainage, diseases of plants, stock breeding, weather prediction. He had to understand farm "economy" and be able to prepare detailed plans for farm investment and improvement.[19]

In 1883 when he was already in late middle age, Knapp decided to practice what he preached. He quit his teaching post at Iowa and became the organizer of a group of investors that bought over a million and a half acres of supposedly worthless marshland in Louisiana and planted it in rice. Ironically, he also predicted, without ever acknowledging the fact, the death of the American small farm he so loved. Knapp became an enormously rich rice planter, not because he successfully practiced the techniques of scientific farming, but because he headed an incorporated agricultural syndicate that farmed on a huge scale. But when Knapp decided to retire from full-time agricultural management to edit the magazine he founded, the *Rice Jour-*

nal, he ignored the lessons he had learned in large-scale corporate farming. Rather, he filled the pages of the *Rice Journal* with praise for family-centered operations. He himself had not gone into Louisiana independently but had instead created one of the South's first successful agri-businesses. Nonetheless, he advised his readers to be as self-sufficient as possible, urging them, for instance, to grow and can their own food in addition to tending the rice they raised for market. As he mused, "I have learned that if you open the front door of the grocery store and stick one corner of a one hundred and sixty acre farm in, the whole farm will slip in quicker than a small boy will crawl under the canvas of a circus tent."[20]

Seaman Knapp did not long remain a gentleman editor of an agricultural magazine. Rather, a plague of insects "slipped him" into another and final career, as a special agent for the Department of Agriculture. There, he pioneered programs of agricultural extension education that reflected the romantic faith in small farming that he displayed in the *Rice Journal,* not the hard-headed assessments about agriculture in an industrial society that had made him wealthy. The implications for publicly supported vocational education would be profound.

In 1903 the Mexican boll weevil, which had been slowly spreading throughout the lower South for a decade, first appeared in enormous numbers to devastate the Texas cotton crop. Congress, spurred by the "mass panic" in southern states, authorized an additional $40,000 for the annual budget of the Agriculture Department, earmarked for an attack on the boll weevil. The network of agricultural college administrators, journalists, and reformist government officials that formed the heart of the Country Life Movement searched for a man to lead the fight against the new insect pest. Seaman Knapp, everyone's first candidate, agreed to accept the assignment when his old friend, now Secretary of Agriculture, James Wilson presented the government's offer as a personal request. Against initial congressional opposition, these two old crusaders then decided that their war against the weevil would not focus on a frantic search for an effective poison, something that would not be discovered for decades. Instead, Agriculture would spend its additional authorization on farm demonstrations in northeastern Texas.

What exactly was the farm demonstration? Knapp's system, which he had promoted privately for decades, turned a local farm into a model for scientific agriculture. Knapp, who remained capable of working fifteen-hour days into his nineties, personally toured each area chosen for a demonstration. He asked local residents for the names of the county's best farmer and best banker. Then he would interview both. He asked the banker, "Would you indemnify one farm against loss, if the owner of that farm tries new techniques of farming that, by greatly augmenting crop productivity, will offset any potential destruction by the weevil?" He asked the farmer, "With this guarantee, will you allow your fields to become demonstration fields?" If both men answered "yes," Knapp would offer, as his part of the bargain, the promise that neither would feel time or money had been wasted. If, as usually happened, the farmer planted seeds distributed by Knapp, cultivated them precisely according to instructions, and discovered at harvest time that his crop yield had at least doubled, he became a missionary for scientific agriculture. He, not a stranger, proselytized his neighbors who, in turn, saw enviable results on the land of a respected member of their own community. To Knapp, "demonstrations" conducted by government bureaucrats on public land were a waste of money.[21]

This was the system that sent the already normally ebullient Wallace Buttrick back to New York "singing with joy!" Within weeks of his initial meeting with Knapp in Texas, Buttrick met with him again in Washington in the office of Secretary Wilson, who informed both that Agriculture had no authority to expand the demonstration work into areas not yet touched by the boll weevil. However, should the General Education Board be willing to fund programs in these areas, the work could be rapidly expanded. Before the meeting ended, Buttrick and Wilson signed a memorandum of understanding that initiated an eight-year alliance between the board and the Department of Agriculture. Between 1906 and 1914 the GEB would spend almost $1 million in "supplements" to the salaries of some six hundred special Agriculture Department farm demonstration agents.

The agreement between Wilson and Buttrick specified that "said agents shall be under the control of said department in every respect as fully as any other agents of the department." However, it also mandated that each agent send a weekly activity report and a monthly detailed expense account to the Board's New York offices with "duplicates of same" to be "filed with the United States Department of Agriculture."[22] The "supplement" scheme hammered out in the memorandum of understanding was actually a ruse. Agriculture paid GEB-supported special agents one dollar per year.

In its initial year, the expanded farm demonstration work involved 545 farms concentrated in Texas and Alabama. By 1912, the year of the program's height, 106,621 farms in fifteen southern states growing either corn or cotton had become "demonstrations." The General Education Board published estimates that in 1912 alone over fifteen thousand people in each participating state directly witnessed the results of scientific agriculture. At the very least the farm demonstrations exposed hundreds of thousands of rural Americans to methods that promised to boost their incomes.[23]

Those methods stressed Knapp's two cardinal rules: use superior seed and cultivate it intensively. Once a farm had been chosen as a demonstration site, its owner received seeds from the special agent assigned to the farm. He also received answers in person to any questions that the Department of Agriculture–reprinted guidelines on proper cultivation might prompt. He learned that he must plow under a cover crop in the fall in order to supply crucial nutrients to the soil. He learned that wide-row planting allowed more light and moisture to reach plants. In signing a contract to receive his seeds the demonstration farmer also vowed within his best ability to practice Seaman Knapp's "Ten Agricultural Commandments":

1. Remove all surplus water on and in the soil
2. Plow under a cover crop of legumes in the fall
3. Use the best seed
4. Space plants properly
5. Practice crop rotation
6. Use natural and commercial fertilizers
7. Produce as much food as possible for family and stock use
8. Buy better machinery
9. Buy better stock
10. Keep totally accurate accounts of the cost of farm operations[24]

The General Education Board argued that the demonstration farms were a "contagious" success.[25] Their message of economic salvation rapidly spread through rural America as hundreds of thousands discovered that the Ten Agricultural Commandments paid material dividends. Nor was there any question that demonstration farms were more productive. GEB official reports quoted U.S. Bureau of Statistics calculations that they doubled average yields in pounds of seed cotton or bushels of corn.[26]

In a printed account of the demonstrations that it published long after the program had ended, the General Education Board called the project a "perfect illustration" of private-public cooperation: "Governmental bodies can with difficulty undertake educational experimentation on radically new lines; unofficial organizations are more receptive of new suggestions, can create here or there the conditions required for an experiment, and, as they are unhampered, can command the advice and the ability needed to inaugurate a novelty. A successful demonstration once made, the work can be turned over to the state."[27] This account begged several questions. First, it did not accurately describe the relationship between the General Education Board and the Department of Agriculture. When Wallace Buttrick enthusiastically embraced farm demonstration in 1906, it was already an established program within the department. The GEB did not, as an "unhampered" unofficial organization, create a program, that, once proven, could be "turned over" to the state. From the beginning, it always was a partner with the state.

Moreover, the General Education Board never proved that the "novelty" of farm demonstrations promoted greater prosperity in rural America. Board records include hundreds of internal reports about the state of agriculture in the United States, but curiously, not one mentioned the relative improvements in farm commodity prices that had occurred after 1898. Instead, all stated that it was the farm demonstration technique, not a spin in an economic cycle, that spurred higher farm income in southern states between 1906 and 1914. Moreover, a farmer chosen to be a demonstrator saw

> his name in the county paper as one of the farmers selected by the United States Department of Agriculture to conduct demonstration work; he receives instructions from Washington; he begins to be noticed by his fellows; he is proud of planting the best seed and doing the best cultivation. When the demonstration agent calls a field meeting at his farm, he begins to feel that he is a man of more consequence than he had thought. Immediately the brush begins to disappear from fence corners, the yard fence is straightened, whitewash or paint goes on the buildings. The man made a good crop, but the man grew even faster than the crop.[28]

GEB reports delighted in anecdote—in stories about "wretched farmer"(s) on "poor piney woodland" who accepted scientific farming and became prosperous, proud, and happy.[29] In truth, the demonstration program recruited relatively few truly wretched rural residents. The selection process followed Knapp's long-established practice that required that agents ask local citizens for recommendations of the most capable and admired farmers in their counties. These people were, most likely, better educated than average, better able to follow Agricultural Commandments 8 through 10—which required capital expenditure for improved breeding stock and better farm machinery—and more willing to create comprehensive financial accounts for their farms.

The demonstration farmers were not wretched and not even very average. A typical farmer in the South, perpetually the nation's poorest farm region, lacked the capital resources to join even the small-scale commercial agricultural revolution the Knapp system endorsed, much less the coming large-scale one that would eventually revitalize American agriculture. The "demonstration," then, enabled those already advantaged to gain additional skills. It did nothing for the poorest farmers in the South, the approximately 30 percent of whites and 70 percent of blacks who did not own the land they worked. Landowners who practiced the Knapp system did not share with their tenants any additional profits brought by increased productivity. In fact, when the South fully embraced mechanized "scientific" farming during the Great Depression, its poorest farmers were displaced, not enriched.

The voices the General Education Board and the Department of Agriculture chose to record may have echoed general sentiment. There is greater reason to suspect they romanticized it. Very few cracks appeared in the official wall of optimism about the efficacy of demonstration work. Not many southern newspapers followed the example of the Stuart, Virginia, *Enterprise* and printed letters from angry farmers who denounced "soft-handed" county agents who spent most of their time in "comfortable steam-heated offices [we the people] are taxed to maintain."[30]

It is well to remember, however, that the General Education Board did not support farm demonstration work to manipulate commodities prices or build the character of farmers. Rather, its stated purpose was to "create underlying conditions favorable to educational development."[31] GEB documents contain dozens of charts showing increases both in annual expenditures for public schools and in percentages of local taxes earmarked for public education.[32] Clearly, southern states spent more money on public schools in 1914 than they had in 1906. However, the GEB never proved that farm demonstrations provided any significant stimulus promoting this trend, and some of the evidence in its archives posed a challenge to any such causal link.

Alabama, the one state involved in the farm demonstration experiments that achieved 100 percent county participation, was also the only state in the South between 1902 and 1907 that showed absolutely no percentage increase in funds raised for education by local taxation. By contrast, Mississippi, a state with only a modest participation in the program, boasted a 117 percent increase.[33] Most likely, it was a period of general agricultural prosperity in states where, unlike the nation at large, most people still lived on farms, not the GEB–sponsored demonstrations, that encouraged greater public willingness to tax for schools.

The cooperative relationship between the Department of Agriculture and the General Education Board ended abruptly in 1914, but not because a significant number of policy makers challenged the efficacy of demonstration education. On the contrary, the direct legacy of the relationship was an almost complete acceptance of the farm demonstrations' much expanded definition of the kinds of education that should become public responsibilities. Between 1914 and 1917, Congress passed two significant pieces of education legislation. One, the Smith-Lever Act, which became law in May 1914, greatly expanded the pilot programs in farm demonstration work funded by the General Education Board. During the previous eight years the GEB had spent $925,750 on such extension work, and now, through Smith-Lever, Congress mandated that the federal government would spend a minimum of $4 million a year—a sum to be matched by state governments.[34]

President Woodrow Wilson signed the second measure, the Smith-Hughes Act, into law in February 1917. Smith-Hughes provided yet more government endorsement of ideas initially funded by the Rockefeller philanthropy. This act mandated the establishment of a Federal Board of Vocational Education to provide national oversight to burgeoning federal and state involvement in various kinds of "practical" vocationally oriented education aimed at adults as well as children and including a wide variety of subjects beyond scientific agriculture. Interestingly, one of the first members of the three-person board was David Houston, former president of Texas A&M and host of the fateful 1906 meeting between Wallace Buttrick and Seaman Knapp. Houston, President Wilson's Secretary of Agriculture, had helped to engineer a revolution in the operating rules for public education. Not only could publicly funded education include an emphasis on teaching practical job skills to adults and children, such education could take place both within and without schoolroom walls. Moreover, for the first time, using a precedent first established by the Agriculture Department and the General Education Board, federal funds became a significant resource to be used for educational purposes.[35]

Given this history, one might easily imagine that congressmen would celebrate the passage of the Smith-Lever Act by inviting Wallace Buttrick and Frederick Gates to Washington to receive the thanks of a grateful nation. Nothing, however, could have been further from the truth. Instead, the halls of Congress rang with denunciation. Thomas Gore of Oklahoma demanded a "divorce of the Government and the General Education Board," because any money coming from the Board or any other Rockefeller philanthropy was unclean—"red with human blood and dripping with human tears."[36] Representative Lewis Martin of New Jersey raged, "I hope the U.S. may be spared from living on the contributions of a Rockefeller. . . . It would be equivalent to a family living on the wages of sin. If we cannot exterminate the cotton boll weevil without recourse to Rockefeller, then a thousand times rather let it destroy the entire cotton crop."[37] Nobody challenged the congressman's emotional rhetoric with the truth: The GEB demonstrations excluded regions infested by the weevil.

Two events in April 1914 prompted these extraordinarily hostile outbursts, one in Colorado, the other in Washington. Ten thousand Colorado miners had, by then, been on strike for months, protesting the refusal of Rockefeller's subsidiary Colorado Fuel and Iron Company to negotiate with the United Mine Workers. On 29 April a pitched battle between armed miners and members of the Colorado state militia called out to protect owners' interests destroyed the tent community of Ludlow, a desolate assembly of pit and canvas dwellings built by the UMW as temporary housing for strikers. By the time the shooting ended, fire had consumed the flimsy structures and forty people were dead, among them thirteen women and children trapped by flames and smothered to death underneath the tents. As word of the "Ludlow Massacre" spread, both John D. Rockefeller Sr. and Jr. faced a public relations disaster of epic proportions.[38]

Quick on the heels of the dreadful events in Colorado came another major embarrassment. Senator William Kenyon of Iowa, a member of the Senate Agriculture Committee, discovered the 1906 memorandum between James Wilson and Wallace Buttrick that provided the framework for eight years of GEB payment of government employees. A furious Kenyon condemned the Rockefellers as the agents of a "silent empire," who wanted to establish an "invisible government—through gifts to education."[39] The senator was not the only public official surprised to discover the details of the arrangement between the General Education Board and the Department of Agriculture. While not technically secret, its existence was, to say the least, not common knowledge. At most a tiny number of top-level Agriculture Department officials, as well as a few members of the General Education Board's New York office staff, knew that hundreds of special agents for the department received their salaries from private philanthropy.

Senator Hoke Smith of Georgia, cosponsor of both the Smith-Lever and Smith-Hughes Acts, was the most vocal advocate for vocational education in Congress. On 23 May, as a verbal melee swirled around him, Smith, not often one to remain silent, quietly stared at his hands. Then he stood to declare to his fellow senators his "astonishment" at Kenyon's revelations:

> I have been familiar with the farmers' cooperative work in my own state and in other southern states. I have met Dr. Knapp. I have seen the work of his demonstrators, but . . . I never knew of this contract until within the last thirty

days. As a member of the Senate, I thought every dollar of the fund came from the National Treasury. . . . The use of this fund has been of great service to the South . . . [but] I think our Treasury is strong enough to pay for anything that ought to be done for the general welfare of the people of this country.[40]

Frantic efforts by General Education Board staff members and trustees to reverse what, by the end of May 1914, had become a tidal wave of vitriolic condemnation of any activity associated with the Rockefeller name largely failed. Trustees inundated Senator Kenyon and his fellow members of the Agriculture Committee with letters and telegrams. Starr Murphy, chief counsel to John D. Rockefeller Sr., expressed utter bewilderment that a "Senator from Iowa would wish to attack a work which had been carried out under the full direction of two such distinguished Iowa statesmen—Secretary Wilson and Dr. Knapp." Moreover, he assured Kenyon, the "only" motive of the General Education Board was "true patriotism. . . . [T]he boll weevil and other conditions created something like a great regional emergency." Surely the senator from Iowa realized that "the Government constantly cooperates with private donors to Red Cross funds in times of great public calamity."[41]

The senator from Iowa, however, remained unconvinced. Indeed, the letter he sent May 4 to Rockefeller trustee and prominent magazine editor Albert Shaw declared that no matter how great the "storm" the money and influence of the Rockefellers could create, he would "simply sit in the boat until the storm goes by." And he would certainly continue, he said, to view John D. Rockefeller Sr. as a villain with an "absolute, apparent lack of all regard for humanity, so outrageous that I should be glad to see the Government revoke any charter [for the General Education Board] it had issued."[42]

Congress did not revoke the Board's charter, but by June 1914 the advocates of Rockefeller philanthropy realized that it would demand a legal separation between the GEB and the Department of Agriculture. At this point they decided to cut their losses and settle for a quiet annulment rather than a scandalous divorce. To secure this end, they unleashed another hailstorm of letters and telegrams, which fell this time on Representative Asbury Lever of South Carolina, chair of the House Agriculture Committee.

Prominent Alabama cotton grower Sydney Bowie was one of Wallace Buttrick's many friends. As such, he responded to the GEB's pleas to lobby Lever in its defense. The idea, said Bowie, that through the "General Education Board, Mr. Rockefeller will acquire a dangerous hold upon the minds of the people . . . is so far fetched and so absurd that I hesitate to attribute any such belief to any intelligent person." Yet, even though he implied that the debate that had raged for weeks on the floors of the Senate and the House was the work of fools and worse, Bowie had resigned himself to defeat and asked Lever for a minor concession, not victory. The wording of the annual agricultural appropriation bill first released by Lever's Agriculture Committee had specifically enjoined the Department of Agriculture from accepting "any money contributed or tendered by the General Education Board or any like organization."

Bowie and other Rockefeller supporters now successfully requested that the Board not be named specifically in the appropriation statute.[43] The final wording of the bill released by the conference committee and passed by Congress on 26 June 1914 spared the General Education Board that additional humiliation. Rather, it appropriated a greatly increased sum of $673,240 for farm demonstration work but then decreed that the Department of Agriculture could only accept "cooperative funds . . . voluntarily contributed by state, county, and municipal agencies, individual farmers . . . colleges . . . local associations of business and individuals within the state."[44]

Obviously, the operative word was *within,* which meant in effect that the General Education Board had been summarily dismissed. Congress had accepted the gift and repudiated the giver. Its actions raised worrisome policy implications. On the one hand, public officials embraced the techniques for teaching scientific farming to adults that Seaman Knapp had invented and that John D. Rockefeller Sr. had supported. But on the other, they engaged in a shabby debate about the latter's character and had decided that even though he had done good, his potential for doing evil was not to be tolerated. The outcome provides a classic illustration of policy making by the American pluralistic state.

Without much acknowledgment of what it had done, Congress passed the Smith-Lever Act in 1914 and endorsed a public policy still in place in the late twentieth century, namely, that the federal government should partially fund programs of vocational education conducted both inside and away from schoolroom settings. Demonstrations provided good, "practical" education. They taught specific skills and promoted general prosperity. The federal government had assumed a new role: as financial patron of vocational education, and on a broader scale than the model of the alliance between the General Education Board and the Department of Agriculture suggested. The Sixty-third Congress accepted this new responsibility, initiating public education policies for which taxpayers would eventually spend billions, not, however, after dispassionate examination of such education's worth, but in a climate saturated with hate-drenched condemnations of John D. Rockefeller Sr.

Why was Senior so despised? Members of Congress found a popular target when they attacked America's richest man, who to millions of Americans represented "commercial sin."[45] That phrase, from journalist Ida Tarbell's famous attack, was only one of many echoing in early-twentieth-century America. The country's citizens could read about Senior's villainies in more than a dozen supposed exposés, of which Tarbell's *The History of the Standard Oil Company* was only the best known.

Rockefeller Sr. was the wealthiest individual in the country after 1910. He was, however, by no means the most venal. He disdained reckless extravagance and had always given generously to good causes, long before the establishment of the Rockefeller foundations. Judged by contemporary standards, his companies were no more unethical than many of their competitors.

How then, can Rockefeller's reputation be explained? It, after all, long preceded the horrible events that occurred in Colorado in 1914. In fact, had another family name been attached to the Colorado Fuel and Iron Company, the national reaction to the Ludlow Massacre might have been different. Repeated, and often very violent, clashes between workers and employers marred the era, and the wives and children of Ludlow were not the first innocent bystanders to die.

Americans, including public policy makers, hated Rockefeller the myth, not Rockefeller the man. The man was elusive. His one published book of reminiscences first emerged in print as a series of plodding homilies to godliness and thrift in *World's Work* magazine. The editor of that journal, a personal friend and a Rockefeller Foundation trustee, probably published Senior's memoirs as a favor. Gripping prose they were not. But these few piously dull essays provided his "fellow citizens" with their only glimpse of Rockefeller as he saw himself.[46]

The public did not rise up, in a groundswell of grassroots rebellion, to call Rockefeller Sr. evil. The overwhelming majority of the country's population never heard him, or saw him, or read a word he wrote. Rather, Americans decided Rockefeller was a terrible man because leading politicians and journalists told them so.

These latter groups probably hated Rockefeller for qualities he really did possess. The founder of Standard Oil was a formidable figure: ruthless against rivals, calm in crisis, coolly remote, implacable, unstoppable. He controlled the most powerful corporate trust in the country but seemed indifferent to the standard rules of American political discourse. He certainly never seemed to understand why Senator Kenyon was so angry to discover that Rockefeller money had paid the salaries of government employees.

This arrogance merited rebuke, and Rockefeller's economic power was dauntingly genuine, not mythical. However, Senior's attackers in Congress also demonstrated faults. In April and May 1914, they shouted and raved and curried favor with constituents with feverish denunciations of tainted money. What they did not do was examine with deliberate care the farm demonstration system itself or question whether it really should be instituted as public policy.

The Rockefeller-funded farm demonstration program, then, illustrates private policy writ largely unchanged and unexamined into public policy. It certainly does not illustrate the machinations of a private and secret empire controlling the American polity. Had that really been true, John D. Rockefeller and his son, both of whom hated publicity and loved decorum, would never have been forced to endure two months of intensely open attack. They would never have felt the need to assign a public relations agent, Ivy Lee, the formidable task of refurbishing the Rockefeller family image.

RURAL PUBLIC HEALTH EDUCATION

Between 1909 and 1914 another Rockefeller philanthropy, the Rockefeller Sanitary Commission, won praise, not vilification, for its battle against a parasitic disease caused in the American South by the hookworm. Rockefeller policy makers certainly wanted to end hookworm infestation, but that was not the primary goal justifying the creation of the Sanitary Commission. The fight against the disease would provide the Sanitary Commission with a "favorable wedge" and allow it to attempt a much larger policy goal: a revolution in rural public health education.[47]

That required the transformation of the still new and little supported institution of the county health department into a powerful new force for public health education. After the hookworm campaign ended officially in late 1914, the Sanitary Commission's successor, the International Health Board (IHB), continued its joint cooperation with county health officials and expanded the original "educational" campaign against hookworm to include parallel attacks on other "preventable" diseases like diphtheria, diarrhea, and enteritis. Only after 1930 did the International Health Board restrict its activities in the American South to concentrate its programs, as its name had always implied, quite incorrectly, abroad.[48]

Once again, the Country Life Commission brought private and public policy makers together. Since 1900, Charles Wardell Stiles, a German-trained scientist with successive appointments at the Department of Agriculture and

Public Health Service, had been conducting a fervent, if usually solitary, campaign for greater public recognition of the connections between worm infestations and disease. In 1909 his appointment as an advisor to the Country Life Commission finally provided Stiles with an interested, and influential, audience. The man most receptive to Stiles's insistence that southern "laziness" was really a form of anemia caused by hookworm was Walter Hines Page, the prominent editor from North Carolina who had recently been appointed by Theodore Roosevelt to the Country Life Commission and was well situated to be an intermediary between the worlds of government and philanthropy. Not only was he extremely well connected politically, he was equally influential in philanthropic circles as a much-admired Rockefeller trustee. In the spring of 1909, after being convinced by Stiles that parasitic diseases were not only a serious problem, but a "preventable" one, Page created an opportunity for the scientist to present a slide lecture to Frederick Gates, Wallace Buttrick, and other key Rockefeller aides at the philanthropy's central New York offices. Stiles's presentation spurred the creation of the Rockefeller Sanitary Commission.[49]

Wallace Buttrick had championed Seaman Knapp to head the farm demonstration work and now played a parallel role in urging the appointment of Wickliffe Rose to head the new Sanitary Commission. Rose was a long-time friend and associate of Buttrick but not a scientist. Rather he was a scholar of classical languages and French, a shy and quiet man who often stayed late at his office to browse through the stacks of books in Greek, Latin, and French he kept for his own after-hours pleasure.[50]

The appointment of Wickliffe Rose, who would remain after the demise of the Sanitary Commission in 1915 to head its successor, the International Health Board, accurately reflected the philanthropy's solution to preventable disease. The weapon was education, not medicine. In 1903 Seaman Knapp had advocated education in scientific farming, not a search for a particular poison, as key to the fight against the boll weevil. In the case of certain kinds of diseases, Wickliffe Rose argued, education was even more crucial.

Drugs might be found to cure a certain category of "filth" diseases spread by "unclean" environments, but, if people returned to those same environments, they would be no better than "sows returning to wallow." Reinfection would be inevitable, and the cost of the drugs would have been wasted. Rather, as Dr. I. A. Shirley of the Kentucky State Board of Health argued, "The object of it all consisted more in teaching how to keep well after treatment than to treat them and turn them loose."[51]

The approach taken by the Rockefeller Sanitary Commission between

1909 and 1914 and continued by the International Health Board between 1915 and 1930 was to create "an effective educational agency" out of county boards of health.[52] But doing this would require a change in public policy. In 1909 most states had established state departments of public health to supervise subordinate boards of health within each county. Most existed as ghost agencies, and nowhere was this more evident than in the South, whose mild winters did not kill the parasites that spread "filth" diseases. In southern states especially, legislatures had organized departments of health, then appropriated little or no money for their operation. Almost no county governments did any better.[53]

Into this near-vacuum marched the Rockefeller philanthropies, eager for another "experiment in Government." Just as the General Education Board never considered undertaking education in scientific farming independently, neither the Sanitary Commission nor its successor, the International Health Board, considered an independent approach to another educational campaign, this one to improve public health. Their choice of an alliance with the county health board, however, provoked no public fireworks.

For one thing, the Sanitary Commission and the International Health Board did not make their relationships with a government agency secret. For another, the public officials with whom Rockefeller philanthropists cooperated were, this time, significantly more independent than were the GEB-supported special agents who sent their weekly reports and expense accounts to Rockefeller offices in New York and "duplicates" to their putative superiors at the Department of Agriculture.

Long before the public relations debacle caused by Senator Kenyon's exposure of this relationship, the Sanitary Commission had established another pattern of philanthropic funding for government-sponsored activity. Between 1909 and 1930 both the Sanitary Commission and the IHB made financial contributions to central state boards of health. The states accepted the moneys with the understanding that they would be used to employ full-time paid county health officers. These new health officers, usually local physicians, reported to county and state health boards. In a reversal of GEB practice, this time the "duplicates" went to New York City.[54]

The Sanitary Commission focused on one disease only: hookworm infestation. It was the campaign against it that provided the model, not merely for cooperative funding with a particular public agency, but also for a new kind of publicly funded education. Between 1909 and 1914 all southern states with the exception of Florida accepted Sanitary Commission funds; Florida had already begun its own program, financed by state property taxes.

In each cooperating state, new county sanitary inspectors emphasized education in preventive medicine and hygiene. Although Rockefeller-funded programs existed everywhere in the South but Florida, archival records for the states of Kentucky and North Carolina are by far the most complete. They serve here as examples of the larger effort.

The Kentucky Health Commissioner felt that he faced not "active resistance but passive disbelief." Summarizing the efforts of dozens of county agents, he continued:

> Our people . . . meet us with no belief in preventive medicine or personal hygiene. . . . The average audience does not believe in the existence of hookworm or other parasites; they do not believe they are infected with these parasites even if they do exist; they do not believe that we could tell it even if they were infected, nor that we could cure them if found. They are not aggressive in their disbelief as the anti-vaccination people are, but they are in a passive state of negation that requires demonstration to overcome.[55]

The demonstrations, the commissioner continued, needed to reach in all directions: "A considerable percentage of both our rural and urban population are illiterate, but this class is rarely more ignorant in regard to the teachings of modern preventive medicine than a large majority of the so-called educated classes."[56] The task was an unenviably difficult one, and it could be accomplished, wrote Wickliffe Rose, only if each county health officer was a zealous, even a "consecrated teacher conducting a school which runs twelve months in the year and has all the people in the county for its pupils. The teaching must be systematic and unceasing."[57]

The activities supervised by the county health officer of Northampton County, North Carolina, provide a typical example of such "unceasing" activity. After Rockefeller officials dissolved the Sanitary Commission in 1915, the International Health Board continued to support the North Carolina Department of Public Health's crusades against hookworm, as well as an expanded roster of diseases that included malaria, typhoid fever, and diarrhea. In 1917, as the nation entered the war, the Northampton County health agent organized evening programs of illustrated slide lectures. At least once a week, he dimmed the lights in a local schoolroom, post office, or library and showed graphic, much-enlarged slides of hookworms and other parasites. Cleverly, he also used slides showing before-and-after photographs of residents of each small town or farming village he visited. These local people often then stood up to a round of applause—to give personal testimonials that the drug treatments they had received and the personal sanitary changes they had made dramatically improved their lives.

Supplementing the regular lectures of the health officer were new programs in the public schools. By the end of 1917 every primary school teacher in Northampton County had agreed to include instruction in the essentials of home sanitation as part of regular course work. Children between the ages of seven and ten were given score cards and required by their teachers to make a "sanitary survey" of their homes at the beginning and close of the school terms. The keys to receiving better marks for home sanitation were two— both relatively simple: Windows and doors should be screened effectively in order to provide some protection from diseases spread by insects, and in the case of hookworm even more important, human waste must not be allowed to pollute surrounding soil and water. That required not just the construction of better privies but, as the North Carolina report emphasized with heavy underlining, "*The creation of a privy sense!*"[58]

How did citizens get a "privy sense?" Most rural health officers agreed: They must cooperate in the sanitation process. For example, once they became convinced that improperly treated human excrement promoted the spread of parasitic diseases, homeowners must build their own sanitary privies with plans and, if necessary, materials supplied by the county health boards. Only then were the new structures likely to be put to effective use. Northampton County even went so far as to issue a "contract" to be signed by both citizen and health officer.[59]

Some county health officers also went beyond soliciting contracts from their fellow citizens. One, William Bridger of Wayne County, North Carolina, promised a "handsome gold watch" to the "man or boy—white or colored" who had assisted, without pay, the "largest number of his neighbors in building or remodeling, their privy." Bridger argued that a good, fly-proof, privy that caused little soil or water pollution could be built according to his plans "by any boy in an hour." Therefore, only people who had built at least twelve privies for neighbors would be entered into the two-month-long competition for the watch. Bridger cautioned, "To win this valuable prize, *Begin Now!* I realize it is the natural tendency among most men to put off until tomorrow all the things that seem not immediately urgent."[60] Unfortunately, the remaining archival record does not reveal whether the males of Wayne County took up Bridger's challenge. It does not note whether privy building fever or even "privy sense" dominated community life during the two months—February and March 1915—designated by Health Officer Bridger as the time frame for the contest, nor does it even indicate whether somebody met his twelve-privy minimum and took home the watch.

Conclusions about the overall effectiveness of the Rockefeller-supported and county-conducted public health education between 1909 and 1930 are also difficult to reach from the evidence available. Were philanthropic reports of the health work justified in claiming victories, as the International Health Board did in 1924, calculating that the people of the South had received a return of six dollars for every dollar invested in public health? Rates of fecal and insect-borne diseases had indisputably dropped, accompanied by marked declines in deaths from typhoid fever, diphtheria, and smallpox.[61] But what caused these "victories" is less clear.

Drug treatment probably did not play a major role, although by 1930 over two-thirds of the 788 southern counties that had a full-time health officer also provided a free drug dispensary that distributed thymol, the medicine used to kill the parasites that caused hookworm disease. The problem was that a large enough dose was almost certain to nauseate and, if taken with alcohol or any foods that contained gravy, butter, or milk, could be lethal. Indeed, people died from taking the thymol cure, though it is now impossible to learn how many. Despite its known dangers, the Sanitary Commission adamantly refused to keep statistics about inadvertent fatalities. In any event, people soon learned for themselves that, at the very least, thymol caused terrible nausea. That alone made them reluctant to complete a full course of tablets. Charles Stiles estimated that well over half the people who received thymol capsules never took them once they got home, and, the county and Rockefeller records, of course, noted the numbers of capsules dispensed, not the number actually taken.[62]

If medicines provided only a small part of the explanation for victories in the battle against gastro-intestinal "filth" diseases, were the publicists for the Rockefeller philanthropies right? Did an aroused public, educated to the dangers of faulty privies, unscreened houses, open rubbish pits, and stagnant water, voluntarily and enthusiastically eliminate these threats? The public pronouncements of Rockefeller officials and county health agents suggested they did, but their private communications hinted at a more complex reality. Dr. J. N. McCormack, Secretary of the Kentucky State Board of Health, in a letter to Rose's assistant, Dr. J. A. Ferrell, noted the slow effect of voluntary education. The average Kentuckian, he said,

> readily understands in his new enlightenment the danger of soil pollution and necessity for those who cough to stop spitting. After a time, he begins to realize

the economic aspect of the thing in a vague way. . . . He begins to understand why the health authorities think the country school houses should be built better than the stock barns, and why the children need fresh air and well-cooked, wholesome food. All this time, it is far easier for him to believe all these things and to know them than to do anything.[63]

Coercion, in concert with education, was what really worked. Rates of infection from fecal and insect-borne diseases dropped far more dramatically after 1913 when many southern states copied North Carolina's initiative and passed laws making it a punishable misdemeanor to disobey any order from a county health officer. After 1913 southerners choosing not to be "educated" about public health faced fines ranging from five to fifty dollars and up to thirty-day jail terms.[64] The problem of hookworm infestation became even more tractable when states again copied the North Carolina legislature's decision in 1918 to require citizens to build sanitary privies. In that state, health officers had the right to inspect and condemn all privies that were not fly-proof or that posed dangers of soil and water pollution. Furthermore, all privies in North Carolina had to be built at least one hundred feet from the nearest well. If a property owner continued to use a condemned privy after thirty days' notice, he faced fines and jail.[65]

Other forms of coercion included the increasingly common decision by local and county public school boards to forbid attendance by children not yet vaccinated against smallpox and typhoid fever. Even Wickliffe Rose, whose faith in the powers of education was unquenchable, admitted that the vaccination orders were victories for county boards of health, not the inevitable decision of better-educated parents. In fact, in a confidential report sent from the field back to Frederick Gates, he allowed that "strong opposition" to vaccination of children existed in some areas.[66]

Private forms of coercion were coupled with public ones. Available records provide no answer, but it would be fascinating to know how many bankers throughout the South followed the lead of the Bank of Grifton in Pitt County, North Carolina. In 1917 it adopted a policy of making loans only to persons who could present evidence that they lived in sanitary surroundings. A successful applicant for a loan had to prove that he lived in a home with a sanitary privy, and that he and all other members of his family had been vaccinated against typhoid fever. He also had to bring in evidence that he and his family were free of hookworm. Were the Bank of Grifton loan officers the only ones who reviewed not only financial assets but also notes from the county health officer attesting to an applicant's hookworm-free stool sample?

It would be equally interesting to know how many tobacco warehouse owners acted as did those of Wilson, North Carolina—who in late 1918 agreed to make loans against the 1919 crop only to families who provided papers from the county health officer verifying their vaccination against typhoid fever.[67]

One must conclude that the early-twentieth-century Rockefeller-supported public health campaigns against filth diseases do not prove indisputably the success of an expanded agenda for public education. Instead, they raise interesting questions about the necessary interactions between threat of sanction and education. Moreover, they pose a challenge to those who would portray the foundations as powerful conspiracies, forcing their will on subordinate public officials, and, through them, an unwary public. The records of the two Rockefeller philanthropies that spearheaded these campaigns reveal negotiation, not domination by one side.

In September 1910 Wickliffe Rose wrote an urgent letter to Dr. Hamilton Jones, Director of the Louisiana State Department of Health, asking if he could not "in some quiet way induce" the governor to change his mind about the pending appointment of Sidney Porter as administrative head of the Louisiana hookworm campaign. Rose asserted that he had nothing personal against the governor's choice, but could not "conscientiously recommend" him since he did not possess the attributes the Sanitary Commission thought crucial: a good medical training and executive ability.[68] When Jones reported back that the governor had no intention of bending, Rose upped the ante. "While I would not presume to dictate to your Board whom it should appoint," he said in his answering letter to Jones, "I would not urge the appointment of any man who was not thoroughly acceptable. No state board thus far has *not* appointed any man without our mutual understanding and agreement."[69]

Wickliffe Rose learned that there is a first time for everything. His correspondence with Louisiana officials about this particular appointment ended on 10 October 1910, when, in a one-sentence note to Dr. Oscar Dowling of the State Board of Health notable for its cold brevity, Rose admitted defeat. "Dear Dr. Dowling," he wrote, "I am now prepared to recommend the appointment of Dr. Sidney Porter as head of the campaign against hookworm disease in Louisiana."[70]

Wickliffe Rose, like so many other progressive reformers, liked to use religious imagery. He wrote often of the immense dedication of the new county health agents, individuals "consecrated" to their cause, bent on "health revival" and "universal human uplift." With "proper management and nursing" they could be "led" by philanthropic support to even greater victories.[71] But if he learned in Louisiana that he could not tightly control state government officials, he also discovered, even if he never publicly acknowledged it, that even lowly county officials were not easily led saints.

Fred Caldwell, a physician hired by the International Health Board to provide it with a confidential report on the progress of health work in the South, spent much of 1919 and 1920 on the road, touring the region, county by county. His discoveries, relayed in detailed reports sent to Rose's assistant, Dr. J. A. Ferrell, suggest a less orderly, but far more plausible, reality. Rockefeller officials, for example, liked to point to Wilson, North Carolina, as a town where the citizenry was absolutely united in support for all aspects of the health campaign. Investigator Caldwell, however, found that the Wilson Sanitary Dairy was anything but. Instead he saw "flies walking in the spout of the separator. In fact, I saw one picked out of the can of milk before it was placed in the bottle filler."[72]

The health officer in Wilson, a Dr. Wickliff, was a "willing" worker, but lacked "training . . . and force of character." He not only "placed faith in the promises" of the dairy owner to screen his premises, he made little effort to enforce the state's new privy law. In fact, Caldwell noted with astonished scorn, "Upon question, Dr. Wickliff said that since the privy law had been passed he had paid no more attention to privy construction." The IHB inspector went on to say that "the privy law is certainly the best thing for the state ultimately, but it certainly has diminished the interest that some of the health officers take in the problem of soil pollution. Some of them say . . . let the other fellow do the dirty work and incur the dislike of the populace."[73]

Fred Caldwell, wreathed with the supposed power of vast philanthropic wealth, could not get Dr. Wickliff of Wilson to initiate charges against privy law violators, nor could he get the county health officer in Raleigh even to talk. Caldwell did not appear there unannounced in hopes of verifying a suspicion that at least one North Carolina health officer was not "consecrated" day and night to human uplift. He had a long-standing appointment. But, the offending health officer "who was ready to leave his office in search of a missing hunting dog . . . did not remove his coat," but instead continued out the door, leaving the representative from the Rockefeller Empire with nothing to do.[74]

Unquestionably, public health education was top-down reform. Nonetheless, a few letters, scrawled in uncertain handwriting on very rough lined paper and found in the records of the Rockefeller Sanitary Commission, raise yet another question about policy making in a pluralistic society, one that is rarely asked by scholars of philanthropy and public policy. In what ways did the "public" use the policy-making process for its own ends?

Clearly, neither A. C. Whitley nor Cola Martin of the tiny rural hamlet of Potecasi, North Carolina, had played a role in the creation of the county health board as an education agency. They were local farmers whose letters to Dr. L. M. Register, the county health agent, reveal only rudimentary literacy. They were, no doubt, members of that great inefficient and undereducated rural class that caused early-twentieth-century government and philanthropic officials such worry. Yet, the uneducated Whitley and Martin seem to have cleverly discovered in the person of the newly appointed county health agent a perfect vehicle for furthering their personal feud. Whitley began what became a volley of letters in August 1917 with a complaint to Health Officer Register that Martin had "thrown" the dead body of a cow within seventy-five yards of his house and, therefore, deserved a fine. Martin, when contacted by Register, was furious, responding that the cow "was burried [sic] about four feet deep. . . . No odor escapes from the hold [sic]. . . . No buzards [sic] has been seen." Charges and countercharges filled Dr. Register's in-box for weeks, and, upon inspection, he could find neither dead cow nor dead cow's grave. Finally, in complete exasperation, he wrote to Cola Martin. Saying that, as a public servant, he was "glad to serve you in any way I can," Register gave notice that he no longer was willing to mediate. He hoped that "you and Mr. Whitley" would get the "cow matter adjusted." As for himself, he wanted no more of it.[75] How many more tens of thousands of "cow matters" existed? What, in aggregate, could we know about all of them, would they say about the impact of public policy?

One impact of this chapter's second case study is clear. Rockefeller support encouraged the permanent establishment of county and state health boards—with educational as well as purely medical missions. In 1909 virtually no state, even in wealthier regions than the South, spent more than a pittance on county health agencies. By 1930 the county health officer was a permanent fixture everywhere, and the appropriations begun by private philanthropy had been largely assumed by state governments. In 1909 Mississippi spent less than five thousand dollars yearly on public health education. By 1930 its annual spending had increased enormously, to an average $200,000. That sum equaled one-third of the entire amount spent in the South by the Rockefeller Sanitary Commission between 1909 and 1914. Mississippi's dramatic increase in spending was typical and reflected the fact that state government had assumed yet another role. Policy decreed that it supervise public health education even though the actual merits of such education remained unclear.[76]

In 1930 the International Health Board announced that "only a few spots" of hookworm infestation remained in the American South. Indeed, it had virtually disappeared, and the IHB could, therefore, focus its health education efforts overseas.[77] However, hookworm still remained. An angry Charles Stiles publicly countered that in many areas of the South infestation rates of 30 and 40 percent remained common.[78] Stiles's crusade had always been to eliminate hookworm from America. Wickliffe Rose's was more complex. For him, hookworm disease was a "favorable wedge" through which to introduce policies that established new educational roles for county government. It was the latter goal that proved spectacularly successful.

EXPANDED PUBLIC EDUCATION FOR NEGLECTED MINORITY GROUPS

Between 1909 and 1930, the Rosenwald Fund and the Russell Sage Foundation spearheaded campaigns to provide equal public educational opportunity for two minority groups in the South, blacks and white Appalachian "Highlanders." Both campaigns provided significant help to people who needed it, although neither achieved its ultimate goal of public support for equal education. Each provokes additional questions about the connections between private wealth and public policy.

During the first decades of the twentieth century, most members of America's elite, and certainly most rich philanthropists, left relatively unexamined the contemporary social prejudice that categorized a wide variety of racial and ethnic groups as their natural subordinates.[79] Many parroted the harsh pseudo-scientific jargon of eugenics. They spoke of the need to "replenish" rural America with a "better stock" than that found among "children whose parents came over in steerage."[80] They saw nothing repugnant in language that urged the development of better human "breeds"—even in communities of hill-country southerners who "owing to peculiar circumstances have remained in a sort of cold storage, though not with the depreciation that we feel takes place in our food under similar circumstances."[81]

In some ways, the prejudices displayed by members of America's elite extended to include everyone but fellow representatives from their own well-educated and well-heeled urban circles. Frank Bachman, dispatched by the General Education Board to study education in the upper South, blithely stereotyped the populace of an entire state in a report sent to Abraham

Flexner: "Kentuckians are extremely individualistic. They love to talk and visit, but work—and particularly intellectual work—[is] repugnant to them. Hence, when any problem is presented to them, they fail to think it through . . . and find refuge in disagreement on minor details."[82]

Such language has led scholars to conclude that as important elite leaders, privileged philanthropists sought education for others less fortunate only as a cement for the status quo—a way to train inferiors for their proper places. Such a conclusion comes easily but is wrong. It exaggerates Progressivism's search for order and neglects its fervor for fairness. It also misunderstands the thought processes of early-twentieth-century elite reformers—who saw no contradiction in their embrace of eugenics and their enthusiasm for expanded educational opportunity. The few philanthropists who sought to use their vast new wealth to prompt social change believed that American institutions needed to provide more—for more Americans. That belief certainly did not make them, by any stretch, social or economic radicals. However, to argue that they spent money only to ensure that things would stay the same is simplistic.

Moreover, a very few seem to have taken a far more sophisticated look at education and social progress. Julius Rosenwald really seems to have come to believe in the necessity of struggling for real equality between the races. John Campbell of the Russell Sage Foundation came to admire the isolated mountain people of Appalachia, not as quaint throwbacks to a purer Anglo-Saxon stock, but as equals. The efforts led by these two men to get publicly funded equal education for these minorities failed. The fact that their foundations supported such a cause provides a challenge to those who persist in making easy generalizations about interactions within the leadership class of the early-twentieth-century state.

The foundation that spent the most money during these decades on black education was not the Rosenwald Fund, but the General Education Board. However, the bulk of the almost $15 million that the GEB earmarked for black education between 1902 and 1930 went to private black colleges that emphasized agricultural and industrial training on models first created at Tuskegee by Booker T. Washington.[83] Although Rockefeller philanthropies were essential partners in public-private alliances that redefined public rural education, most notably in the creation of farm demonstrations and public health education, their spending on education for minorities followed more traditional charitable lines—with an emphasis on generous donations to favored individual schools, especially Tuskegee Institute and Spelman College, named in honor of Rockefeller Sr.'s wife.

While the *Annual Reports* of the General Education Board during these years emphasized that "the Negro needs fairer [educational] treatment," the Rosenwald Fund wanted "equal schools for all."[84] Edwin Embree, president of the fund, summarized its philosophy: "On the grounds of democracy, humanity, and sportsmanship the case for equal schools . . . for all the people is so self-evident that fair-minded men cannot question it. [Rosenwald efforts at reform were rooted] . . . in nothing more ethereal than the good, old-fashioned principle of enlightened selfishness. In modern civilization individuals and groups are closely interdependent. Progress for any group is facilitated or retarded by the progress or backwardness of all other groups."[85]

After 1900, with a fortune secured by the huge success of his Sears-Roebuck Company, Julius Rosenwald began to give generously to black institutions like the Tuskegee Institute. His contributions to such colleges, and his personal friendship with Booker T. Washington, remained life-long. However, by 1917, Rosenwald had also decided that true social change demanded cooperative efforts with the state. It was the public school system, not the private, that became the focus of the Rosenwald Fund's attention.

Between 1917 and 1928 the fund contributed over $18 million toward the construction of 4,190 schools for black children scattered throughout fourteen southern states. In order to qualify for a "Rosenwald" school, a county or local school district had to agree to provide at least half the money for the school's construction, locate it away from the center of a town or village, and guarantee its future maintenance. It also had to follow carefully the architectural plans sent it from the Rosenwald central offices in Chicago and agree that the annual school term be at least five months long. In addition, if local or county school authorities agreed to extend the annual school term to at least eight months' time, the Rosenwald Fund would provide financial aid to construct a residence for one or more teachers.[86]

By 1930 over half a million rural black children studied in clean, well-lit, one-to-six-room brick or clapboard schoolhouses. The creation of a network of such solidly built, modern schools where none had previously existed was a significant achievement on its own merits. Worth noting, however, is the fact that the Rosenwald Fund's goal was far more ambitious—to create a revolution in public funding of education. Julius Rosenwald dreamed that his thousands of well-constructed, cost-efficient schools would "shame" public officials into spending equal, if separate, amounts for the education of black and white children. Moreover, they would spend equal amounts for rural schools and urban schools. No longer would governments anywhere, even in the rural South where over 80 percent of all black Americans lived, be willing to

Cartoon of Julius Rosenwald, by Ralph Wilder, 1912. Courtesy of the Department of Special Collections. University of Chicago Library.

tolerate "shabby buildings—a disgrace to the American public school system—rickety hand-me-down furniture—inadequate teaching equipment—tattered textbooks or no books at all—poorly-trained and abominably-paid teachers."[87]

Julius Rosenwald greatly underestimated the public capacity for shame. The group that joined enthusiastically with the Chicago merchandiser in his crusade to improve public education for blacks was the African-American community itself. Throughout the South, thousands of black church groups, burial societies, and social clubs embraced Rosenwald's invitation to join with him to build better schools for their children. They held bake sales. They passed the plate twice at Sunday services. They gave nickels and dimes. Frequently, black community groups contributed in-kind to help the building projects. Black women's clubs brought hot lunches to the laborers. Parents painted interior and exterior walls. They laid walks and planted flowers. In many small communities, planned one-room schoolhouses became two- or four-room buildings when private black donations supplemented funds committed by government and the Rosenwald Fund.[88] In 1919 Abraham Flexner toured the South with Julius Rosenwald inspecting progress made by the then six-year-old building program. He reported to Wallace Buttrick: "The truth is—as I said to Anne when I got home—'If I see much more of Negroes and Negro schools, and the way they are throwing themselves into it and trying to squeeze 100% value out of what there is in it, I am going to drop the Whites and devote the rest of my life to Negro education.' "[89] Even the dauntingly enthusiastic Flexner could not resist rereading his message and adding "and medical education" before posting the letter. White officials in the South never had to retreat, even in this minor fashion, from an initial rush of support for the Rosenwald schools. They took the private wealth but turned it to entirely different purposes.[90]

Throughout the 1920s, the black historian Carter Woodson periodi-

Red Hill, Rosenwald School, Green County, which received $100 from the Rosenwald Fund. From left to right, the photograph shows the old school building, the new Rosenwald school, the church, and the lodge. General Education Board Photo Collection. Courtesy of the Rockefeller Archive Center.

cally visited southern states for the fund and compiled his assessments of the school building project in an unpublished manuscript report titled "Story of the Fund." Carter astutely saw that "the striking result of Julius Rosenwald rural school construction [is] the effect that it had on whites. The schools thus constructed for Negroes were in many cases superior to those for whites. In some instances, moreover, before there could be erected a comfortable building for the Negroes, one equally good or better had to be erected for the whites, inasmuch as race prejudice was so intense that the Negro building might otherwise be burned down."[91] Woodson continued that local white governments "of course" did not particularly desire to follow in black footsteps. Nonetheless, Rosenwald had spared no expense to hire a team of nationally prominent architects and engineers who had devised good plans for low-cost, easily and well-built rural schools. Local officials, lacking money to employ their own architects, found a perfect solution to their worries about the defects of rural white schools in the Rosenwald plans for rural black schools.[92]

What was the public policy impact of the Rosenwald schools? By 1922 Alabama had established a Division of School House Construction within its State Department of Education, and as a result of action by this division, all Alabama blueprints and specifications followed those first drawn by Rosenwald employees. When the Oklahoma State Legislature passed a "Standard School Building Law" mandating that all rural schools be built to a common plan but appropriated no money for the preparation of such a plan, it was natural that the Oklahoma State Department of Education adopted wholecloth those of the Rosenwald Fund. D. L. Lewis, State Supervisor of Rural Schools of South Carolina, displayed not one hint of the shame the Rosenwald Fund wished to induce. In fact, he actually sent a letter to the philanthropy's Chicago offices. He was "so pleased" with the quality of the fund's plans that he "at once asked permission to use them for white schools. This permission was given us, and their use has rapidly increased among school people for white schools."[93]

Carter Woodson ended his report with the prescient conclusion that it would require "much time" before inequalities in public funding for black and white rural schools would end.[94] Indeed, decades would pass before equal funding became even a stated policy goal, much less a reality. In 1936 Edwin Embree, in a review of the history of the fund published in the *American Scholar*, admitted that after two decades of efforts by his philanthropy, the value of school plant and equipment in the South averaged $157 per white pupil, $37 per black pupil.[95]

Such admissions, however, did not come easily. An exchange of letters between Rockefeller Foundation trustee Jerome Greene and Wallace Buttrick illustrates the more typical spirit of willed disbelief common among even self-declared friends of black education. In January 1914 Greene reported an emotional meeting between Oswald Garrison Villard, head of the National Association for the Advancement of Colored People, himself, and John D. Rockefeller Jr. While considering Villard "earnest" and well-meaning, Greene was sure that he was wrong. He wrote Buttrick, "Both Mr. Rockefeller and I, however, thought he [Villard] was mistaken in the impression he had with regard to the failure of the expenditure for Negro education to advance in proportion to the population—to say nothing of making a relative increase. . . . We should like to put him [Villard] right for his own sake."[96] When Buttrick reported that his search for the requested statistical proof of an increase anywhere in per capita public expenditure for black schools had turned up nothing, Greene, trained as an attorney, responded with another request that would have been viewed in most courtrooms with suspicion. "Well," he wrote, "would it not be possible to secure one or two very competent opinions on that point?"[97]

The "competent" opinion of the day stereotyped other minority groups as well—even one minority among native-born whites. The mountain people who lived in great isolation in the Appalachian range that spanned a 112,000-square-mile area between western Maryland and northern Alabama were the ignorant, bloodthirsty "Hatfields and McCoys" of early-twentieth-century popular imagination. The residents of this area, labeled by the Russell Sage Foundation as America's "Southern Highland," were unquestionably deprived of equal educational opportunity, and John Campbell, a Russell Sage Foundation employee, devoted his career to a thwarted campaign to increase public funding for mountain schools. But if public officials were unwilling to adopt equal funding policies for black and white pupils, they were equally unwilling to consider the special needs of a certain group of particularly impoverished whites, Appalachian mountaineers.

The son of a wealthy Indiana family who had trained for the ministry at Andover Theological Seminary, John Campbell chose not to take a pulpit. Instead, in 1895 he headed south to Tennessee to become a teacher in church-sponsored "mission" schools in remote parts of the Smoky Mountains. In 1908, when the Russell Sage Foundation decided to sponsor travel expenses for members of the Country Life Commission, it searched for a well-respected representative already known throughout the South and found Campbell. He coordinated travel and meeting schedules for the Commission as a full-time Russell Sage Foundation employee, then stayed on to create its Southern Highland Division. The Division and John Campbell were indivisible. When he died in 1919, it ceased to exist.[98]

When he came to work for the Russell Sage Foundation, John Campbell had already spent thirteen years as a teacher, attempting to reach people in the hills and hollows of Appalachia. He accepted the Foundation's appointment, in part, because he had become an advocate of public, not private church-sponsored, education. After years in the field, an exasperated Campbell had no patience with the "mission barrel."

Campbell took delight in describing the "typical" contents of such a gift: two pairs of "frayed duck trousers, a battered silk hat, a dress-coat with stains upon the lapel, indicating that it had not been worn in a prohibition state . . . a great many cigarette pictures—pictures of battle ships, famous race horses, and notorious actresses. Sprinkled as leaves in this mixture were *Bible* cards with the injunction to 'Remember thy Creator.' "[99] Campbell admitted chastising church boards for sending such unwanted rubbish to their rural mission schools. More privately, he turned the stories he told in public about mission barrels into parables. Why, he raged, should church officials accept "the sophistry that because a man is good, inefficient, and a failure elsewhere, he may be qualified for the rural ministry? The country needs men who are not only *good*—but *good for something.*"[100] The poverty-stricken and ill-educated people of Appalachia needed more than religious charity. They needed a good system of public education—but one particularly suited to their needs. During his ten years as Director of the Russell Sage Foundation's Southern Highland Division, John Campbell tirelessly championed the need for such schools.

Before 1930 most public schools throughout Appalachia were ungraded. Except for Maryland, which had a ten-month school law, most were in session a few months of the year at best. Many existed in name only, closed by weather or crop conditions, or by a community's inability to find a teacher. The teachers who did exist were usually "little young girls," teenagers, rarely possessing better than a grammar school education themselves. Most remained with a particular school only a short time, often only a matter of weeks. Even when a public school in a southern mountain community boasted a two- or three-month term, rarely were its students taught during consecutive months, or by the same teacher. Buildings were almost always unheated or poorly heated. Few schools could afford items their counterparts in other areas would have considered necessities. Teachers often struggled to deliver lessons without the help of blackboards, chalk, desks for their students, or textbooks.[101]

Teachers throughout the region rarely received more than a few hundred dollars for a term's work. Nonetheless, teaching jobs offered one of the few ways available in the South's Highlands to earn cash money. Schools, therefore, were "cousined." Kinship counted far more than scholarship; teachers' certificates were easily bought or obtained through political connections, and poverty-stricken mountain communities often parceled out the meager patronage of a school appointment to many competing families. During a typical three-month term, therefore, it was not uncommon for a one-room public school to host from twelve to twenty teachers. Sometimes these "teachers" presided for only a day or two, earned three or four much-appreciated dollars, then left to make way for another.[102]

Poorly trained teachers, political nepotism, and lack of supplies all posed major problems. So too, Campbell argued, did the prejudices often displayed by isolated mountain people. In one report on the state of public education in Appalachia, he described the case of two young women teachers hounded from a mountain school in North Carolina in 1920 after they taught their students that the world was round. They soon faced public charges of "heresy." Obviously, Scriptures said, "The *corners* of the earth are the Lord's." The school's well was poisoned. Rumors flew that the teachers were prostitutes. Parents withdrew their children.[103]

Under such circumstances, Russell Sage's Southern Highlands Division Director concluded that great numbers of the region's people, of all ages, desperately needed more schooling. However, a traditional grammar school structure, while it might work in other parts of the country, would likely fail throughout most of Appalachia. There, "too many mountain youths of eighteen" could barely read and write. If such older teenagers persisted in a desire for education, they would find themselves in classrooms with children of six or eight years old. The few who even tried to face such humiliation usually ended up "discouraged or hardened, to swell before long the ranks of the voters who see no good in taxing themselves to give others education which is " 'no account nohow.' "[104]

Explicitly linking his campaign with that promoted by the General Education Board, Campbell urged southern states to emphasize vocational education and to make more use of the moneys provided after 1914 by the Smith-Hughes and Smith-Lever Acts. Such education, unlike conventional efforts, could reach adults beyond school age, as well as many older pupils who were too embarrassed to sit with small children in the lower elementary grades. It was a key to integrating its poorest whites into the larger fabric of southern and national society. The "folkehoiskoles" or folk schools of Scandinavia provided a model.

Campbell had described these folk schools as the salvation of the "farming class" of Scandinavia. Between 1870 and 1890 countries in this region, especially Sweden and Denmark, had created national systems of schools specifically for their rural populations. First, they required that all children between the ages of seven and fourteen attend free state-supported primary schools. Then, in rural areas all residents over age fourteen could voluntarily attend "folk schools," funded by both private and government contributions. These schools had no age limits, no grades, and no formally mandated curriculums. Very small—limited to about fifty students—the folk schools averaged terms of about ninety days during the winter slow season. Rural Scandinavians eagerly attended them for years to take additional courses in geography, history, literature, or practical subjects—such as new techniques in scientific farming.[105]

John Campbell's vision remained unfulfilled. Most southern states did not begin to establish truly effective systems of compulsory education that included free primary schools for remote mountain districts until the late 1930s. In 1926 seven years after his death, a private school supported largely by the Presbyterian Church opened in Brasstown, North Carolina. Named the John Campbell Folk School and intended as a memorial to its namesake, the school had a short, unsuccessful life and lost most of its students with the onset of the depression. The Russell Sage Foundation viewed it with "sympathetic interest" but gave it no money.[106]

EDUCATION AND THE "RURAL CRISIS"

One final question needs to be added to the others already raised here about relationships between private wealth and the creation of publicly funded programs to educate rural Americans. Did the focus by foundations on education as a cure to the "rural crisis" help establish public policies that ignored more serious, structural problems with the American economy?

The rural crisis identified by the Country Life Movement assumed individual productivity as the key to a better life for farm Americans. Even the pathbreaking Rosenwald and Russell Sage efforts to win equal treatment for blacks and "Highlanders" argued that prejudice had to be fought, not only because it was unjust, but because it contributed to inefficiency and impoverishment.

Foundation-sponsored campaigns and subsequent public policy focused on education and productivity, but productivity was only part of the problem. During the year that Theodore Roosevelt's Country Life Commissioners hurtled by train all over the country, championing the cause of scientific farming, farmers garnered record prices for their wheat, corn, and cotton. For a brief two decades, between 1898 and 1918, consumer demand roughly balanced agricultural output. After World War I, however, farm America once again entered a depression of "overproductivity." After 1920 farmers in areas outside the South shared the desperate plight their fellows in southern states had never really escaped.

Indeed, farmers were not the only Americans who discovered by 1929 that productivity alone was not the key to stability and prosperity. Farmers were not the only ones who became more efficient—and more educated—only to slip into the nation's worst depression, itself, in part, a crisis caused by "overproduction" and serious imbalances in the distribution of national wealth.

Education was one key to the problems of rural America, especially in the American South, the region that the General Education Board, the Rockefeller Sanitary Commission, the Rosenwald Fund, and the Russell Sage Foundation correctly identified as lagging far behind the country. The vocational education policies spurred by these foundations, had they been more widely practiced, might have even further improved the lives of the people they reached. However, the southerners most likely to benefit from the advice of county farm agents or public health wardens were not the area's truly impoverished farmers, a group in which the region's blacks and "Highlanders" were greatly overrepresented. State and county governments rejected or twisted policies that promoted educational equality for minorities. They accepted, at least to some degree, programs that sought to improve the region's productivity by making its citizens better and healthier farmers.

If productivity increases provided no guarantee of good times in other parts of rural America, they may have been a particularly inappropriate solution to the woes of the agricultural South in the early twentieth century. The historian Gavin Wright has argued that improved agricultural productivity had no necessary connection with prosperity in a South where before 1930 a dangerously vulnerable one-crop economy still prevailed. Weak national and international demand meant that great increases in output would have even further depressed world prices for cotton. With few other cash crop options, and a manufacturing sector still in its infancy, the South could not defeat widespread poverty with the weapon of scientific agriculture. Better farming techniques helped the rise of the "New South" after the Great Depression, but they were coupled with a concentration and corporatization of agriculture, urbanization, and industrial development as well.

Despite regional improvements in technology, the decade of the 1920s was one in which the percentage of southern farms under tenancy increased. By 1930, 40 percent of white and over 80 percent of black farmers worked other men's lands and had little hope of dramatically improving their lives. Indeed, the only "escape" available to most of them would be a literal one; they would leave agriculture. Massive numbers would flee the South to seek their fortunes in northern cities, where in many cases they would only transplant, not solve, their problems. Others would stay to find jobs in the industries that finally began to emerge in their home states after 1938.[107]

Even if it did not achieve fully an ambitious agenda that sought justice, health, and prosperity for southern country people, the foundation-sponsored reaction to the "rural crisis" prompted permanent changes in definitions of American public education. So too did the Laura Spelman Rockefeller Memorial's response to another "crisis" discovered by America's leadership elite in the early twentieth century. The "collapse of the home" also prompted private philanthropy to sponsor and public officials to accept innovations in vocational education. This time the training was to be for parenthood, not scientific farming.

THE LAURA SPELMAN ROCKEFELLER
MEMORIAL, PARENT EDUCATION, AND
THE NEW PSYCHOLOGY

D uring the years when Wallace Buttrick and Wickliffe Rose worried about the nation's rural crisis, another group of foundation officials discovered the "collapse of the home."[1] In the face of unprecedented social change, Americans were failing their children. At a time when their guidance was never more desperately needed, the country's parents were bringing up a generation of spoiled future citizens. And the pity was that if they only knew how, they could do better. Society had "almost completely neglected training for parenthood."[2]

This second crisis—in American child rearing—prompted another foundation-sponsored educational initiative: to provide "parent education" in public schools. Once again, a "crisis" first identified by philanthropy became a topic for public policy making. Once again, the attention directed to the problem reflected concerns dominant in the world of the policy-making elite. Southern farmers did not demand agricultural extension education or informational campaigns from county public health departments. Ordinary early-twentieth-century American parents did not ask their leaders for publicly funded training. In fact, the overwhelming majority of American parents probably saw the duties of child care as an unremarkable, if sometimes stressful, part of their lives.

The "rural crisis" was real—a significant disjuncture of opportunity between agriculture and industry. The "crisis" in parent education, however, was really a crisis in the new field of psychology. There, between 1890 and 1925, a generation of psychologists trained at a few elite universities transformed their discipline from a vaguely defined branch of philosophy to an experimental "hard" science. In the process they led an intellectual revolution in perceptions of human nature as well. Human behavior, they had decided, was not instinctual; it could be controlled, and if it could be controlled, careful training of children was absolutely crucial to social progress.

A group of young, ambitious psychologists, members in excellent standing of that new generation, exercised unique influence in one major policy-making philanthropy, the Laura Spelman Rockefeller Memorial (LSRM), and supported efforts to make parent education a part of publicly funded adult education through an alliance with the California State Department of Education. Another example of a foundation-initiated public education policy, parent education, needs to be placed within a larger context. That demands a brief review of the inextricably intertwined histories of parent education and the profession of psychology.

INSTINCT PSYCHOLOGY, BEHAVIORAL PSYCHOLOGY, AND PARENT EDUCATION

William James's *Principles of Psychology*, published in 1890, introduced the study of human psychology to American academics. James, a prominent member of the Department of Philosophy at Harvard University, wanted a text that would inform his students about the "animal roots" of human nature. What he produced was the seminal book in a new professional discipline. Heavily influenced by the ideas of Charles Darwin, James argued that instinct shaped human behavior. Nature, not nurture, determined much of human destiny. Emotions like anger, resentment, and rivalry were largely instinctual. So too, but less obviously, were many other common behaviors: a dislike of unprotected open spaces, a desire to hunt, fear of the dark.

In the first two decades of the twentieth century, G. Stanley Hall, one of James's students, used his position as president of Clark University in Worcester, Massachusetts, to popularize instinct psychology. As flamboyant as James was quiet, Hall argued that the new field provided crucial tools for understanding human growth, especially the stages by which an infant became an adult. If parents understood at what ages their children could be expected to behave in certain ways, they could provide important guidance. Therefore, not just academics, but every parent, should learn the "contents of children's minds."[3]

Parents, according to Hall, should know that those contents were very different depending on a child's age. Human development, in fact, "recapitulated" the species' evolutionary development, and parents should realize that young children were basically still animals. They should be left to play and develop as their instincts demanded. Only after the age of eight had children's minds developed to the point where they could tolerate much restriction or discipline. This meant that formal schooling before that age was not only useless, it could be actually harmful to physical and mental development. Moreover, parents must know that early childhood was not the only period when potential crisis loomed. They should realize that their older children, or "adolescents" as Hall called them, faced a period of unique turmoil—when their primitive instinctual natures warred with other more highly evolved characteristics.[4]

Throughout his career, Hall relied upon questionnaires that asked parents to provide detailed reports about the behavior and speech of their children. Initially these were sent to the faculty at Clark and the residents of Worcester, Massachusetts. But before long, Hall sought a larger sample population and found it in the membership of the new Parents and Teachers Association. Founded in 1897, and known until 1908 as the National Congress of Mothers, by 1915 the PTA had a paid membership of sixty thousand. Overwhelmingly educated white middle-class women, they provided G. Stanley Hall with his most devoted lay followers. Between 1900 and 1930 PTA delegates welcomed Hall as an honored guest to their national conventions. They also met in hundreds of local study groups to study his ponderous books about the biologically imprinted stages of human maturation, and they faithfully mailed in his questionnaires.[5]

The report given by Mary Watts, an Iowa delegate-at-large to the PTA's national convention in 1911, reflected the organization's zealous acceptance of Hall and instinct psychology. If human behavior was largely innate, then obviously careful concern for genetics would produce "Fitter Families for Future Firesides." According to Watts, Iowa had pioneered in a series of events that sought to promote "heredity as a basis for building up the standard for whole families." She enthusiastically assured her fellow delegates that the "time is not far distant" when "humans, like prize live stock, will be registered and pedigreed." As one step in that direction the Iowa PTA had sponsored a contest at that year's Iowa State Fair, in which the family that achieved the highest scores from a panel of doctors and psychologists examining its members' mental and physical health had won a blue ribbon as the "most fit."[6]

The PTA's leadership would continue its support of "instinct" psychology into the late 1920s, but other organizations were not so smitten. The Spelman Memorial would not support "Fit Family" contests, nor would it praise G. Stanley Hall. Instead, between 1923 and 1930 it would promote an entirely different theory about child behavior and a new version of parent education that reflected the direction that the discipline of psychology was taking. By 1918, when John D. Rockefeller Sr. endowed the Laura Spelman Rockefeller Memorial as a tribute to his late wife, Hall and instinct psychology were passé, at least among a small group of university-based psychologists.

Psychologists at the University of Chicago exercised particular influence: first shattering and then re-ordering the profession. The university was another Rockefeller beneficiary, founded in 1891, and almost overnight becoming a notable center for academic research. Rockefeller's millions meant that Chicago's president William Rainey Harper could lure some of the brightest minds in Europe and America to his faculty. He offered enviable terms: salaries better than double the average paid at prestigious institutions like Yale or Harvard, little teaching, ample research facilities. And he got results. Within a decade Chicago was known internationally as a leader in many new disciplines—particularly those of sociology, anthropology, and psychology.[7]

Led by James Angell of Chicago, a group of young psychologists revolutionized the American Psychological Association. In 1900 the association was a sleepy club, its annual meetings attended by a few dozen, mostly elderly, members of university philosophy departments. The retiring president chose his successor. By 1915 the old regime had disappeared, completely defeated. No longer could any lay person merely "interested" in human psychology join. The association would consider for prospective membership only persons with an academic degree, usually a doctorate, in psychology, and now the entire membership nominated and elected the organization's president, who, it was understood, was to promote the association's new creed: Psychology was a science, completely divorced from philosophy.[8]

The revolution promoted by the new generation of psychologists led by Angell was an intellectual as well as an organizational one. John Watson, one of Angell's students, led the attack on instinct psychology. Beginning in 1914 he began to conduct a series of sight and speech tests on infants at the Johns Hopkins University Hospital, and by 1916 he had concluded that instinct theory was untrue, that James and Hall were profoundly wrong. There was, he argued, an immense gap between human behavior and even the behavior of the highest primates. Human and animals did not share a large pool of common instinctual responses. In fact, very little about human behavior was innate. Watson's *Behaviorism* challenged the central thesis of *Principles of Psychology* by concluding that nurture, not nature, determined human behavior.[9]

By 1920 the behaviorists had won, and what they said about human psychology had great implications for parent education. If virtually all human behavior consisted of "conditioned reflexes" learned from environment and training, then the proper education of parents was an even more crucial element of social progress. If, as most behaviorists believed, the first five years of life were the critical ones for the establishment of reflexive patterns of response, children had to be reached and "conditioned" long before they set foot in a schoolroom, and who was in a better position to do the necessary conditioning than the adults most in contact with them: their parents?

If G. Stanley Hall told the mothers who flocked to his lectures that they should let young children develop naturally, fulfilling their instinctual destinies, John Watson told them just the opposite. Young children had no instincts, just reflexes, and during the first years of their lives, they were uniquely malleable. If trained properly, they would grow up to be well-adjusted, happy adults. If trained badly, or worse yet, if left free to do as they pleased, they could be ruined for life. Bad parenting produced bad children. Bad children grew up to be bad citizens. Society's future was at stake.

Unfortunately, parents, especially mothers, usually were "bad parents." Indeed, the latter were "dangerous instruments" who saw a baby's smile as an indication of love, not a conditioned response to touch.[10] They indulged their two-year-olds with hugs and kisses, precisely at the age when toddlers should be kept at a distance. They cuddled when, at most, they should have allowed their young children to shake hands twice a day: once at breakfast, again at bedtime. Their children would forever lack the self-discipline crucial to well-adjusted adulthood. The home was the place where absolutely essential molding of children had to take place, but its adult residents could not be trusted.

Parents had to be placed on "probation." Miriam Van Waters, a behavioral psychologist, titled her popular advice manual, reprinted twice during the 1920s, just that: *Parents on Probation*. In it Van Waters argued that "it is wise to place parents on probation. A nurse or civil service employee is a probationer when he is permitted to carry a limited responsibility and to practice the arts of his profession under supervision, but is thought not yet ready for a final appointment. Parents are in this class." Van Waters thought parents "worthy of help," provided that they "will cooperate."[11] "Cooperation" naturally included a willingness to absorb the lessons contained in her intimidating chapters. For instance, chapter 4, "Nineteen Ways of Being a Bad Parent," began with the stern warning that "of course" there were "well more than nineteen" ways for parents to blunder. Those to be discussed were simply the very worst from a universe of bad "parent habit-patterns." Parents were bad when they let their young chidden spend unfettered afternoons "digging holes . . . in the front yard." They were bad when they neglected to take their children for extensive medical and mental testing. They were supremely bad when they had "a warped view of authority and are thereby unable to make use of social resources."[12]

The child study organization that made use of the "social resources" provided by the behaviorists' advice was not the PTA. It was another group, the Child Study Association of America (CSAA). Founded in 1915 as the Federation for Child Study and renamed in 1923, the CSAA was not the large, national organization its name implied. Unlike the PTA, with its tens of thousands of members, the CSAA remained small, with no more than a few hundred members, most of whom were sophisticated, highly educated, wealthy women scattered in about a dozen chapters throughout the country.[13] At a time when only a tiny fraction of American women earned college degrees, almost 40 percent of CSAA's female members had "at least" four years of college. Virtually all were married to professionals—predominantly lawyers and physicians, and many had backgrounds themselves as teachers or social workers before marriage.[14] From the standpoint of Beardsley Ruml and Lawrence Frank of the Laura Spelman Rockefeller Memorial, they were well suited to conduct the first experimental classes in parent education.

BEARDSLEY RUML, LAWRENCE FRANK, AND FOUNDATION SUPPORT FOR PARENT EDUCATION

John Watson was not the only student of James Angell's to achieve prominence in the 1920s. Another was Beardsley Ruml, who also received his Ph.D. in psychology from the University of Chicago. In 1920 Angell left Chicago to assume the presidency of the Carnegie Corporation. Ruml followed. Angell's tenure with the Carnegie philanthropy was brief and quite unhappy. He began work a year after the death of Carnegie himself, but Mrs. Carnegie was still in control. Angell quickly discovered that anyone who "ran head on" into her was likely to lose. Within months of assuming his new position, Angell privately told his counterpart and friend at the Commonwealth Fund, Barry Smith, that he was immensely frustrated. He would propose plans, confer "with a great many people," receive the approval of the corporation's board of directors, only to find Mrs. Carnegie in victorious opposition.[15] After only one year, Angell left to become president of

Yale University, and the protegés he brought to the Carnegie Corporation went with him. In 1922 Beardsley Ruml, just twenty-six years old, needed a job and found it as director of the newly established Laura Spelman Rockefeller Memorial.

Brilliant and idiosyncratic, Ruml was a man New Dealer Aubrey Williams described as "one of the few—in fact one of the damn few—who made any substantial contribution to the stability of democratic government."[16] By 1922 he was already acquiring the girth that would inspire rumors in the 1930s that Chicago trustees denied him the university's presidency because he was too fat. Ruml, who despised exercise, prided himself on an ability to sit absolutely motionless on a chair for hours "just thinking." Among friends he was famous for his ability to maintain an unmoving slump. As one recalled, "It would have required a taxidermist to give him a smart posture."[17] Ruml spent his immense energy not in physical activity, but in efforts to remake American social science. During his decade at the Spelman Memorial, he gathered together a group of fellow young iconoclasts—psychologists, economists, anthropologists, and sociologists—and used his average annual budget of $4 million to make the LSRM the most important American philanthropic foundation supporting research in social science.

Beardsley Ruml decreed that the social science projects that won the memorial's blessing should focus on practical objectives and on efforts that promised to achieve concrete improvements in life. Before the LSRM merged with the Rockefeller Foundation in 1929, it had supported a wide variety of such "practical" projects. It was a major financial patron of new organizations like the Social Science Research Council, created in 1923 to promote cooperation in the field. Its fellowship programs allowed promising scholars to finish books, attend conferences, and begin professional journals. Universities that sought to develop new departments in fields like sociology, anthropology, or psychology received grants from the memorial. One subject that the foundation particularly encouraged trained social scientists to tackle was child study. That emphasis led logically to memorial support for parent education, but a version of parent education reliant on behavioral, not instinct, psychology.

Psychologists from G. Stanley Hall to John Watson had been crucial to the development of parent education, but the man Ruml hired to direct the memorial's programs in this area was not a psychologist. Lawrence Frank was an economist, trained at Columbia University.[18] Nonetheless, he enthusiastically embraced Ruml's plans to promote behaviorism's versions of child

Beardsley Ruml. Hartley Grattan, "Beardsley Ruml and His Ideas." *Harper's* 204 (1952): 81.

study. Adult education was to be a crucial component of the training of young children. Adults had to realize what truly inept parents they were. Only then could true progress in education of the young occur.

In 1923 the Spelman Memorial distributed the first of what would become annual grants of forty thousand dollars to the Child Study Association of America, which used some of these funds to hire paid staff in its New York headquarters and to sponsor a weekly radio program that featured lectures from experts about proper methods of parenting. Most of the money, however, financed classes and seminars in parent education, the centerpiece of which was an annual ten-day "Institute on Parent Education," held in New York City, which brought together about a hundred CSAA members and a roughly equal number of child study experts. Each institute featured lectures by prominent psychologists, roundtable question-and-answer sessions between parents and child study professionals, and lengthy personal interviews with parents about their child-rearing practices. Parents and invited experts met in small "study groups" to discuss reading assignments that ranged from Alfred Adler's work on "the neurotic constitution" to Boston psychiatrist Douglas Thom's essays on his "habit-clinics." These "child study groups" became the model teaching technique for parent education.[19]

Thom's *Everyday Problems of the Everyday Child* became, along with John Watson's *Psychological Care of Infant and Child,* the bibles that these study groups read. Thom, like Watson, repeatedly warned parents that early childhood was a crucial time, the period that molded individual personalities for the rest of adult life. In his view, moreover, habits were the "tools" parents must use to shape their children for productive futures. A myriad of daily actions, from behavior at the breakfast table to types of play, could be reduced to repetitive formulas, and the children, armed with good habits, could then cope with whatever problems they later confronted.[20]

Reports sent by CSAA officials to Lawrence Frank concluded encouragingly that the use of Thom's and Watson's habit formation techniques brought about significant improvements in children's behavior. Edith V's mother, for instance, had come to her Bronx study group in despair because Edith, age 4½, insisted on keeping a bright light shining in her room all night. When told to go to sleep without it, the child would vomit. Interviews by the social worker who acted as leader of the study group revealed that Mrs. V was "over-serious and without much humor" while Mr. V. was a "pessimistic, easily irritated man." These "bad" parents had unwittingly taught their daughter to be frightened and cautious. She had also learned from them that vomiting was an effective way to get what she wanted, whether that be a night light or extra attention.

When a complete medical exam revealed nothing physically wrong with Edith, the study group leader recommended habit conditioning. First, Edith was made to realize that her parents would respond to vomiting episodes with stern disapproval. Then she learned that she could keep the light in her room on for an hour before bedtime. Next, Edith had to substitute a light in the hall. Finally, she accepted the "habit" that bedtime meant sleeping in the dark. A calmer child who no longer practiced "psychic vomiting" was living proof of the effectiveness of parent education.[21]

THE LSRM AND THE CALIFORNIA STATE DEPARTMENT OF EDUCATION

By the mid-1920s Ruml and Frank had become convinced that LSRM support for parent education had to be extended. Since 1923 one of Ruml's "guiding principles" for the memorial was that "attention should be directed to work which is preventive, rather than remedial. The more fundamentally preventive the better."[22] Parent education seemed to qualify as fundamentally preventive work. After soliciting the opinions of child study experts at the University of Iowa, the University of Minnesota, and the Merrill Palmer School in Detroit, all institutions that received LSRM support, Frank concluded that the new field offered "one of the greatest opportunities for a contribution to the improvement of social life today."[23] Indeed, parent education was not only important for improvements in child welfare, it promised to advance science in general. As Frank noted, "It is safe to say that scientific interest in the small child has been multiplied many times within the past five years. . . . The study of the child as a whole is operating to modify many of the traditional ideas and conceptions of the several branches of science in the direction of a clearer understanding of organic activity."[24]

If parent education had such potential, how could its reach be extended? Frank and his circle of advisors concluded that contact with private groups needed to be supplemented by an alliance with a large public school system. Groups like the CSAA, the YMCA, and the YWCA were all "admirable." But only programs run cooperatively with public agencies could achieve the "systematic support of activities which, once developed and made pervasive in influence, would be fundamentally helpful."[25]

Frank's search for such a fundamentally helpful result eventually led to a cooperatively funded program between the memorial and the California

State Department of Education. Indeed, between 1926 and 1930, California's parent education experiment became, as Lawrence Frank had hoped, a national model. No other state provided such an array of public programs, usually held at night in school classrooms. In all, an average of ten thousand California mothers and five hundred California fathers registered annually for free parent education courses offered under the aegis of state education department sponsorship but with cost-sharing contributions made both by the LSRM and local school boards. Some three hundred child study groups met in fifty-eight California towns and cities.[26]

This was certainly "systematic support." Under the sponsorship of the Child Study Association, a handful of elite women had met in about a dozen groups in several East Coast cities. Under the sponsorship of the state of California tens of thousands of parents met in many hundreds of child study classes. A child study group of six or seven earnest mothers typified attendance at CSAA meetings. California child study groups during these years averaged fifty persons, with many enrolling seventy or eighty parents.[27]

Historian Steven Schlossman has argued that parent education in the 1920s was a feminine phenomenon, and it is true that women overwhelmingly outnumbered men in the California groups.[28] Nevertheless, the California State Department of Education actively recruited men. Ethel Richardson Allen, Assistant Superintendent of Public Instruction in California, who, with Herbert Stolz, the department's Director of Physical Education, was responsible for supervision of the parent education experiment, did not "hold women directly accountable for the progress . . . of the race."[29] Instead, she tried vigorously to get fathers involved in the training of their children, and, to do so, she provided funds to the San Francisco school system to establish "Father's Clubs" that met at night or on weekends. She urged leaders of study groups to make modifications that might appeal to fathers—shorter sessions, a wider variety of discussion topics, and refreshments. Between 1926 and 1930 at least two child study groups composed entirely of men met annually in California.[30]

Finally, then, Lawrence Frank had his opportunity—a large-scale experimental program. However, no notable "improvement in social life" resulted. Rather, the memorial's involvement with the California experiment led first to internal disillusionment and then, by 1930, to foundation abandonment of support for publicly funded parent education.

Examination of the actual workings of the parent education classes helps explain those outcomes. By 1927 a general pattern for the conduct of parent education classes had emerged. The leader of a group was usually a teacher within the city's school system, who received an extra stipend to conduct child study groups in the evenings or, more rarely, on Saturday mornings. Sometimes she was a school nurse. Meeting schedules commonly asked a child study group to meet two hours a week for twelve weeks. During the first two-hour session, most groups received a list of written goals. Although they sometimes varied in details all the lists submitted by Ethel Richardson Allen to the LSRM contained three goals: (1) Develop interest in the study of psychology; (2) Become familiar with reliable sources of information; and (3) Gain control of the problems of human adjustment.[31]

Allen's reports to the memorial did not include transcripts of interviews with class members. Perhaps they did achieve goals one and two. But the Assistant Superintendent for Adult Education emphasized that the state promoted a very "liberal" policy toward "learning methods," and assumed that "general class discussion" and "subgroup discussion" worked just as well as lectures and reading assignments. Necessity, not pedagogy, seems to have prompted the state's flexibility. Statistics gathered in 1926 and 1927 revealed that instructors who took goals number one and two quite seriously and assigned heavy reading and mandatory book reports saw their classes dwindle to a few diehards within the first three weeks.[32]

The wealthy, well-educated mothers of the Child Study Association were willing to plunge into densely written psychological discourse. The far more diverse groups of California parents were not. Even when most classes became informal discussion sessions after 1928, attendance remained a problem. Slightly under half of the parents who enrolled for the classes returned after the second meeting.[33] The precipitous dropout rate might be explained by the fact that most parents wanted to "gain control" of their children more than they wanted to "develop an interest in psychology" or broaden their knowledge of available information about child study. Despite Lawrence Frank's optimistic predictions, the California experiment in parent education provided little firm evidence that a behavioral approach to childrearing really gave average parents better tools with which to reach objective three: success in making their children do as told.

In 1926 the not-yet-married Ethel Richardson had paid a visit to the Spelman Memorial's New York headquarters. Bringing a guarantee that the redoubtable Dr. Miriam Van Waters would be the department's expert consultant, Richardson promised that the parent education program she proposed would "enable parents to rehabilitate the home and make it a modern, efficient institution."[34] The thousands of parents who enrolled for publicly funded parent education in California had a chance to review the nineteen worst ways they could be "bad." Van Waters kept her commitment to Rich-ardson Allen. She actively helped develop the materials that the State Depart-ment of Education provided to all class leaders. Yet it seems that relatively few parents felt they had learned secrets of control or seemed to think their homes were rehabilitated. Significantly, fewer than half bothered to show up for a second class session.

Ethel Richardson Allen recruited Miriam Van Waters, and she repre-sented the California Department of Education in its person-to-person ef-forts to convince Lawrence Frank to fund the state's parent education pro-posal. However, she did not direct the experimental program. Herbert Stolz won that position. He was a physician with a special interest in the relation-ships between physical education and character building for young children, and to further that interest, he had taken a leave of absence in 1923 from his position in California to study with child development experts at the Uni-versity of Iowa whose research was funded by the LSRM. His name, then, was quick to emerge within the Spelman Memorial network of child study specialists. Not surprisingly the program he helped create was one grounded in the creeds of behaviorism and Watson-style child study. Parents who en-rolled in the free parent education discussion groups that began in the fall of 1926 had to check a box on their application forms agreeing to spend at least one hour a week "observing" their children. They were told that if they learned "habit-method" they could obtain "cheerful obedience" from their children.[35] Archival evidence suggests most failed.

Weekly reports that review in detail the activities of five California study groups that met from October through December 1926 provide the best case studies of California parent education in practice. Oakland boasted two parent education groups: one for fathers and mothers, one for men only. The others met in Berkeley, Stockton, and Sacramento. The Berkeley and Oakland groups were the most active, with the highest percentages of parents who not only attended most meetings but also did their homework. This included keeping daily records of their children's sleep patterns, an hour-by-hour diary of all "purposeful activity" by their offspring when awake, written records of "parents' fears—past and present and records of child's present fears," and "time budgets" carefully detailing a wide variety of their own and their children's activities.[36]

The Berkeley group was notable for the gusto with which its mostly middle-class female members threw themselves into discussion and reading assignments. Nonetheless, not even in Berkeley did parents report much success in obtaining "cheerful obedience" through the use of habit-formation techniques. Nor did many solve other behavioral problems, at least as shown on the charts that accompanied group reports.

At the top of each chart was the question, "What are the immediate problems you are interested in solving in connection with the care and training of your child?" Most groups composed lists of from fourteen to twenty problems in child rearing. Many seem universal, common to all generations. For instance, parents wanted to develop truthfulness in their offspring and prevent thumb-sucking, bullying, or "showing off." Perhaps unique to a society not yet completely urban, a great majority of the enrolled parents in these classes also wanted their very young children "not to fear strange people." These charts—with boxes to check marked "The Same," "Worse," "Improved," or "Solved"—reflected a parent's judgment about a child's progress in the specified problem areas.

Groups that kept such good records were, in all likelihood, among the best motivated of all the California child study groups. Yet, the seemingly earnest parents of Stockton or Berkeley reported that, after weeks of carefully applied behavior modification, their whiners, thumb-suckers, and bullies were just as likely to be whiners, thumb-suckers, and bullies. Those who "refused milk" or were "rude to grandmother" remained recalcitrant. Parents did report "improvements"—even a few "solved cases." "Dawdlers over dressing" speeded up, and "too rapid eaters" slowed down, probably because their parents were there, notebooks in hand, recording every movement.[37] Nonetheless, most parents could not boast markedly greater control over their children. For plastic vessels waiting to be "molded," their offspring had proved remarkably resistant.

There was, however, one group whose habits had become modified: the parents. The summary of the "accomplishments" sent to the Spelman Memorial noted that "the attitude of the parents toward their problems was improved. In answer to a questionnaire given each class member on the last meeting day before the Christmas holidays over 90 percent reported that the practice in objective analysis of the behavior problems of their children had lessened both the frequency and intensity of their impatience with their children's behavior."[38]

The children continued to whine, but the parents had developed the habit of patience. This was not what John Watson had predicted, and by 1929 when California Department of Education officials unsuccessfully lobbied the LSRM to continue its grant for parent education past calendar year 1930, their formerly supreme confidence in the potential of behaviorism had begun to wane. Herbert Stolz admitted that "as to whether the individual members of the study groups have derived real and lasting benefit there can be no certainty since objective measurement has not been and probably cannot be made." Also absent from Stolz's 1929 proposal was any Watsonian rhetoric about "control of human adjustment." Instead, the new goal for parent education was far different. Parents who signed up for the free classes could expect, Stolz predicted, to "develop [their] own serenity."[39]

The Spelman Memorial did not find Stolz's arguments persuasive. After 1930 public education officials interested in continuing parent education were on their own. Actually, foundation doubts had begun to surface as early as 1927, primarily because large numbers of psychiatrists condemned the movement as an unscientific fad and filled Lawrence Frank's mailbox with letters expressing their strong skepticism.[40] In March 1927, as a response to their criticism, Frank appointed memorial staff member Sydnor Walker to head an internal "committee of review." Walker, trained as a social worker, guided her committee through a series of discussions that produced a doubtful, troubled assessment of the new field. In a confidential summary of committee deliberations sent to Frank in the form of a series of questions, Walker asked:

1. Is the primary aim [of parent education] to promote child development or development of parents?
2. Why should the Memorial attack this problem rather than that of housing, overcrowding in cities, lack of healthy recreation or any other of the complex factors affecting the child's welfare?
3. Do we know enough about what is desirable human behavior to instruct parents on how to produce it?[41]

Lawrence Frank, the most vocal advocate of parent education within the LSRM, had also begun to develop misgivings, indeed as early as 1927, when the California experiment was only a year old. During a staff retreat held in August of that year, he mused,

I find myself, like many other individuals who have pursued and caught the substance and found they were really after the shadow of the inspiration which had been lost. I think as long as you are pursuing something you don't know whether it is worthwhile doing, you can put pressure to keep on doing it, but after you have gotten the thing more or less to a certain point, there comes a certain amount of let-down that is rather difficult to get over.[42]

Frank's wistful remarks were hardly a ringing endorsement and may have reflected his growing personal understanding of the complexities of child rearing. The pioneering sociologist Helen Lynd, co-author of the famous *Middletown* studies, always thought that "theories of child development in America followed the age of the Frank children. As the Frank children grew older, the theories changed."[43] Frank, not yet thirty-three years old when he joined the staff of the memorial, married in 1917 and had a first child in 1919, followed by others born in the 1920s. Therefore, during the years he first discovered the field of parent education, he himself was the parent of babies and toddlers, upon whom he tried to practice behavior modification. In 1925, for instance, he volunteered his newborn daughter as a subject for Columbia University's home study project in "infant sociology." Myrtle McGraw, a prominent child development specialist, who in 1925 was one of the graduate students sent to the Frank apartment in Greenwich Village, recalled one incident of successful behavioral resistance:

> I'll never forget how funny it was because, if you'll remember, in those days behaviorism's rigidities of management [were] in vogue. . . . [T]humb-sucking was very bad. So when I walked into the baby's [Frank's daughter] bedroom . . . the first thing I saw were these braces on the thumb and those lip-tongue depressors on the elbow so that the baby couldn't get her thumb in her mouth. She was blissfully sucking away on her big toe.[44]

Lawrence Frank was not the first to discover that babies were not as easy to condition as he had imagined, but his views on the matter certainly carried a great deal more weight than those of most other parents. By the late 1920s Frank was encouraging "pre-parenting" rather than "parent" education.[45] He continued to believe that training people in skills of home management and child raising was a worthy goal. Indeed, it should remain a part of publicly funded education. However, the people to be trained were not adults reached through free after-hours study groups. They were to be young girls still in elementary or high school.

The Laura Spelman Rockefeller Memorial exited from its involvement with the California public schools. In doing so, memorial officials suggested a new course of action for parent education that relied, without acknowledgment, on legislation stimulated by previous Rockefeller philanthropic actions. They suggested use of the Smith-Lever and Smith-Hughes Acts, which, since their emergence from congressional battles over decisions made by the General Education Board to provide salaries for hundreds of Agriculture Department employees, had funded an increasingly entrenched system of federal and state cost-sharing for vocational education.

Lawrence Frank, to be sure, had no connection with the entirely separate General Education Board. When the congressional furor over the GEB's joint educational initiatives with the Agriculture Department erupted in 1914, he was an employee of the New York Telephone Company, hired, among other tasks, to help the company create uniform accounting procedures. But if he was not a Rockefeller employee in 1914, Frank was certainly well able to read about a story that filled the pages of newspapers for weeks.

But neither he nor anyone else at the memorial ever suggested a link between the type of programs they now advocated and the actions of another Rockefeller philanthropy. Rather, they wrote about the possibilities provided by Smith-Lever and Smith-Hughes funding as if these funds had always existed—as if the federal government had always had an interest in sharing responsibility for innovative vocationally oriented education with states and localities. Lawrence Frank was not the first, and most certainly not the last, policy maker without any apparent grasp of the history of the policies and programs that his own institution had influenced.

Without any reference to the history of Smith-Hughes and Smith-Lever, Frank circulated a series of memoranda to state officials in California suggesting a new direction for parent education. Through the Federal Bureau of Vocational Education, he noted, the federal government had been promoting the expansion of home economics education in the public schools. Between 1921 and 1927, Congress had continued to expand the program so that, by 1928, the bureau offered to pay half the salary of teachers of home economics in public secondary schools that offered classes for girls over the age of fourteen. Moreover, Congress had increased the funding for agricultural extension work in the states and had interpreted this to include the payment of salaries for home economics demonstrators who would teach part time in rural districts.[46] Hence, there were existing programs that could take over the function of providing education for parenting.

Seaman Knapp, Wallace Buttrick, and Frederick Gates had thought that Smith-Lever and Smith-Hughes would provide publicly financed education in scientific farming. This they did, but they also did much more. Within a decade of their passage, publicly sponsored vocational education had grown tremendously, though no one seemed in charge of any coherent policy governing that growth. By 1930, the LSRM would cut its connections with publicly funded "vocational" education in parent training. It would justify that break by suggesting a new direction: The job of parenthood should be taught in secondary schools and through home demonstrations. It should be taught to teenage girls. It should be, and could be, jointly funded by state, federal, and local governments.

Did California accept the advice? The answer is yes and no. It did incorporate teenaged parent training into public school curriculums, but it also found ways to keep adult education going by making alliances with other organizations. Unforeseen, moreover, was the impact of its mandatory classes in home economics, begun in 1931 and copied in other states, on the emerging profession of home economics.[47]

Variously named "Household Administration," "Home Ecology," "Euthenics," or "Sanitary Science," in addition to the increasingly more common "Home Economics," this new field had begun to make its presence known in American education by 1900. Mostly middle-class women interested in learning more about nutritious food preparation, better sewing methods, and more efficient home management enrolled in the household management and cooking schools that sprang up in most cities. They eagerly read the advice available in more than a dozen new magazines. A few colleges established household arts courses.

Nonetheless, as indicated by its welter of different names, the field was amorphous. Some of its leaders, such as Fannie Farmer, the principal of the famous Boston Cooking School, wanted to emphasize practical skills. They thought that home economics education should remain primarily a private voluntary self-improvement activity of adult women—usually those who were already housewives. Another group, associated with pioneering home economics departments in universities like Cornell and Iowa State, wanted home economics to become a scientific field of study. They wanted home economists to be specialists who could advise industry and government about products used in the home. For these people, home economists should be chemists, skilled in textile analysis, or nutritionists, able to advise corporations about the kinds of additives that would enrich food products. Still others saw the trained home economist primarily as an urban social worker who would teach poor women cooking, cleaning, and other techniques that would elevate blighted neighborhoods' standards of home-making. Few in any camp included child study within their definitions of home economics, and few considered home economics as a subject essentially for young girls.[48]

That changed when home economics training began to appear in public school curriculums, and the fact that the Spelman Memorial saw that training as a fit alternative for voluntary adult child study groups is in itself illuminating. Ethel Richardson Allen had tried valiantly, though without much success, to include men in parent education classes. But when parent training appeared in public schools, it was, to use Lawrence Frank's phrase, "pre-parental" training, addressed to adolescent girls only. Technically, for purposes of funding, it was also vocational education. Yet only girls, it seemed, could train for the vocation of parenthood. Indeed, in an increasing number of states they were required to do so.

So the state of California did accept Lawrence Frank's advice, but only partially. The Laura Spelman Rockefeller Memorial abandoned parent education as adult education. The California Department of Education did not. Instead, it allied with the organization the Spelman Memorial had spurned in the 1920s: the PTA.

Herbert Stolz wrote a lengthy memorandum in 1929 requesting an extension of LSRM support for parent education, in which he listed criteria that would produce better child study groups. The best, Stolz concluded, brought together people from the same neighborhoods, economic status, and social viewpoint. Homogeneity was easiest to achieve when study groups formed from the members of already existing organizations. In cities where leaders recruited through newspaper advertisements, the differences between the enrolled members of the resulting study groups were too great, and discussion faltered. These groups were the ones that recorded the sharpest dropout rates. While "obviously desirable" to have both mothers and fathers studying child raising, mixed gender groups did not work. Most men still shifted the responsibility of raising children to their wives and resented any effort to make them participate seriously. That resentment was "enhanced," even for those few self-selected men who came to the child study classes. Stolz "regretfully" concluded that the small percentage of fathers who attended classes with their wives did not leave more enthusiastic parents. Rather they felt that "the group leader and the mothers . . . conspired against [them]. . . . In discussing problems of child-raising in a mixed group all but a few men feel as unnecessary as their wives would feel in a discussion of the day's events on the stock market."[49]

One "already existing organization," with over a hundred chapters throughout the state of California, was the PTA. Moreover, since the early 1920s it had initiated a series of "Dad's Clubs" open only to men. To officials of the California Department of Education, the PTA seemed the ideal alternative ally to promote parent education. As early as 1929, state educational leaders, like Stolz, had begun to sense the growing coolness of the

Spelman Memorial. Well before they received a formal rejection letter from the memorial's New York headquarters, they had begun to hold meetings with PTA officers.

By 1931 when the financial support of the Rockefeller philanthropy ceased, the state of California had a substitute program ready. In this program, however, the Department of Education's role was far less important and consisted primarily of paying for training classes for study group leaders—classes open only to officers of California chapters of the PTA. Aside from this relatively small commitment, the Department of Education shifted all financial and planning responsibility for parent education to the PTA and local school boards. It collected no weekly reports from local groups and circulated no suggestions for reading lists, discussion topics, or goals.[50]

Under the new management, moreover, parent education ceased to be an exercise in behavior modification. Rather, groups of, for the most part, mothers met to chat, give each other support, and exchange tips. They did not read the latest psychological literature. More typically, they helped plan school picnics and plays. Rather than discussing operant conditioning, they sewed costumes for Grade Three's Christmas Pageant. Prior to this time, PTA groups had not been so closely allied with local school boards. Another long-lasting educational policy had been established. The PTA, ignored during the 1920s by the Spelman Memorial, now had the last laugh. It, and not the Child Study Association of America, was to be the group that became a semi-official adjunct of the local public school.

Parent education, then, became an aspect of an expanded, often mandatory, "vocational" curriculum within public high schools—available only to adolescent girls. It also became an officially sanctioned activity of the local PTA chapter, working closely with a community school board, and eventually it took a third course, again with California in the lead. It became part of the curriculum of junior colleges, which by 1930 flourished as self-conscious alternatives to "elite" higher education and emphasized vocationally oriented courses. At Santa Ana Community College, for instance, parent education reappeared as a for-credit required course titled "The Science of Social Relations."[51]

Officials within the Laura Spelman Rockefeller Memorial did not turn away from parent education because their fears about the collapse of the home had eased. They had begun to believe that, even with proper training, parents alone could not bring up baby. In 1924 Lawrence Frank had thought that well-instructed parents could carry out "in the daily life of the home, the directions and advice of the doctor, nutritionist, the psychiatrist, and all the other profession [sic] and experts concerned with child life."[52] He eventually decided that this faith was misplaced. That conviction led the Rockefeller philanthropies, in concert with the Russell Sage Foundation and the Commonwealth Fund, into the briars of social welfare policy making. These organizations would champion "child-helping" by experts, such as juvenile court probation officers, not mothers. Members of the Sage Foundation would also ally with government officials in the U.S. Children's Bureau to transform the mothers' pensions.

THE RUSSELL SAGE FOUNDATION AND THE TRANSFORMATION OF THE MOTHERS' PENSION

Between 1911 and 1930 forty-six of the forty-eight states enacted "mothers' pension" bills, which provided funds from public revenues to allow needy mothers to raise their young children at home. During the same years that private policy makers at the Laura Spelman Rockefeller Memorial lost their enthusiasm for even the "parent-educated" mother as the ideal "child-helper," public policy makers embraced her. A student familiar with private philanthropy's abandonment of parent education logically might conclude that mothers' pensions would be greeted with open hostility.

In fact, foundation involvement with the mothers' pension movement was far more complicated and illustrates the influence, this time on social welfare policy, exercised by the Russell Sage Foundation. The pensions proved to be plastic vehicles, easily manipulated by organizations with genuine, not rhetorical, policy agendas. Long before the enactment of Title IV of the Social Security Act of 1935, administration of mothers' pensions presaged late-twentieth-century public welfare policy: government-supervised aid to dependent children, not government payments of "service" pensions to mothers.

THE MOTHERS' PENSION MOVEMENT

In 1911 the Illinois state legislature passed a measure that provided cash allowances for needy mothers who required additional funds to care for their children. Within two years, twenty other state legislatures enacted similar legislation. By 1921 forty states had mothers' pensions.[1] Only Georgia and South Carolina lacked a program of public cash payments to indigent mothers without husbands in 1930. The editor of the popular *Everybody's Magazine* explained the phenomenon in one word: It was a "wildfire."[2]

Eligibility varied from state to state. Twenty states enacted bills that made assistance available to families where the father was absent due to desertion, divorce, imprisonment, or death; twenty-three states allowed aid to be given when the father was insane or physically unable to work.[3] Most states required that the children in the family be under the age of fourteen—the age at which, commonly, they could obtain full-time work certificates. All required that the mother be "fit," although definitions of that word were not uniform, except for the provision in all states that a mother living with a man to whom she was not married was "unfit." A few states barred the mother from taking in male boarders, even if relations. Tuberculosis disqualified her in several states, and Minnesota legislators declared that a "fit" mother had to be able to read and write English and prove that she spoke only English to her children.[4]

Despite the seeming breadth of eligibility requirements, actual recipients of mothers' aid were easily categorized. They were urban white widows with at least two children under the age of fourteen. Between 1920 and 1933 the U.S. Children's Bureau conducted the most comprehensive surveys of the implementation of mothers' pensions now available, basing them on a nationwide statistical sample of almost forty-seven thousand recipient mothers, about half of all those receiving aid in 1931. Using these surveys, Children's Bureau analysts concluded that over 80 percent were widows. Ninety-six percent were white, 3 percent were black, 1 percent belonged to "other races." Most of the tiny number of blacks given public aid lived in just two states: Ohio and Pennsylvania. Southern states, where the vast majority of African Americans lived, rarely found any "fit" black mothers. In the entire state of North Carolina only one black woman received mothers' aid and in Florida only three.[5]

Overwhelmingly, the public cash allotments also went to women who lived in urban areas with populations of more than fifty thousand.[6] Such urban widows were not necessarily more fit or more needy than rural ones, but the administration of the laws meant that city dwellers were overwhelmingly favored. Many state legislatures had passed pension bills that authorized cost-sharing between state and localities, with a local or county agency, typically a juvenile court, county welfare board, or, in a few states, a new county organization, a mothers' aid board, deciding which applicants were to receive aid from funds partially provided by the state.

However, while legislators in state capitals were quick to pass bills, they were hesitant about authorizing appropriations. The Minnesota pension law, for instance, provided that the state would reimburse its localities one-third of total expenses, but state lawmakers never provided the money.[7] Given such a situation, common in the majority of states, only a relatively few cities with adequate budgets gave many indigent mothers a pension. Indeed, one analyst has estimated that the majority of mothers who received public payments lived in only nine cities.[8]

The movement peaked in 1931, when an estimated ninety-three thousand mothers received some form of aid, most of it given in the cities of the East and Midwest. How much each woman got varied considerably, but not as much as one might expect from looking at the provisions of the differing state laws. A widow living in Arkansas could legally receive no more than $4.33 per month from any county government, while one living in Massachusetts, the state that authorized the most generous monthly maximum payments, could receive a total of no more than $69.31. Yet this variation on paper was far greater than what existed in reality. Few widows in Arkansas got anything, and few in Boston got the maximum amount allowed under state law. Most recipients of mothers' aid received about twenty dollars a month.[9]

In no state was a mothers' pension a pension, whatever its amount. Although the term was universally used, no state rewarded a certain group of mothers for services rendered in the past, the most common definition of pension. All gave aid for services rendered in the present—daily care of small children—and even the most generous stopped payment as soon as the services stopped, that is, as soon as the children reached an age, usually fourteen, when they could work outside the home for pay. Moreover, no state was generous after 1931. One after another, state by state, county by county, governments abandoned their mothers' pensions programs. Almost none survived after 1934.

A review of the actual operation of mothers' pensions in Massachusetts and Ohio, the two states that led the nation in cash amounts and numbers of pensions offered, illustrates the complexity and confusion that characterized administration of the program in most states. The Massachusetts "Mothers' Aid" law, enacted in 1913, required overseers of the poor in each of the state's towns and cities to allow all "fit" mothers with children under fourteen years to apply for a pension. The overseer, who in many small towns held other

jobs in addition to that of supervising distribution of public relief, interviewed applicants and sent recommendations to the Massachusetts State
Board of Charity. The state board then sent one of its five women "visitors,"
all trained social workers, to conduct a second investigation. Given the load
to be handled by these five individuals, the required second report usually
took many months, sometimes more than a year, to complete. Only when a
widow received a highly favorable review from the overseer of the poor in her
own town as well as from the representative from the State Board of Charity
could she be placed on a list to be considered for a pension, the costs of which
were to be shared equally between her town and the state.

A flood of applications prompted Massachusetts officials to decree that
even if a woman had been deemed suitable by her inquisitors, she could be
categorically excluded from consideration for aid for other reasons. If her answers to questions about her family's circumstances convinced charity officials that her need would continue for less than a year, she was not to receive
aid. This meant that if she had a young teenager, say, a boy of thirteen who
could soon go to work, Massachusetts gave her no mothers' aid. If she had
been deserted by her husband for less than a year, her name could not be
added to lists of approved applicants for aid. In addition, if any of her children
were illegitimate, she could get no aid; if investigators discovered she kept
male lodgers, even relations, she was rejected; and if investigators decided,
even after a woman received a pension, that she was not sufficiently "thrifty"
and "devoted to high standards of home care," they could revoke her aid. Ada
Sheffield, the member of the state's Board of Charity who supervised the five
women visitors assigned to review mothers' aid cases, justified Massachusetts's decision to make its help perpetually conditional on good behavior. In
her words,

> If we grant the aid to any woman whose care of her children will just pass
> muster, we throw away a chance to make these women improve. If, on the
> contrary, we make relief under this law conditional on a fairly high standard of
> home care, we shall find that the mothers will rise to this standard. The fact is
> that a mother of little children who will not attend conscientiously to their
> diet, cleanliness, health, and conduct . . . is not the sort of woman Mas-
> sachusetts wants to help.[10]

Ohio's state legislature also approved a public mothers' pension in 1913,
and, paralleling the actions of Massachusetts's solons, it carefully distinguished
the sort of woman Ohio would help. Under the law, all Ohio counties could
establish their own independent programs, to be funded, if they chose to

participate, by a one-tenth of a mill county tax levy. However, only two county governments, those of Hamilton and Cuyahoga, granted the great majority of the state's pensions, and, not surprisingly, these counties contained, respectively, the state's two largest cities, Cincinnati and Cleveland. As had the Massachusetts legislation, the Ohio mothers' aid law also permitted mothers whose husbands were dead, permanently physically disabled, insane, or imprisoned to apply for public help. In addition, it required that the mother's children be living with her but did not require that she stay home with them most of the time.

In both Cincinnati and Cleveland, county officials established Mothers' Pension Advisory Committees whose members received no public pay but were to help implement the law. In Cincinnati, committee members included a minister, a labor union leader, a public school teacher, the presidents of the United Jewish Charities and the Associated Charities of Cincinnati, and the former president of the St. Vincent de Paul Society. In effect, the most important leaders of the city's leading private charities established procedures for the investigation of pension claims that placed decision making in the hands of sixty social workers, most of whose salaries were paid by religious or philanthropic organizations. The result was a complex gauntlet through which applicants for mothers' pensions had to pass. Each potential recipient of a pension had to fill out a detailed questionnaire—answering questions about her sources of income, including potential financial aid from relatives and other individuals, her health, her children's behavior, her housing, including details of lighting, ventilation, and garbage disposal, and her plans for earning additional income.

After at least three home visits from a social worker, an applicant received a rating. She belonged to either group A, B, C, or D. Group A applicants generally received pensions. Group B women sometimes received pensions, but in the opinion of the investigators their needs were not as urgent. Group C cases were "doubtful," and Group D applicants never received aid. Once officially a recipient, a mother received monthly visits from a Pension Committee social worker who inquired about meals served, church services attended, and types and numbers of books read, to name only three of many dozens of questions listed in Pension Committee guidelines. The aid recipient, after exhaustively discussing her past month's activities, was to wait "apart" while the Pension Committee representative searched her dwelling, looking for "dirt or disorder." Finally, before the visit ended, the pensioner and her social worker were to review together a planned budget for the coming month—checking amounts estimated for rent, food, fuel, carfares, and sundries. In 1914, the Pension Committee oversaw thirteen hundred applications for mothers' aid and granted 358 pensions.[11]

Scholars and the Mothers' Pensions

In recent years, scholars, primarily sociologists and political scientists rather than historians, have discovered the mothers' pension movement and have produced assessments that agree about its origins and disagree about its legacies.[12] Most conclude that mothers' pensions had many supporters and few opponents, and that chief among advocates of pensions were members of women's clubs and editors of women's magazines. When leaders of the Mothers' Congress and the General Federation of Women's Clubs talked about how dreadful a thing it was to tear a child from its mother solely because of poverty, when editors of the *Delineator* cried that the state needed to provide greater safeguards for *"love and the home,"* state legislators listened.[13] In only four years, between 1911 and 1915, politicians in half the states rushed to produce mothers' aid laws. Among the few opponents of pensions were private charities and groups that sociologist Theda Skocpol labels "peak associations" speaking for charities, such as the Russell Sage Foundation.[14] These charities opposed mothers' pensions out of self-interest, worried about loss of control over programs they had already established or intended to create in their own communities.[15]

For sociologists Muriel Pumphrey and Ralph Pumphrey the pensions were a victory for dedicated advocates for the poor. Although they were admittedly poorly funded and available to only a small minority of women, they nonetheless "paved the way for the substantial, regular, assured income under the survivors insurance provision of the Social Security Act now received by millions of full and half-orphans."[16] In a similar vein, Mark Leff argues that mothers' pensions "rebuked" private philanthropy and "undermined the prestige of private charities to such an extent that they never again so confidently asserted their prerogative to define the government-welfare role." Indeed the pensions provided a firm foundation for the idea that government has a duty to establish welfare as a right, "independent of the paternalism of the 'better' members of society."[17]

Less sanguine scholarly judgments challenge these conclusions. All analysts of the phenomenon agree that not even in the most generous of states could a mother with two or more children survive on a government pension alone, and this fact has led Theda Skocpol, as well as political scientists Barbara Nelson and Christopher Howard, to conclude that the pensions, because they often required recipients to be at home most of the time, forced single mothers into dead-end, low-wage work. Forbidden to engage in full-time, well-compensated labor, the poor women who received mothers' pensions were "prodded into low-wage drudgery." They stood for hours over laundry tubs. They sewed on buttons and mended shirts. They made lace.[18]

Scholars disagree not only about the beneficence of mothers' pensions, but also about the government programs they spawned. For Christopher Howard, the mothers' pensions "marked the beginning of the most vilified, most dysfunctional program in the American welfare state." They "sowed the seeds" of Aid to Families with Dependent Children, a program that symbolizes "everything that is wrong with the American welfare state."[19] However, sociologist Ann Orloff concludes, "Far from mothers' pension serving as the precedent for ADC, they served as the precedent for Survivors' Insurance—and ADC . . . took on many of the qualities associated with poor relief."[20]

This body of literature resembles the series of descriptions the blind men gave of the elephant. Ignoring crucial questions, it oversimplifies the nature of support for and opposition to the pensions. Missing in particular is any serious attempt to understand the role played by the organization early-twentieth-century opponents labeled the "Charity Trust": the Russell Sage Foundation.[21]

The mothers' pensions were the product of political manipulation, not national idealism. In no state did public officials ever provide adequate funding. Only a few thousand needy families in even the most generous of states received financial aid in any year between 1911 and 1934. The pension "movement" was really no such thing. No national leader emerged to make pensions a crusade. No organization made establishment of pensions its top priority.

That did not mean that welfare reformers championed any clear alternative to pensions for "worthy" poor women and their children. By the early twentieth century most child-savers condemned the orphanage and boarding-home systems used throughout the previous century. Orphanages, social welfare reformers argued, were overcrowded, unhealthy places that made inadequate provision to train their charges for occupations and life. Children raised in them were often permanently stigmatized. Children's Bureau Chief Grace Abbott reflected a common view among experts when she damned orphanages as institutions controlled by either the corrupt or the untrained. As she said, "The appeal of children is so great that the unscrupulous sometimes use them as a pretext for securing funds. Well-meaning people, ignorant of methods of child care, undertake them with inadequate financial support and little understanding of the problems of children."[22] Increasingly, reformers advocated that, whenever possible, children be kept within homes, and urged the public acceptance of foster, not institutional, care.[23]

If politicians accepted the advice of experts that children should be placed with foster parents, they found it even easier to defend the sacred rights of motherhood, especially when they discovered that they really did not have to foot the bills. Similarly, women's clubs easily found time to pass resolutions approving the idea of pensions at annual conventions but rarely devoted much effort to lobbying government officials actually to make adequate cash payments to large numbers of needy mothers a reality. Magazine editors sold copies with emotional stories about tearful widows and hungry babies.

Scholars have been too easily taken in by the rhetoric of the pensions' putative supporters, including their scorn for the supposedly self-interested opposition of private philanthropy. Indeed, any genuine understanding of the policy impact of mothers' pension legislation requires a careful scrutiny of the far more sophisticated nature of the arguments made by private philanthropy. It also requires investigation of the interesting triangular alliance made between three groups of prominent female social work professionals—an alliance that connected academe, foundations, and government.

Edith Abbott and Sophonisba Breckinridge of the University of Chicago, Mary Richmond of the Russell Sage Foundation, and Julia Lathrop and Grace Abbott of the United States Children's Bureau, unlike their counterparts in state legislatures, were not content to spout praises to motherhood. They had a clear policy agenda. Lacking any real opposition, they used the mothers' pensions to introduce a new public welfare policy. Governments had a duty to aid dependent children. Orphanages were a failure. Foster homes were an alternative to be used only rarely. Children should stay in their own homes. However, those homes had to be "suitable." Only families judged acceptable by experts were to receive public aid. Mothers' pensions were not a woman's right. Rather, they should be a vehicle for government-sponsored supervision of poor children, within their homes, using the techniques of social work case method.[24]

WHO SUPPORTED THE MOTHERS' PENSIONS?

Theda Skocpol has argued that the members of the National Congress of Mothers, the General Federation of Women's Clubs, and dozens of smaller women's clubs wanted to "honor motherhood" by supporting mothers' pensions. They were "upper and middle-class women . . . trying to embrace as sisters, as fellow-mothers, the impoverished widows who would be helped by mothers' pensions."[25] True, the meetings of such groups rang with resolutions in favor of sacred motherhood. However, if the privileged women who led the nation's women's clubs really wanted to be sisters with their less fortunate "fellow-mothers," they demonstrated remarkably little zeal. More likely, such women never really meant their rhetoric about making motherhood a salaried right.

The editors of women's magazines, another privileged group, but one largely male, not female, also found it easy to wax elegiac about the nobility of motherhood. However, the question must be asked: Were their sentiments prompted, at least partly, by desires to boost sales in an increasingly competitive woman's magazine market? In what ways was the most famous of these campaigns, the one waged by the mass-circulation *Delineator*, a clever way to distinguish itself and attract more subscribers to add to its already large list of over one million primarily female readers? After all, Theodore Dreiser, the *Delineator*'s editor, knew a thing or two about milking emotion. By 1911 he was already famous, best known for his novels about fallen women, abandoned wives, and desperate children. To what degree, moreover, did the *Delineator*'s readers justify their subscriptions by associating the journal with a good cause? The majority of the articles in the magazine focused on the newest hats or the season's most becoming coats. Readers probably spent far more time looking at glossy full-color high-fashion features than they did reading articles on social reform.[26]

The "tragic" story of "Mary Morson," a widow living in New York City, became grist for several stories by journalist William Hard. The *Delineator* columnist assured his readers that Mrs. Morson was a real person. Only her name and various other details of her life had been changed to guarantee her privacy. Her husband, an Irish immigrant and stone cutter, died of pneumonia, leaving his young widow and seven children nothing. Mary Morson worked fifteen-hour days; she found one job scrubbing floors, another cleaning feathers for hats. Still, she could not make enough to care adequately for her large family. The baby cried for milk. The oldest, a boy of ten, began to wander the streets. Finally, a "lady from a charity society" convinced Mrs. Morson to give up four of her children. As the broken-hearted mother walked away from these children, now the inmates of an orphan asylum, she knew that from then on "alien hands would pull . . . soft child-bodies close to strange breasts." Her children would no longer know the "joy of direct motherhood." Hard ended his tale of woe with a religious parable: "On canvas and in plaster the Virgin Mother in every city of the world of Christ perpetually holds her child still at her bosom. . . . Our Lord was not brought up in a home maintained by the authorities of Nazareth."[27] Few could resist such high emotion. Few politicians anywhere were as honest as was James T. Begg, the plain-speaking member of the House of Representatives from Sandusky, Ohio. Mothers' pensions, Representative Begg argued, offered "the most wonderful opportunity for a lot of sob stuff."[28]

"Sob stuff" is politically irresistible. It also frequently goes hand in hand with chicanery. Anyone wishing a better understanding of the true reason for the quick adoption of mothers' pensions as public policy should pay closer attention to the arguments marshaled by Mary Richmond, chief of the Russell Sage Foundation's Charity Organization Department, and her allies in private municipal and state charity organizations. Writing in the pages of the *Survey,* the preeminent house organ of the emerging social work profession, as well as in a series of studies financed and published by the Russell Sage Foundation, they argued that the emotional appeal of the pensions made them tools for less high-minded souls. Edward Devine, General Secretary of the New York Charity Organization Society and a contributing editor to *Survey,* also reminded the journal's readers that the issue needed "fewer appeals to instinct" and more "application of intellect." Mothers' pensions might be a popular social movement, but so too, Devine dryly noted, was "the burning of witches."[29]

The application of intellect largely fell to Mary Richmond, and many scholars interested in the history of social work credit her importance. Steven Schlossman rightly calls her "the high priestess of social casework," partly because her textbook, *Social Diagnosis,* first published in 1917, enjoyed nine reprintings between 1917 and 1928 and was, indeed, "the social workers' bible."[30] Available in French and German editions, it was widely used in Europe as well as the United States.[31]

Richmond's influence extended beyond her significant role as a leader of the emerging profession of social work. The longtime general secretary of the Philadelphia Society of Organized Charities, she was already in her fifties when, in 1909, she accepted the invitation of John Glenn, director of the Russell Sage Foundation, to head a new "Charity Organization Department."[32] From 1909 until her death in 1928, she used this position, not only to oversee the transformation of charity societies from the domain of voluntary "lady bountifuls" to the province of trained professional social workers, but also to advance the foundation's position on social welfare policy.

Mary Richmond was an unlikely candidate for the role of influential behind-the-scenes policy maker. An only child whose mother and father died

Mary Richmond. Russell Sage Foundation Collection. Courtesy of the Rockefeller Archive Center.

of tuberculosis before she was ten years old, Richmond grew up a lonely orphan, sharing a cramped one-room tenement flat with an aunt in New York City. When her aunt, who had eked out a meager living as a proofreader for a book publisher, suffered a physical breakdown, the teenaged Richmond was alone in the world. She taught herself bookkeeping, worked twelve-hour days, and attended lectures at the Cooper Union at night. She never went to college, but through talent and sheer force of will, she made herself indispensable, rising from bookkeeper to the general secretary first of the Charity Organization Society of Baltimore, then that of Philadelphia. She succeeded, despite the fact that, like her parents, she fell prey to tuberculosis, which left its mark: permanently scarred lungs. Always frail, Richmond suffered steadily declining health during her final twenty years of life. Illness forced her to take frequent leaves of absence. She wrote parts of many of her books and essays struggling for breath and flat on her back in bed.[33] Those who first met this sickly, sallow-skinned woman might have been tempted to dismiss her as an invalid, but if they did so, would regret it. Mary Richmond was a brainy dynamo, indefatigable in pursuit of her objectives. Richmond's contemporary opponents claimed her objections to mothers' pensions were the self-serving words of a "private lady charity worker" intent on retaining control of relief work, and it is this unfair explanation that has persisted in scholarly work.

Mary Richmond correctly identified the reasons legislators embraced mothers' pensions, noting that like other issues heavy with sentiment and easily manipulated, the pensions were fodder for "shrewd" politicians who loved to "stand up for motherhood." The members of women's clubs "rubbed the lamp industriously without any conception of the temper of the genie soon to appear," and politicians, especially during years when the possible impact of female suffrage was unclear, quoted approvingly from resolutions passed by conventions of the Congress of Mothers.[34] What better to include in speeches than calls to aid defenseless widows and orphans? More than one public official began an oration with the following lead paragraph from *Texas Motherhood Magazine:* "The state is a parent, and as a wise and gentle and kind and loving parent should beam down upon each child alike. At the knee of this great, just *loving mother* . . . no child should beg in vain."[35]

Mary Richmond begged in vain. Her sophisticated arguments about the easy political corruption of sentiment went unheeded as state legislators vied to pass bills honoring motherhood.[36] For Richmond, soldiers' pension legislation provided a cautionary lesson on the dangers of basing policy on appeals to emotion. The original motive for granting pensions to former members of the Union Army was to provide relief to ex-soldiers who had been injured in battle or who suffered diseases directly stemming from their war service. However, in the decades between 1870 and 1910, when legislators began to discuss public pensions for mothers, the soldiers' pensions had grown enormously, expanding eventually to include payments to all discharged Union soldiers and their dependents. In 1913, with three-fourths of the soldiers of the Civil War in their graves, the nation spent $164,500,000 on pensions, making them the largest single item in the federal domestic budget. Moreover, a system of private, special pension acts paralleled general pension legislation, and the names of recipients of these special pensions were kept secret. By the early twentieth century, Congress passed an average of thirty-six thousand individual soldiers' pensions bills a year. Any member of Congress could request that a constituent receive a special allotment, and, on any given day when the House and Senate were in session, an average of two hundred such bills entered the docket.[37]

Mary Richmond denounced the Civil War pensions as corrupt, not so much because they fueled party patronage, but because they tainted the public-policy-making process itself. The American public wanted to care for its aged veterans, but the soldiers' pensions obscured a raid on the treasury. In similar fashion, the mothers' pensions falsely convinced otherwise responsible people that their duties to poor women and children had been fulfilled.

Moreover, Richmond worried that cash grants, even as small as they were, might sow the seeds of dependency. She asked, in a confidential letter to her friend, Joseph Lee, president of the Playground Association of America, "When does a government pension become a hand-out?" "I worked," she continued, "only forty miles from Washington in the days when ex-soldiers were numerous, and I had a chance to see how much energy was crippled, how ineffective their partially or wholly supported lives were."[38]

Legislators found it easy to milk popular sentimentality about fatherless children for political gain. So, too, did lobbyists. No accurate statistics apparently exist quantifying the numbers of persons who embraced the pension scheme for personal gain, but the widely publicized case of Henry Neil, a juvenile court probation officer from Chicago, raises questions. Neil circulated advertisements in newspapers throughout dozens of states between 1911 and 1914 soliciting "women of refinement and ability" to recruit members for an organization he had established, the Mothers' Pension League of America. Neil promised to pay organizers five dollars a day, providing that every day each recruited a minimum of ten new members and collected from each one dollar in annual dues in advance. Neil's advertisement assured organizers that he would be happy to receive "money orders for the amount you collect, less the amount of your pay for organizing."[39] Editors of the *Survey* investigated Neil's literature and found it to be fraudulent. Most of the prominent people listed as members of his league disavowed that status when questioned by *Survey* reporters. Jessie Wilson, for instance, daughter of the president and supposedly an enthusiastic league supporter, released a statement to be printed in *Survey* that noted, "I have taken no active interest in the matter *at all.*"[40]

Henry Neil, for his part, blasted the journal as the tool of the Russell Sage Foundation, which he damned as "reactionary." The truth about the Sage Foundation would be known, he warned, when he published his own "startling" evidence that the foundation was at the root of a conspiracy to suppress information about the huge profits organized charities skimmed from municipal outdoor relief funds.[41] Neil's promised exposé never saw the light of day. He was, no doubt, what the *Survey* claimed: a huckster with a scam. During years when five dollars was a magnificent daily wage, especially for a woman worker, his "investigators" scoured neighborhoods, searching for recruits for the mothers' pension cause. If Chicago charity organization officials were right, he preyed on those least able, but most likely, to give— residents of poor city slums, the people who knew best that the death of a husband could easily plunge a working-class family into financial despair.[42]

How many other Henry Neils existed? That question, probably unanswerable, poses another. To what extent was support for mothers' pensions a classic illustration of the easy corruption of public welfare policy? Mary Richmond's fears were justified. Supporters of mothers' pensions, many undoubtedly unwittingly, created a policy distraction. Politicians in almost every state could praise themselves for honoring motherhood and succoring fatherless children. But the self-congratulations were unearned. In actual application, few public officials, with the exception of those in a handful of big-city governments, provided any significant financial support. In no state did more than a few thousand families receive pensions in any given year between 1911 and 1934.

DID THE PENSIONS MARGINALIZE WOMEN'S WORK?

Scholars who have identified mothers' pensions as a factor pushing poor women into marginal low-wage labor markets echo a fear first expressed by Mary Richmond and her allies.[43] Edward Devine predicted that "the anti-social type of employer who now throws his maimed and mangled workers, his exhausted, worn-out workers, and the widows and orphans of those whom he has slain indiscriminately on the scrap-heap of public relief . . . [would greet] with unholy joy a movement, which by changing the name of this relief . . . makes it more palatable to sentimental reformers, and thus gives the exploiters a new strangle-hold."[44]

Since about half of the mothers' pension bills prohibited beneficiaries from work outside the home altogether or for more than one day each week, yet in no case provided complete financial support, Mary Richmond worried that mothers' pensions would subsidize the sweated industries that employed homebound pieceworkers. Moreover, she mused, "No home [is] remote enough from the freight office and the parcel post to be safe from such exploitation."[45]

Clearly nowhere were pensions adequate to provide women and their children with even basics—such as food, shelter, or clothing. In 1912 Frederick Almy, general secretary of the Buffalo, New York, Charity Organization Society, estimated that an adequate family budget for the poor required a yearly income of not less than $700. The cost of living then escalated sharply during and immediately after World War I, before stabilizing for much of the rest of the 1920s. A yearly minimum of between $700 and $850 remained a common estimate used by social workers of a budget necessary for a family of four that would provide a minimally decent standard of living.[46] Most widows who got mothers' pensions received yearly sums of less than $240.

In 1913 the Russell Sage Foundation published a report analyzing a sample population of 985 widows that Mary Richmond and her assistant in the Charity Organization Department, social worker Fred Hall, had prepared.[47] The two had contacted the nation's twenty largest charity organization societies, asking them to provide detailed information about all widows who had received aid in 1910. Richmond and Hall, using the records of the nine charity organizations that returned complete schedules, concluded that paid outside work provided the best supplement to the aid given widows from either private or public sources. Any measures that forbade such work constituted bad policy.[48]

Indeed, almost half of the widows in the Richmond sample had worked while their husbands were still alive. Earning an average of less than ten dollars a week, the husbands had brought home yearly average wages of about $500, not enough to raise their families above a poverty-level standard of living. When children were still too young to contribute to family income, wives commonly sought ways to supplement their husband's meager wages.[49]

When husbands died, and widows applied to private philanthropy for relief, income received never equaled income needed. Aid from a private charity rarely surpassed $250 per year, and typically private charity organizations urged widows to work, a policy with which Mary Richmond concurred. Eighty-four percent of the 985 widows in Richmond's sample worked regularly for pay, the vast majority at low-wage jobs outside their homes, most often as maids or factory workers. Richmond's widows found these jobs more lucrative and more rewarding than work that would have kept them home-bound. Only a tiny handful kept boarders, did washing, or finished piecework at home. If a widow was healthy, the Russell Sage study urged, she should work. Indeed, "it was unnatural, in her eyes and those of her neighbors, to earn nothing. . . . Although the amount [she earned] be small, sometimes not more than a dollar a week, it gives the mother a stronger influence with her children, and calls forth a special loyalty from them."[50]

Foundation officials, both in municipal charity organizations and at the Russell Sage Foundation, correctly argued that a mother's best chances to contribute to her family's income lay in work done outside her home. They also saw the economic situation of poor widows far more clearly than did politicians—who tended to talk fuzzily about the glories of hearth and home. Social workers like Mary Richmond knew that poor women often worked to supplement their husband's inadequate wages. They knew that when a husband died, the woman's need to work regularly was even more urgent. Only in romantic legislative fairy tales were the coffers of either public or private relief large enough to allow indigent women to stay at home. Moreover, Richmond and Hall made an interesting discovery as they reviewed thousands of pages of records from charity organization societies. In case after case, poor mothers who were in good health reported that they preferred to work outside their homes—at least part time. As one said, "Life can be too dull sometimes." What the mothers wanted, and what the Russell Sage Foundation supported, was adequate publicly sponsored day care for young children, to supplement help needy mothers might receive from neighbors and relatives. Mary Richmond knew that her conclusion that widows preferred to earn outside wages challenged popular prejudices that romanticized a mother's wish to be always home with her children. Indeed, in a letter to her boss, John Glenn, she accurately predicted that her study on widows would be "widely misunderstood and misquoted." Nonetheless, even if the truth was "damaging" to popular myth and subjected the Sage Foundation to public attacks, "the truth should be told." To his credit, Glenn concurred and authorized the publication by Russell Sage of *A Study of Nine Hundred and Eighty-five Widows.*[51]

In any given year between 1915 and 1928 no more than a hundred thousand Americans received mothers' pensions. They constituted fewer than a tenth of 1 percent of the national population. Pension rules probably caused a tiny number of American women to stay home glumly doing washing or piecework when they preferred factory work. The pensions, however, did not marginalize women's labor, except in this very limited way. Occupational opportunities available to poor, badly educated women were already painfully few. During years when the acquisition of a high school diploma was still a hallmark of middle-class status, most poor women had no chance to move into well-paying jobs.[52] Whatever marginalization the pensions actually encouraged was rhetorical. During years when poor women regularly worked outside the home, they still faced charges that such work caused "unwomanly" neglect of family responsibilities. In that sense, the pensions' glorification of woman's place in the home added yet another burden to the shoulders of many poor widows who knew that paid outside jobs provided their only chance of providing a decent life for themselves and their dependents. The language of many pension laws provided yet another legal justification for continued employment restrictions and open gender discrimination in the workplace.

Pension laws did not create the bleak employment prospects facing most poor women. However, they may have played a part in postponing decisions about more constructive welfare policy. The Russell Sage Foundation's Charity Organization Department advocated ideas it argued would be part of such a better welfare policy, including crusades against communicable disease and marriage law reform. It did not suggest that these and other reforms should substitute immediately for mothers' pensions. However, they might eventually make the latter unnecessary.

THE CHARITY ORGANIZATION DEPARTMENT AND WELFARE REFORM

Mary Richmond grew up a fatherless child. She also grew up motherless. No one had to tell her that disease often devastated poor families. Rather than remaining charmed by the chimera of mothers' pensions, she urged that governments at all levels initiate massive campaigns against preventable disease. A third of the widows who composed her case study group of 985 women had lost their husbands to tuberculosis. Most of those husbands were not yet forty years old. Pneumonia and its complications widowed another 20 percent. Other infectious diseases common to poor Americans in the early twentieth century, like typhus and malaria, killed another 10 percent of husbands. Mary Richmond concluded that disease, especially tuberculosis "was the great cause of widowhood." In contrast, industrial accidents killed only 9 percent of the husbands in Richmond's sample population.[53]

She argued that a budget of $50 million could eradicate tuberculosis in New York City, which, with some of the most densely populated residential districts in the world, posed peculiarly difficult challenges to prevention of airborne disease. Tuberculosis killed an average of ten thousand city residents every year, which meant that $50 million spent over a period of five years to defeat tuberculosis would prevent great numbers of women from becoming young widows. If public policy makers joined in a national crusade against tuberculosis, hundreds of thousands of unnecessary deaths each year would be prevented. Moreover, with national coordination and "good social engineering" the costs of each life saved could drop dramatically.[54] Rather than bowing to sentiment and providing small sums to a few widows, policy makers should embrace prevention of widowhood. They should champion measures to improve public health. They should follow the example blazed in the South by the Rockefeller Sanitary Commission.[55]

Edward Devine extended Richmond's reasoning further. The nation should certainly crusade against preventable disease. But it should do more than that. It should take up the cause of national social insurance. Mothers' pensions were an exercise in "self-delusion." Any responsible society should provide outright relief to those who fell by the wayside, those who through physical or mental infirmity could not work, or who had sought, and failed, to find work. Such relief should be the province of the state. For the great majority of Americans who could work, however, there should be a national program of health, old age, and unemployment insurance, to which they, along with their employers, contributed.[56]

The arguments made by Devine, Richmond, and others associated with the Sage Foundation were widely publicized, especially in the pages of the *Survey*. Nonetheless, they found no immediate government champions. Obviously, the fight to gain a national system of old age and unemployment insurance took another two decades to win. The fight for a program of national health insurance still looms.

Another Sage-sponsored policy was better received. Between 1909 and 1928 Mary Richmond became one of the nation's foremost experts on marriage law and succeeded in making that subject one of the dominant concerns of the Charity Organization Department. By 1920 its efforts to collect material on the subject required the hiring of additional staff—including two researchers who had previously worked as investigators for the U.S. Children's Bureau—and by 1928 the Russell Sage Foundation had the best collection of data on the subject in America. Using it, Richmond and her staff published five books, gave speeches at dozens of conferences, and found themselves deluged with offers from state legislatures to testify as expert witnesses on marriage law reform.[57]

The foundation's position was easily summarized. If states tightened their marriage laws, unfit persons would be less likely to marry, and the public would suffer a lighter burden—fewer women widowed or abandoned by men who should not have been allowed to become husbands, fewer diseased children produced by unsuitable parents. The fieldwork that they conducted throughout the country convinced the Charity Organization Department's staff that most states used marriage as an opportunity to gain revenue. In a few states, to be sure, city rather than county governments had taken over the issuance of marriage licenses, and in most there were restrictions on the ages at which marriage could occur. Typically, girls under sixteen and boys under eighteen could not marry legally, but these restrictions were generally worthless.

Few states demanded verifiable proof of age, such as a baptismal or birth certificate. Most allowed a waiver of age restrictions if parents consented. Some states allowed girls as young as twelve to marry if their parents agreed, and parents, in most states, did not have to provide proof of the child's age. The way was open to child marriages, typically involving a very young girl, often as young as ten, married to a man at least three times older who had often colluded with the child's parents to state her age falsely to county authorities. Although spotty record keeping prevented an accurate count, the Russell Sage authorities guessed in 1925 that there were six hundred thousand marriages involving a child under legal age. It was, they said, no more difficult in America to buy a license for a marriage than to buy a license to keep a dog.[58]

In their writings and consultations with public officials Richmond and her staff urged several changes in marriage policy. Child marriage should be abolished. For every tale of a girl who married at fourteen to produce ten children, all leading citizens, there were dozens of stories of ruined lives— unsafe early pregnancies, unhealthy children, incompatible spouses. States should require verifiable proof of age—an attested transcript of a birth certificate, a duly certified transcript of a baptism, or a passport, showing date of birth. Counties must reform procedures that commonly allowed their license issuers to determine fees for marriage documents and to accept those fees in lieu of any salary. Such systems, obviously, encouraged these officials to maximize the number of marriage licenses they issued, and to look the other way if underage applicants appeared.[59]

All states had bureaus of vital statistics. Without having to create a new department of government, states could centralize marriage statistics by requiring that all counties submit to such bureaus complete, verifiable copies of all licenses issued.[60] Moreover, they should require that marriage licenses only be granted in the home county of either the bride or groom. In cases when a couple had legitimate reasons to solemnize a marriage away from their home county or state, they should apply for a double license. Under the scheme devised by the Russell Sage researchers, residents of a state had to meet its requirements for marriage even if they went elsewhere to say their vows. If, for example, a San Francisco man wanted to marry a Philadelphia woman in New York City, he and his fiancée would have to show New York authorities either a valid California or a valid Pennsylvania marriage license. Such a double license system would eliminate the "marriage parlors" usually operated by justices of the peace in small towns within an hour's drive of a major city and intended to provide secrecy on demand. Two Russell Sage investigators, a man and a woman, traveled to six states pretending to be an engaged couple wishing to marry. Operators of most marriage parlors they visited would tie the knot for three dollars, but they told the Russell Sage "couple" that the charge would be six dollars or more if they wished to keep the news of their marriage out of the newspapers.[61]

States should also forbid marriage to anyone suffering a venereal disease. The Charity Organization Department's Associate Director, Fred Hall, enthusiastically endorsed Wisconsin's "eugenic marriage" law, which required that every man applying for a marriage license had to file a certificate by a licensed physician stating that he had thoroughly examined the individual and found him to be free of venereal disease. Significantly, during years when even well-educated physicians' knowledge of syphilis and gonorrhea was highly incomplete, most states ignored questions about a female's role in transmission of these diseases.[62]

These proposals found supporters. In 1919 only Wisconsin required proof of medical examination for venereal disease as a requirement of readiness for marriage. By 1928, the year of Mary Richmond's death, twenty-eight states had passed such laws, although almost all still required testing of males only. Moreover, most had accepted Charity Organization Department suggestions about tightening proof of age requirements in marriage law, and most were now using documents shaped by the work of the Russell Sage Foundation.[63]

Richmond had directed her staff to prepare a folder of mock record forms for use in administration of marriage law. They ranged from "Form A: Application for Marriage License and Record of Same" to "Form D: Official Marriage Certificate" to "Form E: Envelope for Documents" to "Form M: General Follow-up Letter to Each of the Contracting Parties."[64] Thousands of copies of these suggested forms had been circulated among state and county officials, and, by the end of the 1920s, they had become the standard legal tools used by most governments to record American marriage.

The members of the Russell Sage Foundation's Charity Organization Department did not advocate changes in marriage laws or wars against TB as panaceas for the problems of indigent women and children. They did not see these ideas as alternatives that alone would obviate the need for mothers' aid. Some form of publicly funded help would still be needed. However, such aid should only be given after careful investigation, using techniques being developed by the new profession of social work. A quiet alliance between private social workers in the Russell Sage Foundation and public social workers in the Children's Bureau transformed the mothers' pensions. They became the vehicle for inclusion of the casework methods heretofore primarily used by private philanthropy as key elements in public welfare policy.

THE TRANSFORMATION OF THE MOTHERS' PENSIONS

C. C. Carstens, the general secretary of the Massachusetts Society for the Prevention of Cruelty to Children and a frequent consultant to both the Russell Sage Foundation and the Children's Bureau, accurately remarked that "the enthusiast for widows' pensions is indifferent to the rigid enforcement of responsibilities. . . . He is likely to turn easily toward the payment of a lump sum from the public treasury as . . . a remedy for all social ills."[65] Carstens, Hall, Richmond, and other social work professionals affiliated with Russell Sage judged the mothers' pensions to be the cynical product of political manipulation. Nonetheless, they also judged them to be vaguely written laws that, with proper administration, could demonstrate the importance of the science of social work and social work case method. They found allies not only within the municipal charity organizations that had traditionally provided relief to indigent women and children, but also within the Department of Labor, in the Children's Bureau, the special departmental unit authorized by Congress in 1912 to investigate all aspects of child welfare in America.

If Mary Richmond was the "high priestess" of social casework method, she had rivals in Edith and Grace Abbott, Sophonisba Breckinridge, and Julia Lathrop. Together, these women formed an alliance that bridged the worlds of private and public policy makers, connected academe, philanthropy, and government, and transformed the mothers' pensions through policies that gave government the right to determine suitability of homes for children who received public aid.

Unique among highly ranked American universities in the early twentieth century, the University of Chicago wooed talented female as well as male students, not only with the promise that they would be taken seriously but also with the presence of female deans and faculty members and with the availability of financial support for graduate study. Two of those women faculty members, Sophonisba Breckinridge and Edith Abbott, created the first school of social work to be attached to a major research university: the University of Chicago's School of Social Service Administration.[66]

Sophonisba Breckinridge was a member of the politically prominent Kentucky Breckinridge family. Born at the end of the Civil War, a graduate of Wellesley College, and the first woman admitted to the Kentucky bar, she entered the University of Chicago orbit in 1894, first as a graduate student of political economy, later as professor.

Edith Abbott, ten years younger than Breckinridge, was the daughter of a Nebraska attorney. In 1893 the failure of a bank into which Othman Abbott had sunk all his capital precipitated a drastic decline in the family's economic fortunes. Both Edith and her sister Grace, however, refused to accept the crisis as an end to their educations. Edith Abbott taught school, took correspondence classes at the University of Nebraska, and by 1903 was on her way to the University of Chicago to accept first a graduate fellowship, then a faculty position. Her younger sister soon followed.

Julia Lathrop, the daughter of an Illinois congressman, also belonged to the Chicago network. After graduating from Vassar in 1880, she returned to Illinois, moved to Jane Addams's Chicago Hull House, and became an influential member of the Illinois Board of Charities. A longtime friend and colleague of Breckinridge and the Abbotts, she promoted courses in social work method as co-director of the Chicago School of Civics and Philanthropy, and, in 1912, accepted an appointment as the first director of the U.S. Children's Bureau.[67]

If a common tie with Chicago social work education linked Breckin-ridge, the Abbotts, and Lathrop, advocacy of social work training as a legiti-mate social science discipline united all four with Mary Richmond and the Russell Sage Foundation. Moreover, all had enthusiastically advocated the establishment of a federal bureau that investigated conditions under which American children lived and coordinated information about issues that af-fected their well-being.[68]

Florence Kelley, General Secretary of the National Consumers' League, represented the views of many supporters of a national children's bureau when she scolded: "If any stupid, illiterate farmer up near Catskill in New York wants to know something about raising artichokes . . . all he has to do is get his son or the village school master to write to the Department of Agri-culture . . . and he will be supplied with information not only about ar-tichokes, but about every thing relating to agriculture. . . . How different is the situation with regard to children!"[69]

Progressive reformers like Kelley, who were the Children's Bureau's greatest champions, dictated the choice of its first director, Julia Lathrop.[70] The organizational triangle between the University of Chicago's social work de-partments, the Russell Sage Foundation's Charity Organization Department, and the Department of Labor was complete, and operating as a part of it, Mary Richmond, C. C. Carstens, and others at Russell Sage realized that, while state legislators were eager to pass mothers' pensions, they seemed equally quick to forget about them. An administrative vacuum existed, quickly filled by allies at the Russell Sage Foundation and the Children's Bureau.

By the time Congress passed a bill in 1920 authorizing the establish-ment of a Women's Bureau, also within the Department of Labor, a die had been cast. The mothers' pensions were a subject suitable for Children's Bu-reau, not Women's Bureau, investigation. The government's focus, accord-ingly, would be on children, not their mothers. Indeed, Mary Anderson, the first director of the Women's Bureau, did not challenge this demarcation. A Swedish immigrant and former union official, she was an outsider to the social work network of which Richmond, Lathrop, Breckinridge, and the Abbotts were members in such good standing. For practical and ideologi-cal reasons she concentrated her bureau's attentions on young, unmarried women workers.[71]

So, without much struggle, the Children's Bureau retained investiga-tory oversight of the mothers' pensions. Pensioners were not to be judged "even primarily" on their ability to "alleviate material distress." They should be expected to "demonstrate adequate mother care." It was not enough that mothers fed and housed their children, they had to prepare them for "effective manhood and womanhood."[72] The judges of "adequate mother care" were not to be the mothers themselves, but professional social workers, employed by private philanthropy or by the Children's Bureau. They were to be drawn from the expanding ranks of college-educated social workers, a group that found new opportunities and mushroomed by two-thirds in the 1920s. At the end of the decade, its numbers had climbed above thirty thousand, 80 percent of them women.[73]

No one exercised greater influence over this growing professional adolescent than did the trio of Sophonisba Breckinridge, Edith Abbott, and Mary Richmond. The social workers that Abbott and Breckinridge trained at Chicago often found their way to the offices of the Russell Sage Foundation and the Children's Bureau. The alliance was strengthened even further in 1921 when Edith Abbott's sister, Grace Abbott, replaced Lathrop as head of the Children's Bureau.

Typically, when a city or county decided to implement a mothers' pension program, its officials rapidly found themselves overwhelmed with the sheer number of applications. This was the case, for example, in Chicago, one of the few cities in Illinois that distributed a significant number of pensions. There, the juvenile court administered pensions. In 1911 the first year after enactment of the Illinois Mothers' Aid Act, more than 1,450 Chicago women asked for help. Court officials were swamped. With no funds available to hire additional probation officers, they sought assistance from the United Charities of Chicago, which established a "case committee" staffed by social workers whose salaries were paid by Chicago's private philanthropies, not public funds, and within a year this committee had muscled out the thirteen probation officers who were assigned to the court as political appointees. The latter's duties no longer included investigation of applicants for mothers' pensions. This was now the job of "volunteers" on the case committee, who were almost all social workers and who scrutinized the worthiness of applications by following social casework methods. They visited pension beneficiaries frequently, focusing their questions on the care given children. What were they being fed? Had they missed any school? Was their recreation wholesome?[74]

The Chicago pattern, soon to be copied in Cincinnati and elsewhere, was the one championed by the Children's Bureau. In a widely reprinted investigation of the administration of mothers' aid, the bureau's official recommendation was that "the application of family case work technique was crucial to the success of mothers' pensions." When relations between public officials administering mothers' aid and private family-relief agencies were characterized by "great friendliness and mutual confidence," money was well spent. When public officials could not count on the aid of private philanthropies, as was the situation in Massachusetts, casework was "meager and poorly done."[75] At the very least applications languished for months or even years. Cities that used committees of "volunteer" social workers, whose salaries were paid by philanthropies, provided the better model.

Sophonisba Breckinridge and Edith Abbott also co-authored the Children's Department bulletin that became a widely used guide for social workers investigating mothers' aid applications. Not surprisingly, it emphasized rigorous investigatory casework. Using the administration of mothers' aid in the Cook County (Chicago) Juvenile Court as illustration, Abbott and Breckinridge cautioned that at least two months of social work investigation should proceed the granting of any pension. County officials had a choice: They could make a "thorough, which means a slow, investigation," or they could "grant pensions after an incomplete investigation, with the dangers of having to withdraw them later. . . . Those who criticize private charitable agencies for 'taking so much time to investigate' have learned that a public agency must follow the same methods if its work is to be well done."[76]

Abbott and Breckinridge urged that investigators not shrink from awkward questions. Scruples about privacy should not keep them from checking all possible information about an applicant's background. Indeed, they offered a cautionary tale. In one instance, a pensioned widow in Chicago who had appeared to all eyes "a most trustworthy woman" was secretly living with a male lover. Only after repeated questions to neighbors did the social worker in charge of the woman's case find one who repeated gossip about a man on the premises. Needless to say, Abbott and Breckinridge noted approvingly, in this instance careful and repeated casework paid off. Cook County authorities immediately revoked the scarlet widow's public aid.[77]

Further, Abbott and Breckinridge argued that most recipients of mothers' aid cared less for privacy than might be imagined. They were, rather, a different sort of woman, certainly not the kind who earned social work degrees at major universities. In Chicago, recipients received their monthly payments by appearing in person on the designated day at the Cook County Juvenile Court. One might think, Abbott and Breckinridge reported, that such a procedure, where women waited quite publicly, would instill feelings of shame and humiliation. On the contrary, most welcomed the chance to get out of their homes and chat with other women, even if forced to stand in line for long periods. Abbott and Breckinridge assured their readers, "The superior woman has it in her power to avoid much . . . of the publicity by going for her check after the great mass of the women have left."[78]

Politicians rarely spoke in detail about actual mothers' pension recipients. Had they done so, they likely would have agreed with Edith Abbott and Sophonisba Breckinridge. Rather, they sentimentalized motherhood as an unreal abstraction. Meanwhile, social work administrators like Abbott and Breckinridge stereotyped aid recipients as largely inferior. Mary Richmond was one of the few who saw pensioners more clearly, as neither saints nor sinners, but as ordinary women facing financial crises they did not cause.

Ironically, Richmond was a member of the Russell Sage Foundation, the "Charity Trust" against which politicians who professed to support aid to needy mothers loved to rail. If mothers' aid was a painless cause to support, the supposedly sinister "Charity Trust" was similarly easy to attack. Even though the Sage Foundation regularly provided them with free copies of its studies and publications, many members of Congress made it a convenient rhetorical target. Why was it collecting all those statistics? Why was it interested in social welfare issues? What was its secret agenda?

The young Fiorello La Guardia, for instance, then a congressman from New York, made something of a career during the 1920s attacking the Sage Foundation. With its "theories and statistics," it was the "evil heart of the Charity Trust." Although he represented a district that included the "home of the Sage Foundation" and knew that most employees of the foundation were his own constituents, he would "never permit it . . . to monopolize charity and monopolize welfare work."[79]

La Guardia made these remarks on the floor of the House of Representatives in March 1926, over a decade after the Russell Sage Foundation had begun doing just what he feared, with the open approval of hundreds of local, state, and national government officials. As early as 1916, Helen Glenn, a member of the Pennsylvania State Board of Education and chair of the state's supervisory "Mothers' Assistance Committee," had written Mary Richmond

> I am so grateful to you for the copy of the questionnaire for a widow with children and will use it in accordance with your regulations. I will also appreciate so much the case studies of the Charity Organization Bulletin and will use them with care. . . . I am realizing more every day what a debt we owe to charity organization societies and how much the progress of this particular work depends on our close imitation of your methods.[80]

Such "close imitation" meant that politicians' rhetoric and public policy about the mothers' pensions diverged. They always had. Even if few

Americans realized it, the administrators of the pensions had never viewed them as a right of motherhood. Rather, they implemented a de facto policy that would finally emerge openly in the Social Security Act's provisions for aid to dependent children as the doctrine of the "suitable home." The state had every duty to scrutinize with great care the "suitability" of the home the mother provided. In case of any doubt, "the doubt should be in favor of the child." Not all households deserved to be kept together. If public officials, while investigating an application for public aid, decided the mother was unfit and removed a child to the care of a juvenile court or county welfare board, they should be in no great rush to reunite parent and child. When authorities faced a decision whether "to return the child one month, two months, or six months, or even several years later, there are a number of other things to take into consideration. . . . There arises a nice question as to whether a child should be returned even though a home may have gotten somewhat straightened out."[81]

The mothers' pensions had been transformed long before they disappeared, another casualty of the Great Depression. Those who see a great policy gap between them and Title IV of the Social Security Act of 1935 have, like Fiorello La Guardia, paid too much attention to the rhetoric of mothers' pension policy and too little to their actual implementation. The pensions provided very little public money and helped a tiny number of poverty-stricken mothers. Mary Richmond and her supporters were right. The nation's money and attention would have been better directed to crusades against the infectious diseases that created widows or for national health and unemployment insurance. Nonetheless, as policy, the pensions were important, the entering wedge for "suitability" and "eligibility" provisions attached to welfare payments ever since.[82] In advocating such provisions, the Russell Sage Foundation undoubtedly promoted the growth of professional social work. The pensions and their successors provided one group of mostly female Americans with enlarged opportunities as government caseworkers. The women they supposedly helped, poor mothers and their children, received little from either the original mothers' pensions or any of their subsequent permutations. In that sense, both the original and "transformed" mothers' pensions deserved censure. The "worthy widow" gave way to the "suitable home," which in turn led to the "welfare mess," as the early twentieth century turned into the late twentieth century. Policy makers never looked squarely at questions raised by income distribution in America. Rather, they focused their attention on a side issue: criteria for eligibility for aid among those already impoverished.

Victorious in their efforts to reshape the application of mothers' pensions, officials of the Russell Sage Foundation, in concert with allies in other foundations, faced a dilemma. When experts found the home not suitable, where should the child go? Foundation-supported solutions to this question involved a campaign to redefine juvenile delinquency and expand the authority of the new institution of the juvenile court.

FOUNDATIONS, "CHILD-HELPING," AND THE JUVENILE COURT

I f the American home was "collapsing," if the prospects of good results from parent education were doubtful and those from mothers' pensions even dimmer, policy makers in foundations confronted an urgent question: How best could society help children in trouble? Miriam Van Waters, soon to combine her work as a parent educator with an appointment as referee to the Los Angeles Juvenile Court, concluded in 1925 that too many parents deserved permanent probation. Never one to mince words, she warned that "the consequences of those selfish, bewildered adult blunders we call the 'broken home'" were dire. Not only parents needed education. The entire society "must be educated to see the [juvenile] court as the only *force* that can be substituted legally for weakening parental control."[1]

When children's own parents failed, the state, through the juvenile court, should intervene. Officials of the juvenile court would be "wise fathers." They would "treat" rather than punish young persons. They would be agents of salvation, not retribution, for troubled children. Not only would the erring child's life be improved, it was "fundamentally in the interest of the State to save him from a downward career."[2]

Miriam Van Waters was one of many in the early-twentieth-century United States who embraced the possibilities glimpsed in the juvenile court. Among its initial supporters were several of the policy-making foundations. The Laura Spelman Rockefeller Memorial, the Russell Sage Foundation, and the Commonwealth Fund all initiated projects designed to heighten the effectiveness of the juvenile court. This chapter uses their efforts as a lens through which to re-evaluate the history of the first three decades of the American juvenile court—from the establishment of the first such institution in Chicago in 1899 to the disillusioned evaluation of the courts and juvenile delinquency presented at the 1930 White House Conference on Child Health and Protection. As with parent education, foundations accurately predicted the weaknesses of a new phenomenon. By 1930 no major foundation embraced the juvenile court as a solution to juvenile delinquency with any degree of its earlier enthusiasm. Instead, the three whose activities this chapter analyzes had retreated, concluding that the gap between the vision and reality of juvenile courts was simply too wide. Parent education did not die when abandoned, nor did the juvenile court. Each became established social policy, supported with increasing amounts of public funding. Nonetheless early foundation criticisms deserve more attention. Neither contemporary politicians nor later scholars of the juvenile court have paid them sufficient heed.

THE JUVENILE COURT "IDEAL"

In 1899 Illinois enacted the first law bringing together in one jurisdiction—via a special "juvenile" court organized for children's work—cases involving delinquent, neglected, and dependent children. As they had with mothers' pensions, legislators in many other states eagerly copied the Illinois precedent. By 1910 thirty-eight states authorized juvenile courts. By 1930 only the state of Maine lacked a statute allowing the organization of such courts in its counties and cities. At least four thousand separate juvenile courts heard cases.

The underlying principle of mothers' aid was simple: Needy mothers, if worthy, deserved society's support in order to continue to raise their young children at home. Similarly, the two basic ideas behind the juvenile court innovation were easily stated. First, child offenders were not criminals and should not be treated as criminals. Whether called "juvenile disorderly persons," "misdemeanants," or "juvenile delinquents," children brought to juvenile court were to be "reformed," not punished. Indeed, the very "idea of punishment" was to disappear. The juvenile court sought to "exercise parental care" over the delinquent child.[3]

The court, then, substituted for family. Its focus was less on the child's guilt or innocence and more on the creation of a plan of action that would deter further unacceptable behavior. The word "court" itself was a misnomer. Instead, the institution, in principle, acted as would have the best parents in Miriam Van Water's fondest dreams. It studied the behavior of each individual child and devised "treatments." Juvenile delinquency, like tuberculosis, was a preventable disease, demanding concerted, but humane, state intervention.

Second only in importance to the idea that the young delinquent was not a criminal was the principle that jails were not for children. Its advocates argued that the juvenile court existed to keep children from incarceration. Children brought before the court should in the vast majority of cases be allowed to return to their homes, and to daily attendance at school or job, supervised by a new court official, the probation officer.[4] These individuals were not only to visit the boys or girls assigned them regularly. According to typical instructions issued by the Cook County Juvenile Court in 1901, probation officers were also required to supervise their charges' performance at school or at work. Moreover, "[they] must labor with the parents to remove friction, and help them make the home attractive." Finally, they were to be "friends" to each child assigned them, but "friends" who "spoke with greater authority than a teacher or parent."[5]

THE "WILDFIRE" SPREAD OF THE JUVENILE COURT

To meet such job descriptions, applicants for positions as probation officers would have had to be fearsomely efficient saints. With seemingly little concern about the availability of such paragons, state legislators scrambled to join the crusade for juvenile courts; just as simultaneously, they eagerly joined the movement for mothers' pensions. In fact, in many states the two issues were inextricably linked. Each certainly offered irresistible political opportunities. The former allowed advocates to demand that society save its children through the "law of love and not the law of vengeance."[6] The latter provided almost endless opportunities to venerate motherhood.

State legislators championed laws that established juvenile courts and mothers' pensions. In neither case did they require statewide consistency in the application or even the adoption of the enabling legislation. Before 1930 both phenomena truly matched the word so often used in connection with the mothers' pension movement. Indeed, they were "wildfires": spreading rapidly in all directions, with no one in control. Within states, counties, even cities, juvenile courts assumed an infinite variety of forms.

In some areas, they were new, independent courts. In others, juvenile courts became branches of existing criminal courts, especially county and municipal criminal courts. In still others, juvenile courts sometimes were divisions within a noncriminal court with probate or chancery jurisdiction. Some courts dealt only with questions of juvenile delinquency. Others had the authority to adjudicate problems of offenses by adults against children, such as desertion. Some courts administered mothers' pensions and other forms of public aid to needy families. A number reviewed all petitions for adoptions. A few even acted as divorce courts.

No standard definition of juvenile delinquency existed. For the Juvenile Court of Philadelphia, a "delinquent child" was any child who had "violated any law of this state, or any city or borough ordinance."[7] In many other courts the definition was much broader. It included not only children accused of breaking laws, but also those whose habits or surroundings the court deemed unsuitable, if not actually illegal. Such courts had authority over "delinquents" who often were innocent of any legal offense, but who wandered the streets late at night, spent time in "unsavory" places, like taverns or railroad yards, or, overwhelmingly in the case of teenaged girls, were unmarried, but sexually active.

Some courts defined "children" as under age eighteen. In about half the states with legislation allowing juvenile courts, ages could vary, both by gender and individual choice of particular judges. Girls were often still "children" until age eighteen, while boys ceased to enjoy that status at age sixteen or younger. A few courts dealt only with boys. Some juvenile courts did not have jurisdiction over serious crimes committed by children, such as grand theft, assault, or murder, but others did. In still another group, the decision to remand certain juvenile cases was a mutual one, made by the judge of a juvenile court and colleagues from other benches.[8]

Despite these great variations, a few generalizations about the early-twentieth-century juvenile court can be made. Like mothers' pensions, they were almost entirely an urban phenomenon. Rural America did not participate to any significant degree, not even at the small town or county level. Instead, cities with at least twenty-five thousand residents housed more than 98 percent of juvenile courts, and those with populations of over one hundred thousand were the real center for the movement.[9] Except in a few dozen cities, the juvenile court was far more likely to exist largely in name—perhaps as a project of a reform-minded judge, who a few afternoons a month turned his office into a "juvenile court."

Most contemporary reports about the spread of the juvenile court idea neglected to mention this crucial fact. At least initially, reviews of the courts echoed the euphoria of Judge Ben Lindsey, head of the Denver Juvenile Court and the movement's best-known champion. Lindsey's widely reprinted first reports from the bench suggested the triumph of "the principles of [legal] love." Judge Lindsey told his millions of readers that "the boys in the juvenile court of Denver in one year did more to enforce our most important laws—those for the protection of youth—such as forbidding the sale to them

of dangerous firearms, cigarettes, liquor, or immoral literature, than the police department in Denver has done in ten or even twenty years."[10]

The Denver Juvenile Court provided, according to Lindsey, a caring
course in proper republican behavior. Formerly troubled boys became "little
citizens." Studied from "hearts to skins and from skins back to hearts again,"
they learned how to distinguish right from wrong. Aware that the state was
trying to "make men of them, not criminals," Lindsey's boys thrived, and
stayed in school or at their jobs. Out of the hundreds of boys seen, the Denver
court annually sent an average of fewer than twenty deemed incorrigible to
the city's reformatory, the Denver Industrial School. Judge Lindsey boasted,
"We owe it to the boys in the juvenile court that a boy almost takes his life in
his hands to ask anywhere in Denver to buy a 'nickel's' worth of cigarettes."[11]

SCHOLARS AND THE JUVENILE COURTS

For the past quarter century Judge Lindsey's glowing assessment has
taken a drubbing. Scholars interested in the history of the early-twentieth-
century juvenile court have produced a lengthy indictment. It was "ill-
conceived" and staffed by judges who "were compelled to make snap judgments about complex human affairs just to maintain their own dignity and
the illusion of serving society well. Their failures were tragicomic."[12] By
helping to "invent" delinquency, progressive juvenile justice "consolidated
the inferior social status and dependency of lower-class youth."[13] The juvenile
court provided a "broad and far-reaching legal tool for apprehending and
incarcerating young females who violated prevailing moral codes."[14] Perhaps
worst of all, the court, by "camouflaging its action . . . chanting *parens patriae,*
assumed the power to dissolve for a time, and alter permanently, the ties
between impoverished parents and their children. . . . Some of the proponents of the juvenile court were merely sappy and wrong-headed; others
were dangerous, all were wrong."[15] A reader committed to a careful review of
this scholarly literature might reasonably begin to wonder why the nation was
not marching in the streets. He or she could also ask, "Why do the social
historians and legal historians who analyze the early-twentieth-century juvenile court seem to have no knowledge of each other's existence?"[16]

Social historians, led by scholars Steven Schlossman, Joseph Hawes,
Susan Turner, and Mary Odem, have viewed the juvenile court as an outgrowth of progressive reform.[17] Most base their research on careful studies of
a particular juvenile court. Schlossman, for instance, has produced a series of
highly interesting pieces based on the archives of the Milwaukee and Los

Angeles juvenile courts. In collaboration with fellow historian Odem and criminologist Turner, he has illustrated the ways juvenile courts in both cities exercised highly arbitrary power over children who often ended up in their grasp by simply being in the wrong place at the wrong time. For example, James, a teenaged boy caught loitering in a park smoking cigarettes by a factory inspector out looking for someone else, ended up in Milwaukee Juvenile Court—facing not charges of loitering, or even of underage smoking, but of lying to his mother![18]

Schlossman's courts were coercive, but in ways that defy easy categorization as class control. Girls were more likely to be deemed wayward by both judges and parents. Acting in alliance, the latter two often cooperated. Neither judges nor parents, in many cases, wished a job to be a source of too much independence, especially for their adolescent girls. Such daughters in Los Angeles who spent their wages on clothing, movie tickets, or rouge found that it was not a probation officer, but a parent, who brought charges of disorderly behavior against them to the juvenile court. For instance, eighteen-year-old Lydia Walker specifically disobeyed her mother's wishes, quit her job as a telephone operator, and joined a traveling chorus line as a "Broadway Beauty." Acting upon Mrs. Walker's complaint, the Los Angeles Juvenile Court demanded that the dance-crazy girl move back home and return to work at the telephone company. Seemingly far from regarding the court as a tool of middle-class control, Mrs. Walker regaled her daughter's probation officer with a long list of further allegations, including asking for help in forbidding Lydia to use lipstick.[19]

If social historians have depended on the archives of a few famous juvenile courts, legal scholars have viewed juvenile justice as an issue in case law. Social historians interested in putting the courts within the context of Progressive Era reform have debated questions of social control. Legal historians have argued precedents. The latter group has been most interested in the theoretical bases claimed for juvenile court legislation. Many have seen juvenile courts as worthy of scrutiny as a step in the evolution of the famous 1967 Supreme Court decision, *In re Gault,* which required that all due process rights given adults be granted juveniles in juvenile court. Legal scholars, among them J. Lawrence Schultz, Sanford Fox, and Michael Grossberg, have examined the juvenile courts as illustrations of the expanded power of the American judiciary in late-nineteenth- and early-twentieth-century America.[20]

Some legal historians, like Sanford Fox, have argued that juvenile courts simply made concrete ideas about the proper legal treatment of children long present in American society. In terms of procedural change, they were a "myth" that did nothing to change the traditional American practice of blurring distinctions between pauper, vagrant, troubled, and criminal children. All belonged together as potential community problems. Not until *In re Gault* did the Supreme Court decide that children had the right to equal protection under the law. Before 1967 special treatment, or at least treatment quite different from that accorded adults, was the rule at every jurisdictional level.[21]

Others, most notably Douglas Rendleman, have attacked the notion that juvenile courts were a statutory extension of long-standing state claims to *parens patriae* when confronted by children who might pose a threat to community order. Rather than acting as superparent, the juvenile court, in his view, was a direct descendent of English poor law, which allowed the state to apprentice a pauper's child without parental consent. *Parens patriae* was a legal ruse. It justified and made more palatable the old poor law practice of taking children from their parents.[22]

What to make of these investigations of the early-twentieth-century juvenile court? Obviously, while individual works provoke great interest, this body of scholarship possesses serious flaws, over and above the fact that its two main threads, social and legal historical criticism, are almost utterly untied. It exaggerates the ability of elites to maintain social control over their supposed subordinates and ignores the juvenile court as an outgrowth of progressive legal thought. An examination of the involvements of the Russell Sage Foundation, Spelman Memorial, and Commonwealth Fund with the juvenile court during its first three decades focuses attention on crucial connections, questions, and problems that the existing literature largely neglects. How?

First, analysis of foundation involvement clarifies the connections that exist between the transformation of legal theory in the early-twentieth-century United States and the emergence of the juvenile court. Social historians continue to discover the roots of the juvenile court in the actions of progressive reformers—especially campaigns directed by that circle of women social workers and philanthropists whose geographic center was Hull House.[23] Legal historians, strangely, have ignored the ways that progressive legal theory attacked not just nineteenth-century orthodoxy but also motivated a group of scholar-judges to advocate juvenile courts.[24] It detracts little from the contributions of Julia Lathrop, Lucy Flower, or other social activists to recognize that the juvenile court might have been a stillborn dream without the support of prominent members of the bar who wanted to create a court for children that would link "law in books and law in action."[25]

Second, investigation of foundation involvement with the juvenile court movement illustrates the perils of too-intense reliance on case study history alone. Policy-making philanthropists, in league with established allies in the U.S. Children's Bureau, surveyed the juvenile court phenomenon extensively. They discovered that the most famous of these institutions, those in Milwaukee, Denver, Chicago, and Los Angeles (the ones still most studied by historians), were, in truth, quite atypical.

Finally, the foundation embrace of, and then retreat from, the juvenile courts provides a cautionary tale about the frustrations inherent in social policy making. Officials of the Spelman Memorial or the Commonwealth Fund quickly learned, as authors of historical case studies or scholars of legal precedent often still have not, the degree to which the proper question about the juvenile court phenomenon was not "Did it illustrate middle-class social control?" Indeed, with great disillusionment, foundation officials decided that the courts were quite often exercises in bedlam, not control, with policies and actions immensely at variance. The real question foundation disengagement from the juvenile legal reform movement suggests is "Was the juvenile court's 'social control' largely rhetorical?"

THE COMMONWEALTH FUND AND SOCIOLOGICAL JURISPRUDENCE

Scholars have not yet placed the juvenile court within the context of a dramatic change in legal thought in early-twentieth-century America. They should. An examination of the Commonwealth Fund's Legal Research Committee begins that task. This committee, created in 1920 as one of the fund's earliest projects, continued to exist until 1943. However, the years 1920–30 marked its decade of greatest activity. During this period, a group of the most eminent legal thinkers in America met regularly in the fund's New York offices, or at New York City's Yale and Harvard Clubs. These men included future Supreme Court Justices Harlan Stone, Benjamin Cardozo, and Charles E. Hughes, as well as Learned Hand, highly respected judge of the U.S. Second Circuit Court of Appeals, James Parker Hall, dean of the University of Chicago School of Law, and Roscoe Pound, dean of the Harvard Law School and probably the most influential progressive legal theorist in the country.[26] Under Commonwealth Fund sponsorship, this committee initiated ambitious studies of American judicial and administrative law.

Dean Hall chaired the Legal Research Committee, but Dean Pound was its real leader, using it as a forum to generate support for what he called "sociological jurisprudence," a movement that needs to be understood in the context of what it opposed. For most of the nineteenth century, "classical legal thought" had viewed the law as a system of logic, ruled by categories, universal principles, and legal truths. It functioned as society's neutral arbiter, blind to religion, politics, or economic advantage, and wise judges handed down decisions derived from their knowledge of its principles and rules. But in 1905 the case of *Lochner v. New York* prompted the educated American public to pay attention for the first time to a debate that had been brewing in the elite reaches of legal scholarship since the late nineteenth century.

In its majority opinion in *Lochner,* the U.S. Supreme Court declared that a state law in New York regulating the number of hours worked by bakers interfered with the rights of these workers to negotiate favorable terms of employment. But to many observers it seemed obvious that since conditions of employment were overwhelmingly determined by employers, the effect of the decision was to protect the right of bakery owners to dictate hours worked per week. This result caused Justice Oliver Wendell Holmes to issue what became a highly publicized dissent, charging that his colleagues had substituted their own economic ideas about state intervention into employer-employee relations for those supported by duly elected state officials. The salient difference between the two competing economic theories was that the Supreme Court announced its choice to be legally true. Such decision making, Holmes's minority opinion fumed, was arbitrary, arrogant, and an unfair replacement of judicial views for those of a legislature.[27]

Within a few years of the *Lochner* decision, Roscoe Pound had published a number of well-received articles demanding that the views expressed in Holmes's dissent be taken seriously. American law needed to be "sociological," that is, as concerned with outcome as with method. Its practitioners had to be aware of the actual social effects of legal doctrine, which should rest not on fixed rules but on the understanding that constant change within society inevitably altered the context in which the law could be applied. Moreover, judges should realize that jurisprudence could not, indeed should not, be a self-sufficient discipline. They should familiarize themselves with the principles of economics, sociology, psychology, and philosophy. Only then would they be able to abandon the illusion that the logic of the law was separate from the practice of the law.[28]

The memberships of the board and staff of the Commonwealth Fund were well placed to participate in a debate about legal theory. In common with all the other policy-making foundations studied in this volume, they included many with training in the law. George Welwood Murray, a prominent member of the New York Bar, not only drew up the articles of incorporation for the Commonwealth Fund in 1919 and sat for the next two decades as one of its directors, he personally encouraged the fund to support the new "sociological jurisprudence" movement. As a fund director who approved appointments to foundation-sponsored projects, Murray skewed the membership of the Legal Research Committee in Pound's favor.[29] And Pound easily dominated the agenda of a committee that determined its mission to be "re-examination . . . of our entire legal system."[30] In a time of change, moreover, the Legal Research Committee decreed, "It is important that the leadership of this investigation should be entrusted to those whose conclusions will inspire confidence."[31]

Accordingly, the members of the committee, men of such stature within the profession that they expected their conclusions to inspire confidence, began sponsoring studies that repeatedly emphasized the actual practice of law. During the 1920s, the committee produced multivolume studies of the administration of commerce and transportation legislation, railroad regulation, and workmen's compensation laws.[32] And even though it never commissioned research on the specific subject of the juvenile court, the atmosphere in which it conducted its work was one conducive to proposals for changes in the legal system.

Specifically acknowledging the influence of Pound's "sociological jurisprudence" articles in the *Harvard Law Review,* the committee repeatedly argued that the most important task for legal scholars was to answer the question, "*How does the law work?*" It was a simple question, one that "ought to be capable of a definite answer, all along the line, in every applied science. But in law it cannot be answered at all. Indeed it has just begun to be asked."[33]

From its inception, then, there existed within the Commonwealth Fund a climate receptive to cooperation with the new juvenile courts. They were, in line with this new legal thinking, institutions that initially seemed admirable efforts to make law more like an applied science, connected especially to the disciplines of psychology and sociology.

Worth emphasizing too is the fact that judges much influenced by Pound and other legal pragmatists had worked with private charities to create the juvenile courts. The efforts of the Chicago Women's Club and other Illinois philanthropies to establish separate children's courts had gone nowhere between 1895 and 1898, in part because legal advisors thought such courts unconstitutional. Only in 1898, when Hastings Hart, superintendent of the Illinois Children's Home and Aid Society, made a crucial alliance with Judges Julian Mack, Harvey Hurd, and Richard Tuthill, did the juvenile court movement quickly gain momentum. Hart, soon to leave Illinois to spend the rest of his career with the Russell Sage Foundation, convinced his philanthropic co-workers in Chicago that the support of lawyers was crucial and willingly submitted his drafts of the Illinois Juvenile Court Bill to representatives of the Illinois Bar Association, but only after he and Judge Mack had cleverly stacked the deck.

The members of the Bar Association review panel were almost all proponents of "sociological" legal reform. Privately, Hastings Hart groused when Ben Lindsey "allowed the impression to prevail that he was the chief agent in the whole juvenile court movement."[34] To Hart, the flamboyant Coloradan was a publicity-crazy latecomer, but he never vented such opinions publicly. He had known all along that the support of the legal profession was essential if the courts were to succeed.

THE COMMONWEALTH FUND AND THE CHILD GUIDANCE CLINICS

Another crucial ingredient, proponents of the juvenile court agreed, would be acceptance of the idea that the new legal institutions could only work if they incorporated insights into child psychology. Indeed, the premises of the movement held that children were not criminals and were not to be imprisoned, that, instead, they were to be thoroughly studied to determine a proper course of treatment for illegal or unacceptable behavior. And again, this fitted well with the Commonwealth Fund's vigorous promotion of its conviction that not only did law in books need to connect with law in action, but also that "law was so bound up with the social sciences, psychology, and psychiatry that some attempt should be made to determine how far the law [has] deviated from such standards as those sciences have been able to set up."[35]

One result was that between 1922 and 1927 the Commonwealth Fund sponsored seven child guidance clinics scattered across the country. Psychiatrists, psychologists, and at least one psychiatric social worker staffed each clinic. All were "demonstrations," meant to convince citizens of cities and counties with juvenile courts of the crucial importance of careful psychological evaluation of each delinquent child.[36]

The clinics' project began in an atmosphere of great optimism. Within six months of accepting his position as the first director of the Commonwealth Fund, Yale historian Max Farrand reported confidently that he had surveyed his colleagues and sources within the other policy foundations and felt sure that the Spelman Memorial "would not, at least for some time to come, go into the field of delinquency and crime, even of juvenile delinquency." That field, he said, "lies open before us." The new foundation quickly established a "Program for the Prevention of Juvenile Delinquency."[37]

Within a year Farrand had left the Commonwealth Fund to assume a research position with the Huntington Library in California, but the philanthropy's second director, Barry Smith, continued to focus on juvenile delinquency. Smith, like at least one-half of his fellow fund staff members, had a Yale degree. After his graduation in New Haven, he had attended the New York School of Social Work and become financial secretary of the New York Charitable Organizations Society before coming to the fund. Like Mary Richmond at the Russell Sage Foundation, he was an influential figure within the developing world of professional social work and was eager to expand its possibilities. It was he who actively promoted, as part of the fund's Program in Juvenile Delinquency, a proposal to establish a series of experimental clinics staffed by social workers, psychologists, and psychiatrists to help juvenile courts conduct their essential investigations into child personality. The child guidance clinic as adjunct to the juvenile court seemed a perfect tool through which to combine the new foundation's interests in law, social work, and psychology.[38]

Dr. William Healy's Chicago-based Institute for Juvenile Research provided the model for the Commonwealth program. In 1909 the psychiatrist convinced a Chicago philanthropist, Mrs. William Dummer, to cover his clinic's expenses for five years. Freed from the need to seek paying patients, Healy made psychiatric examinations of all children who passed through the Chicago courts and suggested courses of action to its judges. Just as the Great War began in Europe, the Cook County Commission assumed the expenses of the institute.[39]

In January 1922 the Commonwealth Fund announced that the fund stood ready to finance, for five years, psychiatric clinics with a mission to serve juvenile courts. Assignment of clinics would depend on the interest shown by community leaders in the issue of juvenile delinquency and on their assurances that they would make every effort to establish at public expense a permanent court psychiatric clinic.

At the time the fund mailed its proposal around the country to local public officials, the juvenile psychiatric clinic was almost an unknown. Only four such institutions existed. In addition to Healy's Institute in Chicago, there were two clinics in Boston, and one in Baltimore. However, only Healy's clinic worked extensively with a juvenile court. Each of the other three's primary affiliation was with a prominent private teaching hospital.[40]

To head its emerging program, the fund hired psychiatrist V. V. Anderson. Healy himself frequently visited the fund's New York offices as a consultant. The first task was to select sites for the proposed clinics, and between January and April 1922 Anderson and others from the Commonwealth Fund staff traveled the country assessing the dozens of applications sent in by city and county officials. By April the fund had chosen seven cities: St Louis, Norfolk, Dallas, Minneapolis, Cleveland, Los Angeles, and Philadelphia. Between 1922 and 1927 each of the chosen demonstration cities annually received at least $20,000, an exceedingly generous sum, to hire staff members and maintain clinics. Two of the larger cities, St. Louis and Philadelphia, received a yearly average of $26,000 for their programs.[41]

Each clinic supposedly began work committed to Healy's principles for evaluation of delinquency, which stressed the "personality case study" that could only be created after exhaustive investigation of "the facts of ancestry, ante-natal life, childhood development, illnesses and injuries, social experiences, and [all] mental life."[42] At the time, however, both the institutions of the juvenile court and the child guidance clinic were new, staffed by a first generation of professionals. Even had their alliance not involved the complexities of public-private cooperation, problems were inevitable. Not surprisingly, some of the Commonwealth Fund's clinics became battlegrounds for disputes about proper psychological technique in a field where no guidelines really existed and where almost every practitioner was a pioneer. As it turned out, not all the psychologists and psychiatrists affiliated with the clinics agreed with William Healy, or even with each other.

All-out war between psychiatrists, psychologists, and social workers broke out in the Dallas clinic. Its director, Harold Gosline, former head of the Rhode Island State Hospital for Mental Diseases, clashed violently with other members of his staff. Their reports to the Commonwealth Fund supervisors charged that Gosline was an "inflexible" bureaucrat, accustomed to exercising unchallenged authority as the head of a state institution for the insane, with no real interest in children. Staff members warned that Director Gosline intentionally intimidated children, causing many to resist return visits. Gosline vigorously defended himself, denounced his co-workers as lazy, and curried favor with local politicians who sent their own letters to the fund demanding he be kept. The poisonous working climate in Dallas finally ended in 1927 with Gosline's forced resignation. By that date the clinic had only five months left of its five-year grant.[43]

The problems experienced by the other six demonstration clinics never approached the disastrous level of near chaos that characterized work in Dallas. However none of the demonstrations ran an entirely smooth course. In most of the other six cities, politicians interfered in ways that the clinics' psychiatrists and psychologists found unacceptable. After all, their salaries came from the Commonwealth Fund and not local governments, and they bridled at what they perceived to be meddling with their mandate to define the techniques most effective to treat troubled children. They and their foundation patron confronted head-on the realities of policy making in a pluralistic state and did not like it.

One commentator on these battles was the well-known social worker Graham Taylor, who chaired a liaison committee formed between the Commonwealth Fund and the private New York School of Social Work and who accepted an adjunct position with the fund to help with the guidance clinic project. An alumnus, Barry Smith, generously supplemented the school's budgets, kept its administrators carefully informed of fund activities, and considered School of Social Work graduates crucial allies in its efforts to aid the new public juvenile courts. In important ways, Smith's faith was self-delusion. The attitude Taylor and other social workers brought to the work was not one likely to enlist enthusiastic cooperation from the local officials upon whose support the guidance clinics' ultimately depended. In a letter to his sister in 1922 Taylor wrote, "I believe they [the Commonwealth Fund] have put their finger on one of the biggest needs in American life, the need of producing in every possible way . . . a higher level of mental health in children. . . . I think schools and [juvenile] courts and homes are incredibly stupid about the whole thing. Any agency that can point the way through muddleheadedness into a definite plan of action will certainly be doing a large and significant job for the whole country."[44]

Pointing the way out of "muddleheadedness" proved not to be so easy, as Barry Smith discovered when the city comptroller of St. Louis, a Catholic, became an obstacle to implementing plans for that city. Smith speculated in confidential reports to his board that "disgruntled priests" may have been getting to the comptroller. How else to explain the man's opposition to public funding of the guidance clinic? Of course, it was widely known, Smith went on to say, that priests were "occasionally" opposed to psychiatrists on the ground that "they get altogether too much information about their patients, and, from the Catholic point of view, usurp the functions of a confessional."[45]

If a cabal of priests was behind St. Louis's 1927 decision to continue its clinic with but an annual budget of only $13,585, less than half the level previously provided by the Commonwealth Fund, "small-minded" city officials in Norfolk were in back of that city's refusal to give its guidance clinic any money at all, forcing it to close.[46] Smith's internal reports on these problems reflected both a strong anti-Catholic bias and an agreement with Graham Taylor that the politicians with whom they had to deal were "incredibly stupid." They reflected no understanding at all of the dynamics of American politics. If Smith and Taylor truly thought that the benighted citizens of the country's hinterland would kiss their hands for releasing them from a prior state of complete muddleheadedness, then they were the ones who were incredibly stupid.

Indeed, the Commonwealth child guidance clinic project illustrates, yet again, not the actions of a powerful shadow force manipulating the polity, but those of an institution that in basic ways misunderstood the give-and-take involved in social policy making. In the end, only Norfolk decided to abandon its clinic. Yet the six other demonstrations, all of which continued under city funding, never succeeded in convincing fund officials that the almost $1 million they had invested was well spent. The city operations were just not the "right sort," which, as spelled out in Commonwealth Fund reports, meant that they were underfunded, understaffed, and not concerned with the practice of the most up-to-date psychiatric and psychological techniques.[47]

In fact, at least two years before the end of the five-year experiment a number of the Commonwealth clinics had begun to shift their emphasis away from "delinquent" to "normal" children. No exact figures apparently survive, but at least half of the clinics seem to have begun to devote most of their attention to children who were not part of the juvenile court caseload. One indication of the change came in 1925, when the fund published *Three Problem Children: Narratives from the Case Records of a Child Guidance Clinic.*[48] Not one of the three children featured in the publication, who received the pseudonyms of "Mildred," "Sidney," and "Kenneth," had been referred by a juvenile court.[49]

Mildred's anxious mother brought her for treatment when the twelve-year-old girl began to withdraw, silently sitting by herself for hours. Sidney entered the clinic when a teacher, outraged by his "reckless abandonment to autoerotic sex practices, even in the classroom," reported him. Even Kenneth, who had actually gotten in trouble with the law, was not a court referral. At eight he had been hauled into juvenile court for falsely ringing a fire alarm and at age ten had ended up there when caught participating in a grocery store robbery. In each case, Kenneth had been sent home and told to stay out of trouble, an injunction he ignored. Thirteen at the time of his examination by psychiatrists at the child guidance clinic, Kenneth had since "been involved in plenty of minor escapades," but had "not again been in court."

Kenneth's worried mother, not a concerned court officer, sought clinic help. She had married at eighteen, wooed by a good-looking man much her senior who soon revealed himself to be a drunkard and wife-beater. At the time she brought her son to the clinic, Kenneth's mother had not laid eyes on her wandering husband for five years. However, she felt that she saw him every day, since Kenneth not only bore a striking physical resemblance to his father but seemed to have inherited the same charming, lying ways. A mother's fear, not a mandate from the juvenile court, brought Kenneth to clinic psychiatrists' attention.

Three Problem Children claimed each youngster improved dramatically, but the transcripts of the children's cases, which include the "psychological impressions" of their social workers and psychiatrists, suggest mixed results. William Healy had insisted that there was no one cause and no one cure for delinquency. Rather, each individual case needed individual attention, since unacceptable behavior could stem from emotional, physical, or environmental circumstances. Although the Commonwealth Fund psychiatrists agreed that scientific study of problem children demanded close attention to such potential causes of criminal or bad behavior, they discovered there was little they could do to change home or school environments. In Kenneth's case, they seemed to have had little impact even on his emotional frame of mind.

Mildred's father continued to be a hopeless drunk, who passed out regularly and required Mildred to put him to bed, but the girl had, at least, begun to talk on her visits to the clinic. Sidney's divorced mother had been sharing a bed with her thirteen-year-old son and renting the other bedrooms. While she had promised to give Sidney a place of his own to sleep, a surprise visit by a clinic social worker confirmed the presence of another boarder in the room supposedly assigned the boy, raising the suspicion Sidney was back in bed with his mother. On the bright side, the emaciated teenager had gained weight. After a year's treatment, Kenneth's evaluators could not report even such minimal progress. He still had "enormous difficulty bringing his vagrant impulses under control," was still lying constantly, and still skipping school. Indeed, Kenneth, the kind of child for whom the guidance clinics had originally been created, was seemingly the most resistant to psychiatric therapy. A "final impression" concluded bleakly, "[Kenneth] has a furtive look in his eyes that does not inspire trust."

By 1926 committee meetings at the Commonwealth Fund's central offices had also begun to reflect the tone of Kenneth's despairing psychiatrist.

Foundation officials wondered aloud whether they would ever be able to select a "[Juvenile Delinquency] Committee the members of which could work together in harmony and which could secure the cooperation of all the existing organizations and agencies in the field."[50]

Incredibly, even Herbert Hoover managed to be a source of irritation. While Secretary of Commerce, he had become a major figure in the child-study movement. According to an "eyes-only" staff memorandum by Barry Smith, Hoover had been elected president of the American Child Health Association only after promising "generous" support from the funds of the American Relief Association, the organization that he had created after World War I to administer aid to devastated Europe. Hoover, in Smith's account, was a martinet. He dictated Child Health Association policies, salted the organization's staff positions with cronies, and, "in general, made things extremely difficult." His reach, moreover, extended to the child guidance clinics, when between 1924 and 1926, publicity articles about the Commonwealth Fund project were issued by both the Child Health Association and the American Relief Association. The Commonwealth Fund had authorized release of none of this information and found some of it incorrect, especially the implications that Hoover's two organizations were somehow supporting the clinic effort. More maddening still was the fact that quiet protests accomplished nothing. It took "formal objections" from Smith to Hoover himself to get this discontinued.[51]

Compounding the nightmare of professional infighting was the problem of general public incomprehension of the nature of the new fields of psychiatry and psychology. A wry observer of this fact was Charles Hoffman, judge of the Juvenile Court of Cincinnati, Ohio, a prominent advocate of the need to connect the "new psychology" to the juvenile court and a member in good standing of the group of lawyers, judges, and mental health workers frequently invited to fund-sponsored conferences. At one such meeting Hoffman related the story of an exchange that occurred in 1922 when the superintendent of an orphanage "in a southern city" had written asking for further information about a "pump" he understood was used in Cincinnati. The device could be placed in a watertight cell constructed to convince a misbehaving child that if he did not continue pumping madly, he would quickly drown. The orphanage director had heard that, with the help of psychologists, Hoffman's court had been able to build this and several other machines so clever that they could trick children into a state of total obedience. Hoffman assured the Commonwealth Fund audience that the Cincinnati Court possessed neither "pump room" nor any other dark creations of psychological torture. Nonetheless, he dryly noted that the man from the orphanage, eager to get his hands on a "psychological pump" for "inculcation of discipline," was typical of his correspondents. Child psychology, for most, existed in the realm of mysterious shamanism.[52]

By late 1926 the fund had had enough. It decided to end its association with the clinics, the juvenile courts, and city governments. The Program for the Prevention of Delinquency became the Program in Mental Hygiene and Child Guidance. In a long report giving reasons for revision of the fund's programs, Barry Smith noted that not only was the foundation placing decreasing emphasis on the prevention of delinquency, it placed "decreasing emphasis on the *prevention* of anything!"[53]

Instead, the fund decided that its focus should be on professional training and that its primary allies should be private hospitals and universities. Yale University and the New York School of Social Work reaped immediate benefits: large grants that allowed them to greatly expand their fellowship programs to encourage future social workers, psychologists, and psychiatrists.[54] The Commonwealth Fund's faith in "sociological" law and its desire to implement Roscoe Pound's advice to ground legal institutions in the disciplines of social science and psychiatry had not proved particularly infectious, at least in the juvenile courts. The Children's Bureau, which throughout the period produced the most accurate information about the phenomenon, estimated that no more than 7 percent of juvenile courts sought psychiatric advice before making decisions, even though almost every bill authorizing a special court for children justified its existence as an agency that could carefully study each offender's mental and physical condition and prescribe appropriate "treatment," not punishment.[55]

Perhaps the officials at the Commonwealth Fund who launched the child guidance clinics with such grand optimism had not really read Dean Pound's famous essay, "Law in Books and Law in Action." If they had, they might have been advised to ponder carefully the story from *Huckleberry Finn* with which it began. Huck and Tom had decided to rescue Jim by digging under the cabin where he was imprisoned. Huck carried two old picks the boys had found in the back of the cabin, but Tom knew better. From reading he knew that the proper implement for escapes and rescue attempts was a case-knife. The boys dug until midnight with case-knives, and got almost nowhere. Then, Pound interjected, "A light came to Tom's legal mind." As he wrote, "Let Huck tell the rest":

Tom said, "Gimme a case-knife." He had his own by him, but I handed him mine. He flung it down and says, "Gimme a *case-knife!*"

I didn't know just what to do—but then I thought. I scratched around amongst the old tools and got a pickaxe and give it to him, and he took it and went to work and never said a word.

He was always just that particular. *Full of principle.*

Tom, Pound wryly noted, had made "one of the earliest discoveries of the law." After a little struggle with case-knives, communities were likely to keep the principle—"but use the pickaxe."[56]

THE RUSSELL SAGE FOUNDATION AND THE SPELMAN MEMORIAL ASSESS THE JUVENILE COURTS

In alliance with the federal Children's Bureau or in concert with state agencies, both the Russell Sage Foundation and the Laura Spelman Rockefeller Memorial conducted surveys of the juvenile courts that revealed the degree to which most communities embraced their principles, but "continued to use the pick-axe." Their rueful conclusions about the innovation's weaknesses deserve more attention.

In 1912 the editor of the mass-circulation magazine *Good Housekeeping* warned his readers that "professional philanthropists" were eager proponents of the juvenile courts: "The more children the Juvenile Court can tear away from parents . . . the more jobs for high salaried experts, the greater the business for schools of social work. Hence we are given to understand that the Charity Trust hails with satisfaction the swelling numbers brought into the juvenile courts."[57]

The foundation code-named by the American press the "Charity Trust" was the Russell Sage Foundation. In 1909 Hastings Hart, the most important author of the first juvenile court bill, accepted the foundation's invitation to join its staff as head of a new "Child-Helping Department." Already sixty years old at the time, Hart was one of the country's most prominent "child-savers." He had spent decades organizing, and then leading, state charity and children's aid societies in Minnesota and Illinois.[58] But Hart, although a central figure in the creation of the juvenile court, was not its unthinking advocate, nor was the foundation for which he continued to work until his death in 1932. Indeed, the picture *Good Housekeeping* drew of Sage Foundation activities was dead-wrong. Between 1909 and 1930, its Child Helping Department, acting in concert with the federal Children's Bureau, sought to collect accurate information about the juvenile courts. By 1930,

Hastings Hart. Russell Sage Foundation Photo Collection. Courtesy of the Rockefeller Archive Center.

that information thus collected had convinced both Children's Bureau and Sage Foundation child-helpers that the courts were a seriously flawed tool.

Hart launched the activities of the Child Helping Department in a way that garnered tremendous national publicity. He convinced the foundation to fund a major conference on the status of children in America, and in an even greater coup he and coorganizer Homer Folks, then the general secretary of the New York State Charities Aid Association, convinced President Theodore Roosevelt to be the meeting's official sponsor. As he ended his second term, then, Roosevelt presided over the Country Life Commission and the White House Conference on Dependent Children, both paid for by the Russell Sage Foundation. Whatever his private motivations, Roosevelt was too good a politician to miss these opportunities to publicize the Republican Party as friend of both the farmer and the helpless child.[59]

One of the most important recommendations of the conference, which met at the White House on 25 and 26 January 1909, was the creation of a Children's Bureau within the U.S. Department of Labor. Advocates of the bureau wasted no time; dozens descended in force on Capitol Hill to urge passage of authorizing legislation. On 27 January, Julian Mack, who by 1909 had left the Juvenile Court of Chicago for a federal judgeship, argued that it was shameful that the federal government did not give to "the people of this country dealing with children the same information . . . that it gives to those dealing in cattle or those dealing in plants."[60] Homer Folks followed Judge Mack and urged that among the most crucially needed information were details about the juvenile courts. Folks told Congress that he recently had received inquiries from counterparts in England asking him "what we paid probation officers in this country." But, he continued, "I had not the remotest idea. I thought about it and wondered how I would find out. I thought I had better write to the juvenile court judges. Where is the list of juvenile court judges? There never has been such a thing published, as far as I know. Which cities have juvenile courts? Heaven only knows."[61] Theodore Roosevelt, honoring a commitment publicly made during the White House conference, urged Congress to authorize a Children's Bureau. However, not until 1912, after four more years of intense campaigning, did champions of the bureau get their way. President William Howard Taft signed legislation creating the bureau in April 1912.[62]

For the next two decades the Children's Bureau took its mandate to act as a clearing house of accurate information on all issues relating to American children very seriously. The juvenile court was but one of dozens of topics investigated, but since both the first and second chiefs of the new bureau, Julia Lathrop and Grace Abbott, were particularly interested in assessing the court's impact, it was a subject that received consistent attention. The Children's Bureau created not merely the lists of juvenile court judges Homer Folks desired, but a series of prodigiously researched studies that still provide the best review of the courts during their first quarter century.[63]

Julia Lathrop and Grace Abbott maintained warm relations not only with Mary Richmond's Charity Organization Department, but also with Hart's Child-Helping Department. Indeed, their alliance with the latter was in many ways even stronger, nourished by the mutual interest of the government agency and private philanthropy in the actual progress of the juvenile court. Both Lathrop and Abbott attended conferences on the juvenile courts sponsored by the Sage Foundation. Both journeyed to New York regularly at foundation expense as consultants. In turn, Hastings Hart and members of his staff were frequent visitors to bureau offices in Washington. Investigators from the Child-Helping Department helped the understaffed bureau complete its two most important surveys of the juvenile court.[64]

At a conference hosted by the foundation in 1925 to mark the first quarter century of the juvenile court, George Kirchwey, a professor of criminology at the New York School of Social Work, commented that, while a "beautiful ideal," the juvenile courts in most American cities rarely operated according to the principles that justified their existence. Moreover, in the few places where the courts enjoyed adequate funding, those principles often produced doubtful results.[65] The Children's Bureau–Russell Sage surveys agreed.

One basic premise upon which the juvenile court rested was that children were not criminals, but minors needing careful study and treatment. The purpose of the court was not to inflict penalties on children but to save them from further delinquency. Its success depended on understanding the mental, psychological, and environmental problems of each individual child in its care. Yet the Children's Bureau concluded that while scientific study was "indispensable," it rarely occurred.[66] Only a third of American juvenile courts gave children physical examinations. A scant 7 percent attempted mental testing of even some of the children who appeared before them. The few cities with courts that had access to the help of a trained psychiatrist or a psychiatric clinic made studies of a child's mental condition in only a small proportion of cases. Even in Minneapolis, one of seven cities in the country with a Commonwealth Fund child guidance clinic, an average of only two children a week received complete psychiatric examinations. In 1923, for example, the Minneapolis court had heard the cases of over a thousand children, but fewer than one hundred had undergone psychiatric evaluation, and fewer than five hundred had received physical exams.[67]

The emphasis in those courts that required physical exams was detection of venereal disease. After 1919 the Wasserman test was commonly administered, in a few cases to both boys and girls, but in most courts only to girls. Dozens of cities followed the example of the juvenile court of the District of Columbia and required that a physician examine every girl brought into court for signs of gonorrhea or syphilis.[68] Many communities required that any girls found to have sexually transmitted diseases be hospitalized until cured. This was a "treatment," to be sure, but a gender-specific one that rhetorically protected the larger community from the spread of sexual disease. In reality, by mandating confinement and painful topical applications of mercury compounds that often caused internal bleeding, juvenile courts punished girls who had been sexually active.[69]

Interestingly, the Children's Bureau identified the Los Angeles Juvenile Court, the court that has been the subject of more historical case studies than any other, as highly unusual. It was one of a tiny handful of courts in the country with "referees": professional women, usually either psychologists or lawyers, appointed by the court to preside over girls' cases. In a triumph of public relations, the court had hired Miriam Van Waters in that capacity. Although she has been forgotten by the public today, Van Waters, along with Ben Lindsey, was a household name in the 1920s. Her books were best-sellers, her speeches sold out, her newspaper columns avidly read. Her celebrity guaranteed fame for the court she served.

Almost all children in Los Angeles Juvenile Court received physicals; most also took psychological tests. A psychologist hired by the court administered tests four days a week. Not only was Miriam Van Waters a psychologist, most unusually, so was the court's chief judge. The cooperative relationship between the Los Angeles court and the "psycho-pathic" department of the county hospital was uncommonly strong.[70]

The Los Angeles court, unlike most of its counterparts, had a well-organized probation system. Miriam Van Waters even went so far as to distribute questionnaires to children under court jurisdiction asking them to evaluate their probation officers.[71] Although the Los Angeles court was one of the famous few with the funds to allow extensive psychological and physical screening of the children who came before it, there is little proof that better resources brought better results. The Commonwealth Fund Guidance Clinics were hard pressed to demonstrate much success with their "problem children." In similar fashion, the L.A. court did not work a psychological revolution among young miscreants in southern California. Probably its professional staff and thorough examination practices meant most notably that higher percentages of sexually diseased girls within its jurisdiction were forced to undergo hospital quarantine. Hastings Hart had not envisioned the juvenile court as the enforcement arm of mandatory, gender-selective vene-real treatment.

Unlike their counterpart in Los Angeles, most juvenile courts never had sufficient money even to try to provide the scientific treatment theory demanded, not even for young female syphilitics, nor could they provide the careful probationary supervision ideally regarded as equally important. Here too, Children's Bureau investigations discovered an enormous gap between theory and practice. All of the forty-seven state legislatures that passed juvenile court laws between 1899 and 1926 decreed that such a court existed for the purpose of keeping children out of jail and that probation officers were crucial to guide children along the straight and narrow while they stayed at home or on the job. But nowhere did authorizing legislation establish clear qualifications for probation officers.

A few individual juvenile courts established vague employment guide-lines for these supposedly vital figures. Most simply demanded that probation officers be "discreet" or "of good reputation."[72] Almost no courts established minimum education or experience criteria. The court in Buffalo, New York, was one of the rare few that demanded that probation officers have graduated from grammar school and be able to read and write. In almost all cases, the job of probation officer was a political appointment, controlled by the party currently in power.

Compounding problems of political favoritism were low salaries. A wage of $800 to $1,000 per year was common, with only a few courts, like that in Los Angeles, paying its probation officers substantially more, and thus attracting applicants who were, like Van Waters, educated professionals: psychologists, lawyers, or graduates of schools of social work. Only about a fifth of juvenile courts hired full-time probation officers, and fewer than half employed any such officials. When a court had a probation officer at all, it was likely to impose huge caseloads—which made laughable descriptions of probation officers as diligent supervisors of all aspects of their charges' daily activities. It was not unusual for a full-time probation officer to be assigned the cases of two hundred children, and the far more common part-time officers were expected to keep track of from eighty to one hundred children during the average of ten to fifteen hours per week most worked.[73]

In reality the early-twentieth-century American juvenile court was one where few children underwent the supposedly crucial "scientific study" necessary to determine treatment, rather than punishment, nor was the treatment professionally administered. Most did not even receive much help from a probation officer. These individuals were usually tremendously over-worked, scantily educated, political appointees, far more likely to have trouble placing a charge's face than able to devote themselves to individually oriented guidance.

Finally, further attempts to discover what actually occurred in American juvenile courts demonstrated that, in direct challenge to theory, many children were in jail. The Laura Spelman Rockefeller Memorial (LSRM) joined the investigative forces of the Russell Sage Foundation and the U.S. Children's Bureau when it entered into a cooperative arrangement with the State Board of Public Welfare of the Commonwealth of Virginia. The LSRM increased the annual state allocation for the board's activities from $39,000 to $68,000, for the years 1927 and 1928, a budgetary increase of approximately 70 percent, and stipulated that the additional money be used to hire trained statisticians and social workers as full-time employees of the Board's Division of County and City Organization.[74] These new staff members were to "investigate, develop and direct the state juvenile court system, maintaining contact with these courts, providing information, assistance, and supervision as may be necessary for the establishment of modern standards of juvenile court administration."[75]

Accordingly, during the same spring that Sydnor Walker was completing the assessment of parent education assigned her by Lawrence Frank, she was also frequently on the road, traveling between the memorial's New York offices and Richmond, Virginia. As the memorial's liaison, she developed a friendly working relationship with Virginia's Commissioner of Public Welfare, Frank Bane. Soon, she and Bane were exchanging witty, self-deprecatory, "outside-the-record" letters. Bane, for instance, assured Walker that he would not only introduce her to court officials but also to other state citizens whom, he teased, a lady from the North "fully expected to encounter on every hand." A mock agenda for one juvenile court visit included an interview with the "world's champion whittler, who also is quite proficient in other lines—that is, he chews tobacco manfully and can spit ten yards and kill a fly every time."[76]

Despite such personal camaraderie between its private and public coordinators, Virginia's effort to establish "modern" standards of juvenile court justice was a failure. Frank Bane was quick to send charming, personal letters to Sydnor Walker but stalled on delivery of official reports. More than one note from New York began as did Walker's letter of 10 December 1928: "How about that report on last year's activities of the Department of Public Welfare? As I told you, I want merely an informal memorandum, but I want it as soon as I can get it."[77] Sydnor Walker knew the reason for Commissioner Bane's reluctance. After two years of greatly expanded financing meant to regularize juvenile courts, he had little to show for his efforts. Walker's own tours of state facilities convinced her that most officials, including judges and sheriffs, regarded the courts as "jails." Ironically, the very institutions created to keep children out of detention had become places where sheriffs brought runaways, expecting that judges would hold them in custody.

Mandating change was one thing, Walker discovered; achieving it was another. In many counties in Virginia, the old overseer of the poor was still in office, in charge of a budget created by local property taxes, even though the state's Department of Public Welfare channeled state moneys to a new official called the Superintendent of Public Welfare. The situation made conflict inevitable. As locally elected overseers of the poor warred with state-appointed interlopers, the new juvenile court judges were, according to Walker, "left to shift for themselves."[78] Some received no salary and no budget for clerical supplies or probation officers. Others earned sums ranging from $300 to "perhaps" $1,000 a year. The memorial concluded that the juvenile court in Virginia depended almost entirely on the enthusiasm of a particular judge, who usually paid most of its expenses out of his own pocket. Its activities, in most instances, were the voluntary charity work of men who, of financial necessity, maintained full-time legal practices or simultaneously sat as heads of other courts.[79] Public meetings of the Spelman Memorial began to echo those held at its sister institutions, the Sage Foundation and the Commonwealth Fund. At a staff retreat during the summer of 1927, when discussion turned to the subjects of criminology and juvenile delinquency, Lawrence Frank mused, "I must confess that none of the . . . hopes which I started with four years ago have been realized. They have scarcely had time to materialize. On the other hand, I rather feel it isn't merely a question of shortness of time, but rather that the very effort to translate the conception and the practice has exposed perils one didn't anticipate."[80]

The memorial did not renew its two-year grant to enable the Virginia Department of Public Welfare to "modernize" the juvenile court. Indeed, a decision made in 1924 by Hastings Hart presaged the foundation's retreat from the juvenile court movement. After fifteen years as its head, he resigned from Russell Sage's Child-Helping Department, and by 1926 that department had disappeared, replaced by a Department of Social Legislation.[81] Since 1873, when he accepted the job of secretary of the new Minnesota State Board of Corrections and Charities, Hastings Hart had been one of the country's most prominent "child-savers" and champions of juvenile courts.

Prematurely white-haired, but preternaturally vigorous, he had presided over a half century of meetings about juvenile justice. His full-bearded face framed by wire spectacles was nationally well known, even before it appeared on almost every newspaper cover during the 1909 White House Conference on Dependent Children. No one would have rebuked Hastings Hart for a well-deserved retirement after his resignation from the Child-Helping Department. After all, in 1924 he was seventy-three years old. Instead, he continued with the Russell Sage Foundation for another eight years, until his death, as an independent "consultant in penology." It was not child-helping, but construction of better prisons for adults, that engaged Hastings Hart in his final years.[82] He championed the creation of a separate system of federal prisons and lived long enough to see the first significant enabling legislation passed in 1929.[83]

THE 1930 WHITE HOUSE CONFERENCE ON CHILD HEALTH AND PROTECTION

Hastings Hart's refocused career dramatically symbolized the foundation retreat from the troublesome issues of juvenile delinquency and juvenile justice reform. However, members of the educated general public, even of that group of professionals interested in child welfare, did not know much about foundation activities anyway. Foundation officials were not talking, and the press was usually misinformed. So the event that capped the decade for those interested in children's welfare was not the Spelman Memorial's decision to end funding for the Virginia Board of Public Welfare or the Commonwealth Fund's abandonment of child guidance clinics linked to municipal juvenile courts. Rather, it was the White House Conference on Child Health and Protection, held during the third week of November 1930.

This conference stood in sharp contrast to its predecessor, the 1909 White House Conference on Dependent Children. The earlier meeting, funded by the Russell Sage Foundation, had prompted the creation of the Children's Bureau. Its successor in 1930 was held in opposition to the wishes of the Children's Bureau and with the express purpose, according to the agency's chief, Grace Abbott, of destroying it.[84] The proceedings of this conference illustrate another central truth about policy making in a pluralistic state. Not only were policies in practice often wildly different from policies in theory, they also became tools in bureaucratic wars, shaped by personalities as well as by differing ideas.

The bureaucratic conflict in 1930 pitted against each other two of the nation's best-known children's advocates. The public often saw Herbert Hoover and Grace Abbott as working together, but by 1930 they had come to detest each other. Grace Abbott filled frequent letters to her sister Edith with scathing scorn for the "noble Herbert Hoover . . . who weeps over the blind, crippled, and dependent children, children with damaged hearts, and the improperly nourished children, but of course he never thinks of low wages or unemployment. He's too busy being the great humanitarian and friend of children."[85]

Grace Abbott, unlike most subordinates, did not confine her judgments to personal letters. She took her battle public, and the 1930 conference became the scene of a highly emotional struggle between the president and the chief of the Children's Bureau. For many of those involved, a meeting publicized as a national forum on major issues affecting children became, instead, a charged debate over the future of the Children's Bureau. Careful consideration of anything else, including the wisdom of continued support for a separate juvenile court system, became an afterthought.

Abbott had wanted to follow the model created by her predecessor Julia Lathrop in 1919. Then the Children's Bureau had hosted a small conference in Washington, followed by a series of other conferences throughout the nation, sponsored by state agencies and private philanthropies concerned with children's issues. Abbott charged that the White House, using American Relief Association funds, engineered the 1930 conference as a vehicle to attack the Children's Bureau.

That was not true. Herbert Hoover's real objective was to strengthen the Department of the Interior—to make it the kind of super-cabinet agency he had once created at Commerce. Among the expanded functions of a redefined Interior Department would be coordination of national health care policy. Tellingly, Dr. Ray Lyman Wilbur, the Secretary of the Interior, and not James Davis, Secretary of Labor, was Hoover's choice to chair the conference. The Children's Bureau was more an accidental victim of Hoover's ideas about agency reorganization than his direct target, though there was certainly no love lost between the bureau's chief and the president.

Nonetheless, delegates arrived in Washington on 19 November to spend the next week as participants in an all-out bureaucratic firestorm. They had already received printed draft copies of preliminary resolutions passed by each of the conference's 175 committees and subcommittees. One, the Committee Report on the Public Health Service and Administration, recommended that the health work for children done by the Children's Bureau be given to the U.S. Public Health Service, and that the Health

Service itself be expanded and transferred from Treasury to Interior.[86] Since almost everything the Children's Bureau did could in some way be connected to the "promotion of good emotional and physical health" of children, the recommendation, in effect, suggested that the Children's Department be gutted and most of its functions assumed by the physicians of the Public Health Service.

Grace Abbott was a member of the Committee on the Public Health Service, and when its chair, Surgeon General Hugh Cumming, refused to include her fierce minority condemnation with the committee's draft report, she went on the offensive. On 20 November, when Cumming rose to make his oral report, he faced an audience, not just of official delegates, but one packed with Children's Bureau partisans. Many dozens of the bureau's friends from women's associations, private philanthropies, and labor unions showed up to cram extra seats and jam the aisles.[87] Instead of an audience of official delegates drowsing through a lengthy report on proposed changes in federal bureaucratic structure, Surgeon General Cumming faced a sea of hostile faces and a welter of sharp questions. An exchange with Frances Burns of the League of Women Voters reflected the angry tone of the proceedings. When Burns asked whether work done by the Children's Bureau could be transferred to the Public Health Service without additional congressional authorization, Cumming waffled: "This report is a set-up of what in the judgment of that committee constituted a logical sequence in public health organization. There is no legal authority attached to this conference at all. I imagine it would be some time before all of the provisions suggested by the conference will be legislated either by the federal, state, or local authorities." Burns tartly responded: "May I ask as an answer to my question a plain yes or no?"[88]

Alice Hamilton, a well-known reformer who often advised the Department of Labor on industrial poisons, stood up to speak as "one who has been in both social work and public health work." Hamilton, a physician, confessed that she was "utterly unable" to understand the opposition of the Public Health Service to the Children's Bureau. Could it be that the latter's most serious fault was that it was "largely feminine?"[89]

The press had a field day describing the "sex war" between the Children's Bureau and the Public Health Service. According to the *New Republic,* "The women stood with Miss Abbott and won."[90] Indeed, the Children's Bureau did win, at least on this issue. The conference tabled a vote on the report of the Committee on the Public Health Service and decided, instead, to bury its proposals in a recommendation that "at some later time" President

Hoover might wish to appoint another committee to consider questions of Public Health Service functions.

However, in the long term, the Children's Bureau lost its battle with the Health Service. In following decades, the Health Service would gain in importance, while the Children's Bureau's influence would decline. One decision taken by the White House conference presaged that eventual outcome. It declined to support Children's Bureau efforts to revive the Sheppard-Towner Act, which between 1921 and 1929 had provided federal funds for locally administered maternal and baby care.[91]

If Herbert Hoover had ever intended the conference as a vehicle through which to tame his rival, he had underestimated Grace Abbott. She acknowledged no defeat, but rather, true to form, delivered a fiery speech attacking the inequities of the American wealth structure, one in which 76 percent of Americans died leaving nothing at all to their heirs. "Low wages," not "according to some in government . . . absence of thrift or unwise investment," were at the heart of America's worsening economic crisis. Children would thrive again only in a society that "enabled people to buy" and was as concerned with consumption as with production.[92]

The 1930 White House Conference on Child Health and Protection certainly sparked fireworks. The kinds of bureaucratic struggles that usually remained waged quietly became spectacularly public. Nobody missed the fact that Grace Abbott's speech was an attack on Herbert Hoover's assessments of the nation's economy, one year into the Great Depression. A White House conference, for once, became a good story, and the press eagerly seized its opportunity, describing not the dry lists of hundreds of committee resolutions, but the surprise entrance of angry Children's Bureau supporters into what might have otherwise been staid, and staged, committee meetings.

What escaped almost everybody's eye was the fact that the conference accomplished few of its policy objectives. Subsumed by a splashy fight over agency turf, the conference recommendations on a variety of subjects, including juvenile delinquency and the juvenile court, received almost no public attention and quietly disappeared. In fact, the conference's speeches and recommendations on the latter subject echoed the doubts that had prompted foundation retreat from the juvenile court.

Secretary of Labor James Davis, snubbed by Hoover and hobbled by a well-earned reputation as a poor speaker, delivered one of the conference's first major addresses to an almost empty room. Yet, the substance, if not the delivery, of his speech deserved attention, for Davis avoided the usual pleasantries about great expectations and pride in achievements made. Instead, he delivered an unusually frank assessment of the field of child welfare, one that found more confusion and unanswered questions than progress. About the juvenile court Secretary Davis said, "In 1909 [during the first White House conference] the juvenile court was ten years old . . . and was expected to solve the problems that remained unsolved. The juvenile court is now more than thirty years old, psychiatric and child guidance clinics have multiplied, and we are still seeking the road to the prevention and cure of delinquency."[93]

Boston Juvenile Court Judge Frederick Cabot headed the conference committee that investigated juvenile delinquency, and his recommendations echoed those of James Davis. Both found the juvenile court to be a chimerical solution to a larger social problem. Judge Cabot noted,

> We have perhaps been too much of a child-centered society in the sense that we have tried to give to the child an individualism which does not realize that the truest individualism lies in some commingling of what the child has in his own life with the needs of the total group. . . . The handling of the child on the basis of such a philosophy is no longer so much the task . . . of our [juvenile] courts, as it is the task of the entire social group.[94]

After a week of high drama in Washington, delegates to the White House Conference on Child Health and Protection went home to their Thanksgiving dinners. The press soon tired of quoting Grace Abbott. Very quickly everybody, even most historians, forgot the conference had ever been held. That reality, by itself, merits little soul-searching, but it does deserve examination by those interested in understanding the creation of social policy.

The juvenile courts, like mothers' pensions, were the creations of politicians who reaped rhetorical benefits from their supposed support of mothers and children. Their creators never accorded them adequate supervision or proper funding and were not much interested in the flaws they soon displayed. Among the few who decided that the juvenile courts deserved careful examination before they could be proclaimed a success were the members of a small federal agency, allied with professionals working for two private philanthropies. Their investigations should have received wide attention, but they did not.

Few public policy makers, at any level of government, seem to have absorbed the lessons taught by the Children's Bureau. Indeed, during the 1920s and 1930s it fought for its very existence, continuing its surveys on shoestring budgets supplemented by the Russell Sage Foundation. The state of Virginia did not follow the Spelman Memorial's advice to abandon its juvenile court experiment if it could not create a truly modern, statewide system. Instead, the courts continued to proliferate, in Virginia and most other states, as underfunded and badly organized institutions.[95]

Like parent education, the juvenile court was a policy innovation that seemed to employ the advice of highly trained experts to benefit children. Who could be against improving American childhood? Like parent education, it did not live up to glowing, initial expectations. The juvenile courts did not, through probation, "treat and cure" juvenile delinquency. They touted expertise, especially that associated with the "new" psychology, but did not really employ it or even understand it. California parents had not been able to use the insights of behavioral psychology taught them in their parent education classes very effectively. Most did not achieve their primary goal: to control children's misbehavior. The juvenile courts produced similarly disappointing results. Private philanthropy's abandonment killed neither parent education nor the juvenile court, though there is little evidence either deserved to survive.

For decades, historians have been embroiled in debates about social control and Progressivism, asking, "Whom did the Progressives control, and when did they control them?" Far fewer have asked, "When, if ever, did the Progressives manage to bridge completely the gap between their ideas and reality?" Should we be surprised, then, to discover that the early-twentieth-century juvenile court provides another example in which the rhetoric of a social policy has had a remarkably durable afterlife, largely unconnected to its actual effectiveness? Should we be astonished to learn that the policy-making foundations were once again not the all-powerful secret forces so many have claimed them to be, but often-frustrated actors in a play for which no one knew all the lines? One foundation, the Bureau of Social Hygiene, reprised that role by venturing into public health policy, seeking solutions to the "social evil" of prostitution.

THE BUREAU OF SOCIAL HYGIENE:
FROM ANTIPROSTITUTION TO
SEX RESEARCH

By 1929 Grace Abbott had begun to describe the juvenile court as a "great disappointment."[1] Julian Mack, one of the institution's "fathers" agreed. At the movement's first quarter century mark, he sadly concluded that "the juvenile court does not get into action until the child has gone wrong. The fundamental duty of society is to prevent that child from going wrong. . . . Our [task] is the elimination of the causes that lead to the child going astray."[2]

One such cause, according to John D. Rockefeller Jr.'s Bureau of Social Hygiene, was society's mishandling of human sexuality. It was in this area that a great need for new information and policy guidance existed. Between 1911 and 1933 the bureau sought solutions to problems of "social hygiene." By the late 1920s, it had traveled a path from attacks on the "social evil" of prostitution to advocacy of scientifically conducted investigations of human sexual behavior.

This two-decades-long institutional evolution from antiprostitution to sex research deserves attention. For one thing, it illustrates a more sophisticated response to prostitution during the Progressive Era than has generally been acknowledged by scholars. Decades ahead of its time, the bureau concluded that efforts to control prostitution would fail unless linked to a better understanding of human sexuality. For another, it marked the beginnings of a new kind of sex education conducted by public authorities that decreed that not just experts, but average citizens of all ages, needed accurate information about human sexuality, reproduction, and sexually transmitted diseases. Bureau publications were widely distributed by state and county departments of public health, providing large numbers of Americans with the most reliable information available about these subjects. By late-twentieth-century standards, these publications provide a curious blend of insight and misinformation and illustrate the formidable task facing early-twentieth-century sex researchers. When sociologist Katharine Bement Davis, the bureau's longtime general secretary, championed research projects that broadened the boundaries of sex research, she encountered strong resistance. By 1928 she was forcibly "retired" from her position, a victim of concerns voiced by key Rockefeller advisors that the Bureau of Social Hygiene was taking on too many controversial issues. In 1929 Davis's pathbreaking work on the sexual behavior of American women appeared in print, but it was a source of embarrassment to the philanthropy that had funded the research it presented. By 1933 the Bureau of Social Hygiene itself was gone.

The bureau's responses to vice illustrate the potential public-policy-making role that could be played by a private philanthropy exercising leadership in a controversial area. They also demonstrate the limits of such a role. In the case of the bureau, those limits were self-imposed. No government official threatened to raid its offices for evidence of still-illegal birth control information. Its publications would remain in demand long after it ceased to exist. But when Katharine Bement Davis, a woman who truly deserved the label "pioneer," began drawing logical connections between investigations of prostitution and of the sex behavior of completely respectable American women, her search for accurate knowledge became the kind of quest that private philanthropy was reluctant to support. By the early 1930s, John D. Rockefeller Jr. had launched another personal project, the reconstruction of historic Colonial Williamsburg—a change in focus that freed him from the firestorms that accompany emotional topics and controversial policies.

Nonetheless, an examination of his bureau's efforts to affect public policy on charged issues like prostitution and sex education raise important questions, not just about the interactions between private wealth and public life, but about the kinds of limitations imposed on American policy makers, whether they be public or private.

PROSTITUTION AND PROGRESSIVES

John D. Rockefeller Jr. was not the only reform-minded American concerned about prostitution. On the contrary, historians agree that the "social evil" became a national obsession during the first two decades of the twentieth century. Of course, prostitution was not a new phenomenon. Despite the absence of reliable statistics, it is likely that, in the urban populations of the United States and industrialized Europe, the proportion of women practicing prostitution probably reached its greatest peak during the mid- to late nineteenth century. After 1900, as service and white-collar jobs opened to women, prostitution may actually have begun a long-term per capita decline.

However, like the gin bottle, the prostitute was a potent symbol for Progressives. She represented many phenomena that Americans found troubling: the rapid growth of cities, primary home to the influx of alien immigrants in their millions; the supposed decline of religion and family as central to national life; the rise of a new morality shaped by mass advertising.

The prostitute acquired a powerful, but highly contradictory, image in early-twentieth-century America. On the one hand, the popular press often explained her as an innocent victim, young, white, native-born, raised in a respectable home. Lured to the city, this girl-child easily fell prey to the wiles of pimps, who, if they did not literally kidnap her, tricked her with promises of marriage, then forced her into a brothel. Yet side-by-side with this portrait of a farmgirl led astray was another that painted the prostitute in far more sinister colors as a vicious despoiler. This other woman, eager for excitement, lavish clothing, and easy money, actively led men to their ruin. Immoral, lazy, probably feeble-minded, and likely a foreign immigrant, she deserved harsh punishment, not sympathy.[3]

Progressive Era portrayals of the extent of prostitution varied just as dramatically as did its depictions of the "social evil's" practitioners. In Chicago, for instance, different investigators produced figures ranging from a high of sixty-eight thousand prostitutes at work in the city in 1911 to a low of five thousand in the trade. Police departments, mayors' offices, and reform groups in other big cities produced equally confusing statistics. Some experts confidently suggested that there were no fewer than a quarter of a million prostitutes in the country. Others countered that the numbers were much higher or nowhere near so large.[4]

Historians who have analyzed the progressive response to prostitution have come no closer to agreement about the phenomenon. Barbara Hobson has emphasized prostitution as a benchmark by which to note levels of women's political emancipation. During periods, like the early twentieth century, when they fiercely agitated for greater political rights, women encountered a social backlash that focused on the evils of prostitution. Similarly, Mark Connelly has emphasized the symbolic quality of antiprostitution crusades. He acknowledges that red-light districts certainly existed but argues that they caused such an outcry in the early twentieth century because they embodied American anxieties about rapid social and economic change. For Connelly, the phenomenon that most excited the outrage of early-twentieth-century Americans, white slavery, simply did not exist. True, dozens of books and pamphlets with attention-grabbing titles like *The Great War on White Slavery* and *The Cruel and Inhuman Treatment of White Slaves* became best-sellers. True, prominent Americans like Jane Addams urged an all-out national attack on the traffic in shame. In reality, white slave tracts, which depicted the tragic lives of women forcibly kept in prostitution, were fantasies—allegories of the passing of rural America. Moreover, they proliferated as an acceptable form of pornography. Respectable readers who would never allow themselves the real thing could vicariously tour the vice districts and wallow in the details of perverse sex.[5]

Historians Ruth Rosen, Judith Walkowitz, and Leslie Fishbein, among others, agree with Connelly that prostitutes became an often-symbolic focus for progressive reform. A rapidly changing society sought order through reaffirmation of traditional moral values.[6] However, these scholars believe that white slavery did exist. If the country harbored hundreds of thousands of prostitutes, counted among them were, at a minimum, tens of thousands of women who had been lured into prostitution through false promises of marriage, employment, or help for family members and kept in the trade under duress, imprisoned at the least by economic debts and fear.[7]

Both Connelly and Rosen cite one of the most well known of early-twentieth-century vice investigations, the report submitted by a special grand jury convened in New York City in 1910 and led by John D. Rockefeller Jr. Connelly argues that this report "found no evidence of an organized white slave traffic in the New York City area."[8] Rosen, in striking contrast, declares that "the Rockefeller Grand Jury presentment documented the existence of an extensive, informal white slave trade across the country."[9] Who is right?

JOHN D. ROCKEFELLER JR. AND THE WHITE SLAVE GRAND JURY

The American public never was able to read the hundreds of pages of conclusions and transcribed testimony produced by what everybody soon came to call the "Rockefeller Grand Jury." These were never published, but they do exist, even though neither Mark Connelly nor Ruth Rosen seem to have consulted them. The authors of the two most authoritative studies of

Progressive Era prostitution cite, instead, brief secondhand accounts of the jury's decisions found in contemporary newspapers and magazines.[10]

An examination of the actual documents produced by the Rockefeller Grand Jury supports the conclusion that significant numbers of women were lured to and kept in prostitution. The documents reveal more, however. They provide a carefully crafted series of policy recommendations on the "vice question," which indicate strongly that Progressives like John D. Rockefeller Jr. wanted to go beyond simply closing down the red-light districts. They also suggest that the portrait of Progressives as reformers who "never really confronted the causes" of prostitution needs amendment.[11]

The origins of the Rockefeller Grand Jury lay in charges that New York City was the worst of the nation's many Sodoms, indeed, national headquarters for white slave rings that operated throughout the country and in Europe. During the 1909 mayoral elections, the alleged presence of white slavery in the city became a major issue. Although the Tammany candidate, William Gaynor, became New York's new mayor, he faced running a city in which reform-slate candidates had won all five borough presidencies. One of Gaynor's first acts was to impanel a grand jury of twenty-three citizens with John D. Rockefeller Jr. as its foreman to investigate white slavery.

Grand jury investigations, like blue ribbon commissions, often become tools of politicians eager to assuage public worry about an issue without actually doing anything. In fact, in the long term, the Rockefeller Grand Jury played this role. In the short term, Mayor Gaynor discovered in Rockefeller Jr. a man with his own agenda and unlimited funds to supplement the city's budget for investigation. Called into session initially for three weeks, the grand jury actually sat for six months, calling hundreds of witnesses between January and June 1910.

In some ways Rockefeller Jr.'s leadership of the "White Slave" Grand Jury functioned as his public coming-of-age ceremony. Shy and serious, John D. Rockefeller Jr. was his father's only son. His four sisters never figured equally in their father's plans. Alice died in infancy, Bessie in 1906 at age forty. Alta and Edith survived, married wealthy men, and took no active role in either the family businesses or their philanthropies.[12]

John D. Rockefeller Sr. always intended his one male heir to inherit the bulk of his fortune and responsibilities but took his time about delegation of either, without, it seems, arousing his son's resentment. Even when making entries in private journals, Rockefeller Jr. described his father in unvarying tones of hero worship and never complained about the fact that it was not until 1909, when he was already thirty-five years old, that he received his first large gift of Rockefeller securities.[13] Clearly this long delay did not stem from any lack of willingness on the part of son to help father. Indeed, Junior was painfully eager to begin his apprenticeships as philanthropist and business-man. Upon his graduation from Brown University in 1897, he declined the European tour taken by many of his friends. Instead, he appeared at the family's downtown New York offices at 26 Broadway, ready to go to work.

Despite his diligence, John D. Rockefeller Jr.'s first decade as a formal participant in the Rockefeller enterprises, marred by financial failure and deep personal anxiety, was not a happy one. Junior's first attempt at personal management of a securities portfolio proved disastrous. Duped into buying highly overvalued leather stocks, he lost well over a million dollars, a debt the senior Rockefeller had to cover.[14] In 1904 Junior suffered a complete nervous breakdown, living in seclusion for many months, before able to return, even part time, to regular work.[15]

John D. Rockefeller Sr. impressed almost everyone who met him as a patient man, eerily calm in moments of crisis, perfectly willing to wait. According to his son he was also someone who "never gave any substantial amount to any individual unless he was convinced that he or she was capable of handling it wisely."[16] To both the creator of and heir to the Rockefeller fortune it may have seemed best that the former was nearly eighty years old and the latter approaching forty before any genuine shift of funds or power occurred. Once begun, however, the transition of authority from father to son was relatively rapid. In 1909 John D. Rockefeller Jr. personally owned assets in real estate, stocks, and bonds of several hundred thousand dollars. A decade later, he controlled wealth of almost half a billion dollars. Senior, by 1920, had completed the disposition of his immense fortune, dividing it equally between his son and his foundations.[17]

The John D. Rockefeller Jr. who headed the "White Slave" Grand Jury, then, was finally a man on his own, in personal control of vast wealth, apparently released from a decade's prison of self-doubt and a lifetime of carefully exercised parental control. By all accounts, he took lively personal charge of the jury's investigations. Rockefeller's provision of supplemental funds allowed grand jury members to interview hundreds of witnesses and hire fourteen full-time undercover detectives.

Did an organized traffic in women exist in New York City? The Rocke-feller Grand Jury's answer was no. It decided that no organized white slave syn-dicate trading in the bodies of unwilling women existed but announced that white slavery did exist, "carried on by individuals acting for their own individual benefit. . . . [T]hese persons are known to each other and are more or less informally associated." Indeed, one of the jury's detectives, who presented himself on the street as a brothel owner, was able to "buy" two young girls, one for sixty dollars and the other for seventy-five dollars. Belle Moore, an infamous New York madam, boasted to another jury investigator that "little girls" were readily available through her many contacts in orphan asylums.[18]

Members of the jury were certainly aware that, since the mid-1890s when prostitution became a perennial target of reform crusades and an issue in city elections, New York City had mounted several efforts to eradicate the "social evil" by closing its red-light district, the Tenderloin, a concentrated neighborhood of brothels, saloons, cheap hotels, and dance halls. They knew also that New York's segregated vice district, in common with counterparts around the country, was a relatively recent phenomenon.

Before about 1850, most prostitutes probably walked the streets of cities, personally soliciting their customers. The emergence of prostitution as a high-profit "commercialized" business in the mid- to late nineteenth century encouraged third-party investment in brothels, whose number skyrocketed everywhere, leading New York and hundreds of other cities to pass municipal ordinances that required that any building used for "immoral purposes" be sealed under judicial supervision.[19] These measures brought results in New York City and elsewhere. Brothels, the most visible sign of prostitution's existence, were far less numerous in most big American cities in 1910 than they had been in 1890 or 1900. However, the grand jury presentment cautioned against optimism. The decline of the brothel, it said, had in direct fashion strengthened the influence of third-party male procurers, in the early twentieth century usually called "pimps" or "cadets."[20] Indeed, the grand jury argued that

> [the] business [of prostitution] has developed to this point that it depends on the man. Most of the prostitutes in town are dependent on a man who brings trade, and this man terrifies these women so, and, in many cases they are bound to him by affection, strange as it may seem, so that if she would not break away on account of her affection, she would be afraid to break away on account of what would happen to her from the rest of the pimps who are in the same business.[21]

Prostitutes had almost no chance to forsake one pimp for another. The "unwritten" but "distinct" understanding among the latter was that "a woman belongs to a man, and nobody must interfere [even] if he kills her."[22] Marcus Braun, a special immigration inspector for the federal Department of Commerce and Labor, sent the grand jury hundreds of pages of documents he had collected during seven years of investigation of prostitution in America and Europe. In a cover letter to Rockefeller, he wrote that with the closing of red-light districts, prostitutes

> are driven into tenements and private houses, they are hounded by dishonest police officials, by janitors, landlords, saloon-keepers, and professional bondsmen. What wonder they fall into the hands of pimps and cadets who assume the part of lover and protector, but in reality become heartless masters. . . . In my seven years experience as an investigating official of this government I [have] failed to find any organized traffic in women, nor do I believe, with the exception of sporadic cases, innocent girls are sold or driven into this life, but nevertheless, I regard every prostitute in this country more or less of a white slave, just because of the conditions enumerated above.[23]

Consequently, instead of praise for a city that had boarded its bordellos, the Rockefeller Grand Jury presentment suggested a program of further action. It suggested that police sweeps should focus not on the prostitute, even if she had "adopted the profession with eyes open and by choice," but on the "so-called pimp." He, and not the women he controlled, was the "vile" heart of prostitution. Further, "Serious consideration [should] be given to the introduction into the curriculum of the public school, carefully prepared courses for boys and girls, having for their object proper instruction in matters of sex." Finally, a special commission should be established to study all laws relating to prostitution in both America and Europe, with "a view to devising the most effective control of the evil."[24]

These recommendations were sensible, reflecting the work of jurors firmly directed by John D. Rockefeller Jr. They neither sentimentalized nor vilified the prostitute but sought ways to challenge an "evil" system whose greatest beneficiaries were male procurers. Rockefeller's jury condemned the pimp. It did not go so far as to berate the legions of male clients whom, ultimately, the pimp served. Nonetheless, the jury's suggestions should have been adopted. They were not. Instead, Judge Thomas O'Sullivan, part of the Tammany organization, initially refused even to accept the jury presentment, arguing that Rockefeller's group had been asked to answer just one question: "Did organized traffic in women exist in New York?" It was not supposed to introduce a new policy agenda as well as bring indictments against fifty-four pimps. Only when the press reported Rockefeller's angry challenges to O'Sullivan in open court did the judge relent enough to accept the present-ment. However, he read the names of those indicted only in closed session and quickly buried the jury's recommendations.

Mayor Gaynor's formal dismissal of the grand jury emphasized only one element of its work. The dismissal statement, quickly sent by the mayor's office to newspapers around the country, thanked the jurors for their "per-sonal sacrifices," but noted that "in return for it all you must have the pleasing consciousness that they were given for a city in every way worthy of your best efforts. Your answer to the main question submitted to you is a merited rebuke to the slanderers of the cleanest, greatest city of the world."[25]

By 1911, when it became clear that none of the recommendations of the "White Slave" Grand Jury would be followed, Rockefeller Jr. had be-come convinced that local governments were basically corrupt. For months, as jury foreman, he had listened to undercover investigators report that bribes from pimps easily bought police silence or an elected official's blind eye. The fact that almost all of those indicted by his jury soon won acquittals only further convinced Junior that solutions to the problem of prostitution would not come through alliance with municipalities.

THE BUREAU OF SOCIAL HYGIENE AND THE AMERICAN SOCIAL HYGIENE ASSOCIATION

Instead, Rockefeller decided to establish another Rockefeller philan-thropy, this one to be dedicated to investigation of issues of "social hy-giene" and committed to work with private research groups as well as public officials, but at the state, federal, and even international, rather than municipal level. Acting as trustees of the new Bureau of Social Hygiene were Rocke-feller Jr., his good friend the prominent New York banker Paul Warburg, and Rockefeller family attorney Starr Murphy.[26] Although not formally incorpo-rated under the laws of the state of New York until 1913, the new foundation actually had begun operations by the winter of 1911, and by 1912 had ac-quired a new board member, prison reformer Katharine Bement Davis. From 1917 to 1928 she acted as the organization's de facto director and gen-eral secretary.

First on Rockefeller's agenda was a merger of existing organizations interested in social hygiene questions, including control of venereal disease and sex education as well as remedies to the problem of prostitution. At the time of the Bureau of Social Hygiene's creation, two major national organizations of this sort existed, themselves already the products of decisions made by several late-nineteenth-century societies to consolidate. One was the American Vigilance Association, headed by Clifford Roe, a former assistant state's attorney in Chicago, whose widely reprinted accounts of his battles against white slave lords gave him the status of a pulp magazine popular hero in the early twentieth century. Roe's organization had attracted a broad spectrum of reform-minded Americans by focusing on the drafting of laws to penalize commercialized vice. A second organization, the American Federation for Sex Hygiene, led by a physician, Prince Morrow, and with a membership largely drawn from the medical community, saw its primary mission as a crusade against "the diseases of vice," especially syphilis and gonorrhea. Junior had contributed substantially to and become a member in good standing of both organizations. Using that leverage, he played a crucial role in masterminding the merger that created the American Social Hygiene Association.

Throughout 1912 and 1913 Rockefeller bombarded the members of both organizations' boards with letters and telegrams. In a letter written in late 1912, for example, he argued, "Whenever existing organizations working along similar lines can be combined, such combination is in the interest of economy of management and efficiency in operation." Indeed, were the federation and the Vigilance Association to remain separate, each would "waste time and money."[27] By July 1913 Rockefeller was applying yet more pressure. He warned that "I should not feel justified in lending my name or the endorsement of my financial support to a work of this character which I did not believe was being done in the way which was best calculated to bring about success."[28]

By December 1913 Rockefeller had won. The American Vigilance Association and the American Federation for Sex Hygiene joined and filed articles of incorporation as the American Social Hygiene Association.[29] Charles Eliot, former president of Harvard University and already a trustee of the Rockefeller Foundation, served as the new organization's first president, to be succeeded by William Welch, the Johns Hopkins University physician, medical education reformer, and president of the Rockefeller Institute for Medical Research. From the beginning, the roster of officers and boards of directors for the American Social Hygiene Association comprised a Who's Who of policy-making foundations and their friends. Roscoe Pound was a vice president. Jerome Greene served as treasurer. Representatives from the Russell Sage Foundation and the Commonwealth Fund sat on the association's Board of Trustees.[30]

KATHARINE BEMENT DAVIS AND THE LABORATORY OF SOCIAL HYGIENE AT BEDFORD HILLS

There was, however, one female face in the association's leadership ranks, its second vice president, Katharine Bement Davis, who, while new to the world of organized philanthropy, was not an unknown. Largely forgotten today, she was one of the most admired women in early-twentieth-century America. In 1915 the Women's Board of the Panama Pacific Exposition voted her one of the three most famous women in America. A poll sponsored in 1922 by the League of Women Voters recognized her as one of "the twelve greatest living American women."[31]

Davis, with Edith Abbott and Sophonisba Breckinridge, was a member of the first generation of women to earn doctorates in social science from the University of Chicago. A student of Thorstein Veblen, Davis received a Ph.D. in "political economy" in 1900, graduating cum laude as the author of a dissertation that compared the lives and wages of a group of German agricultural workers that had stayed in Bohemia with another that had migrated to the United States. She was by then a mature woman of forty, having already worked for years as a grammar school teacher, settlement house worker, and city housing inspector. Soon after finishing her work at Chicago Davis won an appointment as the first superintendent of the New York State Reformatory for Women at Bedford Hills, a new model prison for women located in Westchester County, New York.[32]

Her work at Bedford Hills brought Davis and John D. Rockefeller Jr. together. In 1911 the Bureau of Social Hygiene did not yet formally exist, but Rockefeller had already made a real name for himself as foreman of the "White Slave" Grand Jury. His status as a prominent antiprostitution figure was known, and within reform circles word of his interest in creating a new organized philanthropy spread. Hoping to gain his support, Davis sent Rockefeller what she described as a "tentative plan for the establishment of a research laboratory and clearing house for the study of young women convicted in the criminal courts of New York."[33] Since over 75 percent of the three hundred–some women housed during an average year at Bedford Hills were convicted prostitutes, Davis suggested her "study of young women" might hold the keys to the causes of prostitution.

The "laboratory" Davis outlined would house women convicts for one to three months, during which time they would undergo intensive study by a team of psychiatrists, nurses, and social workers. Each inmate would answer a battery of questions about her social background. Who were her parents?

Katharine Bement Davis. R. F. Photo Collection. Courtesy of the Rockefeller Archive Center.

What was the "social and moral condition" of her family? Was she religious? Social workers would return to each prisoner's old neighborhood to seek verification of her answers, and in the meantime each inmate would undergo an extensive series of physical and mental tests—to determine her health, intelligence, and potential suitability for a wide variety of occupations. Needless to say, a career in prostitution would not be an option.[34]

Intrigued by this proposal, Rockefeller Jr. soon journeyed to Westchester County to meet Bedford Hills's superintendent. He left much impressed, describing Davis as a "woman of rare mental endowment, combined with a large heart, deep sympathy and an unusual amount of common sense."[35] Convinced that Davis's proposal could make "important contributions to a fuller knowledge of the conditions ultimately responsible for vice," Rockefeller authorized aides to purchase eighty-one acres of land that abutted the reformatory grounds and begin construction.[36]

By the time the Bureau of Social Hygiene became a formally incorporated entity in May 1913, the Laboratory of Social Hygiene was a reality, a compound that included housing for staff, cottages for the prison inmates, and a research building. Later, the laboratory would expand, adding a psychiatric hospital. Between 1912 and 1918 these facilities, including buildings, roads, and improved grounds, were paid for by John D. Rockefeller Jr. and then leased to the state of New York. State officials were in possession of structures that, after all, imprisoned convicted prostitutes and other criminal wards of the state. Nonetheless, the state paid no rent to the Bureau of Social Hygiene, providing only for the food and clothing expenses of inmates during their stays at the laboratory, as well as a salary for the matron who acted as a guard. Rockefeller provided for all other costs, including the salaries for an all-female staff that, by 1917, numbered twenty professional women and included psychologists, psychiatrists, sociologists, social workers, and statisticians.

Initially, news from Bedford Hills was optimistic. Prominent journalists flocked to Westchester County to see innovative prison reform and "social hygiene" experimentation for themselves. Ida Tarbell's reaction was typical. She described Davis as a woman for whom the word "dynamic" was an understatement. Rather, the Bedford Hills superintendent was "radium—that's what she is."[37]

According to Tarbell, Davis was certainly a woman able to work wonders with "the Bedford type." Almost always young, usually under age twenty, the typical Bedford Hills inmate arrived "dirty, disorderly, and afflicted with vermin and diseases of the street."[38] The prevalence of head lice meant that new prisoners could be easily identified by their closely cropped hair. These "untrained, shiftless girls," accustomed only to earning "easy money," were transformed by the regime at Bedford Hills. Within a year, said Tarbell, Davis's combination of close individual attention, remedial vocational schooling, and healthy doses of labor out-of-doors began to work miracles. Formerly foul-mouthed, syphilitic prostitutes spent their days learning basic math and grammar, raising pigs and flowers, draining swampland for a vast five-acre vegetable garden, and pouring concrete. Their old friends on the street would have been unable to recognize them, especially those inmates whose record of improvement merited an invitation to a weekly ritual: tea with the prison superintendent in her parlor. Meeting in a cozy room, each of these young women in her hair ribbons and starched checked dress sipped a cup of tea and stirred it with a spoon Davis had inherited as a family heirloom. Perhaps, Tarbell mused, "If one could get down to the bottom of evil-doing among these girls, it is possible that in more than one case it might rest on the fact that nobody before ever thought her fit to use a silver spoon."[39]

What better site for a serious effort to understand and remedy the causes of vice? In fact, reality proved horribly different. Indeed, Tarbell's celebration of Bedford Hills, published as the lead story in the December 1912 issue of *American Magazine,* hinted at the trouble to come. While lavishing praise on Katharine Bement Davis, Tarbell also noted that Bedford Hills was shamefully overcrowded, with more than three hundred prisoners living in quarters built to accommodate fewer than two hundred. Her article not only featured photographs of happy former prostitutes tending their carrots, it also included shots of inmates forced to sleep on cots crammed into hallways, linen closets, even between toilets.[40]

Terrible overcrowding, however, did not doom the Bedford Hills experiment, Katharine Bement Davis's departure did. In 1913 even as carpenters were still putting the finishing touches on the laboratory's new and renovated buildings and as staff members had, for the most part, just arrived to begin work, she decided to accept an offer from New York's new reform-slate mayor, John P. Mitchel, to become the city's first female commissioner of corrections. By January 1914 Davis had left Bedford to assume her duties in New York City, and while she remained deeply interested in the Laboratory for Social Hygiene, she was no longer head of the prison to which it was attached.

Davis's successor as head of the laboratory, Mabel Fernald, sought to continue her predecessor's careful plans for mental, physical, and social testing of inmates. However, she soon found herself caught in a power struggle with Edith Spaulding, the psychiatrist who headed the hospital included within

the laboratory complex. An advocate of experimental hydrotherapy techniques meant to thwart impulses toward prostitution, Spaulding encouraged
hostile relations between her medical staff and the team of social workers and
statisticians directed by Mabel Fernald.

Social histories of new inmates were made and intelligence tests administered, but since Spaulding's real interest lay in establishing a program of
water cures, more and more inmates sent to the laboratory for testing ended
up making prolonged visits to its psychiatric hospital. While there, they were
often forced to take as many as eleven baths a day, each lasting up to two
hours. Such "cures" subjected a significant number of inmates to truly abu-
sive treatment—in the name of ultimately discredited "science."

To add to the laboratory's already considerable internal woes, the new
superintendent of Bedford Hills, Marian Moore, was an old-style prison
matron who viewed Davis as a soft-headed reformer. Convicted prostitutes,
Moore believed, deserved punishment, not tea. In practice the prison's new
superintendent effectively nullified the mandate of the Laboratory for Social
Hygiene to explore the causes of prostitution and implement programs to
save its practitioners. Backed by Rockefeller money, the laboratory continued
to exist, but it was a ghost institute. Moore refused to use any of the information collected by laboratory staff members and did her best to thwart their
efforts to see all incoming prisoners. Investigators from the New York State
Board of Charities accused Superintendent Moore of imposing a regime at
Bedford of excessively harsh punishments, including the shackling of unruly
prisoners and the introduction of bread-and-water diets as punishment for
trivial offenses. Inmates reported being strung up on hooks and blasted with
cold water hoses in winter.[41]

In 1917 Katharine Bement Davis accepted John D. Rockefeller Jr.'s
offer of full-time employment with the Bureau of Social Hygiene. She became its general secretary and in this role undertook the painful task of ending
the bureau's ill-fated relationship with the New York State Reformatory for
Women at Bedford Hills. As was the case with many other projects funded by
Rockefeller philanthropies, the bureau had intended the Laboratory of Social
Hygiene as a demonstration, which after proving itself, would be continued
by the state. That, however, never happened. Despite Davis's diligent efforts
as lobbyist, New York state legislators wanted nothing more to do with the
Laboratory of Social Hygiene. By 1918 Bedford Hills was not a model prison
in anyone's imagination. For many, it constituted a nightmare. The Bureau of
Hygiene ended its support for the laboratory, but, unable to sell the buildings
immediately to the state of New York, John D. Rockefeller continued to

"rent" the complex he had spent over $200,000 to create to the New York Commission on Prisons for one dollar a year. Not until 1924 did New York authorities relent, and, for a price far below their market value, buy the laboratory structures as a prison for women drug offenders.[42]

To say the least, the Laboratory of Social Hygiene at Bedford Hills did not fulfill John D. Rockefeller Jr.'s initial expectations. To conclude that it did not discover "scientific, humane, and less wasteful" solutions to the problem of prostitution would be putting it mildly.[43] From beginning to end the experiment was a fiasco. However, such a shaky start did not convince Rockefeller Jr. to abandon his interest in solutions to the problem of vice.

THE BUREAU OF SOCIAL HYGIENE AND PUBLICLY SUPPORTED SEX EDUCATION

From his first involvement with public policy making as foreman of the "White Slave" Grand Jury, John D. Rockefeller Jr. was convinced that publicly supported sex education would play a crucial role in the elimination of prostitution. Subsequently, as he became more involved in social hygiene activities, he also listened carefully to the advice of physicians who warned that not only was vice a moral evil, but it also posed a serious medical threat to society. Ignorant of the dangerous risks posed by venereal diseases that prostitution and other forms of promiscuity encouraged, Americans had to be educated about sexual diseases and sexual hygiene. They desperately needed unembarrassed and clear information based on the best-available scientific research. To provide such information, the Bureau of Social Hygiene decided to work with state departments of public health. In addition, it began to support basic "sex research." Such research was decades ahead of that conducted by any other private institution or public agency. Eventually, it proved to be too controversial even for the Rockefeller Foundation and led to the demise of the bureau.[44]

As early as the 1880s American "social purity" organizations like the White Cross had supported publicly funded sex education, especially for children. Such groups, however, viewed such training as a key to the maintenance of traditional morality. They emphasized the need to teach children to avoid sexual behavior, not to teach them to understand it, and decreed that the ideal relationship between a man and woman, even as spouses, was the sexually chaste one of son to mother or brother to sister. Children should be taught that even indulgence in sexual fantasy, not to mention the actual act, was dangerous. Boys had to learn that they had no more of an animal need for sex than did girls. Both would be physically and mentally most healthy when morally pure, which generally meant sexually abstinent. Sexual activity in marriage should always be procreative, never recreative.[45]

A speech delivered by the American Social Hygiene Association's first president, Charles Eliot, reflected this traditional emphasis on maintenance of moral standards. Like most nineteenth-century social purity crusaders, Eliot emphasized the need to make "boys understand that chastity is just as admirable and feasible in a man as in a woman." He also echoed the vague approach of such reformers to actual explanation by suggesting that sex instruction could easily be accomplished "without ever leaving the vegetable kingdom." For children not quite satisfied with discussions about insects carrying pollen from one flower to another, "the nesting habits of birds and their care of offspring are highly instructive."[46]

Charles Eliot was one officer of the American Social Hygiene Association; Katharine Bement Davis was another. It was Davis, with her emphasis on public health rather than public morality, who was the organizational officer with closer access to John D. Rockefeller Jr. In turn, he was a man who needed little persuading. Even before he had met Davis, Rockefeller had begun exercising his considerable influence to change the course of sex education. Indeed, he wasted little time with subtlety in his letters to key members of the Social Hygiene Association. As the association's "largest financial supporter," he wanted it made clear that "men of the old school would be a hindrance rather than helpful" to the progress of the social hygiene effort.[47] Eliot, in many ways, was such an "old school" social purist. The association soon replaced him with William Welch, one of the country's most prominent advocates of new approaches to medical and sex education.

Between 1914 and 1926 two publications funded by the Bureau of Social Hygiene and published under the aegis of the American Social Hygiene Association received wide distribution. Each was available to the general public for a nominal cost of ten cents. More important, state public health departments could receive as many free copies as they wished. At least one-third of the country's state departments of public health distributed *Some Inf'mation for Mother* and *Social Hygiene vs. the Sexual Plagues.*

The Indiana State Board of Health went much further. It reprinted the latter, now subtitled *The Rapid Invasion of the American Home: The Direful Consequences of Sex Secrecy and the Obligation of Parents and the State to Protect the Rising Generation.* As an official publication of the Indiana Board of Health this Rockefeller-sponsored pamphlet went through four editions. At least one million copies were printed for distribution throughout the state. Every Indiana public school district received tens of thousands of free copies.[48]

Charles Eliot's nostrum about the "highly instructive" lessons of nesting birds was not lost on journalist John Gavin, the author of *Some Inf'mation for Mother.* Gavin acknowledged the clichéd piece of advice, but in an interesting way. He mocked it. Originally published in a March 1914 issue of the *Survey, Some Inf'mation* enjoyed a remarkable afterlife. The American Social Hygiene Association acquired its copyright from *Survey* editors. With Bureau of Social Hygiene funding, the association reprinted Gavin's little parable many times. It appeared in over a hundred newspapers, went into six pamphlet editions, appeared as a reissued publication over the names of twenty state boards of health and fifteen state departments of education, and was still available in 1933 when the Bureau of Social Hygiene closed its doors.

What did it say? Structured as a conversation between a little girl of seven and her kindly older relative, *Some Inf'mation* provided parents and teachers with a gentle, unembarrassed example of "how to properly answer the questions of a child about reproduction." Watching a summer's afternoon catch of fish being gutted on a stump, the little girl naturally asks, "What's that?" when confronted with a mass of yellow-pink roe. To which her relative, named the Iconclast by Gavin, replies, "That's thousands of eggs." And when asked, "What's that—that white thing? That isn't eggs, is it?" the Iconoclast answers, "No, that's not eggs, that's milt." The little girl shakes her head in puzzlement and them smiles triumphantly. She now knows that when the mother bird lays her eggs, the father bird flies in and spreads his milt over them. "No," the Iconoclast explains, "The father bird puts the milt on the egg before the mother-bird lays it." When told how that could be possible, the little girl exclaims, "I do believe I've seen them doing it. I thought they were always fighting." "They were not fighting." Then, with the mess of fish half-gutted, the little girl becomes thoughtful and asks, "Where do cats lay their eggs? I'd awfully like to see a cat's egg. Mother says cats are very secret about their eggs." "Ah," says the Iconoclast, "your kittens weren't fresh-hatched. The cat's egg never leaves the mother's body at all. The nest is inside the mother cat." Moreover a human baby, "stays in its mother-nest until the time comes for it to be born, just as the kitten does." Gavin's simple, but highly effective, sex education lesson ends with the little girl saying,

> Now why didn't mother tell me that when I asked her? She said it was a terrible secret, and that I mustn't talk about it to anybody else but her, and then she told

me about flowers and pollen and bees, and I got all mixed up. I couldn't see what bees had to do with babies—except to sting 'em. . . . You'll have to 'xcuse me now; I've simply *got* to give mother some inf'mation![49]

Almost a century after its first appearance, *Some Inf'mation for Mother* could still serve well as a guide to teaching young children about human reproduction. By contrast, the information contained in *Social Hygiene vs. the Sexual Plagues* is a curious mixture, certainly no longer of value as a teaching aid. As a serious attempt to present the most accurate evidence available about sexuality and sexual disease, it documents the very imperfect quality of early-twentieth-century knowledge about these subjects, even among the country's best scientists, while reflecting the era's new concern with sex education as one of the best tools to promote general public health, under grave danger from the venereal diseases spread by prostitution and promiscuity.

In the decades since World War II, Americans have come to regard syphilis and gonorrhea as relatively minor physical inconveniences, cured in most cases with one huge dose of penicillin. If, however, they are compared to AIDS, a sexually transmitted disease that terrifies the late twentieth century, the two former diseases reemerge as they appeared to educated people before the discovery of penicillin in the 1940s.

As late as 1910, the remedies proposed by physicians for sexual disease and sexual malfunction were not much better than those their colleagues in the seventeenth century might have used. For instance, in the early twentieth century a common medical recommendation to a male who complained of impotence was that he wear a tiny leather belt studded with sharp tacks, to be tied tightly around his penis. Treatments for syphilis were not much less grisly. Usually, a doctor injected a solution of a potassium or mercury iodide directly into the genital organs. Not only was this treatment spectacularly painful, it usually led to complications: commonly, loss of teeth, inability to use the tongue, and bleeding bowels. One textbook still used by some American physicians until about 1915 described the curvature of the penis upon erection that sometimes was a symptom in men suffering advanced cases of gonorrhea and then suggested, "To straighten the organ, it should be laid with the curve upwards on a table and struck a violent blow with a book."[50]

By 1920, the best-trained American doctors had begun to use arsenic-based compounds, like Salvarsan, to treat venereal disease. Compared with being struck violently with a book, a patient might have regarded a regime of Salvarsan as a major improvement. Nonetheless, both it and other drugs in use before 1930 usually caused side effects. Most patients experienced intense nausea. Moreover, as is the case with experimental drugs used to attack AIDS in the late twentieth century, Salvarsan and its cousins were extremely expensive, effectively limiting their use to those who could afford them.

Given the social stigma surrounding venereal disease, accurate statistics are notoriously elusive, but it is likely that more men than women received drug treatments, ranging from injection of mercury to doses of Salvarsan. In the early twentieth century, before Wasserman testing at time of marriage for both sexes became common, a significant percentage of women who suffered from venereal disease were probably misdiagnosed when they sought medical advice, since neither they nor their physicians realized the symptoms of early venereal infection in females, especially in the case of gonorrhea. A large number of the complete hysterectomies performed on women before 1920 may have been a physician's solution to long-term syphilitic or gonorrheal infection.

Before penicillin, no foolproof cure for syphilis or gonorrhea existed. However, beginning in the late nineteenth century, scientists began to recognize the true nature of these diseases. Only in the early twentieth century, and then only within the small community of medical investigators working in the country's best hospitals, did the full range of problems caused by each begin to be understood. Physicians like William Welch knew that syphilis often entered a latent stage, only to reemerge years later to do virulent damage to bones, blood vessels, skin, and nervous system. They knew that men and women could transmit venereal disease even if neither showed any visible symptoms of infection. They knew that pregnant women with gonorrhea could unknowingly blind their newborns. These medical leaders knew, as a large number of physicians still did not, that nitrate of silver applied to the eyes of a gonorrheally infected baby could save her sight.[51]

Sex education, then, was crucial. *Social Hygiene vs. the Sexual Plagues* warned that "vicious, popular ignorance" was helping to spread venereal infection and produce "misled men" who would "just as leave have [syphilis or gonorrhea] as a bad cold."[52] The hundreds of thousands of readers of *Social Hygiene vs. the Sexual Plagues* also learned that there were "no more dangerous disease breeders than prostitutes."[53] Yet they were urged not to support the most popular Progressive Era "solution" to prostitution, the abolition of red-light districts. Indeed,

> Prostitutes unduly oppressed, seek cover and practice clandestine prostitution, often in the midst of respectability. Clandestine prostitution is much more dangerous to public health than open prostitution, for in clandestine prostitu-

tion, the hygienist has no power to cope with secret foci of disease. When not regulated too severely, there is a natural tendency among prostitutes to come together in a special locality. In early days prostitutes were burned at the stake, drowned, scourged, branded, flayed and tortured in diverse ways. But as one writer has stated, if all the prostitutes in the world were to be removed today, on the morrow the ranks would be filled with fresh recruits.[54]

Only "general and persistent education" could deter prostitution.[55]

In prescribing proper sexual behavior, *Social Hygiene vs. the Sexual Plagues* warned men to avoid prostitutes, not only to avoid disease themselves, but also to protect their wives and children from infection. That advice paralleled the kind given in dozens of other purity manuals common in the early twentieth century. However, in some ways, the sex education offered in this book was well ahead of its time. The vast majority of early-twentieth-century "social purity" manuals treated masturbation as a dread evil, never to be indulged in, and warned boys that their friends would soon notice the telltale signs of self-abuse. A chalkish complexion and sunken eyes, however, were only the first and least of possible symptoms. Traditional, morally oriented, early sex education tracts regularly included tales of masturbators who had lost all mental control and ended their days in asylums.[56] In dramatic contrast, *Social Hygiene vs. the Sexual Plagues* argued, "The evils of masturbation have been grossly exaggerated. It is wrong to terrify the mind of youth with the formidable insanity specter." If fathers believed in the "untrue threat of the madhouse," they would go so far as to say to sons, "If you have to do a thing of that kind, go to some first class house."[57] Such advice, based on ignorance promoted in the name of social purity, inevitably increased the nation's population of syphilitics.

Social Hygiene vs. the Sexual Plagues offered equally untraditional advice on many other sexual topics, although some of it, unlike the very modern sounding conclusions about the potential harm of masturbation, dated the pamphlet as a creation of a scientific community with much still to learn about sexuality and sexual disease. Still, even if in hindsight some of this advice was inaccurate, it had a significant impact on public health policy. For example, the pamphlet argued that sexual disease could be prevented by a medical procedure then rarely practiced in America. Noting that "the Jewish race is remarkably free from syphilis," it urged the widespread adoption of the custom of infant circumcision. While the technique did not guarantee total protection against venereal infection, when circumcision of baby boys "is performed at an early age, the skin of the part becomes toughened—becomes somewhat like the palm of the hand. In case of exposure [to syphilis] the skin does not easily abrade. . . . The syphilitic poison does not find entrance to the circulatory system."[58]

In 1900 probably fewer than 2 percent of the nation's males were circumcised, the vast majority of them Jews or Moslem immigrants from North Africa, almost all for religious reasons. Between that date and 1930, physicians affiliated with American Social Hygiene Association led a campaign to convince public health officials to promote the practice as not only hygienic, but as a prophylactic against the diseases of vice. A direct link cannot be made between the publications promoted by the association and the Bureau of Social Hygiene and the growing acceptance among physicians of circumcision as a measure to promote public health. Yet, it is clear that state departments of public health, the public agencies most receptive to the ideas of the two private organizations, were leaders in the effort to gain acceptance in America for widespread circumcision of male infants. By 1930 the number of circumcised male babies had already begun to increase, though the technique did not become a commonplace practice until after World War II, when, for the first time, most American baby boys entered the world in hospitals rather than at home.[59]

KATHARINE BEMENT DAVIS AND SEX RESEARCH AT THE BUREAU OF SOCIAL HYGIENE

The most important private-public alliance to promote sex education as beneficial to public health took place between the Bureau of Social Hygiene and state departments of public health, which distributed its pamphlets, often with no acknowledgments as to their source. Those who knew sometimes wrote directly to John D. Rockefeller Jr. to congratulate him. For example, Julia Richman, a district school superintendent for New York City, used bureau pamphlets obtained from the New York State Department of Public Health as the heart of a pilot program of sex education in fourteen public grammar schools. With this help, Richman reported such training was "where it belonged—right into the elementary schools before the children reach the danger line."[60]

By early 1922 Katharine Bement Davis, as general secretary of the Bureau of Social Hygiene, might have had reason for pride. The bureau's decade-long program of sex education seemed to be winning converts around the country. Instead, Davis worried. She saw a different kind of "danger line." Despite every effort to be accurate, was the bureau giving Americans proper advice about sexuality and sexual disease? She reported to Rockefeller, "Our knowledge of sex is in a chaotic state. Concerning a matter of prime importance to the individual and the race, we are largely dependent upon opinion rather than established fact. . . . It remains that trained specialists, having most to do with sex problems, are unable to agree upon fundamental questions. This condition can have but one basis, namely, inadequate scientifically derived data."[61]

Davis urged Rockefeller to expand his support for basic sex research, especially for the efforts already begun, in the late fall of 1921, through the establishment within the National Research Council of a Committee for Research in Problems of Sex. The council had been created in 1916 as a branch of the National Academy of Science to oversee defense-related research projects during World War I, had survived the conflict, and by 1921 had become a sponsor for a wide variety of scientific research projects. Until 1933, the Committee for Research in Problems of Sex received its entire budget, over $670,000, from the Bureau of Social Hygiene.[62]

However, as early as 1922, Katharine Bement Davis was openly expressing frustration with the committee's agenda. Theoretically, its interests included six fields: physiology, psychology, psychopathology, biology, sociology, and anthropology, but in truth the "hard" scientists dominated. Of the five voting committee members, only Davis was not affiliated with a university's science department or medical school, and in committee deliberations questions most of interest to social scientists never received more than a perfunctory hearing. Psychologist Robert M. Yerkes, not sociologist Katharine Bement Davis, exercised the most influence in setting the committee's course. By 1922 it was already clear: The emphasis would be on research done in animal populations. Most of the committee's grants funded projects that emphasized medical experiments conducted on monkeys and rats by biologists and psychologists. They measured the effects of radiation on the sperm counts of primates and studied the sexual glands of rats. Yerkes himself examined the effects of castration and gonad transplantation in monkeys.[63]

Katharine Bement Davis did not dispute the value of such animal studies. She felt, however, that they did little to promote the essential work of the Bureau of Social Hygiene: the understanding of *human* sexuality. In 1923 Davis not only began a massive investigation of sexuality in American women herself, she allied the bureau with another research committee much more sympathetic to her point of view. The Committee on Maternal Health

(CMH) was the brainchild of obstetrician and birth control advocate Robert Dickinson. Together with fellow dissident gynecologists, surgeons, obstetricians, nurses, and a few general practitioners, Dickinson created a vehicle to promote the study by trained specialists of all aspects of human sexuality. The CMH, with headquarters in New York City, operated within a climate of general professional hostility to its activities. The American Medical Association (AMA) would not formally even consider contraception as a medical problem until 1937.[64]

In 1925 Dickinson mocked his fellow physicians in a speech given before a meeting of the AMA. "It is," he said, "not a little curious that about the pivotal point of the physiology of sex, science should develop its sole timidity." We physicians, he continued, exhibit "our greatest shyness, not of the bizarre, the extreme, the abnormal or the diseased, but of the average and usual sex practice of mankind."[65] Those practices, the Committee on Maternal Health declared, should be investigated, and could be investigated with "dignity, decency, and directness."[66]

Despite "steady antagonism," moreover, the committee did initiate a formidable program of research and legislative lobbying.[67] By 1928 the organization had produced numerous articles and research papers on such topics as gonorrheal sterility in women, causes of male infertility, masturbation in humans, and techniques to improve the practice of therapeutic abortion.[68] It had also adopted as one of its highest priorities the development of techniques of effective birth control based on the general principles of "putting the care of the woman" into her own hands and "fitting a vaginal device replaced and removed by her as needed."[69] Throughout the 1920s its members lobbied state and federal legislators to abolish legal restrictions on all forms of birth control. Contraception, they argued, was a social good, not a social evil.[70]

Hence, at a time when the biologists and psychologists who controlled the Committee for Research in Problems of Sex were ignoring Katharine Bement Davis, the leaders of the Committee on Maternal Health were effusively thanking her for her "cordial" decision to put "her unpublished material at our disposal."[71] Indeed, Robert Dickinson publicly praised her research as "epoch-making."[72]

And it was. Her research led to a lengthy book finally published in 1929, which, under the title *Factors in the Sex Life of Twenty-two Hundred Women,* examined almost every aspect of the sexual experience of Davis's sample population of over two thousand American women.[73] It also appeared in journal articles throughout the 1920s and in this form became well known to Davis's contemporary colleagues in the small world of serious social-science-oriented sex research.[74]

In both her articles and in the massive *Factors in the Sex Life of Twenty-two Hundred Women,* Davis emphasized one theme: that "except on the pathological side . . . sex is scientifically an unexplored country."[75] To complete her book, she had first created a female advisory committee, consisting, among others, of university professors, physicians—including the woman who headed the Pennsylvania State Department of Health's Division of Child Health—and several prominent psychologists.[76] Then, working with such advisors, she created a sample population of "normal" women, using funds from the Bureau of Social Hygiene to compile a master list of twenty thousand women, half of them married, half unmarried, with their names taken from the membership rolls of chapters of the General Federation of Women's Clubs, the National League of Women Voters, and the alumnae registers of women's colleges. What Davis sought was a large sample population of typical, rather than atypical, women. Prior to her creation of this sample population almost all knowledge of female sexuality came from records kept by physicians who worked in institutions for the retarded or insane. In contrast, all the members of Davis's group were "[women] of good standing in the community, with no known physical, mental, or moral handicap, of sufficient intelligence and education to understand and answer in writing a rather exhaustive set of questions as to sex experience." They lived in every state in the country and in a variety of environments, from big cities to farms, but all were adults, with an average age of thirty-seven and a modal age of thirty.[77] Each of the women on Davis's original list of twenty thousand names received a letter asking if she would be willing to cooperate by filling out questionnaires on her sex experience. About one-fifth of these women agreed to participate and became the subjects of several years of intense study. This sample group was certainly skewed by race, education, and class, given the techniques used to create it, but compared to the female populations of insane asylums, Davis's women were undeniably more "normal."

In both of Davis's groups, the one thousand married women and the twelve hundred unmarried women, interest ran high. Many respondents not only filled out the lengthy questionnaires regularly sent them, but supplemented their answers by inserting additional sheets of comments. In the end they produced "many thousands" of pages of this kind of unsolicited, additional detail as well as tens of thousands of pages of completed questionnaires.[78] It took Davis and the statisticians she hired years to tabulate and analyze this material, and when she finally published her book in 1929, Davis hoped it would be seen as a beginning, not an end. "It goes without saying," she said, "that hundreds, yes thousands of other correlations [from these case histories] would be possible." *Factors in the Sex Life of Twenty-two Hundred Women* could be a "way-mark, with which future studies may be compared."[79]

The body of work that Katharine Bement Davis produced with bureau support between 1923 and 1929 was indeed a "way-mark" in a new field of social-science investigation. Many of Davis's hypotheses directly challenged conventional wisdom. After years of scrutinizing tens of thousands of pages of anonymous answers to her questionnaires, she concluded, for instance, that most normal American women probably practiced "auto-eroticism" or masturbation. At least two-thirds of the women in her samples found masturbation a pleasurable way to release tension. Far from fearing the insane asylum, this same two-thirds did not even admit any feelings of wrongdoing or shame. Only about 5 percent were troubled enough to seek advice, through books or their physicians, on ways to stop the practice.[80]

Moreover, Davis discovered that very frequent intercourse seemed to cause no physical or mental damage. *Social Hygiene vs. the Sexual Plagues* warned that "excessive intercourse is silly, vulgar, brutal, and destructive."[81] Davis disagreed. She classified ten of the married women in her sample of one thousand as "sexual athletes." This group reported intercourse kept up daily or at least every other day over a period of many years. *Factors in the Sex Life of Twenty-two Hundred Women* reported that investigators could discover no ill effects from such behavior, despite the fact that most physicians still accepted as undisputed "truth" the supposed connection between sterility and frequent intercourse. Davis's study, in contrast, found no lessened fertility. Indeed, a group of ninety women among her married case histories who reported that they experienced intercourse at least once, and often, many more times, each day, seven days a week during their early years of married life, seemed, if anything, to experience much higher fertility rates than those found in the total sample group of one thousand married women.[82] Finally, Davis concluded that homosexuality among entirely respectable American women was probably far more widespread "than is generally suspected."[83]

The original edition of *Factors in the Sex Life of Twenty-two Hundred Women*, appeared clearly identified on the title page as a "publication of the Bureau of Social Hygiene."[84] However, almost immediately, the bureau sought to distance itself from the project it had funded. While it had exerted great energy to find a wider audience for *Social Hygiene vs. the Sexual Plagues,* it provided no publicity budget for *Factors.* When the book, brought out by the well-known New York publishers Harper and Brothers sold well anyway, bureau staff members refused requests from researchers to see Davis's questionnaires. In fact, at some point someone destroyed them all.[85]

Raymond Fosdick, the longtime Rockefeller advisor who assumed the presidency of the Rockefeller Foundation in 1936, was probably the major actor in the strange drama that surrounded the conclusion to Katharine Bement Davis's years of pioneering research. Fosdick felt that Davis's work would saddle the Rockefeller philanthropies with unwanted public attention. A man who had enjoyed the complete trust of John D. Rockefeller Jr. ever since his first assignment as an investigator hired in the wake of the "White Slave" Grand Jury to look more deeply into the causes of prostitution, Fosdick argued that Davis had to go. She was sixty-eight years old and suffering increasingly poor health, but her "retirement" was clearly a forced affair.[86]

Lawrence Dunham, Davis's successor, filled the role of caretaker. In 1931 the Bureau of Social Hygiene implemented a de facto policy of letting all grants expire without renewal. The bureau continued to exist as a legal entity until 1940, but, except on paper, it was dead by 1933—its offices shuttered, its furniture sold, its former employees dispersed.[87]

What lessons does the history of the Bureau of Social Hygiene offer to students of public policy making? In 1913, as he announced the incorporation of a new family philanthropy, John D. Rockefeller Jr. waxed optimistic. In light of his experience as foreman of the "White Slave" Grand Jury, he concluded:

> The forces of evil are never greatly alarmed at the organization of investigating or reform bodies, for they know that they are generally composed of busy people, who cannot turn aside from their own affairs for any great length of time to carry on reforms. . . . So the conviction grew that in order to make a real . . . improvement in conditions a permanent organization should be created, the continuation of which would not be dependent upon a temporary wave of reform . . . but which would go on, generation after generation. . . . It also appeared that a private organization would have, among other advantages a certain freedom from publicity and political bias, which a publicly-appointed commission could not so easily avoid.[88]

Of course the Bureau of Social Hygiene did not go on, generation after generation. It lasted twenty years.

There were identifiable villains behind the fact that the bureau did not become a "permanent organization." Some were public officials who thwarted attempts by a reform-minded private organization to make an alliance. A photograph of Superintendent Moore of the Bedford Hills women's prison apparently does not survive in available records. It is easy, however, to fantasize her with cruel eyes and a hatchet chin. But all the bureau's enemies were not external.

Under Katharine Bement Davis, the bureau advised that American society could only cope with sexual "evils" if it better understood human sexuality itself. Under her leadership, the bureau's transitions from antiprostitution investigations to sex education to sex research itself were logical and sophisticated. Had the Bureau of Social Hygiene continued to promote no-holds-barred research into human sexuality and sexual disease, the benefits to society might have been substantial. What would have happened if, beginning in the 1920s, "generation after generation" of public health officials had copied Indiana's State Board of Health? What if, as early as the 1930s, not just Indianans, but most American citizens, were advised by public health officials dedicated to massive publicity campaigns linking accurate information about sexuality and sexual disease to good public health policy?

Theoretically, Davis headed an organization freed of the snares of "publicity and political bias" that inevitably constrained public agencies. In fact, her bureau's history demonstrates yet again the more complex reality of private wealth's influence on public life. Despite the specter of Superintendent Moore up in Westchester County lashing her prisoners to hooks or of New York City judges giving known pimps a quick ticket back to the street, public officials did not force the bureau to close. In fact, by the end of the 1920s, its sex education advice was increasingly in demand. It is well to remember that, despite bureau efforts to pretend it did not exist, *Factors in the Sex Life of Twenty-two Hundred Women* sold briskly. Moreover, the many Americans who bought it could not depend on a private philanthropy's subsidized charge of ten cents.

Within the network of Rockefeller philanthropies Davis was a leader, but she had too few followers and several very influential opponents. Davis's internal enemies, like Raymond Fosdick, did not see the Bureau of Social Hygiene as politically neutral, but as a potential source of unwanted attention. Moreover, at a time of upheaval within the entire family philanthropic organizational structure, Fosdick found Junior willing to listen when he urged the Rockefeller heir to regroup and reassess his commitments. While logical, John D. Rockefeller Jr.'s decision forced a foundation retreat from the cutting edge of a field of scientific investigation his patronage had significantly influenced.

Fosdick's ascendancy to leadership within the Rockefeller Foundation signaled another, larger change, one even a younger and more vigorous Davis would have been unlikely to prevent. The major reorganization of the Rockefeller philanthropies under the umbrella of the Rockefeller Foundation in 1928–29 represented not just a decision to create a more closely centralized organizational structure. It had ideological implications as well and, in important ways, symbolized incorporated philanthropy's coming of age. After 1930, as mature institutions, foundations were far less likely to nourish very experimental work in a dramatically new field like sex research. They began to play the roles that would distinguish their participation as policy makers during the New Deal and after: as seekers of compromise and the middle ground. Men concerned about bad publicity replaced men like the fiercely exuberant and vocally incautious Frederick Gates. Such leaders found fewer and fewer important staff positions for controversial innovators like Katharine Bement Davis.

John D. Rockefeller Jr. continued to express interest in issues of birth control and sex research after the demise of the Bureau of Social Hygiene but gave only token amounts to organizations promoting either cause. For instance, his annual check of twenty thousand dollars to the Planned Parenthood Federation of America, successor to Margaret Sanger's American Birth Control League, was minuscule compared to the millions he had personally donated to the Bureau of Social Hygiene.

When the Rockefeller Foundation, encouraged by John D. Rockefeller 3d, returned after World War II in a serious way to the field of sex research, its focus was global, not local. World overpopulation, not American syphilis, was the crisis for which it sought solutions.[89] By the time "population planning" supplanted "sex research" as the phrase of choice, officials in the Rockefeller philanthropies concentrated on programs for India, not Indiana. Most public health officials in this country had probably forgotten that the Bureau of Social Hygiene ever existed. The public health policy for which a Rockefeller philanthropy made a sustained "generation after generation" effort did not involve decision making about social vice and human sexuality, but rather involved the far less controversial subject of publicly funded recreation.

FOUNDATIONS, RECREATION, AND
THE PUBLIC'S MORAL HEALTH

J ohn D. Rockefeller Jr., spurred into action by his leadership duties on the "White Slave" Grand Jury, created the Bureau of Social Hygiene to attack the moral evil of prostitution. Two decades later, by the time the bureau shut its doors, it had shifted emphasis, and had come to view the "social evil" primarily as a public health issue, only secondarily a challenge to American morality. The far more successful campaigns led by the Russell Sage Foundation and the Laura Spelman Rockefeller Memorial to promote government-sponsored recreation were, in interesting contrast, dominated by discussions of morality. Organized recreation was crucial to the public's moral as well as its physical health. Fit Americans best exemplified civic virtue.

Before the twentieth century, local, state, and federal governments devoted very little attention to recreation as a public responsibility. Indeed, for much of the eighteenth and nineteenth centuries most people viewed leisure as idleness, a tool of the devil. For public moneys to be spent to organize the leisure-time pursuits of the republic's citizens would have struck the average policy maker as absurd. Nonetheless, by the end of the 1920s such activities were commonplace. Over eight hundred cities had "recreation departments" that collectively spent over $32 million of the public's money. Millions of children and adults played in city-owned playgrounds, parks, golf courses, swimming pools, and tennis courts. Millions were members of municipally sponsored baseball, basketball, horseshoe, and football leagues. Even greater numbers participated in huge public pageants.[1]

By 1925 all but seven state departments of education had mandated that some form of "motor skills testing" be included in the curriculums of public schools. A majority of American school children hopped, threw balls, and ran potato races under the watchful eyes of a new type of teacher: the "physical educator."[2] By the middle of the decade, even the federal government had become involved as a sponsor of publicly funded recreation. Declaring that recreation should be "a federal function" and that the country needed a "national recreation policy," President Calvin Coolidge created a National Conference on Outdoor Recreation.[3]

Activists in the Sage Foundation and the Spelman Memorial spurred these dramatic developments and in the process created new definitions of civic duty and public health. Underpinning this foundation-led revolution in public policies about leisure was a new "philosophy of play," which equated the development of muscles with the creation of morals.[4]

THE "PHILOSOPHY OF PLAY"

Early-twentieth-century ideas about the role of play in the lives of children and adults need to be placed within two contexts. First, they must be understood as a sharp departure from traditional American notions about leisure. Joseph Lee, the wealthy Boston reformer who, with the Sage Foundation's Luther Gulick, created the theories upon which the early twentieth century's recreation movement rested, argued that "all other races live a little as they go along. [Only Americans] are forever postponing our life in our devotion to the means of living. With us it is always jam yesterday and jam tomorrow, but never jam today."[5]

In truth, nineteenth-century Americans could not so easily be damned as work-obsessed. They did play. However, play was a subject about which most felt conflicted. Many Americans continued to make a long-established cultural equation of leisure with laziness. As believers in, if not always practitioners of, the Protestant Work Ethic, they accepted the idea that if an adult had time to enjoy himself, he had time to work harder, and they thought that children with free time were on their way to mischief.

Most nineteenth-century children played games of their own construction. The older generation's very limited involvement in such activities was primarily a negative one. If they thought about child's play at all, most nineteenth-century adults imagined ways to restrict it. For themselves ideal "play" was sedentary. Men and women alike were passive spectators at speeches, plays, and concerts. Largely male crowds gathered to watch wrestling and boxing matches. They loved horseraces and cockfights. They played cards.

Such uses for leisure time usually included gambling and almost always involved a bottle of whiskey. Indeed, drinking heavily together may have been the most common form of recreation indulged in by nineteenth-century males. Boys quite literally learned to drink at the sides of their fathers, often accompanying their elders to taverns when they were as young as five or six years old. They were part of a culture that did not begin to impose age restrictions on alcohol consumption until the 1870s, and often they played games that imitated adults' recreational lives, one of the most popular being "militia." In this, boys imitated their elders, substituting sticks for rifles on their shoulders, but consuming very real rounds of whiskey at game's end.[6]

Before the twentieth century most Americans would have regarded the notion that play was essential to proper moral development as ludicrous. The recreation movement, like its early-twentieth-century cousin, parent education, emerged as an offshoot of the equally new discipline of psychology. That is the second context in which it should be placed. Neither of the play movement's two most prominent leaders was a trained psychologist, but both were widely read, enormously influential popularizers of psychological theories ranging from instinct theory to behaviorism. Joseph Lee took a law degree from Harvard University in 1883 but never practiced. The fortune he inherited from his family's banks enabled him to devote his entire adult life to reform crusades. He championed birth control. He petitioned state legislators to provide free lunches in every public school. Most important, he advocated publicly funded playgrounds.

Luther Gulick, a physician, was a tireless advocate of playgrounds as well. Like Mary Richmond, Hastings Hart, and other key staff members, Gulick came to the Russell Sage Foundation in middle age with an already well-developed national reputation. By the time he accepted the foundation's offer to form one of its first departments, he was America's best-known advocate of the positive benefits of recreation and physical exercise.[7] Lee's *Constructive and Preventive Philanthropy* and Gulick's *A Philosophy of Play* outlined the ideas of a movement that linked "muscles and morals."[8]

Physically, Joseph Lee and Luther Gulick could not have been more different. Lee, tall, thin, and elegant, looked the part of a Boston blue blood, while Gulick was short, rumpled, and decidedly middle class, troubled by a heart murmur and plagued by migraine headaches. Emotionally, however, the two men were virtually identical twins. Each was the kind of man awed co-workers described as fiercely combative and absolutely convinced of the rightness of a cause.[9] Each raised the function of play from an activity to be viewed skeptically, to an essential ingredient in the development of well-balanced and politically democratic human beings.[10] Crucial to play "philosophy" was a belief that physical, emotional, and moral development were inextricably connected. As Gulick argued, "The chief discovery of recent years in regard to the emotions is that they are, first of all, 'states of body.' The mind has only a second-hand relation to them. It enters at the end, not at the beginning."[11]

If society wanted emotionally stable, morally responsible citizens, it had, first of all, to direct the play of its young. Following at least the rough outlines of behaviorism's belief in habit formation, play theory urged that children not only be provided with places to play, but with planned and carefully supervised activities. Children left alone would not play wholesomely. Joseph Lee warned that they actually preferred "grizzly" forms of amusement. After years of watching youngsters play in the streets and alleys of Boston, he was convinced that the city's favorite child's game was "funeral," the centerpiece of which was always an "interment" of one unfortunate.[12] If Boston's children were digging graves for each other, New York's were happiest playing craps, which, according to Luther Gulick, if not the boys of the Lower East Side, was "useless physiologically and bad morally."[13]

For play to be a source of benefit rather than a source of evil, adults had to provide children with better games and careful instruction. Unaided children, with their unformed muscles and emotions, would never gain the kind of self-control they needed to become useful workers and productive citizens. As Joseph Lee pontificated, "The boy without a playground is father to the man without a job."[14] Moreover the boy without a playground would never understand the type of freedom necessary to maintain democracy. Gulick argued:

> There is real freedom on the playground, because a child must either play by the rules or be shut out by those in charge. . . . The kind of control which people exert upon one another is, to be sure, external control—and external control does not develop morality. But the external control of the playground differs from the control of the home or the school: the child is free to leave if he chooses. [If a boy] stays, controlling his temper and playing according to fair ideals, he learns self-control, not simple obedience. . . . Self control of the higher type is primarily developed under the conditions of the playground.[15]

Yet, Lee, Gulick, and many progressive allies argued, those children most in need of lessons in self-control and proper moral behavior were unfortunately those least likely to enjoy organized play. Far from spending regular time on playgrounds, the nation's poor children regularly worked brutally long hours in fields and factories. This was a point made in a 1913 *Survey* editorial that mocked the "play trust" formed by the nation's largest canneries, who in their vegetable-processing sheds were providing a "glorious opportunity of play which we might envy for our own children." There, ten-year-old Milly Vaconti "frolicked making bean toys" on average twelve hours a day, from 4:30 in the morning until 9:30 at night. Yet this "ungrateful wretch" could only murmur, "I'm awfully tired." On Sundays "some more lenient parents allowed a few hours recreation to their children," but Milly's "orthodox" mother, just arrived from Sicily, kept her home from the cannery bean sheds to help with washing.[16]

If organized play was important to the development of its young, it was also essential to "conserve the morals" and help bring together the nation's adults, especially as the country included more and more new residents like Mrs. Vaconti.[17] Prominent politicians and government officials soon joined reformers and echoed the rhetoric of the philosophy of play. As governor of the state of New York, Charles Evans Hughes publicly worried that "we cannot, as our population becomes congested, keep men good by force."[18] They would only be "kept good" if they believed they belonged to a common society, as players belonged to a team, and speaking in 1924, President Coolidge agreed. "We have," he said, "a national interest in recreation. There is no better common denominator of a people. In the case of a people which represents many nations, cultures, and races, as does our own . . . recreation is bound to wield a telling influence for solidarity of the entire population."[19]

Many play advocates thought that if cities introduced programs of planned recreation, they would not only integrate their burgeoning and diverse populations, they would reduce crime and encourage habits of fitness and efficiency that would make city dwellers better workers. Self-described progressive businessmen agreed. Companies like National Cash Register or U.S. Steel had, as early as 1900, pioneered a new approach to employer-employee relations that included benefits as well as wages. Programs often featured subsidized housing, free medical care in company clinics, libraries within factories, and profit-sharing schemes. Almost all emphasized recreation as another benefit and provided such activities as company-sponsored baseball teams, golf courses, hiking trails, and weekend dances. However, such firms employed only a fraction of the nation's urban workforce, and the recreational opportunities they offered extended only to the relative handful of children of their own employees. The Milly Vacontis of America were not included. Municipal governments needed to supplement the "welfare work" progressive businesses had begun.[20]

Millions of city people, both natives and new arrivals, were crowded together into rented, yardless, and gardenless apartments that offered little chance for wholesome play. Only a very few worked for companies that provided gym equipment or organized baseball leagues. Rather, after long hours of labor most returned home via streets that offered temptations on every side, luring them to waste leisure hours passively in "dissipation, not recreation."[21]

As commercialized leisure became big business, the "moral injury" of "perverted leisure" became an ever more dangerous threat.[22] Urban Americans had an increasing array of ways to amuse themselves. In 1916 Russell Sage Foundation officials surveyed all forms of commercial recreation available to New Yorkers and estimated that the city's residents spent over $100 million in dance halls, theaters, private clubs, baseball stadiums, saloons, excursion boats, and houses of prostitution. Interestingly, the foundation's survey report did not separate amusements favored by the rich and the poor. It recognized, moreover, that commercial recreation would not disappear: "The Harvard Club and Yale Club will still go on. When Maud Adams plays *Peter Pan* the theaters will be filled. When Ty Cobb knocks the ball over the fence, [Americans] will be in the bleachers to see him do it. As long as the circus has elephants and giraffes, men will still go to the circus."[23]

In 1922 the motion picture business was only twenty-five years old, but it already possessed the kind of capital to pay Charlie Chaplin weekly wages of $13,500.[24] Joseph Lee damned the nation's "pathetic" love of commercialized spectator games. He scorned the "American mania over professional baseball and the hysteria of our big football games, in which strong men weep over a game which they have never played and very imperfectly understand."[25]

Joseph Lee frequently ranted against movie houses and professional sports, but other advocates of the "philosophy of play" thought that many forms of commercial entertainment had their place. Nonetheless, all agreed that some actively promoted immorality; others, while not morally harmful, encouraged Americans to passivity. The best forms of recreation, ones that deserved public subsidy, were those that pushed the country's citizens to be active. People amused themselves when they sat in a dimly lit movie. They learned the skills of self-control and group loyalty crucial to democracy when they played on baseball or basketball teams, when they sang in glee clubs, or when they played a role in a community pageant. Americans needed free time, but, even more they needed leaders to tell them how best to spend it. Leisure alone could lead to evil. As Joseph Lee cautioned, "Napoleon could not conquer Europe without rations. But how long would it have taken his rations to conquer Europe without Napoleon? How many valiant potatoes could have done the trick?"[26]

For many reformers, moreover, the "play question" was not one of immigrants and cities alone. Throughout the nation, except in the South, farmers had become ever more reliant on machinery, which allowed them to expand their holdings, but forced them to work harder than ever. If urban Americans encountered a welter of entertainment choices, many of them dangerous, expensive, or worthless, rural people faced lives of bleak isolation, characterized in Julia Lathrop's words by "deadening" boredom. Her agents, sent to compile statistics for studies of child and maternal welfare, returned with reports of farmwives who had not been to town for six, eight, or more years and who could not remember the year in which they had last enjoyed even one break from a seven-days-a-week work routine. One "old farmer," Lathrop recounted, left his wife a patient in a Minnesota state hospital for the insane, saying sadly, "I do not know where she could have caught it. She has not been off the farm for ten years."[27]

Of course, Lathrop, like so many other early-twentieth-century students of the "rural crisis," was a sophisticated city dweller. However, unlike most in the Country Life Movement, she neither patronized nor romanticized rural people. Her agents allowed the women they interviewed to speak for themselves, and their own words resonated with loneliness. The "philosophy of play," then, in theory, was all-inclusive, offering help for a farmwife's isolation, or an impoverished immigrant girl at work, as well as wholesome alternatives to taverns and movie palaces for urban adults. In reality, its advice rarely applied to anybody but men and boys in cities, overwhelmingly the same group to which corporate "welfare work" benefits had been extended.

Play organizers presented confused analyses of recreation's role in the lives of all the country's girls and women, be they in cities or on the farm. Luther Gulick argued that the desire to "throw straight and hard" was masculine. However, as a doctor, he acknowledged that "this is not because of man's special adaptability. A man's shoulder joint is not very different from a woman's. In fact, what differences there are in the joint itself seem to be in favor of the woman."[28] From this one might conclude that Gulick was either mistaken about the desire being masculine or about the close interrelation between the moral, nervous, and muscular systems of human beings.[29] But instead of acknowledging either, he speculated vaguely in his most widely circulated book, *A Philosophy of Play,* that, while he could discern no truly important variations in male and female muscular growth, perhaps women developed different "instinct feelings." For a man whose prose usually leaped off the page, filled with vivid analogies and sharp warnings, his advice to American girls and women was curiously half-hearted: "Indiscriminate basketball is certainly bad. Home basketball is good. The ground between the two is debatable."[30] Only Jane Addams confronted the issue of play for females squarely: "The opportunity which the athletic field provides . . . is the basis for a new citizenship and in the end will overthrow the corrupt politician. In fact, I see no other way of overthrowing him in a crowded city quarter where people's prejudices are easily played upon. . . . If girls were voting, I would, of course, say the same for them."[31]

Most play organizers were far less forthright than Jane Addams. They ignored questions raised by female muscles. They talked about the needs of the entire nation's population for wholesome physical activity, when they really meant men and boys. At best, a few advocated programs of mild activity for women, such as group singing. One of Luther Gulick's protégés, James Naismith, invented the game of basketball. He and Gulick together produced the definitive rule book for the new sport. Both praised it as the ideal team game, the best way to inculcate civic spirit in America's citizens. Nonetheless, Gulick revealed to his readers that "I have seen the most cultivated and mature young women lose complete control of themselves . . . in a game of basketball."[32] So much for games as a key to self-control, at least where half the population was concerned. In fact, play organizers, including the game's inventors, praised the development of special, constrained rules for women's basketball, which effectively limited the amount of running, dribbling, and bodily contact allowed female players.

If play organizers publicly noted their indecision about the effects of "indiscriminate" basketball on women, they rarely doubted their conclusions about anything else. Joseph Lee, for instance, did not want merely to reform the dangerous recreational habits of his working-class inferiors. He firmly believed that many fellow members of the Harvard Club were "potatoes" as well. Perhaps he should have ruminated further about Napoleon? After all, Europe did not remain conquered, and the French emperor's "potatoes," when force-marched into Russia, were not particularly enthusiastic.

The evidence available does not indicate that the play philosophers inspired average Americans to exchange seats at the movies with places as members of teams bent on developing democratic virtue through the enthusiastic playing of group games. But the planned play advocates did achieve great success with a smaller group of people: government policy makers at local, state, and federal levels. No nineteenth-century government had a recreation department or a recreation policy. By 1930, hundreds of cities, the majority of states, and the federal government embraced publicly funded recreation. The American people did not demand that their governments adopt such policies. During the 1920s, city recreation superintendents routinely warned each other that citizens would initially view municipal ball teams or tennis courts as unnecessary frivolities. Only gradually would the voters come to value them.[33]

Once again, as was the case with the Knapp System, parent education, and many of the other social policies treated in this volume, an elite imposed a public policy, expecting that, once trained, other Americans would accept and then embrace it. And indeed, millions of Americans did come to endorse the "philosophy of play," though not necessarily for the reasons its advocates urged. By the onset of the Great Depression millions of Americans had adopted an idea most citizens would have considered strange in 1900. They expected their cities to build baseball diamonds in municipal parks. They enthusiastically played roles in huge public pageants. They wanted lifeguards at state-owned lakes so their children could swim in safety. They thought that federal lands should be used for recreation, not just mined for minerals, or leased for grazing. A transformation in attitudes had taken place, and doing much to create the context for this was an alliance between the Laura Spelman Rockefeller Memorial, the Russell Sage Foundation, and the Playground and Recreation Association of America.

THE SPELMAN MEMORIAL, THE SAGE FOUNDATION, AND THE PLAYGROUND AND RECREATION ASSOCIATION

The Bureau of Social Hygiene funded the American Social Hygiene Association. In addition, executives of one served the same function for the other. In important ways the two formed one organizational unit. A similar close alliance bonded the Laura Spelman Rockefeller Memorial, the Russell Sage Foundation, and the association both patronized, the Playground and Recreation Association of America. In 1906 Luther Gulick, then director of a fledging physical education program for the New York City public schools, convinced fellow play advocates Joseph Lee, Jane Addams, Jacob Riis, and Henry Curtis to meet together to plan strategy in Washington. This small group decided a national organization could best promote the cause.

Initially, the new organization existed in name only. But in 1907 the Russell Sage Foundation incorporated, and, as one of his first actions, the director of the new foundation, John Glenn, contacted Luther Gulick with a job offer. Would he resign his position with the New York public schools to direct the Russell Sage Foundation's recreation studies? Gulick agreed but asked to continue as the president of the Playground Association. He recruited two key aides, Clarence Perry, a former special agent with the U.S. Immigration Service, and social worker Lee Hanmer to help him plan the work of the Sage Foundation's new Department of Child Hygiene. From the beginning the department worked very closely with the Playground Association. Hanmer continued to be a field secretary of the association until 1912, released from full-time work by the Sage Foundation, but paid a full-time salary. Moreover the foundation paid most of the other expenses incurred by the Playground Association, including the publication of the association's journal, *The Playground*.

In late 1911 Gulick decided to resign from the Sage Foundation in order to devote his attentions full time to the organization he and his wife had founded in 1910. However, this organization, the Camp Fire Girls, continued to cooperate with the Playground Association, as did other already-established youth organizations such as the Boy and Girl Scouts of America, the YMCA, and the YWCA. Also in 1911, seeking to broaden its range of activities and public influence, the Playground Association changed its name to the Playground and Recreation Association of America (PRAA), and under Lee Hanmer, Gulick's successor, the Sage Foundation's Department of Child Hygiene underwent a corresponding name change, becoming the Department of Recreation.[34] In 1912 Luther Gulick formally left both his director's position at the Sage Foundation and the presidency of the Playground and Recreation Association, to be succeeded by Joseph Lee who continued as head of the organization until his death in 1937.

Unlike Gulick, the son of middle-class Presbyterian missionaries, Lee was extremely wealthy, and under his leadership, the Playground and Recreation Association acquired a board of directors of similarly privileged individuals, including Ellen Scripps, heir to the Scripps-Howard publishing fortune, and Harold Swift, of the Chicago meat-packing family. Like Lee himself, many members of the association's board regularly contributed tens of thousands of dollars to the organization, with the result that their donations provided, on average, about a quarter of the association's yearly budget. Until 1922, the Russell Sage Foundation met most of the rest of the PRAA's costs. After that year, the new Spelman Memorial committed $50,000 annually to association activities. In addition, it pledged a million dollars to a $3 million endowment used by the Playground and Recreation Association to expand its field work with city governments.[35]

FOUNDATION-SPONSORED FIELD WORK AND MUNICIPAL RECREATION

Officials of the Spelman Memorial, the Sage Foundation, and the Playground and Recreation Association agreed that their primary goal was the creation of new public policies. City, state, and national government officials needed to learn how crucial recreation was to good social order, and as social worker Howard Braucher, longtime executive secretary for the association, put it in a speech delivered in 1916, the purpose of the organization's "private experiments" was to demonstrate "the value so that government could be persuaded to take over." In Braucher's words,

> We believe in government. The future of our country depends on building up habits of working through government. We are willing to stake all on government because we feel that government is so important. We have dealt with men who sell their votes. We have been unable to persuade them not to because they think of government as negative. We want them to think of government as a positive force working for the good of the people. Under any other philosophy of government I see no possibility of averting social revolution. I should be willing if necessary to see [recreation programs] less efficient under government, rather than slightly more efficient under private management. Building up confidence in government is *fundamental*.[36]

The officials Braucher and his allies sought first to reach were those closest to the citizenry, in city government. They did so by employing a staff of thirteen traveling agents known as field secretaries.

These individuals, mostly male social workers, provided the crucial link between organized philanthropy and city government. Given the connections play organizers constantly made between male muscularity and civic development, Clarence Perry's guidelines for hiring a field secretary were most interesting. Of course, an applicant should have "plenty of energy and enterprise," but Perry did not want what "you would strictly call the red-blooded type of man." Instead, the foundation's emissaries, in fact recreation workers in general, should play "the role of political boss, not political leader." Perry mused, "According to my notion a political boss does not work so much by the 'hurrah boys method' as by patient study and observation, tactful suggestions, and skillful wire-pulling."[37] Clarence Perry, Lee Hanmer, and the people they hired were clearly "political boss" types. Of all the significant leaders within the organizational triangle formed by the Spelman Memorial, Sage Foundation, and Playground and Recreation Association, only Joseph Lee definitely was not. He, however, served as the movement's highly colorful figurehead, not as a behind-the-scenes "wire-puller."

The PRAA initiated its field secretary system in 1913, but it had only just begun to operate nationally when the country entered World War I. Until 1919 all efforts focused on the war. Raymond Fosdick, on leave from his duties at the Rockefeller Foundation, headed a presidentially appointed Commission on Training Camp Activities and recruited recreational specialists from the PRAA, as well as the YMCA and other private organizations, to devise a program of wholesome recreation for the troops. According to Fosdick, "Leisure time activities make . . . a contented army, and an army is not a fighting army until it is a contented army." He dispatched athletic directors to every stateside military camp, civilian aides responsible to the commanding officer, and urged that the boxing lessons, glee clubs, and baseball games be continued when the men sailed for Europe. Indeed, even though "some old Indian fighters down in the War Department" fought the innovation, America, Fosdick declared, supported his efforts to send a "singing army" to France.[38]

The war had a crucial impact on the play movement. Not only were over a million and a half men drafted into the army and thus exposed to planned recreation, large numbers of public officials, from the mayors of over one hundred towns in the neighborhood of training camps to governors, members of Congress, and the president himself, had been exposed to a full dose of the philosophy of play. Moreover the widely publicized information that the military had rejected almost one-half of all potential draftees as physically or mentally unfit raised a national furor and gave politicians strong reason to be receptive to play theory's edicts about sound minds in sound bodies.

Consequently, the PRAA's field secretaries were deluged with requests for help, as local officials in hundreds of communities vied to establish recreation programs. Each secretary was responsible for a region that included at least thirty cities with populations over ten thousand. Most visited, on average, two cities a month, each for about two weeks. Person-to-person advice was the heart of the system. Howard Braucher confided to Beardsley Ruml, "Many of the best recreation leaders are not nearly so good at obtaining suggestions from reading as they are at obtaining their education from word of mouth. The nature of recreation is such that it draws to the movement this kind of individual. Therefore it is of much greater importance in this movement than in most movements to provide for personal contact."[39]

But the handful of PRAA agents had many more mayors begging for personal contact than they could possibly accommodate. The Playground and Recreation Association decided to provide help only to cities with recreation committees that included members both of the business community and city government already in place. Moreover, each city assigned an agent had to have a minimum population of ten thousand residents. In reality, no cities with fewer than twenty thousand people received visits from the hardpressed association field secretaries.

Once accepted as a candidate for a municipal recreation survey, a city hosted an agent who spent the next ten to fifteen days promoting the cause of tax-supported recreation in nonstop fashion. One field secretary sent to Hartford, Connecticut, gave sixty speeches in nine days to groups ranging from the Rotary Club to the Jewish Welfare Board, urging each to put pressure on city officials to expand the community's public recreational opportunities. Speech-making and friendly arm-twisting occupied his evenings; during the day he collected data on city residential patterns and land costs, to be compiled by the Sage Foundation's Department of Statistics. Hartford officials, in due course, received detailed maps that suggested ideal locations for ballparks, playgrounds, baths, and other facilities.[40]

Joseph Lee suggested that cities met the field agents as saviors. "It is feeding the hungry," he said. "Every bit of information answers a question; almost every one determines a policy."[41] The agents' confidential reports suggested that Clarence Perry's less sanguine assessment was the more accurate one. Many field secretaries found that mayors and other city officials were hardheaded, practical men, not inclined to add items to municipal budgets until they were convinced that their constituents would approve. In their attempts to convince local politicians, agents emphasized that organized recreation would create physically and mentally superior workforces that would inevitably attract new business and bring jobs. When companies searched for new factory locations they would pass over cities without organized recreation.[42]

Some agents reported quick success. Waltham, Massachusetts, became almost immediately "recreation-minded." Its new recreation director, John Leary, a former professional baseball player, was "almost worshipped" by all the city's boys. Waltham's mayor found ways every year to increase the municipality's recreation budget. By 1924 it even included funds for a "married couples' gym class." On the other hand, the superintendent of parks in neighboring Springfield supported a city-sponsored team games program only as a way to impose his incompetent son as its director.[43]

Despite the kinds of petty politics displayed by Springfield, Massachusetts, officials, the "municipalization" of recreation promoted by the Playground Association agents was a significant success. In 1900 only three cities in the country, Boston, New York, and Chicago, had municipally owned and supervised playgrounds. Many more had parks, but like New York City's Central Park, they were not meant to be sites for active recreation. In the late nineteenth century, landscape architects, most famously Central Park's creator, Frederick Law Olmsted, had allied with urban reformers to create tens of thousands of city parks throughout the country. From the grand to the modest each existed primarily as a green oasis, in which frazzled urbanites could reclaim their pastoral heritage. The big cities that hired park wardens instructed them to keep their visitors quietly on the paths or benches. Parks were for contemplation and rest, not group exercise and vigorous games.

By 1929 a policy revolution had occurred. Taxes for play had become a commonplace within municipal budgets. Not many urban Americans enjoyed the panoply of activities the Los Angeles Recreation Commission offered its citizens. Angelenos could work out with weights at city-owned gymnasiums, folk dance or do the Charleston at municipal dance halls, use public bowling alleys, boxing rooms, baseball diamonds, and basketball courts. When they were tired after all this activity, they could retire to one of six city bathhouses to relax in a steam or salt-water bath. Use of any of these facilities was free.[44]

Other municipalities offered more modest recreation programs, but compared to what most had provided in 1900, the change was enormous. Over eight hundred cities had recreation departments. Additionally, at least that number had included recreation as a responsibility of public welfare or parks departments. Almost every town in the country with twenty thousand residents or more had at least one community-owned and supervised playground. In any year after 1925, an average of one million adults and close to two million children played on city-sponsored sports teams.[45]

There is obviously no way of knowing how many, if any, of these people were learning lessons of group loyalty and democratic spirit as play organizers predicted. Joseph Lee himself provided, unwittingly, proof that play was probably not so easy to direct to such foreordained ends. In his description of a "model" Boston playground established in 1909, Lee mentioned that play organizers had included a variety of large and small benches, meant to be used by youngsters for rest between their carefully scheduled games. The children, however, had other ideas. Within weeks of their installation, the benches had become a toboggan slide—the big benches forming the ramps, the small ones, turned upside down, serving as sleds.[46] If children made their own uses of organized recreation, did adults? Did democratic virtue, along with sweat, gild the brows of the men and women who attended the Waltham, Massachusetts, married couples' gym classes? Did they have an entirely different agenda? We don't know. What is clear, however, is the emergence of a new social policy: municipally sponsored, tax-supported public recreation.

THE RUSSELL SAGE FOUNDATION AND PAGEANTS

In the late twentieth century, publicly sponsored recreation still includes ballteams and exercise classes. What it is far less likely to feature is the recreational event that the Russell Sage Foundation promoted as quintessentially beneficial: the public outdoor pageant. Every summer between 1907 and 1930 hundreds of America's communities, from small towns to big cities, hosted pageants.

Prior to the Sage Foundation's active promotion, many towns had enjoyed kinds of civic celebrations that included some elements found in the early-twentieth-century pageants. Nineteenth-century Americans gathered on summer evenings, especially on the Fourth of July, to hear patriotic orations. Even more important, they loved grand parades. When they celebrated the Glorious Fourth or Washington's Birthday, they stepped in formation down their streets and avenues. In big cities such patriotic holidays called out crowds of thousands of marchers, often organized by occupation or ethnicity.

Important contemporary events demanded a procession, though parades were largely male affairs. Women usually stood on the sidelines as spectators. The bigger the reason for celebration, the larger the parade. For instance, the men of New York City marked the opening of the Erie Canal on 5 November 1825 with a mammoth parade. Over fifty thousand marched; at least a million crowded the streets to watch. The city's butchers led, dragging squealing hogs behind them; occupying the positions of greatest status at the end of the march line were many of New York's most prominent physicians and clergymen, as well as most of the faculty of Columbia University.

By the 1880s, however, the parade's importance as an all-inclusive symbol of community-wide celebration had declined significantly. In many areas citizens no longer marched even on the Fourth of July. Instead, the parades that continued in the late nineteenth and early twentieth century were more narrowly partisan. Interestingly, as the parade became more commonly a ritual used by those championing a particular cause, women, for the first time, enthusiastically joined the marching ranks. Tens of thousands of suffragists used the time-honored public tradition of a procession to demand the vote. Members of the Knights of Labor marched to demand recognition of their right to organize. But fewer and fewer communities participated en masse as marchers and spectators in parades that were primarily symbols of democratic unity.[47]

Early-twentieth-century pageant supporters wanted to revive the American civic tradition of whole towns joined in parade. They often justified a return to parades as a "safe and sane" alternative to Fourth of July celebrations spent exploding firecrackers and firing rifles. As Luther Gulick argued, "It is reported from apparently trustworthy sources that more persons have been sacrificed in celebrating the Fourth of July than were fatally injured in the War of Independence itself."[48]

However, pageant advocates, especially within the Russell Sage Foundation, had a grander vision, not encompassed simply by a reintroduction of marching in the streets. Pageants were to be all-inclusive celebrations that certainly could include parading but would also involve dramatic skits, grand historical re-enactments, concerts, athletic contests, and a variety of other activities. The key to a successful pageant was the degree to which it involved a significant number of a community's citizens in active cooperation.

Some spectacles were truly spectacular. In 1909, for example, in celebration of the three-hundredth anniversary of Henrik Hudson's first exploration of the Hudson River, New York City sponsored an elaborate fifteen-day pageant involving one million schoolchildren and six million adults. The program involved three huge land parades, and one by water, naturally on the Hudson. Almost two hundred replicas of period sailing ships sent from eight nations escorted the "Half Moon" on its river journey. Nor did the pageant end with New York City's fete in September. It continued throughout the fall in all the principal cities along the river and ended in November with ceremonies in Albany.[49]

Early-twentieth-century pageant organizers obviously felt that Hudson's voyage deserved a splashy celebration. However, they deemed no historic theme unworthy, as long as it involved a big cast. For instance, in July 1915, over five thousand of the citizens of Lincoln, Nebraska, costumed as grasshoppers and wildly flapping their "wings," reenacted the destruction of the community's corn crop in 1870. In 1912 similarly impressive masses from Schenectady, New York, paraded as lightbulbs to celebrate General Electric's decision to locate another major factory in their midst.[50]

Chauncey Langdon, who combined an interest in playwriting and set design with a career as executive secretary of the New York state branch of the American Red Cross, became the Sage Foundation's most important consultant on pageants. Luther Gulick, a longtime friend, had recommended that the foundation provide funding for Langdon's "demonstration" pageants, meant to show communities how to stage events that would emphasize civic "harmony" and shared purpose. There is no evidence that Langdon played any central role in orchestrating the pageants in Lincoln or Schenectady, but he was a major advisor for the pageant first presented by the citizens of Tarrytown, New York, in 1909 and continued as an annual summer celebration through the mid-1920s, drawing participants from both the town and surrounding communities in Westchester County, becoming in its heyday a small-scale classic of the genre that well illustrates it.

Whether they involved hundreds or thousands of amateur actors, pageants usually focused on local history, in ways that could involve large numbers of different groups. "Stages" were suitably vast: fields on the edge of town, meadows, or riverfronts. In Westchester County, for example, the pageant was staged in several sites on three successive days between 2 and 4 July with the big crowd scenes taking place on orchard land that included a lush meadow near the Hudson River. In such an idyllic setting, the first players to appear were bands of Mohawks, ready to negotiate the sale of property to land-hungry Dutchmen. Then, in chronological order followed Anne Hutchinson and her fellow refugees from Massachusetts Bay, searching for safe exile; George Washington's Revolutionary War encampment near White Plains, New York, complete with dozens of horses and full-size tents; the capture of Major André; and finally, a "dinner party" with literary recitations at Washington Irving's home, "Sunnyside," located a few miles down the road from the pageant's primary site among the apple trees.

Over three hundred and fifty Westchester County citizens snared major roles, with "fierce" competition for favorites, like George Washington or Washington Irving. The supporting cast varied from performance to performance and from year to year. Sometimes the Mohawk negotiations involved more than a hundred braves following their chief through the woods. Other years, the Indians, Boy Scouts in homemade leggings and feathers, opted to be young patriots, assisting in a crowded capture of Major André. More continuous was the use of male extras in battle scenes, either as revolutionaries led by Washington, or as British Redcoats under General William Howe, and there were always opportunities for interested women and girls to sew costumes and appear as Puritan goodwives in the crowd that banished Anne Hutchinson, or to mill among the Mohawks as suitably dressed Dutch matrons.

While it survived, the Westchester Pageant was an event that occupied thousands of area residents' energies for months. The journalist Mary Fanton Roberts reported that weeks before the actual event, Westchester citizens began to appear on streets and town squares in costume, squeezing dozens of rehearsals into their regular routines. Uninitiated visitors might stare in wonder at fifty or sixty bare-chested Indians, tomahawks in hand, on commuter trains and streetcars. They might glimpse several hundred British troops practicing marching or musketry. They might discover Mrs. Nathaniel Hawthorne chatting with Anne Hutchinson in front of the meat counter at the local grocery.[51]

By 1925 fewer and fewer towns and cities held such pageants, and by 1930 they had almost disappeared. Summer celebrations certainly continued, especially in ethnic communities and small towns. Increasingly, however, the central focus of such festivals was commercial. Organized by business leaders to tout a product for which an area was famous, Cherry Blossom Days, Maple Sugar Weekends, and their many variations appeared. In direct contrast to the early-twentieth-century pageant, most who attended these kinds of festivals were essentially spectators, not active players, there to enjoy entertainment or purchase items available for sale.

The partisan parade reappeared during the Great Depression. Across the country, millions of Americans marched in favor of the NRA, the CIO, or dozens of other causes. But those not in the streets singing "Solidarity Forever" tended to retreat inside, to their radios. When they ventured out to explore their history, they did so increasingly by visiting restored or re-created historical "towns." In 1929 Henry Ford dedicated Greenfield Village, Michigan, a collection of actual nineteenth-century buildings he had authorized to be bought, painstakingly dismantled, and then reconstructed on the outskirts of Detroit. In 1930 Salem, Massachusetts, opened its re-creation of seventeenth-century Salem to the public. John D. Rockefeller Jr. was, by then, deeply involved in one of the era's most famous restoration efforts, that of Colonial Williamsburg. In these and other places, visitors were again spectators, not actors. They stood behind ropes or quietly on sidewalks listening to costumed "interpreters." In this new kind of "historic re-enactment" the parts were all played by paid professionals. The role of average citizens at Greenfield Village, or Salem, or Colonial Williamsburg was a limited one. They paid their entrance fees and watched.[52]

Supporters of the older Progressive Era pageants had called them "dramas of democracy."[53] They had not worried much about the fact that the history they presented was highly romanticized. Like their predecessors, the early-nineteenth-century parades, their primary goal was not historical authenticity. Rather, both celebrated civic community. Progressive reformers, like those in the Russell Sage Foundation's Department of Recreation, thought that play was best when it was an active group pleasure, not a passive, solitary one. They thought that people who spent "wholesome" leisure time together would be better workers and better citizens. Their visions of the possibilities of pageants, like progressive expectations of organized play, or even of human nature, were pierced with self-contradictions and burdened by excessive optimism.

Nonetheless, the pageant's disappearance should be mourned. The many millions of late-twentieth-century Americans who spend their free hours slumped before television screens or immured within the "virtual reality" of cyberspace rather than engaged in the actual life of their communities could learn lessons from the Sage Foundation's now-forgotten pageant and recreation pamphlets.

Almost all, like one published in 1910 under the title *The Exploitation of Pleasure,* shared a common theme: "Joy is power."[54] Moreover, it could be a source of democratic civic strength, as well as of individual satisfaction. True joy demanded that members of a community connect physically and emotionally. People who actively celebrated together acknowledged each other as fellow Americans, often across high barriers of economic, religious, and ethnic difference. The Russell Sage Foundation's "play philosophers," wrong about many specifics, were right on this essential point: that acknowledgment mattered. It did then. It does now.

STATE STANDARDS FOR PHYSICAL FITNESS

The community historical pageant, regrettably, died. However, many other features of the "municipalization" of play supported by the Russell Sage Foundation, the Spelman Memorial, and the Playground and Recreation Association became entrenched in city government. And even as they were doing so, the movement's leaders, especially at the Spelman Memorial, were seeking to align other levels of government in support of publicly sponsored recreation and physical fitness. If America's youngsters were not minimally fit, then all the hard-won municipal playgrounds, parks, golf courses, and gymnasiums would be wasted on a future generation of flabby adults.

In 1919 no state department of education mandated standards of physical fitness and physical education to be met by public primary and secondary schools. By 1928 forty, the vast majority, did. The Spelman Memorial, in cooperation with the American Physical Education Association and the National Amateur Athletic Federation, was a crucial force behind this successful campaign to impose first-ever statewide fitness standards on public school children. It was an effort that increased the importance of physical education in public schools at the same time that it transposed the philosophy of play's ambiguities about recreation for women into public policy.

The term "physical education" was one that relatively few Americans had heard as late as 1920. But as early as 1885 the American Physical Education Association had been founded by a Yale University physician and had begun holding yearly conferences attended by those interested in educating the body as well as the mind. World War I energized the association, just as it had supplied the PRAA field secretaries with far more pleas for help than they could possibly answer. Before the war, the Physical Education Association had been a sleepy group of fewer than two hundred school principals and college professors, but by 1917, thanks to the shocking news that great numbers of the nation's draft-age males were physically defective, it had enrolled over two thousand members, including hundreds of public school superintendents as well as directors of state education departments. By that time it was poised to begin a new role, and, after 1922, acting in concert with the Spelman Memorial, it became one of the nation's chief advocates of a new idea: that physical education be included within state minimum curriculum guidelines. In addition, it argued that mandatory physical education courses should follow statewide standards so that physical fitness of children could more accurately be judged.[55]

Between 1923 and 1928 the Spelman Memorial funded the Physical Education Association's campaign to make "motor ability testing" part of every public school's annual evaluations of its students. During those years the association's Motor Ability Committee, which included representatives from the memorial, tirelessly lobbied state departments of education and state legislators, arguing that "motor ability" was essential to physical fitness and health. It was an accurate predictor of later skills and employability in various occupations and secured the skills crucial for a well-rounded future adult recreative life. Finally, and central to the creed of play philosophy, it provided the key to "fundamental team skills . . . that aid in developing social and moral values."[56]

The association recommended eight groups of activities that public school teachers could use to test a child's motor abilities. They were: (1) free exercises (without use of hand apparatus), (2) calisthenics (with use of hand apparatus), (3) marching, (4) dancing, (5) track, (6) team game activities, (7) tumbling, and (8) swimming.[57] Taken together, these would show whether the child's body had been properly educated, and to promote their usage the association distributed elaborate recommendations for achievement standards for every grade and provided many pages of specific information about how tests were to be conducted in each motor skills area.[58]

"Potato races" provide an example of the association's precise guidelines and were especially recommended as an excellent, and inexpensive, way to test category two: calisthenics skills with use of hand apparatus. According to the instructions, boxes four inches deep with bases no more than twelve inches square were to be placed on stands two feet high, spaced at distances thirty-one feet apart. No fewer than sixteen boxes were to be used, and each was to be free-standing, in no way fastened to a floor or floor covering. The child being tested then received potatoes to hold in each hand and was required run around each box in turn, while passing the potatoes from hand to hand. Children in grades one through six were to race with one potato in each hand. Those in grades seven through nine had to repeat the performance, but with three potatoes in each hand. Those in grades ten through twelve had to run while transferring a total of ten potatoes from hand to hand. No rubber mat or any other nonskid floor covering was allowed, and points were to be deducted if a competitor dropped a potato or moved a box.[59]

The U.S. Army in 1917 and 1918 did not utilize potato racing in its testing regimes. Had it done so, perhaps its already troubling estimates about the percentages of American young men who were physically unfit would have skyrocketed. Nonetheless, the massive failure rates reported were sufficiently alarming to spur numerous state legislatures to pass physical education laws that demanded standardized tests for fitness be distributed and monitored by state departments of education. Between 1917 and 1923, thirty-two states passed such laws. By 1928 eight more had followed suit.

Clearly, the Army's judgments about draftees were a major factor prompting this outpouring of new state laws. Without the appalling news from the War Department, which caused politicians and the general public alike to worry about the apparent presence of an entire generation of physically defective Americans, the American Physical Education Association's crusade to include physical education as a mandatory part of public school curriculums would have continued to flounder. Nonetheless, with Spelman Memorial backing, the association was able to make good use of an opportunity. It blanketed the country's state education departments with its criteria.

Not surprisingly, many of these department administrators, faced with legislative mandates but lacking increases in their own budgets, adopted the association's standardized testing schemes whole-cloth. These guidelines were age and grade ranked. They were also gender specific. Spurred by the "physical fitness" crisis the Army had apparently discovered, state education departments readily accepted the Physical Education Association's standardized testing programs. In doing so, they also, again with little debate, accepted their inherent attitudes about women and physical activity.

Crucial to these attitudes was an ambivalence about the good done women who participated in stressful physical activity, an attitude especially apparent in the new National Amateur Athletic Federation, first organized under the auspices of the Secretary of War at a 1921 meeting in Washington. Dedicated to "physical education, healthful recreation, and sound ideals of Sportsmanship," the federation created separate men's and women's divisions, and by 1924 had succeeded, with Spelman Memorial financial backing, in getting its rules for women's sports accepted by ten state departments of education.

A public policy with far-reaching impact had been accepted, with little discussion and at the behest of a group of self-appointed private experts who decreed not only that the physical activities of girls and women should be different from those enjoyed by boys and men, but that they should be grounded in different philosophies. The former should be encouraged to compete strenuously, as long as they jousted for the honor of a team, not simply for individual glory, but under no circumstances was female competitive spirit to be encouraged.

In 1924 a national conference hosted by Mrs. Herbert Hoover, sponsored by the Women's Division of the Amateur Athletic Federation, and funded by the Spelman Memorial underscored this basic tenet. Conference participants vigorously condemned tournament games for girls and received with "great excitement" the news that four southern state departments of education, in Alabama, Georgia, Mississippi, and Tennessee, had decided to abolish statewide high school girls' basketball tournaments. One conference speaker reported that girls' teams in those states had in many instances traveled two hundred or more miles from home, then played for three days and three nights in tournament elimination rounds. The girls themselves, she reported in disbelief, thought "that they have the gayest time."[60]

Such "gay" times were to be eliminated, for the girls' own good, even though the games were popular with the players, their audiences, and hometown politicians. One unnamed state school superintendent "finally put an end to the tournaments" in his district, reported Lillian Schoedler, executive secretary of the Women's Division, but he had done so only after receiving the "armament" of the Amateur Athletic Federation's warnings about the dangers to girls' physical development by participation in highly competitive games.[61] Luther Gulick was dead by 1924, but his fears about "indiscriminate" basketball lived on. The worries he expressed in *A Philosophy of Play*, enshrined as policy, meant that girls' games would involve less jumping, less throwing, less running, and less fun.

The Bureau of Education within the U.S. Department of the Interior explicitly warned, "Because competitive athletics are for them a new and especially exciting form of adventure, women have entered into these sports with an intensity which has added to the fear for their welfare."[62] A few outstanding American women athletes, like the great Babe Didrikson, triumphed despite all odds, but the legacies of foundation-sponsored play theories would constrain the recreational and sports activities of several generations of America's women. The same progressive reformers who were so intent on creating "rugged, national vitality" cheered when public school administrators forbade girls' tournament games, issued edicts to physical education teachers that they were not to allow any girls to "indulge intensive training," and advised that national and international competitions for women and girls "are inopportune."[63] It was the policy, not the competition, that was inopportune.

THE SPELMAN MEMORIAL AND THE NATIONAL CONFERENCE ON OUTDOOR RECREATION

The final group of foundation-influenced recreation policies considered here has had a far more salutary long-term impact on American life. For four years, between 1924 and 1928, the Spelman Memorial met the research and conference costs of an organization that Secretary of Commerce Herbert Hoover called "semi-official . . . one which receives no Federal financial support, but does receive the earnest cooperation of . . . various Federal Departments."[64]

This organization, the National Conference on Outdoor Recreation, owed its existence to Colonel Theodore Roosevelt, son of the former president and, in 1924, occupant of a federal office to which his family had and would continue to lay informal claim. He was President Coolidge's Assistant Secretary of the Navy, and, like his father, was an ardent conservationist. Roosevelt Sr. wished to expand federal park lands to save priceless natural resources for posterity; Roosevelt Jr. wanted to use them for recreation as well. Moreover, he wanted to conduct a comprehensive survey of all federal lands, which in 1924 amounted to more than one-sixth of all land in the continental United States, to determine the ways they "could be used in terms of human service, not in terms of money." He thought that national policy makers should view outdoor recreation as a "needful national institution for the promotion of the bodily, mental, and spiritual welfare of all the people."[65]

Spurred by Roosevelt, Coolidge convened a national conference on outdoor recreation in May 1924. All federal agencies with responsibility for public domain lands participated. More significantly, the fact that more than one hundred private organizations sent representatives indicated the importance of resource conservation and use issues to a growing segment of the American population. Grassroots environmentalism did not begin in the 1960s. In 1924 organizations influential in the late twentieth century, like the Sierra Club and the Audubon Society, already thrived. The delegates from these and dozens of other groups dedicated to preservation and wise use of America's scenic and wildlife treasures came to Washington as natural allies of government officials like Colonel Roosevelt. At the end of its planned three days of meetings, the National Conference on Outdoor Recreation concluded that a "national recreation policy" was necessary, but that it could not be formulated in a matter of a few days. Instead, conferees announced an ambitious four-year agenda of surveys and investigations to determine what role federal lands should play in "nation-recreation-planning."[66]

The policy-planning group that tried to complete this task, and that continued to call itself the National Conference on Outdoor Recreation, sought private wealth for the creation of public policy. Chauncey Hamlin of the Playground and Recreation Association wrote Beardsley Ruml requesting financial support for the organization's work; he assured the Spelman Memorial's director that "the country is looking to the National Conference on Outdoor Recreation for leadership in developing a federal policy on this important question."[67] Hamlin and Roosevelt cochaired the conference, and L. F. Kneipp, Assistant Forester of the U.S. Government, acted as the organization's executive secretary.

The Spelman Memorial was its financial patron, but Roosevelt found space for conference offices within the Navy Department. The Secretaries of War, Interior, Agriculture, Commerce, and Labor were also members of an affiliated committee, and over forty private organizations, ranging from the

U.S. Chamber of Commerce to the Playground and Recreation Association, American Physical Education Association, Boy Scouts, Audubon Society, and Boone and Crockett Club participated in conference surveys and deliberations.[68] Representatives from these groups, as well as government officials, served as members of the eighteen committees through which the conference conducted its work.[69]

Given such a Byzantine structure, complaint was inevitable. Robert S. Yard, executive secretary of one of the conference's organizational sponsors, the National Parks Association, groused in a letter to his membership that "politics" rather than "purity of spirit" dominated the conference's agenda. He considered the organization's four-year effort a failure. It was not. Indeed, Yard was more accurate when he conceded that it was hard to understand "how it lasted."[70]

That any conference on federal recreation policy that included the competing bureaucracies of the Forest Service, the National Parks, the Bureau of Indian Affairs, the federal Land Office, and eight other agencies responsible for management of some part of the public domain did not dissolve within weeks was impressive. Its survival is even more notable since warring officials competed for conference attention with over forty, highly diverse, private groups. That conference organizers even attempted to reconcile the clashing views of such sponsoring groups as the America Bison Society, Sierra Club, American Automobile Association, and U.S. Chamber of Commerce invokes admiration.

Indeed, some federal agencies responded to conference queries with suspicion. The head of the Forest Service initially refused to comply with its requests for statistics about possible recreational use of public lands supervised by his agency. He did not want federal forests "overrun with campers." The chief of the Land Office argued that his agency assumed no responsibility for the nature of lands taken up by settlers, who were solely responsible for their use. This policy, he continued, could be more consistently followed if his employees "knew nothing" about the characteristics of land in the public domain. Consequently, he had no idea whether any of them possessed recreational possibilities.[71]

Groups like the Izaak Walton League and the Wild Flower Preservation Society lobbied conference leaders to ban tourist roads from national parks and forests. They condemned the nation's "blind hysteria for auto highways everywhere." National recreation policy should not fall victim to "fool road building" but should require that those seeking to use federal lands for pleasure do so on foot, horseback, or by canoe.[72] Needless to say, the membership of the American Automobile Association felt differently.

At their first official meeting conference leaders determined that their objective was to establish a "definitive" policy to govern the use and development of lands and natural resources under federal control and the expenditure of federal funds for purposes relating to outdoor recreation. Moreover, they hoped to "correlate" the activities of various branches of the federal government in the performance of duties that related to or influenced recreation. Over the next four years, Herbert Hoover, in his capacity as Secretary of Commerce and an honorary chair of the conference, kept in touch with its work. In May 1929, as the nation's new president, he received its official report in which it did recommend a clear policy: to dedicate "the public lands of the United States to the forms of use which yield the highest net return in permanent public benefit and human service; decision in each given case to be based on social as well as economic grounds, on collective as well as individual welfare."[73] Four years earlier, Calvin Coolidge had inaugurated the conference's work by announcing that "Our aim should be to place the chance for out of door pleasure within the grasp of the rank and file of our people, the little man as well as the big man."[74] To a remarkable degree, the Conference on Outdoor Recreation set in motion policies that reinforced that goal.

The conference during its brief life oversaw first-ever national surveys of municipal park and recreation systems and produced similar recreational surveys of state and federal lands, including all lands in the public domain, as well as national parks, monuments, forests, game refuges, and Indian reservations. The conference drafted and succeeded in shepherding through Congress a bill that allowed states, counties, and municipalities to acquire title at nominal cost to unappropriated federal lands it had classified as chiefly valuable for recreation purposes. Moreover, it successfully persuaded Congress to authorize the enlargement of the boundaries of several existing national parks, including Yellowstone, Mt. Rainier, Sequoia, and the Grand Canyon National Parks. It proposed, and Congress agreed, to create two new national parks, Shenandoah in Virginia and Great Smoky in North Carolina and Tennessee. Finally, it recommended, and Congress passed, a bill creating a National Arboretum in Washington.[75]

Calvin Coolidge had justified his creation of a National Conference on Outdoor Recreation by saying that against a "great and growing public demand for a place in the shade" was a "national trend toward reduction of the total available recreation areas as the process of conversion to industrial and economic development goes on."[76] As a result of the conference's actions, more public "places in the shade" existed in 1929 than in 1924. Moreover, an even more significant policy had become accepted: The nation should not only conserve its most beautiful public lands—it should use them intelligently as places of "wholesome" play.

RECREATION AND THE "RURAL CRISIS" REDUX

The alliance examined here between the Spelman Memorial, the Russell Sage Foundation, and the Playground and Recreation Association successfully engineered a revolution in recreation policy at local, state, and federal governmental levels. Worth noting in conclusion, however, is the fact that these policy changes overwhelmingly affected urban, not rural, Americans. This volume's case studies began with an examination of the "rural crisis," the Country Life Movement, and the birth of publicly sponsored vocational education. Fittingly, they should end there as well.

The urban elite who ran the country's government systems and established its few policy-making foundations did not want country people to head to the cities. They wanted to create public policies that made rural life more prosperous and attractive. The vocational education policies examined in chapter 2 did not do that; neither did the far more successful recreation policies discussed here.

Indeed, the subject caused the small number of play theorists who even discussed recreation for rural areas to flounder. Henry Curtis, a vice president of the Playground and Recreation Association and the Superintendent of New York City's public playgrounds, recognized that country people were often isolated and lonely and had little to do but work. He thought that regional "social centers" would help but conceded that many farm areas were unlikely to be able to afford them.

Without acknowledging the irony, Curtis recommended the "motion picture" as a "wonderfully effective teacher of moral lessons."[77] The same man who urged New York City's residents to scorn dimly lit motion picture theaters in favor of team sports and group singing thought that Thomas Edison's "Home Kinetoscope" could bring recreational salvation to the nation's rural population. A country church congregation or village council, he thought, should be able to afford its cost of only sixty-five dollars. Granted, commercial movies could not be shown on the machine. Even those made to accommodate its special one-inch film format "flickered." Nonetheless, Curtis brightly concluded he had recently enjoyed two Kinetoscope features. One portrayed the life of Moses; the other illustrated the differences in red blood cells after their infection with African sleeping sickness.[78] There is no evidence that many country people followed this or Curtis's other recommendations in his *Play and Recreation for the Open Country.* Perhaps those who read the book concluded they could have an equally jolly time following Wickliffe Rose's detailed instructions for building a sanitary privy. If demographics, and not policy recommendations, are to be believed, many rural adults, and even larger percentages of their young, began instead to plan their escape to the nearest town.

CONCLUSION/THE FOUNDATION COMES OF AGE

In 1929 Herbert Hoover appointed the five members of his President's Research Committee on Social Trends and charged them with an unprecedentedly ambitious mission—to assess in detail the direction of American culture. They were, said a *New Republic* editorialist, "qualified spies sent out to discover the nature of the country."[1] What they found was a nation torn by unequal rates of change—almost as if "the parts of an automobile were operating at unsynchronized speeds."[2]

The dramatic contrasts in organization and disorganization to be found side by side throughout American life provided Hoover's investigators with a theme to unify their massive report. It also provides a way to understand the roles played by the policy-making foundations. They were, most importantly, new institutions moving at a far faster pace than many other parts of the political structure, and because they were not yet synchronized as a part of an American polity, they first inspired confusion and fear. That fear, however, was largely unfounded. The foundations investigated here never constituted a shadow government, not at the beginning of the century nor at the beginning of the New Deal, and by the time Herbert Hoover ceded office to Franklin Roosevelt, the initial reaction to them had softened, if not entirely disappeared. By 1932 politicians more readily accepted organized philanthropy's place at the policy-making table. These foundations, in turn, became more astute, and often quite cautious, players in a pluralistic system that demanded power be shared and symbols be acknowledged.

Three topics, the failure of the Rockefeller Foundation to gain a federal charter, the activities of the U.S. Commission on Industrial Relations, and the public-private alliance created within Herbert Hoover's Research Committee on Social Trends, illustrate this process. Each provides a vehicle through which to make final judgments about private wealth's impact on public life in early-twentieth-century America.

THE ROCKEFELLER FOUNDATION CHARTER CONTROVERSY, 1910–1913

John D. Rockefeller Sr. could not have chosen a worse time to petition the U.S. Congress to incorporate another family philanthropy to be known as the Rockefeller Foundation, with a broadly stated purpose to "promote the well-being of the peoples of the United States and . . . of foreign lands." It was on 2 March 1910 that the bill's sponsor, Senator Jacob Gallinger of New Hampshire, announced that the proposed foundation, with an unspecified "significant" endowment, would be Senior's greatest gift yet to the nation and the world.[3] Not surprisingly, skepticism, rather than gratitude, greeted Gallinger's speech. In March 1910 the same federal government that Rockefeller was asking to grant a charter to his new philanthropy was demanding the dissolution of the vast Standard Oil empire as an illegal conspiracy in restraint of trade. After years of litigation and appeal, which had produced over fifteen thousand printed pages of testimony entered into federal circuit court records, the great Standard Oil case had entered its final stage—its ultimate appeal to the Supreme Court.[4]

Rockefeller Sr.'s decision to seek a federal charter was made in the face of protests by his longtime chief legal advisor, Starr Murphy. In Murphy's view, the idea of a philanthropy dedicated to the broadest of goals, the benefit of all human life, was a good one. He also liked the possibility that such an organization might eventually be used as an organizational device through which to consolidate all Rockefeller giving. But with seven federal suits against Standard Oil working their way through the courts, the Rockefellers' personal attorney counseled a low profile. The time was just not right, he pleaded, to petition Congress.

Practical legal reasons buttressed some of Murphy's objections. A federally chartered corporation would receive its incorporation papers in the District of Columbia, and as a "citizen" of the District, the new philanthropic organization would not be able to sue in federal court. This, worried Murphy, might cause serious problems in the future. Should a state legislature pass a law the foundation deemed hostile, it could find no refuge in the federal courts for redress.[5] Murphy's real concerns, however, were political. He thought that President Taft would curry favor on Capitol Hill by letting it be known quietly that he opposed a federal charter for a Rockefeller interest.

White House opposition, he said, was unlikely "to be open." But Murphy correctly predicted that "if it is concealed, it will be even more effective for that reason."[6]

Rather than face a potentially embarrassing firestorm in Washington, the Rockefellers should, Murphy insisted, seek a charter from the New York state legislature. The laws of the state expressly granted corporations of any type the right to do business in foreign countries, and state policy granted broad powers to charitable corporations, barring them only from breaking existing law and requiring them merely to file certificates explaining their activities with the state's supreme court. Moreover, the New York state legislature granted all charitable corporations an absolute exemption from taxation. Finally, and to Murphy, most important, "Mr. Rockefeller is much better known in this state, and . . . little political capital could be made by attempting to hold up a charter simply because his name was connected with it. . . . The state is open to big things in a financial way, and the influence of men of large affairs is apt to be more potent in the legislature of this state than in any other legislative body in the country."[7]

Rockefeller Sr. was certainly well aware of the hostility his business activities aroused. By 1910 Standard Oil was not only the most controversial of the great American trusts; it was among the most powerful—worth at least $660 million, able to produce forty thousand barrels of refined oil per day, and with control over hundreds of thousands of miles of company-owned pipeline and a vast world market serviced by the trust's fleet of one hundred tankers. Its practices had long aroused interest and fear. Since Ida Tarbell began publishing a series of articles about him in *McClure's,* Senior had emerged in American public imagination as the evil head of this corporate empire. He routinely received death threats and slept with a revolver under his pillow. Giving in to worried friends, the family had finally hired private guards from the Pinkerton Agency to accompany them when in public.[8]

Rockefeller Sr. should have followed his attorney's counsel. Instead, he accepted the advice of Jerome Greene, a newer member of his inner circle. General Education Board Trustee President Charles Eliot of Harvard University had brought his assistant to Frederick Gates's attention, and Greene, who acted as the university's chief administrative officer, reprised that role at the Rockefeller Institute for Medical Research before moving to the family offices.[9] In his new capacity as a personal aide, Greene convinced Rockefeller Sr. that Congress would see a federal charter not as an attempt by a powerful family to escape government control. Just the opposite. A request for such a charter would indicate that the Rockefellers were actually "courting" government supervision and that they had faith in the good will of the representatives of the entire population.[10]

Such "faith," if genuine, was misplaced. Senior may even have had a premonition of the public outcry to come. On the very day that Senator Gallinger introduced his bill, the elder Rockefeller met the press in New York City. Never garrulous, he could not be coaxed by reporters into disclosing his dreams for the proposed new foundation. Rather, he "smiled" and refused specific questions: "Just at this time, I don't care to have anything to say. I'll wait until I see what they are going to do there. However, you may rest assured it is not anything that'll do harm to anybody."[11]

Less than a week after Gallinger's introduction of a request for federal incorporation of a new Rockefeller philanthropy, the Senate's Committee on the District of Columbia favorably reported the bill back to the full body.[12] Such an auspicious beginning, however, quickly stalled, halted by a storm of public protest, exactly the "political" reaction Starr Murphy had anxiously prophesied. "Old Rockefeller," the *Los Angeles Record* thundered, wanted to use philanthropy to "squeeze himself, his son, his stall-fed collegians and their camels, laden with tainted money, through the 'eye of the needle.'"[13] A congressional charter would put the government behind Standard Oil and provide endorsement to the terrible methods by which Rockefeller Sr. had accumulated his immense fortune.

When newspapers across the country were not making biblical analogies to the inequities and dangers of concentrated wealth, they turned to Greek myth and repeatedly referred to the proposed Rockefeller Foundation as a "Trojan Horse," laden with menace to democracy.[14] Exasperated staff members in the Rockefeller family office belatedly realized what Starr Murphy had known all along: If Senior "had come out in favor of the Ten Commandments" many members of Congress would have taken to the floors of both chambers to denounce him.[15] On 22 March 1910, less than three weeks after its introduction, Senator Gallinger withdrew his Rockefeller Foundation charter bill.

The attempt to gain federal incorporation did not end there but would continue for three more years. Acting upon the advice of friendly critics, most prominently Edward Devine of *Survey,* the Rockefeller family office drafted a revised bill, and in June 1911 Gallinger placed it before the new Senate at its first session. The amended charter proposal specified that the total amount of the proposed foundation's endowment would be limited to $100,000,000, and that Congress would have the right, but not the duty, to dissolve the philanthropy and distribute all its funds as it chose after one hundred years. Moreover, a majority vote in a group composed of the president of the United States, the chief justice of the Supreme Court, the president of the Senate, the Speaker of the House of Representatives, and the presidents of Harvard University, Yale, Columbia, Johns Hopkins, and the University of Chicago could veto the election of any person to the new foundation's board of trustees.[16]

The Senate, however, did not pass the bill even as amended. Once again, timing was all-important. Weeks before the reintroduction of the Gallinger bill into the Senate's docket, the Supreme Court had finally decided the Standard Oil appeal and had decreed that the corporation's structure violated the Sherman Antitrust Act. The high court gave Standard Oil six months to divest itself of all its subsidiaries. The trust dissolved, and its investors received shares in thirty newly created, supposedly independent companies. The impact on Rockefeller Sr.'s huge fortune was dramatic. It vastly increased yet again.

This was not the outcome anybody welcoming the death of the oil trust would have predicted. In fact, when the separate Standard companies began trading stock on Wall Street, the market exploded in approval. In the biggest bull rally for a single stock issue in all of American history, the stock prices skyrocketed. The value of Standard of Indiana, for instance, tripled within a week. Rockefeller Sr., as a major stockholder in the new "Standards," garnered spectacular profits. In the space of a few months his personal worth probably increased by at least $200 million.[17] He became the nation's first billionaire. To many in Congress he seemed more dangerous than ever. The Supreme Court seemed to have delivered him a victory, not a defeat. John D. Rockefeller Sr. was more unstoppable and richer than ever, his wealth greater than that possessed by anyone in American history.

After two embarrassing Senate votes, the Rockefeller interests should have accepted defeat. Instead, uncharacteristically, Frederick Gates gave Rockefeller Sr. some very bad advice. He wrote the latter that he and President Taft had been invited in May 1911 to the same Bryn Mawr College dinner party. Although the subject never came up directly, Gates harbored the impression that the White House would no longer oppose a federal charter, and he urged Senior to reintroduce the bill, several times if necessary: "Even should it fail in successive sessions . . . I can see nothing but good from such agitation. It certainly cannot harm you. Your beneficent purpose will be manifest. . . . [It] will call the attention of wealthy men everywhere to their duty."[18] Rockefeller Sr.'s agreement to continue resubmitting his request for a charter to Congress called his philanthropic efforts to national attention all right, but again, only of the most painful sort.

In January 1912 Jerome Greene took over the family office's efforts to obtain a federal charter, leaving his position as general manager of the Rockefeller Institute. If the politically savvy Starr Murphy, who had reluctantly presented the charter case to the Senate in 1910 and 1911, could not win, then the politically still-innocent Greene was doomed from the start. Many years later, as the seasoned executive director of the Rockefeller Foundation, Greene recalled that "with the self-confidence and assurance of youth, I thought I had learned the ropes in Washington and was ready to tackle a more difficult job."[19] The victory inspiring him to aim higher had been his success in getting a private pension bill for his disabled brother through Congress. But Congress, after all, passed thousands of such bills every year. A federal charter for a foundation attached to the hated Rockefeller name was entirely another matter.

Rockefeller Sr.'s power was real; his wealth was enormous. If it is true that momentous events are best seen in miniature, his charter request might have provided an opportunity for a thoughtful consideration by the nation's leading politicians of economic trends and policies. Congressmen could have debated the proper public responses to great private fortunes. The unexpected aftermath of the dissolution of Standard Oil might even have prompted serious discussions about tax policy or the necessity to revise anti-trust legislation. Nothing remotely like this happened. Instead, the final debate on a federal charter for the proposed Rockefeller Foundation echoed the previous two.

The charter bill presented to the House of Representatives in February 1912 was essentially the same proposal that had been rejected by the Senate in June 1911. When the House Judiciary Committee reported the bill out for full debate, in April 1912, members of the House rivaled their Senate colleagues and staged yet another contest in vivid name-calling. Several dozen representatives led by Robert Fowler of Illinois pushed, shoved, jumped in place at their desks, and demanded that their opinions about Rockefeller Sr. be heard.

Fowler's repeatedly shouted invective, "Viper, viper; he is a viper!" set the tone. Jerome Greene only gradually came to understand that all the shouting was not even over a yea or nay final vote. Fowler had achieved a legislative sleight of hand. The Rockefeller Charter bill had come up before the House on a Unanimous Consent Calendar. Since, obviously, not all members of the body agreed to consent to actually debate it, the bill was stricken from the House's April calendar.[20]

During the summer and fall of 1912 Greene received a crash course in congressional procedures that led him to write in despair to a friend. "The stupidity and cowardice of members of the House," he said, "is enough to make angels weep."[21] Greene learned the difference between Unanimous Consent and Suspension Calendars, the necessity of courting the Speaker to achieve recognition of a move to suspend rules, and the importance of accurately timed telegram campaigns to secure a particular politician's interest. He came to understand that the new Speaker of the House, Champ Clark of Missouri, was immensely ambitious and that flattering talk about "his presidential boom" got good results. He realized that many southern politicians, shown balance sheets for the amount of money spent by the General Education Board in their states, could be counted as allies. When the bill finally came to a vote in the House on 20 January 1913, southern Democrats did provide the winning majority.[22]

Yet when the bill returned to the Senate in March 1913, Greene learned that the support of southern congressmen was not enough. In the upper house, he faced the determined opposition of several important senators, including William Borah of Idaho, Robert La Follette of Wisconsin, and Hoke Smith of Georgia. This unusual partnership of a conservative isolationist Republican, a liberal midwestern Progressive, and a populist southern Democrat had been formed in the climate of national unease caused by a frighteningly bloody wave of strikes and labor violence that had engulfed the country since October 1910, when a massive bomb destroyed the Los Angeles *Times* building, killing twenty people and shattering windows throughout the city.[23] Borah, La Follette, and Smith were adamant: any government endorsement of the Rockefellers would encourage more unrest. The three led a successful filibuster that prevented the charter proposal from ever coming to a vote in the Senate.

On 3 March 1913 the Sixty-second Congress was scheduled to adjourn. At 8:30 P.M. that day an exhausted Jerome Greene arrived on the floor of the Senate, which was still in session, but with only two senators present, one of whom was Hoke Smith, orating about the virtues of Georgia's peaches. Greene, seeing Smith "in possession of the field, hauled down the flag and took the eleven o'clock train for New York."[24]

After three years of frustration, the Rockefeller office finally followed Starr Murphy's original advice and petitioned the New York State Legislature for a charter. Greene approached Robert Wagner, the Republican leader of the state senate, who told him to get Senator William Foley to introduce the bill. As Greene described it, "I went . . . prepared with an abundance of arguments and data, but had no sooner started to inflict them upon him when he stopped me with the remark, 'Say, write a letter.' When I started to walk away, he called me back and said, 'Say, don't make it more than one page.' "[25]

The bill was quickly introduced and passed in both houses unanimously, taking far less time than a measure that prohibited bootblacking in New York after 3 P.M. on Sundays.[26] In fact, the legislature passed the charter bill with such speed and so little discussion that conspiracy-minded critics of the Rockefellers persisted for years in charges that no charter had ever been issued. As late as 1926, Julius Rosenwald, a Rockefeller Foundation trustee, received letters demanding that he resign from an organization "whose widely proclaimed charter . . . is as nonexistent as the lost tribes of the Children of Israel."[27] The charter did exist, but it came at the price of painful political lessons. When Jerome Greene sent him a draft of a possible public notice about the plans of the new foundation, John D. Rockefeller Jr. replied, "When things are really going and something definite has been accomplished let us make a public announcement, but in my judgment, not before. Especially would I be disposed to avoid publicity at this time in view of the political, and social, and financial unrest of the country and also in view of the fact that the charter was not secured from Congress but from the state."[28]

Rockefeller Jr.'s fervent wish to spend time "in the privacy of our own office, rather than before the public eye" was to be denied.[29] Instead, no sooner had one struggle between Rockefeller philanthropy and a government institution ended than another began.

THE ROCKEFELLER FOUNDATION AND THE U.S. COMMISSION ON INDUSTRIAL RELATIONS, 1913–1915

Between 1913 and 1915 a congressionally authorized investigatory body, the U.S. Commission on Industrial Relations, explored the causes of American industrial violence. Its chair, Frank Walsh, singled out the Rockefeller family's "huge philanthropic trusts as a menace to the welfare of society." Indeed, Walsh charged that they were "attempts to present to the world, as handsome and admirable, an economic and industrial regime that draws its substance from the sweat and blood and tears of exploited and dispossessed humanity."[30]

Interestingly, though, organized philanthropy was at least partly responsible for the creation of the Industrial Relations Commission. When California officials arrested John McNamara, national secretary of the Bridge and Structural Iron Workers and his brother James, charging both with masterminding the dynamiting of the *Times* headquarters, organized labor reacted with outrage. Convinced of a frame-up, A. F. of L. President Samuel Gompers raised money for a defense fund and hired famous Chicago attorney Clarence Darrow to represent the accused. The resulting trial riveted national attention, especially when it ended in a shocking surprise: John McNamara's courtroom confession that he had planned the bombing. The McNamara case prompted Edward Devine of *Survey* to call together reformers, industrialists, and union leaders in a series of symposia on the causes of unrest in America, and the Russell Sage Foundation, longtime financial patron of *Survey,* soon joined in the call for a national commission on industrial relations.

So did Julius Rosenwald, who provided operating funds for a fifty-three person committee organized by Devine to lobby Congress to create a federal Commission on Industrial Relations. As Russell Sage's director John Glenn explained, "Bad as dynamiting is, it is a comparatively small feature of our present-day history. We . . . only dimly realize the extent of growing evils which threaten national life. Labor questions must be dealt with in an intelligent and practical way, or our national vitality . . . will be sapped. . . . Only government can get at the whole truth through its power to compel testimony and enter private premises. . . . I believe only by commissions shall we . . . lay a foundation for discovering proper remedies."[31]

Congress agreed. Within six months after prison doors closed on the McNamara brothers, it had enacted legislation authorizing the president to nominate, subject to congressional approval, a nine-person commission, three each from labor, management, and the general public, with a mandate to submit a report within three years. The new U.S. Commission on Industrial Relations received a $100,000 budget, the right to hold hearings anywhere in the United States, and the ability to subpoena any witnesses it chose to question. In August 1912 President Taft signed the bill but delayed announcing his choices for commission membership until after the November election. It was a mistake. After November 1912, Democrats did not want to grant the now-lame-duck president many prerogatives, and a Senate filibuster prevented Taft's nominees from ever receiving approval.[32]

Once inaugurated, Woodrow Wilson retained some of Taft's proposed appointments but also made several changes, one of which dramatically altered the nature of the commission. The president nominated Frank Walsh, a prominent Kansas City trial attorney, as one of its three public representatives, as well as chair. Before Wilson's announcement, rumors had circulated that the commission's chair would be the eminent jurist Louis Brandeis, but Brandeis may have offended the president by his insistence on giving Frank Bohn, editor of the *International Socialist Review* and a former I.W.W. official, a seat.[33] Wilson knew that naming a labor radical would alienate the A. F. of L. Perhaps by naming Walsh, a Democratic member of the Kansas City Board of Public Welfare, who was widely known to be friendly to moderate socialism, he hoped to facilitate a consensus.

With Brandeis as its head, the commission might have had an entirely different history. But Walsh quickly made it a forum for his strongly held views and in the process bitterly divided its membership and weakened its final influence. Walsh's fellow members representing the public were University of Wisconsin economist John Commons and Daisy Harriman, whose fortune came from banking and railroads and whose influence with Wilson stemmed from her public support for him, rather than Champ Clark, during the Democratic Convention of 1912. Representing labor were prominent members of mainstream trade unions: Austin Garretson, president of the Railroad Conductors, James O'Connell, head of the A. F. of L.'s Metal Trades Department, and John Lennon, the A. F. of L.'s treasurer. Of the businessmen, one, Frederick Delano, was a Chicago resident and former president of the Wabash Railroad; another, Thurston Ballard, was a Louisville, Kentucky, mill owner; and the third, Harris Weinstock, was a clothing merchandiser from San Francisco.[34]

In the fall of 1913, the members of this commission met together for the first time, and in the winter of 1914, armed with a supplemental budget of $200,000, they began their work in earnest, choosing a two-pronged approach to fulfill its mandate to uncover the causes of America's labor unrest. Professor Commons assembled a team of researchers, many of them his former students, and set them to work collecting evidence. Would a typical wage for an American adult male support a family? How often did the average worker face unemployment? What kinds of conditions occurred in American workplaces? What kinds of housing, food, and recreation could American workers afford? While its Research Division assembled answers to these and hundreds of other questions in Washington, commission members themselves took to the road. Between March 1914 and February 1915, they conducted official hearings in dozens of cities, concluding with a series of dramatic sessions held in January and February 1915 in New York City.[35]

Again, timing proved fateful, for even a nation numbed by three years of unprecedented industrial violence reacted with horror in the spring of

1914 to what could only be described as class warfare in the coal fields of Colorado. In 1913 and 1914 strikes had turned into bloody riots all over the country, from the silk mills of Paterson, New Jersey, to the hop fields of California. In Colorado, however, many observers believed that civilian government itself had collapsed. Strung out along isolated canyons, the state's mining camps were squalid company towns, whose owners forbade their employees to construct their own dwellings but instead forced them to pay high rents for flimsy shacks or leaky sod dugouts. Streets were unpaved, adequate sanitation almost unknown. In some camps, parts of dead rats regularly appeared in pump water, and in others, human feces floated in cesspools overflowing onto main streets. Typhoid outbreaks were common. Workers who protested these abominable conditions risked the loss of job, housing, and even the right to remain in a state where mine operators rigged elections and openly controlled politicians. When the United Mine Workers sought to organize the coal fields of Colorado in 1913, nobody was surprised that operators refused absolutely to negotiate.

Instead, both sides prepared for war. By the fall of 1913, some ten thousand miners had piled their pitifully few possessions into carts, and, by late 1913, moved into tent colonies established by the U.M.W. One of the largest, at Ludlow, housed about a thousand striking workers, their wives, and children, all of whom lived in large pitlike trenches dug into the ground and covered by canvas sheeting draped on tree trunks. At least half of the state's coal miners were now in rebellion, and Colorado operators prepared a counterattack. Led by the largest company, Colorado Fuel and Iron, mine owners built trenches around their properties, deployed privately hired detectives, installed searchlights, bought hundreds of machine guns, and convinced Colorado's governor to call out units of the National Guard for further protection. Strikers, in turn, openly acquired weapons. Disaster was virtually inevitable.

It came on 20 April 1914 at the Ludlow colony when a fierce battle erupted between guardsmen and strikers. For over twelve hours miners and troops hid behind the large mounds of dirt left when the pits had first been dug, raining fire on each other, while hundreds of women and children huddled underground between them, seeking safety in the muddy holes that served them as temporary housing. In the melee, the canvas coverings of the three largest pits caught fire, and soon, the entire tent colony was an inferno of choking black smoke. Women and children stumbled around blindly, trying to escape. Not all did. Rescuers found the burned bodies of two women and eleven children in the rubble.[36]

These charred remains became for many Americans a potent symbol.

They thrust the fact-finding travels of the Commission on Industrial Relations onto the front pages of the nation's newspapers. Frank Walsh promptly
changed its schedule and held its first major hearings in Denver, not Chicago,
in order to question directly union leaders, government officials, and mine
owners about the Ludlow debacle.

From the very beginning, then, the shadow of the Ludlow Massacre
hung over the commission's inquiries, and, since Colorado Fuel and Iron was
a Rockefeller-owned subsidiary, so too did the name of America's most hated
man. Rockefeller Sr. owned 40 percent of the company's stock as well as
much of its bonded debt, while Junior, Starr Murphy, and Jerome Greene
represented him on its board of directors. Rockefeller control of Colorado
Fuel and Iron provided Frank Walsh with a chance to exercise his oratorical
skills. Traveling throughout the country with his fellow commissioners,
Walsh repeatedly gave interviews naming the Rockefeller empire as the evil
heart of economic wrong in the country. In October 1914, when he received
word that Rockefeller Jr. had hired former Canadian labor minister Mackenzie King to conduct a far-reaching study of problems of industrial relations,
Walsh became convinced that the younger Rockefeller sought to thwart the
efforts of his commission.[37]

Rockefeller Sr.'s petition to Congress to grant a charter for the Rockefeller Foundation coincided with efforts by the Department of Justice to
dissolve Standard Oil. Rockefeller Jr.'s decision to fund studies of industrial
relations coincided with the investigations of American industrial relations
already being conducted by a federal commission. Both actions reflected
political naiveté much more than they did efforts by either man to use philanthropy as a cloak behind which to hide business misdeeds. Yet it seems all too
clear that both were also spectacularly ill timed and ill advised. By January
1915, when the members of the Industrial Relations Commission arrived in
New York City, Frank Walsh had decided to focus his final hearings on the
menace posed by foundation philanthropy.

Neither the Rosenwald nor Commonwealth Funds existed in 1915,
though Julius Rosenwald testified before the commission when it held hearings in Chicago and earned favorable comment as a fair employer. The major
foundations Walsh proposed to investigate were those established by Andrew
Carnegie, John D. Rockefeller Sr., and Olivia Sage. Andrew Carnegie appeared to answer questions about his philanthropies as did John Glenn for the
Russell Sage Foundation.[38]

Despite his statements to the contrary, Walsh's purpose was not a dispassionate investigation of the activities of major foundations. Andrew Carnegie

seized the occasion to play to the audience. Ignoring Walsh, the old man smiled broadly, turned his back on commission members, and began a rambling speech on the beauty of women's faces, the necessity of woman suffrage, and the glories of spring in Scotland. As a flamboyant trial attorney, Frank Walsh knew when he had a witness he could not control. Moreover, "Merry Andrew" was never his real target. In short order, Walsh thanked Carnegie for his time and dismissed him.[39]

John Glenn arrived ready to answer any questions but instead spent most of his time listening quietly to praise for his efforts as a member of the committee organized by Edward Devine that had originally lobbied Congress to create the commission in the first place. Had they wished to do so, commission members could easily have learned that, from its inception in 1907, the Russell Sage Foundation had been allied with Rockefeller philanthropies, sharing information, advice, and long-term goals, but these connections were never explored. John Glenn quickly realized that the so-called commission investigation of American foundations was really to be a loaded examination of the Rockefeller philanthropies.

That did not mean he absented himself once dismissed from the witness stand. After all, the commission hearings were open. When Glenn was unable to attend personally, he delegated numerous staff members to take notes and hired a court stenographer to produce for Russell Sage files a complete transcript of each day's testimony. By the end of February 1915 over a dozen Russell Sage Foundation staff members had filed lengthy reports with Glenn.

Acting as a Greek chorus to the main dramatic action, these Russell Sage Foundation officers spared no one on a commission they judged to be inept and hopelessly politicized. For Clarence Perry, the commissioners were a "body of people engaged in taking pot shots at game which they have not yet clearly located."[40] According to Franz Schneider, of the Department of Surveys, Walsh was "suprisingly young . . . and with an air of cheapness about him . . . not big enough for the job"; unionists O'Connell and Garretson were "failures"; O'Connell was "not a clever questioner"; and Garretson "has a funny loud bellowy way of asking questions." Professor Commons was, as usual, absent, and Daisy Harriman was, as usual, "posing." Harris Weinstock tried hard, but "was not able."[41]

Russell Sage staffers drew a damning portrait of commissioners who acted like poorly prepared court examiners seeking to discredit evidence rather than learn the truth. They described an atmosphere of discourtesy and disarray, where Walsh chewed gum noisily or ostentatiously read newspapers when a witness answered questions in ways that displeased him. Other commissioners frequently looked over their mail, shuffled papers, and sorted clippings.[42] No wonder Andrew Carnegie had felt free to turn his back and deliver a speech on the splendors of womanhood.

Edna Bryner, a Russell Sage statistician, accurately observed that "I do not feel [Walsh] desires to know the truth about foundations, how they conduct their work, and what the results to the community are, but rather to catch them doing something that can be construed as premeditated evil."[43]

Although the commission called dozens of others witnesses, Walsh's focus was clear: the Rockefellers and their employees and the "premeditated evil" of the Rockefeller philanthropies. Rockefeller Sr., however, proved, in his own way, as difficult to challenge as Andrew Carnegie. He portrayed himself as long retired and unable to "speak intelligently on affairs of business." Yes, he was a trustee of the Rockefeller Foundation. But he never attended its meetings, and if staff members like Jerome Greene or Starr Murphy journeyed to Senior's Tarrytown, New York, estate, they came merely to enjoy sociable dinners with his son.[44] Senior was not literally lying. He did indeed stay away from the family's New York City's offices at 26 Broadway, but, by no means, was he the disinterested old gentleman his self-portrait described. Until at least 1916, he received regular reports on all Rockefeller companies. Moreover, he had only just begun to transfer significant assets and authority over both family philanthropic and business enterprises to Junior.

Deprived of a target by Rockefeller Sr.'s successful evasion tactics, Frank Walsh turned his attention to Rockefeller Jr. and the Rockefeller Foundation's executive administrator, Jerome Greene. During two days of relentless questioning of Junior, Walsh sought to demonstrate that the Rockefeller businesses and philanthropies were indistinguishable. Both controlled great wealth. Neither was subject to significant public scrutiny. Indeed, Walsh badgered Junior into admitting that the divisions in the roles he played as philanthropist and corporate director were "irregular": "I might spend all of today on matters bearing on the Foundation. I might spend no time for a week. I might spend tomorrow, half an hour on matters connected with the General Education Board."[45]

When Walsh portrayed the Rockefeller philanthropies as huge entities on whose boards sat only trusted members of the family's inner circle of advisors, responsible only to their employers and not the public, Rockefeller Jr. answered, "The larger the foundation is, the safer it is because the more sure it is to attract very general public interest."[46] But he admitted that Rockefeller philanthropic boards did include significant numbers of salaried employees or business associates of the family. Moreover, the boards met rarely. To Walsh's question, "Are the minutes of the meetings printed?" Junior answered, "The minutes of the meetings are typewritten and sent to the—I am not sure whether they are sent to the members, or simply laid on the table at current meetings. I have forgotten which."[47]

Turning next to the executive secretary of the Rockefeller Foundation, Walsh sought to reinforce his developing picture of the Rockefeller philanthropies as remote organizations, free of meaningful public control and able to do what they wished with vast tax-exempt resources. Peppering Jerome Greene with a series of questions for which he demanded a "yes" or "no" answer, Walsh asked,

> Q: Could the foundation conduct propaganda against trade unions?
> A: I can imagine it making a start in that direction; I cannot imagine anything more atrocious.
> Q: That is, your answer is yes, that the Foundation might, if it wished, conduct a propaganda against trade unionism?
> A: Yes.[48]

After a series of such questions, as Walsh probed to discover the theoretical limits of the Rockefeller Foundation's power and suggested that at some time in the future the philanthropy might become a champion of free trade, or protectionism, or socialism, or Buddhism, or the programs of the Democratic or Republican Party, Greene angrily exploded:

> A: Yes, Yes: I have got the opportunity of going out into the street and firing off a gun and killing somebody.
> Q: [Interrupting]: The misuse of a legally granted power, to go out and kill a man?
> A: What I mean is liberty to do wrong . . . is the commonest attribute . . . of complete human liberty. Persons who have entrusted to them important responsibilities have the power for a while by complete lapse of ethics, morality, and law of doing a lot of mischief, but it does not take any particular legal knowledge to know that.[49]

As Greene's furious response demonstrated, Walsh had spent days destroying a straw man. He offered no proof that the Rockefeller Foundation or any of the other Rockefeller philanthropies posed a menace to democracy but showed only that their actions were not subject to a majority vote of the American people, which nobody had ever denied.

Yet in an ironic way Frank Walsh's attack on the Rockefeller philanthropies paved the way for a greater acceptance of philanthropy's place as one of many public policy makers. Given the scope of the inquiry, Walsh felt that the American people would agree that his investigations proved organized philanthropy to be a danger to polity and society. In fact, not even all his fellow commissioners agreed with him. In January 1915 Franz Schneider of the Russell Sage Foundation prophetically sized up the members of the Commission on Industrial Relations and predicted that they would be unable to complete a final report. "Their morale," he concluded, "is not high. They waste a lot of time in amateurish interrogation and do not seem to have much of a grip on their problem."[50]

In late February 1915, faced with an August 1915 deadline to complete their investigations, submit an official report, and disband, the members of the commission split into warring camps. Walsh fired Charles McCarthy, the Wisconsin-trained historian Commons had secured to head the commission's research team, charging him with secretly coaching John D. Rockefeller Jr. for his appearance before the commission, pointedly noting that the two men had been friends since their undergraduate days together at Brown University.

Walsh never produced definitive evidence that McCarthy had acted in an illegal or even an unethical manner. All he had were several letters from McCarthy to Rockefeller Jr. containing pleas from McCarthy that the latter cease his own independent industrial relations investigations. McCarthy was naive to send them, as Junior was naive to hire Mackenzie King while the members of the Commission on Industrial Relations barnstormed the country. When Walsh replaced McCarthy with Basil Manly, a former publicist for the A. F. of L., the discord that had always simmered just below the surface within the commission exploded into very public rage. Commons and other commissioners rushed to McCarthy's defense. Frederick Delano resigned in disgust. Each side held bitter press conferences.[51]

As a member of the committee that had urged the establishment of a Commission on Industrial Relations in the wake of the Los Angeles *Times* bombing, prominent journalist Lincoln Steffens had argued that crucial to the body's success would be the careful choice of its members. They should, to be sure, represent employers, employees, and the public. However, all should be distinguished and open-minded citizens willing to listen and learn. "We must," Steffens urged, "see why a labor man throws a brick. The question is not 'who did it?' but 'what did it?' "[52]

Commission members could not even agree about "who" did it, much less "what did it." The body's final report included not one, but two separate statements, one crafted by Basil Manly and sanctioned by Walsh, Lennon, O'Connell, and Garretson. The other, written by John Commons, was signed by Harriman, Weinstock, Ballard, and Richard Aishton, the Illinois manufacturer who had replaced Delano during the commission's final few months of existence. Indeed, there were really seven final reports, since the three labor members, and two representatives from business chose to supplement their signatures with written dissents.

The report authored by Basil Manly argued that unjust distribution of wealth was the primary cause of industrial unrest in the country. Americans believed in the "fundamental" idea that "income should be received for service, whereas, in fact, it bears no such relations. He who serves least, or not at all, may receive most."[53] Working girls went hungry on fifteen-cent suppers, while the rulers of "invisible industrial principalities" engorged themselves. The structures of these "petty kingdoms" of wealth, including philanthropic foundations, should be destroyed through new systems of confiscatory inheritance taxes. Foundations, far from being beneficial to society, allowed the very rich to keep yet more of the wealth that really belonged to the American people. The funds that foundations administered were ill-gotten gains, won through low wages or high prices.[54]

While it was ultimately desirable that all foundations be abolished, the Manly report urged Congress in the short term to enact legislation providing that all incorporated charitable organizations whose charters empowered them to perform more than a single specific function and whose funds exceeded $1 million be required to secure a federal charter. The Rockefeller Foundation, already denied a federal charter, "should be taken over and used by the State for the creation of public works that will minimize the deplorable evil of unemployment . . . for the creation of sickness and accident funds for workers, and for other legitimate purposes . . . directly beneficial to the laborers who really contributed the funds."[55]

Far from damning foundations, however, John Commons argued that "many of these endowments in private hands have a beneficial effect on the work of governmental institutions."[56] The chief cause of industrial unrest, he maintained, was not low wages, but conflicting, ambiguous, unenforced, and unenforceable laws. Government had to do better if the American people were to retain confidence in it, and foundations, by collecting accurate information, could help government in the essential immediate task of restoration of public faith. "While recognizing the justice of much of this demand for [them]," Commons and his supporters urged that legislatures not enact any new laws affecting topics like wages, hours, or unemployment. First, the nation had to engage experts to recommend better methods of enacting, interpreting, and administering laws.[57]

Employer representatives Ballard and Weinstock signed the Commons report but in supplementary statements made clear their strong belief that yet a third primary problem explained the high level of conflict between workers and employers in America. Although it was true that some employers were "guilty of much wrongdoing," contests for supremacy between rival unions had bloodied the country. After all, had their colleagues forgotten that a bomb set off by a union official brought the Commission on Industrial Relations to life?[58]

The commissioners need never have spent almost three years' time and hundreds of thousands of dollars. The conclusions they reached about the causes of industrial violence were the ones they brought with them when appointed. Labor representatives and their ally Frank Walsh blamed greedy plutocrats. Businessmen blamed the unions. Academics demanded further study. Nobody paid attention to any of them, and the final report of the Commission on Industrial Relations quickly disappeared, subsumed by the preparations for the war that the United States finally entered in 1917.

HERBERT HOOVER'S RESEARCH COMMITTEE ON SOCIAL TRENDS, 1929–1932

The Great War against Germany had begun, but, effectively, the war on the Rockefeller family ended. To use Carl Sandburg's apt phrase, "the fierce white light" of attention the nation had focused on Rockefeller Sr. as evil symbol of an age began to fade. Indeed, Sandburg himself stopped writing articles about "Poison Ivy Lee" and the other "soft-handed, long-headed, high-salaried" lawyers, preachers, and newspaper men who surrounded the "cruelest" businessman in America.[59]

In 1915 the faction within the U.S. Commission on Industrial Relations led by John Commons called for another major governmentally appointed commission—this one to be comprised of experts who would study all aspects of national life. Without the knowledge that such a complete compilation of data about social conditions would unearth, Commons feared that laws would remain unenforceable words on paper. In 1929, a little more than a decade later, President Herbert Hoover created just such a commission: the President's Research Committee on Social Trends. The fact that the Rockefeller Foundation provided a $600,000 grant to sustain the committee's work over three years, between 1929 and 1933, was never secret. Rather, it

John D. Rockefeller Sr. in Carl Sandburg's "The Two Mr. Rockefellers—and Mr. Walsh."
International Socialist Review 16 (1915): 19.

was widely reported in the press.[60] Moreover, committee members, in their sixteen hundred page final report as well as in thirteen supporting volumes of published documents, acknowledged that the foundation's help was crucial.

By 1929 Rockefeller Sr. had turned ninety and was very frail. Nobody seriously challenged any more the veracity of his statements about retirement. He had fully turned over his affairs to Rockefeller Jr., who, in turn, no longer mixed business with philanthropy but devoted himself full time to the latter. Junior had considerable talent, but he was not a man shaped in his father's mold. He would never inspire the same kind of awe and dread, nor would the companies and philanthropies that continued to bear the Rockefeller name.

The Rockefeller Foundation did not fund the investigations of the Walsh Commission. Instead, its leaders came before it as hostile witnesses answering subpoenas. It did back the work of Hoover's committee, which among dozens of other topics judged the state of industrial relations in America. The decade that separated the work of these two presidentially appointed fact-finding groups had allowed a gentler Rockefeller image to begin to emerge. Frank Walsh heaped scorn on the Rockefeller Foundation as menacing enemy territory within an "evil industrial principality." Wesley Mitchell, the Columbia University economist who chaired Hoover's Research Committee, thanked the foundation for its "generous support."[61] Such a dramatic change in public pronouncements is worth noting, but it does not suggest that foundations had taken over social policy making. Whether hated or thanked, the Rockefeller Foundation, in common with a few other charitable foundations, consistently wanted to shape social policy. However, it never unilaterally controlled any significant aspect of domestic public policy making, neither when seen as enemy, nor when praised as friend.

The massive report issued in 1933 by Hoover's committee was one of the most serious efforts any nation has ever made to take a truly candid self-portrait.[62] Unlike their predecessors on the Commission on Industrial Relations, Hoover's appointees tried to be impartial experts, obeying their chief executive's frequently repeated mantra: "Sound data makes sound policy."[63] President Wilson should have denounced his commission for incompetence but did not. President Hoover should have praised his but did not.[64]

Politics determined both presidents' decisions, and political considerations, above all, sealed the fate of the final reports of the Commission on Industrial Relations and the Research Committee on Social Trends. Both disappeared almost instantly, as if hundreds of thousands of dollars had never been spent, as if armies of experts had not been consulted, as if, in each case, three years and forests of paper had not been devoted to the cause.

The fact that the Rockefeller Foundation hated the conclusions of one and sponsored those of the other did not make either an effective tool for social policy making.

Nonetheless, Herbert Hoover, the quintessential technocrat, explicitly intended to create such an aid to domestic policy making. He wanted to appoint leaders of new fields in social science to direct the most ambitious review of American life ever undertaken. Shortly after his inaugural, he asked French Strother, a member of the White House administrative staff, to seek private funding for this vastly ambitious project. Strother looked first to the Rockefeller Foundation. In October 1929 he contacted George Vincent, president of the foundation, urging his support for a "programme of scientific research into fundamental phases of social relations . . . to produce a rounded and explicit picture of the whole American social scene, with such a wealth of facts and statistics and conclusions as to form a new and unique basis of thought . . . for those officers of government who [like President Hoover] have a special responsibility in relation to such problems." Vincent, in turn, requested that the proposal be judged by the director of the foundation's new Division of Social Science, Edmund Day, a former Harvard economics professor who had replaced Beardsley Ruml when the Spelman Memorial merged with the Rockefeller Foundation.[65]

In fact, Day already knew about Hoover's plans. A month before, his friend, University of Chicago sociologist William Ogburn, had written "informally and not exactly for your files." He had, Ogburn said, been invited to dinner at the White House along with Wesley Mitchell, University of Chicago political scientist Charles Merriam, University of North Carolina sociologist Howard Odum, and the director of the Russell Sage Foundation's Department of Surveys, Shelby Harrison. This group of eminent social scientists had been asked to assemble because Hoover was "very much interested in doing something in a large way in fields . . . touching human welfare." Promising to keep Day fully informed of all developments, Ogburn ended his confidential letter with regret: "Personally, I am very sorry to have a situation such that you can't very well accept an invitation to the White House, so left your name off."[66]

Some of the old bad odor still clung to the Rockefeller name, but notably, Shelby Harrison's name was not left off, and he, along with the other four men summoned to Hoover's dinner in September 1929, accepted another presidential invitation: to constitute the Research Committee on Social Trends. Day, moreover, was quick to lend his enthusiastic support, and in short order the Rockefeller Foundation agreed to fund Hoover's project. Not only did it grant outright the money necessary to cover the committee's costs for research, conferences, travel, and publication, it also provided help in kind. Lawrence Frank, who had moved from the now defunct Spelman Memorial to the General Education Board, received a two-year fully paid leave to work as a researcher for the committee. Several members of the Social Science Division labored for months at a time compiling materials to send to William Ogburn, who had assumed the job of head editor for the project's publications, and both Frank and Sydnor Walker wrote chapters that appeared in the committee's final report. Significantly too, all of this support was openly given. Frank's and Walker's names, along with their Rockefeller affiliations, appeared under their chapter titles, just as did the names of all other authors. The only constraint seemed to be the one evident at the project's start, namely, that it was best that a representative of the Russell Sage Foundation, not the Rockefeller Foundation, sit as an actual committee member.[67]

The initial press reaction to the announcement that Hoover had appointed yet another commission was generally enthusiastic. Historian Mark Sullivan, writing in the New York *Herald Tribune Magazine,* predicted that the research committee would produce "results such as may cause this to seem, a quarter century from now, the most important aspect of American history that coincided with the Hoover Administration."[68] Of course, Will Rogers kept things in perspective. He wrote:

> I always felt there was only one thing that could possibly defeat Mr. Hoover's capable management of our affairs, and that was when he ran out of practical men to put on commissions. Sure enough, he is getting short-handed. Yesterday's commission didn't have a practical man on it. Every one was a college professor. It's to find out "what has brought the social changes in our lives here lately." Knowing college professors, he gave them three years to agree on an answer. I could have told him before sundown: buying on credit, Ford cars, too many Republicans, Notre Dame coaching methods, and two-thirds of Americans, old and young, thinking they possessed "it."[69]

Even without Will Rogers's blessing, the members of the Committee on Social Trends began work with high hopes, sure that they would create a body of data that would be used to shape social policy in conformity with the altered conditions of life. Although Mitchell and Merriam acted as chair and vice chair of the committee, the sociologists Ogburn and Odum were its true leaders. Together they contacted hundreds of fellow academics, as well as government researchers, legal theorists, and economists and statisticians working in the private sector. More than five hundred such experts contributed to the research and publications efforts of the committee.

Ogburn had assured Edmund Day that "as a man of experience" Hoover would not be "inclined to butt in on details."[70] He was wrong. Indeed, if he had studied the committee's relationships with the six commissions he had already appointed by December 1929, when the creation of the Committee on Social Trends was announced, Ogburn would have learned that Hoover or a designated alternate practiced micro-management of all bodies associated with the White House. Hoover had appointed narrowly focused groups—a commission appointed, for instance, to consider joint federal-state solutions to the problem of building a bridge across San Francisco Bay. He had also created those with a broad mandate—a commission organized to promote overseas sales of American goods. However, each of Herbert Hoover's commissions was expected to keep in close touch.[71]

For instance, when Hoover decided that it would "strengthen public feeling" toward its work if the committee included a woman member, he personally wrote to Wesley Mitchell arguing that such an appointment should be quickly made.[72] Odum and Mitchell recommended that he appoint Neva Deardorf, head of the research division of the New York Welfare Federation. They knew that Deardorf was unknown outside of the academic community, so both additionally agreed that if Hoover wanted "some eminent woman whose function would be advisory membership rather than working membership" he should choose Jane Addams.[73] The president appointed neither but instead surprised the men on his committee with his decision to name public health activist Alice Hamilton of the Harvard Medical School.[74]

Hoover's concern about the absence of a woman on the research committee reflected a fact insufficiently acknowledged by the hundreds of experts at work surveying America's social trends. The president was not a disinterested fellow social scientist, and his agenda was, above all, a political one. William Ogburn proved a better prophet when in another confidential letter sent before the formal appointment of the research committee, he speculated to Shelby Harrison that "Hoover has ambition of doing something conspicuous in this field [of human welfare] to offset the growing myth about his having a cold engineering mind."[75]

By 1932 Edward Hunt, an undersecretary in the Department of Commerce who often acted as the president's trusted liaison with appointed commissions and attended almost all of the Committee on Social Trends meetings, could have reported back to the White House that the emerging report on American social trends was not likely to be politically helpful in the coming campaign. Charles Merriam admitted privately that recommending social policies as the depression worsened seemed ever harder. "We started out with faith, you know, of walking on the waters," he said, "but we fell in a little bit as we went along."[76]

Merriam's comment unwittingly summarized the Rockefeller Foundation's agenda as well. Its support of the social trends committee reflected a belief that carefully and scientifically collected information was a key to good social policy making. Herbert Hoover's faith in the connections between "sound data and sound policy" echoed that view, but Hoover had no chance to implement policies derived from the mountain of evidence his experts created. The Rockefeller Foundation was to learn that data alone would not float on the waters of political pluralism. The research committee's policy advice did not just "fall in a little bit." It sank out of sight.

By 10 November 1932, when page proofs of the research committee's huge final report were first available, Herbert Hoover had suffered a bitter defeat. William Ogburn wrote French Strother, "I am so sorry that it is coming so late. But we are dealing with a study with policies that will be still in process of formation or reformulation by our children, policies that will be before not just one session of Congress but many. I am sure of this, and I hope that the work will be a legacy from President Hoover to the many policy makers of the future."[77]

The final report of the President's Research Committee on Social Trends did in fact grapple with questions that would plague its authors' children. Divided into three parts, on America's material heritage, its human resources, and its social organizations, the report contained predictions about social trends that would prove remarkably accurate. America's population growth, it said, would continue a long-term decline, and use of contraception would increase. The divorce rate would climb dramatically, but the prospect of divorce would not deter the vast majority of the nation's citizens from marrying and then remarrying. The country would continue to be a bread-basket for the world, but its number of farms would grow fewer and fewer, to be replaced by ever-larger agricultural operations run like big businesses. New chemical and genetic discoveries, especially those related to the regulation, growth, and functioning of human hormones, would revolutionize medical treatments. The United States would continue to be a country whose citizens' professed moral beliefs were often at odds with their behavior. The America of 1932 was a "land of prohibition and easy divorce, strict censorship and risqué plays, scientific research and laws forbidding the teaching of the theory of evolution, contraceptive information legally outlawed but widely utilized." These and similar social contradictions would mark American life in years to come.[78]

But, in the depths of the depression, politicians were not interested in judging the accuracy of academics' guesses about social trends, even though a better understanding of how their nation's institutions had developed might have made them wiser when they made short-term, as well as long-term, decisions. What they wanted in the winter of 1932 were solutions to the Great Depression, and these the research committee's final report did not offer. Indeed, in his editor's foreword, William Ogburn gloomily noted: "A change in the distribution of income which put more purchasing power in the hands of wage earners would enormously increase the market for many staples and go far toward providing places for all competent workers, but for the near future we see little prospect of a rapid increase of wage disbursements above the 1929 level. Another possibility is a great expansion of exports; but in a tariff-ridden world that seems a dim hope."[79]

In January 1933 the final report was available in print, and over the next two years tens of thousands of additional pages of charts, tables, interview transcripts, and other documentary materials would be published as supplements to its twenty-nine lengthy chapters. The new Roosevelt administration, however, did not wish to be attached to a project that had been so closely identified as a mandate from a now thoroughly discredited Herbert Hoover. The report's massive collection of social science evidence, optimistically created as a blueprint for social policy making, quickly disappeared from public sight, to rest, unused and soon forgotten, on the shelves of government documents rooms in the nation's major libraries. In a rough draft for the final report's chapter on public welfare activities, Howard Odum sadly and accurately concluded, "Social science is no help in getting elected," and noted, again correctly, "The main influence of social science upon government is probably exerted by others than social scientists in government, and through the many ill-trained, more than the few well-trained."[80]

Between 1929 and 1932 hundreds of well-trained social scientists produced a monumental guide to domestic policy making full of useful insights, but they could not force any politician to use it. The fact that the Rockefeller Foundation underwrote the project was irrelevant. Since the final report so quickly vanished, nobody commented on one interesting fact: despite an attempt to cover every aspect of American domestic life, the bulky study almost ignored the subject of foundation philanthropy. Sydnor Walker had originally called her chapter "Organized Philanthropy and Social Work," but the final version that actually appeared carried the title "Privately Supported Social Work" and emphasized the development of community chests as typifying trends in social work.[81] Nonetheless, Walker's few comments about organized national policy-making philanthropy were accurate: "There are critics of particular foundations and of some of their specific programs, but in general, little dissatisfaction is now evidenced. A congressional investigation of . . . the Rockefeller Foundation in 1915 was tangible proof of the apprehension then felt concerning foundations. In 1932 the chief criticism is that foundations . . . rule out various programs in controversial fields."[82]

Between 1915 and 1932 the few foundations interested in social policy making had quietly become part of the process of governance—now more likely to be scolded for their caution than for their supposed attempts to exercise plutocratic control of the nation's political institutions from the shadows.

FINAL THOUGHTS

This volume has studied the impact of the private wealth controlled by seven national policy-making foundations over American social-policy-making processes. Between 1903 and 1932 their comparatively huge financial resources gave these institutions significant access at all governmental levels, from city halls, to state education departments, to federal agencies. As demonstrated here, sometimes that access resulted in foundation ideas becoming policy. Other times it did not. Moreover, policies initially embraced, but later repudiated, by foundations often continued to thrive anyway. In a pluralistic political system characterized by divided power, rarely was just one entity a policy's sole author, and almost always the impact of implemented policies confounded prediction.

The foundations studied in these pages supported publicly funded vocational education to promote a variety of goals—many unfulfilled. The Knapp System and informational campaigns against filth diseases did not make early-twentieth-century southern farmers prosperous and content to stay put. Parent education did not achieve its grandiose aims. In some cases, initial foundation enthusiasm for such programs quickly waned. Nonetheless, late-twentieth-century American governments, at local, state, and federal levels, remain sponsors of an ever-expanding list of vocationally oriented education schemes. In like manner, the juvenile court has remained a fixture among American legal institutions, despite the fact that its first sponsors, private philanthropies, retracted their endorsement.

Other social policies still in effect also originated as foundation proposals. In these cases, however, foundations successfully persuaded skeptical government officials to accept their ideas and remained enthusiastic. As the twentieth century ends, great numbers of politicians decry welfare as a national disaster but fewer challenge the foundation-sponsored principle that transformed the mothers' pensions: that trained investigators should categorize the "fitness" and supervise the lives of public aid recipients with dependent children.

Publicly funded recreation, first a foundation campaign, has also become accepted. The national park and forest systems remain among the most popular of all federal initiatives, not least for the varied recreational opportunities they offer. State and local politicians threaten to cut well-liked recreation programs when they advocate the need for bond issues or tax increases, aware that their constituents endorse as public policy ideas once embraced only by private wealth.

Finally, some late-twentieth-century public policies remain haunted by the same kinds of disputes that caused both their private and public sponsors to abandon them in earlier decades. Government-funded AIDS education remains as controversial as did some of the efforts by early-twentieth-century social hygienists to promote better popular understanding of the real nature of syphilis. The idea that public institutions, like schools or health agencies, should distribute information about human sexuality still attracts opponents.

If there is one link between all of the topics raised within these pages, it is that foundations consistently championed the importance of the neutral expert as the ideal government official. Swayed by objective evidence, not partisan passions, such an individual would promote the best kind of public policy making. In fact, in such a government, policies would inevitably result from the rigorous use of social science method. They would be deductive conclusions made by those trained to analyze all relevant sources of information.

In the early nineteenth century many governments openly embraced the spoils system. In such a world political loyalty was the characteristic most prized in officeholders. For decades Andrew Jackson's idea that any American citizen could serve in any government post reigned. Political hacks were not the only ones who agreed that "rotation in office" was beneficial to the maintenance of democracy.

Americans, said Henry James, ate the fruit of the tree of knowledge during the Civil War and lost their innocence. After 1870 fewer and fewer of them championed the notion that party membership could provide a basis for choosing public leaders. Throughout society careers once taught by apprenticeship closed to all but those with the proper credentials. Physicians needed medical degrees, lawyers had to prove they had passed examinations, and while qualifications for government service were still vaguely defined, political parties began to decline in power. In the mid–nineteenth century elections had been crucial events, attracting the attention and participation of almost all eligible voters. By the late nineteenth century, that had begun to change, and when women finally won the national franchise in 1920, they simply copied their brothers and fathers. Members of both genders, in greater and greater percentages, failed to vote, and the principle of merit, as a crucial qualification for government service, won increasing acceptance. At least in theory, government should be in the hands not just of loyal Democrats or Republicans, but *good* Democrats and Republicans.

Finally, between 1900 and 1930, governments began to consider the nonpartisan expert indispensable to their practical operations. In a sense, from the mayor's mansion to the White House, government institutions had finally "professionalized," at least rhetorically. That was a foundation idea, but it was not just a foundation idea. To say that foundations alone invented the government expert would be to misunderstand the convoluted nature of public decision making in early-twentieth-century America. But private wealth certainly played a role in creating this changed paradigm for the conduct of public life. An overwhelming faith in the advice of experts linked the foundation-sponsored innovations in education, social welfare, and public health policy these pages have explored.

This volume ends with the defeat of Herbert Hoover and the beginning of the New Deal. The year 1932 truly marked a turning point, and not just for relationships between private wealth and public life. Government, not the political party, became an ever more important part of the lives of millions of individual Americans. A relatively small federal bureaucracy mushroomed. The public members of private public-policy-making alliances controlled far more money and possessed significantly greater power. However, throughout decades of change from the 1930s to the 1990s, one "ideal" remained constant: the neutral, highly trained "expert" was a more worthy member of government than a mere "politician."

In 1920 the American electorate finally became one that accurately could be called "We the people." But we the people marched away from the polls, not toward them. By the 1990s small minorities, sometimes as few as a quarter of the nation's potential voters, decided the outcome of major elections. Had "we" decided the nonpartisan experts knew best? Did "we" no longer feel polity and society were the same? Had long traditions of American anti-intellectualism and hatred of bureaucracy, always a force in the nation's history, strongly resurfaced to reflect public disillusionment with all forms of government—elective and appointive? After all, the same sorts of "experts" the Progressives glorified brought late-twentieth-century America the Vietnam War and a massive federal debt. But if both politicians and the experts who served them were discredited, what new paradigm for representative government could emerge?

The small group of people who created the foundations this volume has examined possessed an intellectual gift lost to many in the late twentieth century. With a fierce kind of optimism we now find peculiar, they believed people could be better, that governments could be better, that society could improve. Not only did they believe that, they thought that American society could crumble unless its people searched, as Frederick Gates might say, "at a *hot* pace" for answers to their problems. "Take the advice of trained experts" was one solution these foundation policy makers proposed. One wonders what advice Frederick Gates would now give, could he speak from the grave? What answer would he now give to a question raised by William Ogburn in the final report of the Research Committee on Social Trends: "What is the relation of democracy to the expert in [government] administration?"[83] The fact that this question still demands scrutiny, perhaps now more than ever, links late-twentieth-century policy makers with those studied here.

NOTES

CHAPTER ONE—FOUNDATION PHILANTHROPY AND PUBLIC POLICY MAKING IN THE EARLY-TWENTIETH-CENTURY UNITED STATES

1. Simon Kuznets, "Long Term Changes in the National Income of the United States since 1870," *Income and Wealth*: Series II (Baltimore, 1952), 50–55; Steven Ruggles, "The Transformation of the American Family Structure," *American Historical Review* 99 (1994): 103–28; U.S. Department of Commerce, Bureau of the Census, *Public Use Microdata Samples. United States. Technical Documentation* (Washington, D.C., 1992).

2. Alan Pifer, *Philanthropy in an Age of Transition: The Essays of Alan Pifer* (New York, 1984), 106.

3. Autobiographies include Andrew Carnegie, *The Autobiography of Andrew Carnegie* (Garden City, N.Y., 1909); Frederick Gates, *Chapters in My Life* (New York, 1977); Abraham Flexner, *I Remember* (New York, 1940). Typical biographies include Abraham Flexner, *Henry S. Pritchett: A Biography* (New York, 1943); Raymond Fosdick, *John D. Rockefeller, Jr.* (New York, 1956). Among the best known of the institutional histories are John Glenn, Lilian Brandt, and F. Emerson Andrews, *The Russell Sage Foundation* (New York, 1947); Edwin Embree and Julia Waxman, *Investment in People: The Story of the Julius Rosenwald Fund* (New York, 1949); Raymond Fosdick, *The Story of the Rockefeller Foundation* (New York, 1952); Abraham Flexner and Esther Bailey, *Funds and Foundations: Their Policies, Past and Present* (New York, 1952); Frederick Keppel, *The Foundation: Its Place in American Life* (New York, 1930).

4. Glenn et al., *The Russell Sage Foundation*.

5. Ibid., 3

6. Gates, *Chapters in My Life, 206.*

7. Alan Gregg quoted in Fosdick, *The Rockefeller Foundation, 29.*

8. John Ensor Harr and Peter Johnson tell the story in *The Rockefeller Century: Three Generations of America's Greatest Family* (New York, 1988), 85–88.

9. Versions of this motto, used in 1913 to describe the work of the new Rockefeller Foundation, appeared in explanations of the work of most of the major foundations of the period. As early as 1914 the phrase had become a press cliché. See "Newspaper Files: 1905–1920," Rockefeller Family Archives, Series 2, Subseries

"Rockefeller Boards," Box 19, Folder 190, Rockefeller Archive Center, Tarrytown, N.Y. (hereafter RAC).

10. For example, Raymond Fosdick, *Adventure in Giving: The Story of the General Education Board* (New York, 1962), 12.

11. Gates, *Chapters in My Life,* 188.

12. Wright Babcock (letter to the editor), *Survey* 28 (1912): 984.

13. Ibid.

14. "The Dangers of Foundations" (26 Mar. 1910), copy in Rockefeller Family Archives, Series 2, Subseries "Rockefeller Boards," Box 25, Folder 255, RAC.

15. "Hillquit Non-Partisan Committee of One Thousand for the Children of New York City and Their Schools," Pamphlet, RAC Pamphlet Files, Box 3, Folder 38, RAC.

16. Merle Curti and Roderick Nash, *Philanthropy in the Shaping of American Higher Education* (New Brunswick, N.J., 1965); Daniel Fox, *Engines of Culture: Philanthropy and Art Museums* (Madison, Wis., 1963). The Carnegie Corporation and the Carnegie Foundation funded the research for Ellen Lagemann's two studies: *Private Power for the Public Good: A History of the Carnegie Foundation for the Advancement of Teaching* (Middletown, Conn., 1983); *The Politics of Knowledge: The Carnegie Corporation, Philanthropy, and Public Policy* (Middletown, Conn., 1989).

17. The final chapter of this book will explore the impact of the commission on foundations in much greater detail.

18. For further information about foundations and tax policy see Gary Scrivner, "One Hundred Years of Tax Policy Changes Affecting Charitable Organizations," in D. L. Gies, J. S. Ott, and Jay M. Shafritz, eds., *The Nonprofit Organization* (Pacific Grove, Calif., 1990), 126–32.

19. Pifer, *Philanthropy in an Age of Transition,* 7.

20. For further information about foundation reaction to the Tax Reform Act of 1969 see Peter Dobkin Hall, "Dilemmas of Non-Profit Research," *Philanthropy Monthly* 11 (1989): 10–13; John Ensor Harr and Peter Johnson, *The Rockefeller Conscience: An American Family in Public and in Private* (New York, 1991), 293–99.

21. Darwin Stapleton, "Plumbing the Past: Foundation Archives Are Becoming an Invaluable Resource," *Foundation News* 1 (1987): 67–68. Seven of these eleven foundations have deposited their archives with the RAC. Most significant of these non-Rockefeller-related philanthropies are the Russell Sage Foundation and the Commonwealth Fund.

22. The two best of these articles are Barry Karl and Stanley Katz, "The American Private Philanthropic Foundation and the Public Sphere, 1890–1930," *Minerva* 19 (1981): 236–70; idem, "Foundations and Ruling Class Elites," *Proceedings of the American Academy of Arts and Sciences* 116 (1987): 1–41.

23. Lagemann, *Private Power for the Public Good;* idem, *The Politics of Knowledge;* John McClymer, *War and Welfare: Social Engineering in America, 1890–1925* (Westport, Conn., 1980); Steven Wheatley, *The Politics of Philanthropy: Abraham Flexner and Medical Education* (Madison, Wis., 1988); Martin Bulmer, Kevin Bales, and Kathryn Kish Sklar, eds., *The Social Survey in Historical Perspective, 1880–1940* (Cambridge, 1991). For an extensive list of secondary sources on foundations see the bibliography.

24. Karl and Katz, "Foundations and Ruling Class Elites," 34–35.

25. Among social scientists debate has been most fierce when private charitable foundations figure as elements in controversies over neopluralist theory and structuration theory. For further discussion of such theories see Leo Pantich, "Recent Theorizations and Corporatism: Reflections on a Growth Industry," *British Journal of Sociology* 31 (1980): 159–87; Kirsten Gronbjerg, "Patterns of Institutional Relations in the Welfare State," *Journal of Voluntary Action Research* 16 (1987): 64–80; Clark Gordon and Michael Dear, *State Apparatus, Structures, and the Language of Legitimacy* (London, 1984).

26. Jennifer Wolch, *The Shadow State: Government and the Voluntary Sector in Transition* (New York, 1990), 25.

27. Martin Bulmer, "Philanthropic Foundations and the Development of the Social Sciences in the Early Twentieth Century: A Reply to Donald Fisher," *Sociology* 18 (1984): 572–79.

28. Donald Fisher, "The Role of Philanthropic Foundations in the Reproduction and Production of Hegemony," *Sociology* 17 (1983): 224. See also Fisher, "Boundary Work: Toward a Model of the Relation of Power/Knowledge," *Knowledge* 10 (1988): 156–76; idem, *Fundamental Development of the Social Sciences: Rockefeller Philanthropy and the United States Social Science Research Council* (Ann Arbor, Mich., 1993).

29. Robert Arnove, "Introduction," in Robert F. Arnove, ed., *Philanthropy and Cultural Imperialism: The Foundations at Home and Abroad* (Boston, 1980), 1.

30. Fisher, "The Role of Philanthropic Foundations," 233.

31. For a sampling of this debate see Fisher, "The Role of Philanthropy"; idem, "Philanthropic Foundations and the Social Sciences: A Response to Martin Bulmer," *Sociology* 18 (1984): 581–87; Bulmer, "A Reply to Donald Fisher"; Salma Ahmad, "American Foundations and the Development of the Social Sciences between the Wars: Comment on the Debate between Martin Bulmer and Donald Fisher," *Sociology* 25 (1991): 511–20. Ahmad summarizes the debate and sides with neither camp. However, she offers no alternative interpretation. For discussion of Gramsci see Alastair Davidson, *Antonio Gramsci: The Man and his Ideas* (Sydney, 1968). For discussion of Gramsci's influence see Karl and Katz, "Foundations and Ruling Class Elites," 4–7.

32. Russell Marks, "Legitimating Industrial Capitalism," in Arnove, ed., *Philanthropy and Cultural Imperialism*, 89.

33. Quoted in Teresa Odendahl, "Independent Foundations and Wealthy Donors: An Overview," in Teresa Odendahl, ed., *America's Wealthy and the Future of Foundations* (New York, 1987), 14.

34. For analyses of contemporary foundations see Odendahl, ed., *America's Wealthy and the Future of Foundations*; idem, *Charity Begins at Home: Generosity and Self-Interest among the Philanthropic Elite* (New York, 1990); Waldemar Nielson, *The Golden Donors: A New Anatomy of the Great Foundations* (New York, 1985). Kenneth Rose, Assistant Director of the Rockefeller Archive Center, supervised a 1988 survey of the thousand largest foundations in America. Of the 390 respondents, only 50 (12.8%) had deposited their records in an archive or otherwise made them available for independent scholarly research. The survey, whose results appeared in 1990, reinforces the

argument of Odendahl and others that most foundations are small, local entities, interested in doing good works, with very little or no interest in public policy making. See Kenneth Rose, "Results from the RAC Survey of the 1000 Largest American Foundations," Background Papers for "Foundation Archives: Information, Access, and Research" Conference Co-Sponsored by the Council on Foundations and the RAC, 9 Jan. 1990, Conference Transcript, RAC.

35. Given a lack of definitive tax or other financial records, most of these figures are rough estimates. See Merle Curti, Judith Green, and Roderick Nash, "Anatomy of Giving: Millionaires in the Late 19th Century," *American Quarterly* 15 (1963): 416–35; Robert Bremner, *American Philanthropy* (Chicago, 1988), 85–127; Gies et al., *The Non-Profit Organization*, 61–90.

36. For a discussion of the connections between taxation and charitable giving see Joseph Pechman, *How Taxes Affect Economic Behavior* (Washington, D.C., 1981).

37. For a discussion of nineteenth-century patterns of charity see Kathleen McCarthy, *Noblesse Oblige* (Chicago, 1982); Kathryn Kish Sklar, "A Call for Comparisons," *American Historical Review* 95 (1990): 1009–14; Mary Jo Deegan, *Jane Addams and the Men of the Chicago School: 1892–1918* (New Brunswick, N.J., 1988).

38. "Foundations and Endowments," typed draft of report for *Bulletin of the Russell Sage Foundation Library,* Aug. 1926, in Records of the Russell Sage Foundation (hereafter RSF), Series 3, Box 34, Folder 274, RAC. For a discussion of the uniquely American nature of charitable foundations see Arnove, *Philanthropy and Cultural Imperialism,* 4–5.

39. "Confidential Conference of Trustees: April 29, 1928," typed minutes, Appendices A and B, Papers of Julius Rosenwald (hereafter Rosenwald), Addenda 1: Rosenwald Fund, Box 2, Folder 1, Archives of the University of Chicago, Regenstein Library, Chicago, Ill. (hereafter UC).

40. Ibid. Appendices A and B discuss in detail the "best available estimates" of amounts expended by these forty largest foundations and list all capital endowments. See also "Rockefeller Gifts," Rockefeller Family Archives, Series 2, Subseries: Rockefeller Boards, Box 19, Folder 190, RAC; "Remarks of the Retiring Chairman, April 6, 1939," RAC Pamphlets File, Box 3, Folder 38, RAC; Edward Devine, "Memorandum of Purposes," typed manuscript, Dec. 1906, RSF, Series 2, Box 2, Folder 11, RAC; "Appropriations for Philanthropic Purposes: Appendices," *Historical Sketch of the Commonwealth Fund* (1963), RAC Pamphlets File, RAC. The quotation from Olivia Sage can be found in Glenn et al., *The Russell Sage Foundation,* 20.

41. Glenn et al., *The Russell Sage Foundation,* 3.

42. Robert DeForest to Olivia Sage, 10 Dec. 1906, RSF, Series 2, Box 2, Folder 11, RAC.

43. "Minutes, Trustees' Meeting: April 26, 1930," Rosenwald, Addenda 1: Rosenwald Fund, Box 2, Folder 7, UC.

44. Mary Richmond to John Glenn, 18 Jan. 1914, RSF, Series 3, Box 13, Folder 112, RAC.

45. Frederick Gates to Charles Eliot, 30 Dec. 1910, Papers of Frederick Gates (hereafter Gates), Box 1, Folder 21, RAC.

46. "Special Confidential Memorandum of the Kinds of Things That Should

Be Supported by Foundations," typed manuscript, 23 July 1930, unsigned (Edwin Embree?), Rosenwald, Addenda 1: Rosenwald Fund, Box 3, Folder 6, UC.

47. The standard (and best) works are Lagemann, *Private Power for the Public Good* and *The Politics of Knowledge.* See also Edward Berman, *The Influence of the Carnegie, Ford, and Rockefeller Foundations on American Foreign Policy: The Ideology of Philanthropy* (Albany, N.Y., 1983); Richard Heyman, "The Role of the Carnegie Corporation in African Education" (Ed.D. diss., Teachers College, Columbia University, 1970); Donald Critchlow, *The Brookings Institution: Expertise and the Public Interest in a Democratic Society* (De Kalb, Ill., 1985); Ronald Tobey, *The American Ideology of a National Science 1919–1930* (Pittsburgh, 1971).

48. It should be noted that the Carnegie Endowment for International Peace was established in 1910, but like the IGR and the Institute of Economics, it had little influence. Moreover, as an agency interested in promoting international law and organization, its activities lie outside the limits of this volume's focus. For information about early Carnegie-funded forays into "government research" see Critchlow, *The Brookings Institution.* See also Nielson, *The Golden Donors,* 4–11, 133–44.

49. For discussion about the reactions to "Wealth" see Lagemann, *Private Power for the Public Good,* 30–35; Joseph Frazier Wall, *Andrew Carnegie* (New York, 1970), 806–20. The Wall biography is by far the best yet written about Carnegie. For the essay itself see Andrew Carnegie, *The Gospel of Wealth and Other Timely Essays,* ed. Edward Kirkland (Cambridge, Mass., 1962), 20–40.

50. As late as 1988, in a new edition of his *American Philanthropy,* probably the historical work about American philanthropy most commonly used in college classrooms, Robert Bremner once again listed the document as one of great importance in the creation of scientific philanthropy (100–102). In the context of its arguments, the phrase "scientific giving" more properly belongs to the senior Rockefeller. It appeared in his printed essays as early as 1909. See John D. Rockefeller Sr., *Random Reminiscences of Men and Events* (New York, 1909), 147.

51. John Rockefeller Sr. to John Rockefeller Jr., 25 Apr. 1917, Rockefeller Family Archives, Record Group 2, Series: "JDR, Jr., Personal," Letterbook 3, RAC.

52. Harr and Johnson, *The Rockefeller Century,* 502.

53. Carnegie, *The Gospel of Wealth,* 33–38. Many of the prominent philanthropists studied in this book espoused a version of religion that involved support for a version of the Social Gospel, whether they were Christians or Jews, whether they specifically employed the phrase. Frederick Gates was typical when he wrote in his autobiography, "Under the influence of modern science and the higher criticism of the *Bible* [I] came to disbelieve altogether in the peculiar tenets of the Baptist Church. . . . But I still called myself a Christian. My religion became and still is, simply the service of humanity in the Spirit of Jesus." Gates, *Chapters in My Life,* 205.

54. Lagemann, *The Politics of Knowledge,* 6.

55. Lagemann, *Private Power for the Public Good,* 24.

56. Ibid., 53–85. It should be noted that by 1913 Flexner, disgusted by conflicts at the Carnegie Foundation, had switched allegiances and was working for the Rockefeller Foundation. Lagemann admits that the Mann Report on the state of the profession of engineering reached only a "narrow audience" and "was not of great

interest to groups outside the profession" (85). For Flexner's own account of his departure from Carnegie employment see *I Remember,* 170–84.

57. Any such involvements would have condoned "socialism." Pritchett even saw state restrictions on the labor of young children as "socialistic." Lagemann, *Private Power for the Public Good,* 175–77.

58. I have used Lagemann's own words (*The Politics of Knowledge,* 7) since I believe she largely fails to make her case that the corporation had indeed accomplished much more than a string of policy failures prior to 1930.

59. Ibid., 116–22; quotation on 118.

60. Graham Adams tells the story in his *The Age of Industrial Violence, 1910– 1915: The Activities and Findings of the United States Commission on Industrial Relations* (New York, 1966), 160–61.

61. John D. Rockefeller Jr., "Recollections of My Father," typed notes, Aug. 1920, Rockefeller Family Archives, Record Group 2, Series "JDR, Jr., Personal," Letterbook 3, RAC.

62. Representative copies of suppressed phony interviews can be found in Rockefeller Family Archives, Series "Rockefeller Boards," Subseries "Rockefeller Foundation," Box 24, Folder 250, RAC.

63. Carnegie was not, however, an active board member and rarely attended meetings. See "Remarks of the Retiring Chairman, April 6, 1939," RAC Pamphlets File, Box 3, Folder 38, RAC.

64. Gates, *Chapters in My Life.*

65. Frederick Gates, "The Purpose of the Rockefeller Foundation with Suggestions as to Policy of Administration," typed report, 1906, Rockefeller Family Archives, Record Group 2, Series: "Rockefeller Boards," Box 19, Folder 198, RAC.

66. "Memorandum by Mr. Gates," 28 Feb. 1910, Rockefeller Family Archives, Record Group 2, Series "Rockefeller Boards," Box 19, Folder 198, RAC. Frederick Gates refrained from every conventional obscenity. However, as a voluble man, he invented all kinds of highly personal substitutes. His co-workers soon realized that the word "retail" scrawled on a report meant doom, that it was Gates's highest indication of scorn. See, for instance, Alan Gregg, "Appraisal of Foundations," 26 Mar. 1949, RF, Record Group 3, Series 900, Box 28, Folder 155, RAC. Did Ellen Lagemann know of Gates's withering, special use of the word when she wrote that "[Frederick Paul Keppel] ran the Carnegie Corporation more as a retail shop with many valued and welcome clients than as a scientific bureau involved in national affairs"(*The Politics of Knowledge,* 101)?

67. Lagemann, *The Politics of Knowledge,* 161.

68. See also the comments of Gates, Abraham Flexner, Raymond Fosdick, and Beardsley Ruml, "Memorandum on Conference at Gedney Farms," 18–19 Jan., 1924, typescript, Records of the Rockefeller Foundation (hereafter RF), Record Group 3, Series 900, Box 22, Folder 165, RAC.

69. "General Memorandum," October 1922, unsigned (Beardsley Ruml?), RF, Record Group 3, Series 910, Box 2, Folder 10, RAC.

70. Gates, *Chapters in My Life,* 33–47.

71. Quotation cited in David Hammack, *The Russell Sage Foundation: A Guide*

to the *Microfiche Collection* (Frederick, Md., 1988), 1. Many of the basic published sources about these foundations have already been cited in note 3. In addition, see Steven Cohen, "The Pittsburgh Survey and the Social Survey Movement: A Sociological Road Not Taken," in Kathryn Kish Sklar, ed., *The Social Survey in Historical Perspective,* 245–69; A. McGehee Harvey and Susan Abrams, *"For the Welfare of Mankind": The Commonwealth Fund and American Medicine* (Baltimore, 1986).

72. For information on Ruml's career see Papers of Beardsley Ruml (hereafter Ruml), Series 2, Box 2, Folder 1, UC. For information on Embree and Rosenwald see Rosenwald, Addenda 1, Rosenwald Fund, Box 2, Folders 2 and 3, and Box 32, Folder 8, UC.

73. Papers of Edith and Grace Abbott, Box 31, Folder 10, UC.

74. Commonwealth Fund Director's Reports, 1 Mar. 1921, unprocessed reports, Records of the Commonwealth Fund (hereafter CF), RAC.

75. John Glenn to Mary Van Kleeck, 19 Sept. 1920, RSF, Series 3, Box 15, Folder 132, RAC.

76. Raymond Fosdick, "Our Machine Civilization," typed notes for speech, Rockefeller Family Archives, Record Group 2, Series "Rockefeller Boards," Box 25, Folder 257, RAC.

77. Ibid.

78. Frederick Gates, "Competition vs. Cooperation," undated typed manuscript, Gates, Box 1, Folder 13, RAC.

79. Frederick Gates, "On Corporation Privileges," undated typed manuscript, Gates, Box 1, Folder 17, RAC.

80. Mary Richmond to John Glenn, 12 July 1926, RSF, Series 3, Box 34, Folder 274, RAC.

81. Luther Gulick to John Glenn, 30 Sept. 1912, RSF, Series 3, Box 13a, Folder 119b, RAC.

82. Karl and Katz tell the story in "Foundations and Ruling Class Elites," 24–25.

83. Ibid.

84. "Documents # 178–182," Rosenwald, Box 55, Folder 2, UC.

85. For Gates's account see his *Chapters in My Life,* 160–82.

86. Samuel Gompers, "Sycophancy and Callousness," *American Federationist* 22 (1915): 514–15. For scholarly discussion of the "Ludlow Massacre" see Howard M. Gitelman, *Legacy of the Ludlow Massacre: A Chapter in American Industrial Relations* (Philadelphia, 1988).

87. For biographical information about Ruml see Ruml, Series 1, Box 1, Folder 1, UC.

88. For biographical information about Ayres see "Biography of Leonard Ayres," typed manuscript, RSF, Series 3, Box 13, Folder 118, RAC.

89. Good books on this subject include Susan Ware, *Beyond Suffrage: Women and the New Deal* (Cambridge, Mass., 1981); idem, *Partner and I: Molly Dewson, Feminism, and New Deal Politics* (New Haven, Conn., 1987); Martha Swain, *Ellen S. Woodward: New Deal Advocate for Women* (Jackson, Miss., 1995).

90. For biographical information on all original trustees see "Biographical Files," RSF, Series 3, Box 4, Folder 37, RAC. Schuyler quoted in Glenn et al., *The*

Russell Sage Foundation, 10. For further information about these women and other female professional employees of the Sage Foundation see "Biographical Files," RSF, Series 3, Box 4, Folder 37, RAC. Mary Richmond headed the Charity Organization Department. Mary Van Kleeck headed the Department of Industrial Studies. Helen Gould, one of the foundation's original trustees, served until 1936. Laura Lee served from 1926 to 1938. All other trustees were male. Glenn et al., *The Russell Sage Foundation,* 669–70.

91. Raymond Fosdick, for instance, once received a letter from a deranged woman accusing John D. Rockefeller Sr. of being a compliant witness to her seduction by the "completely degenerate" Harry Emerson Fosdick, the eminent theologian and Senior's pastor at New York City's Riverside Church and Raymond Fosdick's brother. Although Raymond Fosdick, who assumed the presidency of the Rockefeller Foundation in 1936, would, by the 1920s, be increasingly concerned about avoiding controversy and maintaining good public relations, he could still forward the letter to his brother with a note: "Dear Harry: Here is a letter that came to me from one of your girl friends. Of course, I can't keep up with your affairs." Quoted in Robert Miller, *Harry Emerson Fosdick: Preacher, Pastor, Prophet* (New York, 1985), 307.

92. Emphasis in original, "Private Memorandum," 20 Apr. 1891, Records of the General Education Board (hereafter GEB), Series 1, Subseries 5, Box 716, Folder 7386, RAC.

93. James Angell to Beardsley Ruml, 25 Jan. 1918, Ruml, Series 1, Box 1, Folder 1, UC.

94. Quotation from Fosdick, *Adventure in Giving,* 18.

95. Beardsley Ruml, "Notes on Foundation Problems," typed manuscript, 23 Dec. 1952, Ruml, Series 2, Box 8, Folder 2, UC.

96. Alan Gregg, "Appraisal of Foundations," typed manuscript, 26 Mar. 1949, RF, Record Group 3, Series 900, Box 28, Folder 155, RAC.

97. Max Farrand to Edward Harkness, 19 Feb. 1919, Correspondence Files, unprocessed correspondence, CF, RAC.

98. Harry Pratt Judson to John D. Rockefeller Jr., 13 Nov. 1913, Rockefeller Family Archives, Record Group 2, Series "Rockefeller Boards," Box 25, Folder 256, RAC.

99. Abraham Flexner, "Foundations: Ours and Others," 3 Jan. 1924, typed, paginated manuscript, 8, RF, Record Group 3, Series 900, Box 22, Folder 165, RAC.

100. Charles Merriam, "The Aid Which the Social Sciences Can Render to National Planning," typed draft of report, undated (1933?), Papers of Charles Merriam (hereafter Merriam), Series 6, Box 172, Folder 2, UC.

101. Flexner, "Foundations: Ours and Others," 16.

102. Jerome Greene to Arthur Woods, 30 Sept. 1930, Records of the Laura Spelman Rockefeller Memorial (hereafter LSRM) Series 3, Subseries 7, Box 85, Folder 894, RAC.

103. Jerome Greene to Thomas Appleget, 8 Oct. 1930, LSRM, Series 3, Subseries 7, Box 85, Folder 894, RAC.

104. Wickliffe Rose, Memorandum, 13 Mar. 1913, RF, Series 3, Subseries 908, Box 14, Folder 149, RAC.

Chapter Two—Foundations, the "Rural Crisis," and the Birth of
Publicly Funded Vocational Education

1. Wickliffe Rose, Memorandum, 3 Mar. 1913, Records of the Rockefeller Foundation (hereafter RF), Series 3, Subseries 908, Box 14, Folder 149, RAC.

2. For discussions of the state of American agriculture during this period see David Danbom, *Born in the Country: A History of Rural America* (Baltimore, 1995); William Bowers, *The Country Life Movement in America: 1900–1920* (Port Washington, N.Y., 1974), 10–25; Donald Tweton, "The Attitudes and Policies of the Theodore Roosevelt Administration toward American Agriculture" (Ph.D. diss., University of Oklahoma, 1964); Alfred True, "A History of Agricultural Education in the United States: 1785–1925," Miscellaneous Publication 36, Department of Agriculture, Washington, D.C., 1929.

3. Remarks of Frederick Russell, Transcript, Meeting of Rockefeller Foundation Officers and Directors, Princeton, N.J., 29–30 Oct. 1930, RF, Record Group 3, Series 900, Box 22, Folder 166. Capitals in original, RAC (hereafter Remarks of Frederick Russell).

4. William Link, *A Hard Country and a Lonely Place: Schooling, Society, and Reform in Rural Virginia, 1870–1920* (Chapel Hill, N.C., 1986), 125. For other examples of how scholars have treated this topic see Lagemann, *The Politics of Knowledge;* idem, *Private Power for the Public Good;* Roger Geiger, *To Advance Knowledge: The Growth of the American Research Universities, 1900–1940* (New York, 1986); Ronald Goodenow and Arthur White, eds., *Education and the Rise of the New South* (Boston, 1981); James Anderson, *The Education of Blacks in the South, 1860–1935* (Chapel Hill, N.C., 1988); John Heffron, "Science, Southernness, and Vocationalism: Rockefeller's Comprehensive System and the Reorganization of Secondary School Science Education, 1900–1920" (Ph.D. diss., University of Rochester, 1988); Wayne Urban, "Organized Teachers and Educational Reform during the Progressive Era: 1890–1902," *History of Education Quarterly* 16 (1976): 35–52; Daniel Levy, ed., *Private Education: Studies in Choice and Public Policy* (New York, 1986); Thomas James and Henry Levin, eds., *Comparing Public and Private Schools: Institutions and Organizations* (New York, 1987).

5. Mary Van Kleeck, Internal Memorandum, Records of the Russell Sage Foundation, Early Office Files, Department of Industrial Studies, 1911–1926, Box 15, Folder 133, RAC. Emphasis in original.

6. Remarks of Dr. Mary Sloop, School Superintendent, Crossnore, N.C. Typed Speech Transcript for Conference of Southern Mountain Workers, 4–6 Apr. 1923, Knoxville, Tenn., 10, RSF, Series 3, Box 16, Folder 138, RAC.

7. For one example of such language see the description of "health revivals" in "Report of the Educational Work for 1913 by the State Board of Health of Kentucky," Records of the Rockefeller Sanitary Commission (hereafter *Sanitary*), Series 2, Box 3, Folder 90, RAC.

8. John Campbell, "Confidential Report of the Southern Highlands Division," RSF, Series 3, Box 16, Folder 136.

9. *Asheville Citizen,* 13 Aug. 1919; copy of newspaper in RSF, Series 3, Box 16, Folder 136.

10. Edwin Embree, "The Business of Giving Away Money," *Harper's Monthly*

161 (1930): 329. Embree, in a characteristic and unsolicited letter to Julius Rosenwald, once remarked, "You [Rosenwald] are often unreasonable . . . and too prone to fits of temper." However, Embree concluded, "You [Rosenwald] are the least timid rich man I know." This was high praise from Embree. Embree to Rosenwald, 21 Aug. 1931, Rosenwald, Box 33, Folder 9, UC.

11. For a copy of the report sent to Congress see "Report of the Country Life Commission," Senate Document 705: Sixtieth Congress, Second Session, 1909. An abridged version of the report was finally published decades later: *Report of the Commission on Country Life with an Introduction by Theodore Roosevelt* (Chapel Hill, N.C., 1944); Contemporary assessments include "The Farm Commission," *Independent* 63 (1908): 1012–14; Carnegie, "The Country Life Commission: How Much Did It Accomplish?" *Country Gentleman* 74 (1909): 231–35. Scholarly assessments include Clayton Ellsworth, "Theodore Roosevelt's Country Life Commission," *Agricultural History* 34 (1960): 155–72; Bowers, *The Country Life Movement in America*, 25–44. The best treatment of rural reaction to the Country Life Movement is David Danbom, *The Resisted Revolution: Urban America and the Industrialization of Agriculture, 1900–1930* (Ames, Iowa, 1979).

12. Wickliffe Rose, Internal memorandum, 3 Mar. 1913, 6 RF, Series 3, Subseries 908, Box 14, Folder 149, RAC.

13. Typed report, "The County Health Service" (unsigned but probably by Wickliffe Rose), 1912, 9, RF, Series 3, Subseries 908, Box 14, Folder 149, RAC.

14. Watson Rankin, Confidential memorandum, "Recommendations in Regard to Appropriations for Rural Health Work in North Carolina, 1919," Records of the Rockefeller Foundation: International Health Board, Record Group 5, Series 2, Box 17, Folder 95, RAC (hereafter IHB).

15. "Remarks of Frederick Russell."

16. Fosdick, *Adventure in Giving*, 40; see also Fosdick, *The Rockefeller Foundation*, ix–xiii.

17. Fosdick, *Adventure in Giving*, 40.

18. Joseph Bailey describes this meeting in *Seaman Knapp: Schoolmaster of American Agriculture* (New York, 1945), 213–18.

19. Ibid., 89–92. See also Seaman Knapp, "The Mission of Cooperative Demonstration Work in the South," Department of Agriculture, Office of the Secretary, Circular 33, Washington, D.C., 1910.

20. Bailey, *Seaman Knapp*, 130.

21. For a good description of the farm demonstration system see Seaman Knapp, "Farmers' Cooperative Demonstration Work and Its Results," *Proceedings of the Ninth Conference for Education in the South* (Richmond, Va., 1906).

22. The exact figure is $925,750; *The General Education Board: An Account of Its Activities, 1902–1914* (New York: General Education Board, 1930) (hereafter GEB 1902–14), 48. The RAC Library houses a complete collection of all GEB-published *Annual Reports*, which began with this belated compilation. For details of the agreement between Wilson and Buttrick see "Memorandum of Understanding between the United States Department of Agriculture and the General Education Board for Cooperation in Extending the Farmers' Cooperative Cotton Demonstration Work,"

in Rockefeller Family Archives, Record Group 2, Series, "Rockefeller Boards," Box 15, Folder 148, RAC.

23. The fifteen states included all the states of the Old South as well as Oklahoma, West Virginia, and Maryland. GEB 1902–14, 37–38.

24. GEB, 1902–14, 29.

25. Ibid., 38.

26. Ibid., 50.

27. Ibid., 49–50.

28. Ibid., 31–32.

29. Ibid., 30

30. Quoted in Link, *A Hard Country and a Lonely Place,* 168.

31. GEB 1902–14, 181.

32. Confidential memorandum, "Opportunities for Cooperative Aid," (1907), Records of the General Education Board, Series 1, Subseries 5, Box 720, Folder 7410, RAC (hereafter GEB).

33. Ibid.

34. The best available (though highly flawed) account of the history of the Smith-Lever Act is Perry Mock, James Chrisman, and Arthur McLure, *Education for Work: The Historical Evolution of Vocational and Distributive Education in America* (Charlotte, N.C., 1985), 58–60.

35. Ibid., 60–70. *Education for Work* never notes the role played by the controversy over the GEB but instead exaggerates Smith's promotion of vocational education during his two terms as Georgia's governor.

36. *Congressional Record,* 5 June 1914, 51: 9897.

37. Ibid., 23 May 1914, 51: 9891.

38. The most thorough account of the incident is Gitelman, *The Legacy of the Ludlow Massacre.* The conclusion of this book provides much more information about the infamous "massacre" through its analysis of foundations and the Commission on Industrial Relations.

39. Charles Little to B. W. Hunt, 29 May 1914. This letter summarizes a speech by Kenyon that contains the quoted phrases. Rockefeller Family Archives, Record Group 2, Series "Rockefeller Boards," Box 15, Folder 148, RAC.

40. *Congressional Record,* 5 June 1914, 51: 9895.

41. Starr Murphy to William Kenyon, 5 May 1914, Rockefeller Family Archives, Record Group 2, Series "Rockefeller Boards," Box 15, Folder 148, RAC.

42. William Kenyon to Albert Shaw, 4 May 1914, Rockefeller Family Archives, Record Group 2, Series "Rockefeller Boards," Box 15, Folder 148.

43. Sydney Bowie to Asbury Lever, 30 May 1914, Rockefeller Family Archives, Record Group 2, Series "Rockefeller Boards," Box 15, Folder 148, RAC.

44. *Congressional Record,* 26 June 1914, 51: 12180.

45. Ida Tarbell, *The History of the Standard Oil Company* (New York, 1904), 231.

46. Most of the essays were later collected into Rockefeller's only published book, *Random Reminiscences of Men and Events.* For a list of books condemning Rockefeller Sr. see Harr and Johnson, *The Rockefeller Century,* 58–60. The historian

John Ettling has argued Rockefeller so inspired the hatred of his fellow citizens because they sensed that at heart he was "too much like them." They saw someone who, like themselves, seized the main chance, but talked in pious cant. See Ettling, *The Germ of Laziness: Rockefeller Philanthropy and Public Health in the New South* (Cambridge, Mass., 1981), 183–84. I find this and similar arguments about Rockefeller's remarkable unpopularity dubious at best. Did Americans really see someone they so disliked because he was really the face in the mirror? Isn't self-deception more common than genuine self-revelation? Moreover, Rockefeller was strikingly unlike anybody. He wasn't one bit like the "average" American. He was far smarter, far more ruthless, better educated, and better organized. He wasn't even like most "average" rich Americans, who kept all their money, or, at most, gave in conventional ways to conventional good causes.

47. RF, Series 3, Subseries 908, Box 15, Folder 155, RAC.

48. Ettling focuses on the history of the Sanitary Commission only and ends his study with the year 1915. In many ways the cooperative work done between county agencies and the IHB between 1915 and 1930 is even more interesting. Though this chapter will not emphasize the relationship, the IHB sporadically also worked with a federal agency, the U.S. Public Health Service. In 1919, for instance, Congress eliminated the sum of $50,000 from the appropriations bill for the Public Health Service— a venerable congressionally established institution that, in the nineteenth century, primarily provided care for disabled military veterans. By the early twentieth century the Public Health Service, however, had also embraced an "educational" mission. So when it faced cuts in its 1919–20 "malaria education" budget, it sent four of the five employees who had been doing the work to the IHB. The International Health Board hired these men, then "loaned" them back to the Public Health Service. The care with which contracts were drawn in 1919 perhaps reflected IHB concern after the farm demonstration debacle of 1914. There was no question that the four men were IHB employees though they worked as "advisors" to the Public Health Service. As a 1919 report sent to the Rockefeller philanthropy's central offices noted, "This shows the kind of cooperation which is possible with a federal department if the department head desires such cooperation." Memorandum, "Relations with U.S. Public Health Service," 30 June 1919, Rockefeller Family Archives, Record Group 2, Series "Rockefeller Boards," Box 15, Folder 148. For a history of the U.S. Public Health Service see Fitzhugh Mullan, *Plagues and Politics: The Story of the United States Public Health Service* (New York, 1989).

49. Ettling, *The Germ of Laziness*, 97–113.

50. Ibid., 114–15. See also Roy Acheson, *Wickliffe Rose of the Rockefeller Foundation: 1862–1914, The Formative Years* (Cambridge, 1992).

51. "Report of I. A. Shirley," 1 Jan. 1915, *Sanitary*, Series 2, Box 3, Folder 93, RAC.

52. "Report to John A. Ferrell," 18 July 1911, *Sanitary*, Series 2, Box 6, Folder 117, RAC.

53. Ettling, *The Germ of Laziness*, 118–21.

54. Confidential memorandum, "Regarding the Extent to Which International Health Board Funds Can Legally Be Employed in Supporting Health Work

Also Supported by the U.S. Government," 13 Sept. 1923, RF, Series 3, Subseries 908, Box 14, Folder 149, RAC.

55. "Report of the Educational Work for 1913 by the State Board of Health of Kentucky," *Sanitary,* Series 2, Box 3, Folder 90, RAC.

56. Ibid.

57. Wickliffe Rose, "Memorandum on the County Health Service," 1912, RF, Series 3, Subseries 908, Box 14, Folder 149, RAC (hereafter Rose 1912).

58. Memorandum, "Development of Public Health Work in North Carolina," Jan. 1918, IHB, Record Group 5, Box 64, Folder 1918 N.C. Reports, RAC.

59. In 1917, for instance, the heads of more than two hundred families in North-ampton County, N.C., signed the following agreement with the county health officer:

Recognizing that a large number of deaths that yearly take place in North-ampton County are entirely *preventable,* I, the undersigned do hereby agree to cooperate with the County Health Department as follows:

I agree to build a sanitary privy according to directions . . . to improve my well so as to keep surface water and polluted soil out of it, and to screen my house.

The Northampton County Health Department, in turn, agrees to do the following free of all cost to me:

Examine the family for hookworm disease.

Vaccinate the family against typhoid fever.

Have a representative visit and inspect my home and point out the best meth-ods of sanitation to protect the family against infectious diseases.

"Report of the Bureau of County Health Work of the North Carolina Board of Health for July and August, 1917," IHB, Record Group 5, Box 64, Folder North Carolina Reports, RAC.

60. "Open Letter to Friends," 8 Feb. 1915, IHB, Record Group 5, Series 1, Box 7, Folder 95, RAC.

61. "Investment in Public Health," Jan. 1924, IHB, Record Group 5, Series 2, Box 17, Folder 96, RAC.

62. Ettling, *The Germ of Laziness,* 164–67, 213.

63. J. N. McCormack to John Ferrell, 16 Sept. 1913, *Sanitary,* Series 2, Box 3, Folder 90, RAC.

64. See, for instance, "Penalty Rule: Chapter 62, Section 22: Public Laws, 1911 N.C. and as Amended, Chapter 181, Section 10, 1913," copy in IHB, Record Group 5, Box 64, Folder North Carolina Reports, RAC.

65. Ibid.

66. Wickliffe Rose to Frederick Gates, 22 Nov. 1911, IHB, Record Group 5, Series 2, Box 17, Folder 95, RAC.

67. Memorandum, "Results Accomplished," IHB, Record Group 5, Box 64, Folder North Carolina Reports, RAC.

68. Wickliffe Rose to Hamilton Jones, 1 Sept. 1910, *Sanitary,* Series 2, Box 3, Folder 94, RAC.

69. Ibid., 10 Sept. 1910.

70. Wickliffe Rose to Oscar Dowling, 10 Oct. 1910, *Sanitary,* Series 2, Box 3, Folder 94, RAC.

71. Rose 1912.

72. "Report of Fred Caldwell to John A. Ferrell," 2 Feb. 1920, IHB, Record Group 5, Series 2, Box 17, Folder 95, RAC.

73. Ibid.

74. Ibid.

75. The above sequence of letters can be found in *Sanitary*, Series 2, Box 63, RAC.

76. "Remarks of Frederick Russell."

77. Ibid.

78. Ettling, *The Germ of Laziness*, 209–11.

79. Walter Hines Page to Wickliffe Rose, 20 Feb. 1912, *Sanitary*, Series 1, Box 3, Folder 38, RAC. In trying to lure Rose to his son's North Carolina home for a vacation, Page told Rose: "We'll walk; we'll ride horseback; motor; golf; swap lies; have the kids sing and play. . . . 'Go long nigger . . . Ain't yer got imaginat'n 'nuff to 'magine yer own?' . . . I implore you [to come]. It'll make you over. We'll be new men. Hookworms will eat out of our hands."

80. Speech Transcript, Speech of William Frost (President of Berea College), reprinted in *Berea Quarterly* 18 (1903): 6. A complete collection of the published Berea College *Berea Quarterly* newsletter can be found in the Berea Library Archives, Berea College, Berea, Ky. (hereafter BA).

81. "Meeting of the Berea Association of New York at Carnegie Hall," Transcript of Speeches, Feb. 1911, "Berea Association Speeches," BA. The quoted exchange occurred between Seth Low, Mayor of New York City, and William Cady, President of the Berea Association.

82. Frank Bachman to Abraham Flexner, 19 Sept. 1923, GEB, Series 1, Subseries 1, Box 82, Folder 723, RAC.

83. Fosdick, *Adventure in Giving*, 107.

84. This quotation from the GEB's Annual Report for 1914–15 is typical of many similar phrases in antecedent and subsequent reports. The General Education Board, *Report of the Secretary for 1914 and 1915* (New York, General Education Board), 38. Complete File of AR in RAC Library.

85. Edwin Embree, "Education for Negroes: Divided We Fall," *American Scholar* 5 (1936): 319.

86. Edwin Embree provides an overview of the project in Embree and Waxman, *Investment in People;* see also idem, "How the Negro Schools Have Advanced under the Rosenwald Fund," *The Nation's Schools* 1 (1928): 37–44.

87. The description occurs in Embree, "Education for Negroes," 319. Rosenwald Fund officials regularly used the word "shame" in private discussions of their policy goals. See Edwin Embree to Julius Rosenwald, 26 May 1931, Rosenwald, Box 33, Folder 9, UC.

88. Embree and Waxman, *Investment in People,* 30–48.

89. Abraham Flexner to Wallace Buttrick (1919), GEB, Series 1, Subseries 2, Box 303, Folder 3171, RAC.

90. Ibid.

91. The Woodson manuscript is divided into typed chapters, but the pagination between chapters is not sequential. Carter Woodson, "Story of the Fund,"

chapter 8: 1, Rosenwald, Box 33, Folder 1, UC (hereafter Woodson). For more information on the career of Carter Woodson see Jacqueline Goggin, *Carter G. Woodson: A Life in Black History* (Baton Rouge, La., 1993).

92. Woodson, ch. 8: 1–10.

93. Ibid., ch. 8: 1–16; quotation on 8.

94. Ibid., ch. 10: 7.

95. Embree, "Education for Negroes," 318.

96. Jerome Greene to Wallace Buttrick, 7 Jan. 1914, GEB, Series 1, Subseries 2, Box 353, Folder 3651, RAC.

97. Jerome Greene to Wallace Buttrick, 10 Jan. 1914, GEB, Series 1, Subseries 2, Box 353, Folder 3651, RAC.

98. Biographical information on John Campbell can be found in RSF, Series 3, Box 16, Folder 136, RAC.

99. John Campbell, "Mountain and Rural Fields in the South," undated, probably 1916(?), RSF, Series 3, Box 16, Folder 136, RAC.

100. Ibid.

101. John Campbell, *The Southern Highlander and His Homeland* (New York, 1921), 264–65.

102. Ibid., 265–66.

103. Ibid., 267–68.

104. Ibid., 295.

105. Campbell and his wife Olive were actually on board ship in New York harbor in August 1914, ready to depart for a long-anticipated trip to Denmark to investigate folk schools under the aegis of Russell Sage support, when World War I intervened. The voyage was canceled. John Campbell never got to Scandinavia, but Olive did. After her husband's death, she traveled, with RSF funding, to Denmark, Sweden, and Finland in 1924. Her report on the folk schools of Denmark is summarized in speech transcript, "Address at Southern Mountain Workers' Conference," 9 Apr. 1924, RSF, Series 3, Box 16, Folder 138, RAC.

106. Glenn et al., *The Russell Sage Foundation*, 282–84. The Carnegie Foundation funded "mountaineer education" in this period as well. However, the contributions of Andrew Carnegie buttress this book's contention that, before 1930, the Carnegie philanthropies practiced largely traditional, distributive charity or sought influence over private organizational policy. Rather than promote a new public educational policy in Appalachia, Carnegie provided generously for Berea College. Berea's president, William Frost, was a well-connected northerner, a former minister who lobbied Woodrow Wilson and Andrew Carnegie personally for funds for the private college. When "kind friends" sent him on recuperative summer vacations to Scotland, beginning in 1904, Frost received luncheon invitations to Carnegie's Scotland estate, Skibo Castle. The canny Frost, in private notes, recounted the way he played on Carnegie's jealousy of other philanthropists' donations. When told in 1913 that he "had given a great deal, and at times when it counted the most" but that he had not made the largest individual contribution to Berea, Carnegie quickly wrote Frost a check for "$63,000, the precise amount necessary to top any other philanthropic giving between 1904 and 1912." It was his long personal association with Frost, not public-policy-making objectives, that opened Carnegie's checkbook on

this occasion. Such almost ad hoc giving characterized the Carnegie philanthropies until the mid-1930s—more than a decade after their creator's death. Berea College Records: Office of Development, Record Group 5, 23, William Frost, typed notes, "Three Interviews with Carnegie," Box 4, Folder 3, BA.

107. For information about the plight of southern farmers and black and white migration from the South see Danbom, *The Resisted Revolution*, 20–45; Douglas Flamming, *Creating the Modern South: Millhands and Managers in Dalton, Georgia, 1884–1984* (Chapel Hill, N.C., 1992); Neil Fligstein, *Going North: Migration of Blacks and Whites from the South, 1900–1950* (New York, 1981); Jack Temple Kirby, *Rural Worlds Lost: The American South, 1920–1960* (Baton Rouge, La., 1987); Peter Gottlieb, *Making Their Own Way: Southern Blacks' Migration to Pittsburgh, 1916–1930* (Urbana, Ill., 1987).

CHAPTER THREE—THE LAURA SPELMAN ROCKEFELLER MEMORIAL, PARENT EDUCATION, AND THE NEW PSYCHOLOGY

1. Edward Barrows, typed report, "Why a Deductive Study of Child Life in New York Is Needed," 1 Aug. 1923, Records of the Laura Spelman Rockefeller Memorial (hereafter LSRM), Series 3, Subseries 5, Box 28, Folder 1923, RAC.

2. Ibid.

3. G. Stanley Hall, "The Contents of Children's Minds," *Princeton Review* 11 (1883): 249. For discussions of James, Hall, and "Instinct Psychology" see Carl Degler, *In Search of Human Nature: The Decline and Revival of Darwinism in American Social Thought* (New York, 1991); Dorothy Ross, *G. Stanley Hall: The Psychologist and Prophet* (Chicago, 1972); David Krantz and David Allen, "The Rise and Fall of McDougall's Instinct Doctrine," *Journal of the History of the Behavioral Sciences* 9 (1973): 66–76. For discussions about the emergence of the new profession of psychology from the established discipline of philosophy see Daniel Wilson, *Science, Community, and the Transformation of American Philosophy, 1860–1930* (Chicago, 1990).

4. For further discussion about Hall's growing fascination with adolescence, a term he introduced into widespread usage, see Ross, *G. Stanley Hall*, 300–345.

5. Historians have largely ignored the subjects of the PTA and parent education. Two exceptions are Mary Madeleine Ladd-Taylor and Steven Schlossman. See Mary Madeleine Ladd-Taylor, *Mother-Work: Ideology, Public Policy and the Mothers' Movement, 1890–1930* (Ann Arbor, Mich., 1987), 72–127. Steven Schlossman's work is the best available on parent education and includes interesting insights about the LSRM and parent education, though, as will be noted, this chapter challenges some of his conclusions. Most useful are Steven Schlossman, "Before Home Start: Notes toward a History of Parent Education in America, 1897–1929," *Harvard Educational Review* 46 (1976): 436–67; "The Formative Era in American Parent Education: Overview and Interpretation," in Ron Haskins and Diane Adams, eds., *Parent Education and Public Policy* (Norwood, N.J., 1983), 7–39; "Philanthropy and the Gospel of Child Development," *History of Education Quarterly* 21 (1981): 275–99; "Philanthropy and the Gospel of Child Development," in Gerald Benjamin, ed., *Private Philanthropy and Public Elementary and Secondary Education: Proceedings of the Rockefeller Archive Center*

Conference (Tarrytown, N.Y., 1980), 15–23. The latter two articles are identical. Schlossman's article in *Parent Education and Public Policy* is a slightly revised version of "Philanthropy and the Gospel of Child Development." Schlossman does not seriously address the issue of public policy making; rather he focuses on the LSRM's interaction with private organizations, primarily the Child Study Association of America.

6. "Iowa Health Fair Idea Taking Root: Mother's Delegate Here Says," report in LSRM, Series 3, Subseries 5, Box 43, Folder 450, RAC.

7. For discussions of the influence exercised by the University of Chicago during this period see Hamilton Cravens, *The Triumph of Evolution: American Scientists and the Heredity-Environment Controversy* (Philadelphia, 1978), 25–46; Daniel Kevles, "Foundations, Universities, and Trends in Support for the Physical and Biological Sciences," *Daedalus* 121 (1992): 195–235. John Jordan provides a fascinating analysis of the entire range of "technocratic progressivism" that included psychology among its principles in his *Machine-Age Ideology: Social Engineering and American Liberalism, 1911–1939* (Chapel Hill, N.C., 1994).

8. Cravens, *The Triumph of Evolution*, 180–99.

9. John Watson, *Behaviorism* (New York, 1925).

10. John Watson, *Psychological Care of Infant and Child* (New York, 1928).

11. Miriam Van Waters, *Parents on Probation* (New York, 1927), 4, 5. Estelle Freedman's splendid biography of Miriam Van Waters corrects decades of historical neglect. See Estelle Freedman, *Maternal Justice: Miriam Van Waters and the Female Reform Tradition* (Chicago, 1996).

12. Ibid., 59–80.

13. For discussion of the CSAA see Schlossman, "The Formative Era in Parent Education," 16–34.

14. "Comparison of Entries Made on Registration Cards by Members" (typed membership statistics sent to LSRM), LSRM, Record Group 3, Series 5, Box 28, Folder 291, RAC. For example, in 1920, only 16,642 women earned college degrees out of a national female population of 52,170,000. *Historical Statistics of the United States: Colonial Times to the Present* (New York, 1976), 9, 386.

15. Barry Smith to Edward Harkness (undated, probably Jan. 1921), Correspondence Files of Edward Harkness (unprocessed), CF, RAC.

16. Aubrey Williams to Beardsley Ruml, 2 Jan. 1940, Papers of Beardsley Ruml (hereafter Ruml), Box 1, Folder 1, UC.

17. The description can be found in E. B. Garnett, "Beardsley Ruml Has Never Worked, Except with His Mind," Box 1, Folder 1, Ruml, UC.

18. The best information about Frank can be found in the transcripts of a series of interviews with Frank's colleagues and friends by Milton Senn. The complete transcripts are in Milton Senn Oral History Collection, History of Medicine Division, National Library of Medicine, Bethesda, Md. For an edited collection of these oral histories see Milton Senn, "Insights on the Child Development Movement in the United States," *Monographs of the Society for Research in Child Development* 40 (1975): 34–161 (hereafter Senn, *Monographs*). A valuable dissertation that discusses Frank is Stephen Cross, "Designs for Living: Lawrence Frank and the Progressive Legacy in American Social Science" (Ph.D. diss., Johns Hopkins University, 1994). For an over-

view of LSRM activities during the 1920s, see typed transcript, "Staff Meetings held in Hanover, New Hampshire, August 24–27, 1927" LSRM, Series 2, Box 3, Folder 41A, RAC.

19. "Annual Reports of the Child Study Association of America," LSRM, Record Group 3, Series 5, Box 28, Folder 291, RAC.

20. Douglas Thom, *Everyday Problems of the Everyday Child* (New York, 1927). See also idem, "Habit Clinics for Children of Pre-School Age," *American Journal of Psychiatry* 79 (1922–23): 31–38.

21. "Summary of Study #11," LSRM, Record Group 3, Series 5, Box 28, Folder 291, RAC.

22. Typed manuscript, "Review of Child Study and Parent Education," Jan. 1929, LSRM, Series 3, Subseries 5, Box 43, Folder 446, RAC.

23. Lawrence Frank, "Report to the Trustees of the Laura Spelman Rockefeller Memorial," LSRM, Series 3, Subseries 5, Box 30, Folder 315, RAC.

24. Lawrence Frank, Internal Memorandum, "Child Study and Parent Education," Sept. 1926, LSRM, Series 3, Subseries 5, Box 30, Folder 315, RAC.

25. Lawrence Frank, "Report to the Trustees of the Laura Spelman Rockefeller Memorial, LSRM, Series 3, Subseries 5, Box 30, Folder 315, RAC.

26. The programs averaged an annual cost of $30,000. Of that amount, the LSRM paid $7,500. The California State Department of Education paid $2,000. Local school boards made up the difference. Memorandum, "Financial Support for the Program," LSRM, Series 3, Subseries 5, Box 27, Folder 281, RAC.

27. "Appendix A: Tabulation of Data Concerning Parent Education Discussion Classes Maintained in California," LSRM, Series 3, Subseries 5, Box 27, Folder 281, RAC (hereafter "Tabulation").

28. See Schlossman, "Before Home Start," 449–56.

29. Ibid., 449.

30. Ethel Richardson Allen, "General Description of an Experiment in Parent Education Carried on by Direction of the Superintendent of Public Instruction of the State of California: Upon a Grant made by the Laura Spelman Rockefeller Memorial," LSRM, Series 3, Subseries 5, Box 27, Folder 281, RAC.

31. Ibid.

32. Ibid.

33. "Tabulation."

34. Ethel Richardson, Memorandum, "Set-up of Proposed Parent Education Program," 29 Mar. 1926, LSRM, Series 3, Subseries 5, Box 27, Folder 280, RAC.

35. Copies of application forms can be found in LSRM, Series 3, Subseries 5, Box 27, Folder 280, RAC.

36. Will C. Wood (Superintendent of Public Instruction for the State of California) to Beardsley Ruml, "Report of Progress," Jan. 1927, LSRM, Series 3, Subseries 5, Box 27, Folder 280, RAC (hereafter "Report of Progress").

37. Ibid.

38. Ibid.

39. Herbert Stolz, "Report on an Experiment in Parent Education," 15 Dec. 1929, LSRM, Series 3, Subseries 5, Box 27, Folder 280, RAC (hereafter Stolz 1929).

40. For Frank's discussions of the objections of psychiatrists see Lawrence

Frank, Memorandum, "Child Study and Education of Parents," 24 Mar. 1927, LSRM, Series 3, Subseries 5, Box 30, Folder 316, RAC. In general, psychiatrists who wrote to Frank thought that parent education was too vaguely defined to be of any good to either parents or children.

41. Sydnor Walker to Lawrence Frank, 10 Mar. 1927, LSRM, Series 3, Subseries 5, Box 30, Folder 316, RAC.

42. Remarks of Lawrence Frank, typed transcript, "Staff Meetings held in Hanover, New Hampshire, August 24–27, 1927," LSRM Series 2, Box 3, Folder 41A, 158, RAC.

43. Senn, *Monographs,* 22.

44. Ibid., 28.

45. Lawrence Frank, confidential memorandum, "Child Study and Parent Training" (this typed title is followed by a handwritten subtitle, "What Is Child Care?"), LSRM, Series 3, Subseries 5, Box 30, Folder 315, RAC.

46. Ibid.

47. "Report of Vierling Kersey to the Secretary of the Laura Spelman Rockefeller Memorial," 17 Dec. 1931, LSRM, Series 3, Subseries 5, Box 27, Folder 281, RAC.

48. For discussions of the early home economics movement see Emma Weigley, "It Might Have Been Euthenics: The Lake Placid Conferences and the Home Economics Movement," *American Quarterly* 26 (1974): 79–96; see also "Interview with Pauline Park Wilson Knapp," in Senn, *Monographs.*

49. Stolz 1929.

50. In 1931 the state of California paid only $800 for this type of training for study group leaders. See Gertrude Laws, "Annual Report of the Los Angeles Office of the Bureau of Parent Education," Appendix C: 1930, 1931, LSRM, Series 3, Subseries 5, Box 27, Folder 281, RAC.

51. Ibid. For information on the junior and community college movements, see George Vaughan, *The Community College in America: A Short History* (Washington, D.C., 1985); George Baker, ed., *A Handbook of the Community College in America: Its History, Mission and Management* (Westport, Conn., 1994); Maurice Weidenthal, *Who Cares about the Inner City? The Community College's Response to Urban America* (Washington, D.C., 1988).

52. Lawrence Frank, typed notes, "Parent Training," 26 Mar. 1924, LSRM, Series 3, Subseries 5, Box 30, Folder 315, RAC.

Chapter Four—The Russell Sage Foundation and the Transformation of the Mothers' Pension

1. "Ten Years of Mothers' Pensions," *Survey* 49 (1923): 634–36.

2. "Wildfire Spread of Widows' Pensions: Its Start, Its Meaning, and Its Cost," *Everybody's Magazine* 32 (1915): 780.

3. The best statistical summary of the mothers' aid phenomenon can be found in U.S. Department of Labor, Children's Bureau (hereafter CB), *Mothers' Aid,* 1931, Publication 220 (Washington, D.C., 1933). The twenty states are Colorado, Florida, Indiana, Kansas, Kentucky, Maine, Massachusetts, Michigan, Mississippi, Missouri, Nebraska, Nevada, New Hampshire, New Mexico, North Carolina, Rhode Island,

South Dakota, Virginia, Washington, and Wisconsin. Other very useful CB publications are U.S. Department of Labor, CB, *Proceedings of the Conference on Mothers' Pensions,* Publication 109 (Washington, D.C., 1922); U.S. Department of Labor, CB, *Standards of Public Aid to Children in Their Own Homes,* Publication 118 (Washington, D.C., 1923). Note: The complete publication numbers assigned to these documents by the U.S. Government Printing Office are cited in the bibliography.

4. CB, *Mothers' Aid,* 1931, 15–28; in addition to the above states, Ohio, Oklahoma, and Oregon.

5. Ibid., 12–14. This 1931 study of 46,597 families receiving aid, in the estimate of Children's Bureau statisticians, presented evidence on about half of all families receiving mothers' aid in that year. No information on race was available in six states.

6. Ibid., 28–29. See also U.S. Department of Labor, CB, *The Administration of Mothers' Aid in Ten Localities,* Publication 184 (Washington, D.C., 1928).

7. "Ten Years of Mothers' Pensions," 635.

8. Winifred Bell, *Aid to Dependent Children* (New York, 1965), 13. The cities were Boston, Chicago, Cleveland, Detroit, Los Angeles, Milwaukee, New York City, Philadelphia, and Pittsburgh. Bell bases this estimate on statistics compiled in 1934–35 by advocates lobbying for the Social Security Act.

9. CB, *Mothers' Aid,* 1931, 28–33.

10. Ada Sheffield, "Administration of the Mothers' Aid Law in Massachusetts," *Survey* 31 (1914): 645. Sheffield's extensive report in this issue of *Survey* provides the details of the law's administration discussed here.

11. T. J. Edmonds and Maurice Hexter, "State Pensions to Mothers in Hamilton County, Ohio," *Survey* 33 (1914): 289–90; George Adams, "Mothers' Pensions," *Ohio Bulletin of Charities and Correction* 21 (1915): 18–22.

12. A few scholars pioneered investigations into the topic earlier, but most published the analyses cited here after 1982. See Bell, *Aid to Dependent Children,* 1–25; Ann Vandepol, "Dependent Children, Child Custody and the Mothers' Pension Movement: The Transformation of State-Family Relations in the Early Twentieth Century," *Social Problems* 29 (1982): 221–35; Ladd-Taylor, *Mother-Work;* Seth Koven and Sonya Michel, "Womanly Duties: Maternalist Politics and the Origins of the Welfare State in France, Germany, Great Britain, and the United States, 1880–1920," *American Historical Review* 95 (1990): 1076–1114; Mark Leff, "Consensus for Reform: The Mothers' Pension Movement in the Progressive Era," *Social Service Review* 47 (1973): 397–415; Ann Orloff, "Gender in Early U.S. Social Policy," *Journal of Policy History* 3 (1991): 249–82; Christopher Howard, "Sowing the Seeds of 'Welfare': The Transformation of Mothers' Pensions, 1900–1940," *Journal of Policy History* 4 (1992): 188–227; Theda Skocpol, *Protecting Soldiers and Mothers: The Political Origins of Social Policy in the United States* (Cambridge, Mass., 1992); Barbara Nelson, "The Origins of the Two-Channel Welfare State: Workmen's Compensation and Mothers' Aid," in Linda Gordon, ed., *Women, the State, and Welfare* (Madison, Wis., 1990), 123–51; Muriel and Ralph Pumphrey, "The Widows' Pension Movement," in Walter Trattner, ed., *Social Welfare or Social Control? Some Historical Reflections on "Regulating the Poor"* (Knoxville, Tenn., 1983), 51–64; Sonya Michel, "The Limits of Maternalism: Policies toward American Wage-Earning Mothers during the Progressive Era," in Seth Koven and Sonya Michel, eds., *Mothers of a New World* (New York,

1993), 277–320; Libba Gage Moore, "Mothers' Pensions: The Origins of the Relationship between Women and the Welfare State" (Ph.D. diss., University of Massachusetts–Amherst, 1986); Wendy Sarvasy, "Beyond the 'Difference versus Equality' Policy Debates: Postsuffrage Feminism, Citizenship, and the Quest for a Feminist Welfare State," *Signs* 17 (1992): 329–62.

13. See, for instance, Skocpol, *Protecting Soldiers and Mothers,* 432–40, which includes lengthy quotations representing both groups.

14. Ibid., 425.

15. For elaboration of this argument, common to almost all scholarly literature that examines the pensions, see Ladd-Taylor, *Mother-Work,* 227–40.

16. Pumphrey and Pumphrey, "The Widows' Pension Movement," 62.

17. Leff, "Consensus for Reform," 411, 415.

18. Nelson, "The Origins of the Two-Channel Welfare State," 142; Skocpol, *Protecting Soldiers and Mothers,* 476–77.

19. Howard, "Sowing the Seeds of 'Welfare,'" 188, 218.

20. Orloff, "Gender in Early U.S. Social Policy," 273.

21. No scholar mentioned here has used the archival records of any foundation or private charity organization. At least, the notes in the materials examined above make no reference to any such research. It should be noted that, in contrast to the foundations examined in chapters 2 and 3, which conducted a variety of programs but maintained a body-of-the-whole organizational structure, the Russell Sage Foundation organized itself into departments. Between 1907 and 1930 the Sage departments were Recreation, Education, Child-Helping, Southern Highlands, Charity Organization, Remedial Loans, Consumer Credit Studies, Women's Work-Industrial Studies, Statistics, Surveys and Exhibits, Social Work Interpretation, Arts and Social Work, and Delinquency and Penology. Departmental influence within the foundation waxed and waned. At all times, however, the Charity Organization Department was an important unit within the foundation.

22. Edith Abbott, *The Child and the State, II* (Chicago, 1938), 17.

23. Indeed, Mary Ladd-Taylor admits that "the pension movement did not generate any major leaders or spokeswomen" (*Mother-Work,* 244). Mark Leff agrees and says, "The [pension movement] was characterized by polycentricity, with no national coordinating committee or national leader" ("Consensus for Reform," 405). For discussions of institutional alternatives and the generally bad reputation of orphanages by the early twentieth century see Susan Tiffin, *In Whose Best Interest? Child Welfare Reform in the Progressive Era* (Westport, Conn., 1982), 60–87; Dee Kilpatrick and Robert Roberts, eds., *Child Caring, Social Policy, and the Institution* (Chicago, 1973).

24. No scholar whose work is here reviewed mentions the potential alternative of the Women's Bureau, authorized as an agency of the United States Department of Labor in 1920. This is a subject dealt with later in this chapter. For further information on the Women's Bureau see Judith Sealander, *As Minority Becomes Majority: Federal Reaction to the Phenomenon of Women in the Work Force, 1920–1963* (Westport, Conn., 1983). A few scholars have noted the presence of Edith Abbott and Sophonisba Breckinridge, but they have misunderstood their roles in the mothers' pension debate. Historian Sonya Michel argues, for instance, that "Sophonisba Breckinridge and Edith Abbott, who had been central to the formulation and passage of pension legisla-

tion, suddenly found themselves boxed out—helpless to influence administration. Workers from private charity agencies moved in, establishing harsh investigative routines and protocols of constant surveillance" (Michel, "The Limits of Maternalism," 301). Mary Richmond was preeminently one of the "workers from private charity." However, she was Abbott's and Breckinridge's soul-mate, not their enemy. Moreover, as this chapter seeks to demonstrate, the latter two women were most certainly not "boxed out" of influence over the administration of the mothers' pensions.

25. Skocpol, *Protecting Soldiers and Mothers,* 479.

26. For an interesting estimate of Dreiser's editorial strategies see Harold Jambor, "Theodore Dreiser, the *Delineator,* and Dependent Children," *Social Service Review* 32 (1958): 33–35.

27. William Hard, "Motherless Children of Living Mothers," *Delineator* 81 (1913): 19–20.

28. "Remarks of Representative Begg Excerpted from the *Congressional Record,* February 8, 1926," copy in RSF records, Series 3, Box 38, Folder 317, RAC.

29. Edward Devine, "State Funds to Mothers," *Survey* 29 (1913): 747–48.

30. Schlossman, "Before Home Start," 457. See also Daniel Walkowitz, "The Making of a Feminine Professional Identity: Social Workers in the 1920s," *American Historical Review* 95 (1990): 1051–75; Clark Chambers, "Women in the Creation of the Profession of Social Work," *Social Service Review* 60 (1986): 1–33.

31. John Glenn, "Notes on Miss Richmond," RSF, Series 3, Box 13, Folder 114, RAC. For another discussion of the influence of *Social Diagnosis* see E. Wayne Carp, "Professional Social Workers, Adoption, and the Problem of Illegitimacy: 1915–1945," *Journal of Policy History* 6 (1994): 161–84.

32. Glenn, "Notes on Miss Richmond."

33. "Mary Richmond: Tribute," *Family* 9 (1929): 320–21.

34. Mary Richmond, "Motherhood and Pensions," *Survey* 29 (1913): 778.

35. Ibid., 776. Richmond cites an editorial that appeared in the Nov. 1912 issue of *Texas Motherhood Magazine.*

36. Even some scholars have oversimplified her views on corruption. Theda Skocpol, for example, dismisses Richmond's analogy between mothers' and soldiers' pensions: "Concerned with the possibilities of political corruption, she [Richmond] did not consider the differences between the cross-class male constituency helped by Civil War pensions and the impoverished female constituency that would benefit from mothers' pensions" (*Protecting Soldiers and Mothers,* 426). Richmond, however, was concerned about a political system swayed by forces in addition to the obvious ones generated by direct lobbying or the search for votes.

37. Richmond, "Motherhood and Pensions," 778–79.

38. Ibid., 778. Mary Richmond to Joseph Lee, 10 Apr. 1916, RSF, Series 3, Box 13, Folder 114, RAC. Mary Glenn, wife of John Glenn and a prominent social worker in her own right, echoed these worries about dependency. If a society became comfortable with the idea of the state assuming the care of indigent women without husbands, but with children, she asked, would "strong members of families no longer feel obliged to support weak?" Mary Glenn, "Relief of Needy Mothers," Remarks at Conference on Charities and Corrections, *Proceedings,* 1914, 452–53.

39. "Henry Neil: Pension Agent," *Survey* 29 (1913): 559–60.

40. "The Henry Neil League for Mothers' Pensions," *Survey* 29 (1913): 849. Emphasis in the original.

41. "Henry Neil Declares Reports Have Been Suppressed: Attacks Russell Sage Foundation," *New York Times,* 2 Mar. 1913, 3.

42. "Henry Neil: Pension Agent," 560.

43. Theda Skocpol expresses a common view when she says, "Mothers' pensions truly boomeranged on the intentions of their original supporters by pushing poor women into marginal wage-labor markets" (*Protecting Soldiers and Mothers,* 476).

44. Edward Devine, "Pensions for Mothers," *Survey* 30 (1913): 460.

45. Richmond, "Motherhood and Pensions," 775.

46. Frederick Almy, "Public Pensions for Widows," *Child* 5 (1912): 51–54. See also Paul Douglas, *Real Wages in the United States: 1890–1926* (New York, 1930).

47. Mary Richmond and Fred Hall, *A Study of Nine Hundred and Eighty-five Widows Known to Certain Charity Organization Societies in 1910* (New York, 1913).

48. Ibid., 8. The nine were in New York City, Philadelphia, Boston, Baltimore, Buffalo, Minneapolis, Atlanta, Cambridge, Mass., and Colorado Springs.

49. Ibid., 10–16.

50. Ibid., 22–25; quotation on 21.

51. Ibid., 20. See also Mary Richmond to John Glenn, 13 Aug. 1912, RSF, Series 3, Box 13, Folder 112, RAC.

52. The percentage of professionals in American society was still quite small. Moreover, between 1890 and 1920 that tiny percentage remained relatively stable— 3.78 percent of the national population in the former year—up to 4.4 percent in the latter. As late as 1970, official census estimates judged only 13 percent of the nation's workers to be professionals. The mushrooming of professional jobs in America is, indeed, a very recent phenomenon. In any decade, and certainly in the early twentieth century, the majority of those professionals—with well-paid, interesting, "nonmarginal" jobs—were men. A few of the new professions that emerged between 1870 and 1930, such as nursing, teaching, librarianship, or social work, became dominated by women. Without exception, these professions paid badly. In the 1920s an experienced, usually college-trained, social worker earned slightly less than a skilled male industrial worker who had a grade-school education and who had, typical for the era's working-class men, begun full-time work at age fourteen. An elite few, like Mary Richmond, in leadership positions at foundations with generous salary schemes, earned as much as $150 per month. Most averaged much less—about $90 per month. In sum, mothers' pensions played little role in marginalizing the already marginal. See Laurence Veysey, "Who's a Professional? Who Cares?" *Reviews in American History* 3 (1975): 421. For discussion of incomes earned by female professionals between 1900– 30 see Walkowitz, "The Making of a Feminine Professional Identity"; Penina Glazer and Miriam Slater, *Unequal Colleagues: The Entrance of Women into the Professions* (New Brunswick, N.J., 1987); Barbara Melosh, *The Physician's Hand: Work Culture and Conflict in American Nursing* (Philadelphia, 1982).

53. Richmond and Hall, *A Study of Nine Hundred and Eighty-five Widows,* 13.

54. Ibid.

55. Richmond, "Motherhood and Pensions," 779.

56. Devine, "Pensions for Mothers," 458–59.

57. Fred Hall and Elisabeth Brooke, *American Marriage Laws in Their Social Aspects* (New York, 1919); Mary Richmond and Fred Hall, *Child Marriages* (New York, 1925); idem, *Medical Certification for Marriages* (New York, 1925); idem, *Marriage and the State* (New York, 1929); Geoffrey May, *Marriage Laws and Decisions in the United States* (New York, 1929).

58. Richmond and Hall, *Child Marriages,* 66–138; idem, *Marriage and the State,* 338.

59. Richmond and Hall, *Child Marriages,* 131–44.

60. Richmond and Hall, *Marriage and the State,* 340–41.

61. Ibid., 92–209.

62. Hall and Brooke, *American Marriage Laws in Their Social Aspects,* 1–40. Chapter 6 more thoroughly discusses new early-twentieth-century public health approaches to the subject of venereal disease.

63. Glenn et al., *The Russell Sage Foundation,* 316–17.

64. For reproductions of all of these forms see Richmond and Hall, *Marriage and the State,* Appendix A.

65. C. C. Carstens, *Public Pensions to Widows with Children: A Study of Their Administration in Several American Cities* (New York, 1913), 28.

66. For information on the status of women at the University of Chicago see Ellen Fitzpatrick, *Endless Crusade: Women Social Scientists and Progressive Reform* (New York, 1990), 1–130.

67. For information about the Abbotts, Lathrop, and Breckinridge, in addition to *Endless Crusade,* see Robyn Muncey, "Gender and Professionalization in the Origins of the U.S. Welfare State: The Careers of Sophonisba Breckinridge and Edith Abbott," *Journal of Policy History* 2 (1990): 290–315; Jacqueline Parker and Edward Carpenter, "Julia Lathrop and the Children's Bureau: The Emergence of an Institution," *Social Service Review* 55 (1981): 60–77; Lela Costin, *Two Sisters for Social Justice* (Urbana, Ill., 1983); Ellen Lagemann, *A Generation of Women: Education in the Lives of Women Progressive Reformers* (Cambridge, Mass., 1979).

68. In 1909 the Russell Sage Foundation was not yet two years old. Nonetheless, it was already energetically pursuing its mandate—to investigate social conditions in America and promote effective public policy. In that year, the foundation provided financial support for research and travel expenses incurred by Theodore Roosevelt's Country Life Commission. It also endorsed and partially funded another presidential initiative, the White House Conference on the Care of Dependent Children. Two hundred experts interested in the problems of dependent children, including Hastings Hart, director of the Child-Helping Department of the Russell Sage Foundation, attended. Chief among the conference's recommendations was the establishment of a federal agency to coordinate information about America's children. In a very direct way the establishment of the U.S. Children's Bureau in the Department of Labor grew out of the energy generated by the 1909 White House Conference, even though Congress delayed final passage of the necessary enacting legislation until 1912. Beginning in 1909 supporters of a Children's Bureau, many of whom had attended the White House Conference, steadily lobbied for an agency, both in speeches before the House and Senate as well as in print. Theda Skocpol is correct when she notes that most scholars have misleadingly identified this conference as the impetus for the mothers'

pensions. Its more important impact was to promote a Children's Bureau (*Protecting Soldiers and Mothers,* 667). For information about Russell Sage Foundation involvement, see "Memorandum Respecting the Plans of the Children's Department of the Russell Sage Foundation for 1909–1910," RSF, Series 3, Box 14, Folder 122, RAC.

69. "Transcript of Remarks of Florence Kelley in Favor of HR Bill 24148, Jan. 27, 1909," in Papers of Edith and Grace Abbott, Box 38, Folder 1, UC.

70. For histories of the Children's Bureau see Kriste Lindenmeyer, "A Right to Childhood: A History of the U.S. Children's Bureau, 1912–38" (Ph.D. diss., University of Cincinnati, 1991); Nancy Weiss, "Save the Children: A History of the Children's Bureau, 1903–1918" (Ph.D. diss., University of California–Los Angeles, 1974). It should be noted that, until 1914, some opposition to Lathrop surfaced on the grounds that, as director of an agency engaged in investigations of infant mortality, diseases of children, and similar subjects, she should have medical training. See "Statement of Mark Foote" in Abbott, Box 38, Folder 2, UC.

71. For more information about Mary Anderson's career in the Women's Bureau see Sealander, *As Minority Becomes Majority,* 15–145.

72. CB, *Administration of Mothers' Aid in Ten Localities,* 5.

73. Walkowitz, "The Making of a Feminine Professional Identity," 1054.

74. For descriptions of the activities of the Case Committee see Carstens, *Public Pensions to Widows with Children,* 24–29.

75. CB, *Administration of Mothers' Aid in Ten Localities,* quotations on 25–26, 25, and 26, respectively.

76. U.S. Department of Labor, CB, *Administration of Aid-to-Mothers' Law in Illinois,* Publication 82 (Washington, D.C., 1921), 22.

77. Ibid., 22–23.

78. Ibid., 24.

79. "Statements of Fiorello LaGuardia, March 8, 1926," copy in RSF, Series 3, Box 38, Folder 317, RAC.

80. Helen Glenn to Mary Richmond, 18 Jan. 1916, RSF, Series 3, Box 13, Folder 112, RAC.

81. C. C. Carstens, "Summary of Discussion," U.S. Department of Labor, CB, *Standards of Child Welfare: A Report of the Children's Bureau Conferences of May and June, 1919,* Publication 60 (Washington, D.C., 1919), 351.

82. The "suitable home" provisions of the Social Security Act of 1935, as well as their administration through federal-state partnerships, proved one of the most durable legacies of the original Title IV. The provisions survived the depression and became in most places a permanent part of AFDC. This was true in states that extended public aid most generously as well as in states with highly restrictive programs. See Bell, *Aid to Dependent Children,* 20–40.

CHAPTER FIVE—FOUNDATIONS, "CHILD-HELPING," AND THE JUVENILE COURT

1. Miriam Van Waters, "The Juvenile Court from the Child's Viewpoint," in Jane Addams, ed., *The Child, the Clinic, and the Court* (New York, 1925), 219, 222–23 (emphasis in original, hereafter *Clinic*). This volume provides a published transcript of

papers delivered by participants at a 1925 Russell Sage Foundation–sponsored conference, held to mark the first quarter-century of the American juvenile court.

2. Julian Mack, *Legal Problems Involved in the Establishment of the Juvenile Court* (New York, 1912), 198.

3. Frances Bjorkman, "The Children's Court in American City Life," *Monthly Review of Reviews* 33 (1906): 306. Other contemporary assessments outlining the principles of the juvenile court include Katharine Lenroot, "The Evolution of the Juvenile Court," *Annals of the American Academy of Political and Social Science* 105 (1923): 213–22; Abraham Beitler, "The Juvenile Court in Philadelphia," *Annals of the American Academy of Political and Social Sciences* 21 (1902): 271–88; Evelina Belden, "The Boys Court of Chicago: A Record of Six Months' Work," *American Journal of Sociology* 20 (1915): 731–44; Paul Furley, "The Juvenile Court Movement," *Thought* 6 (1931): 207–27.

4. On the theory of probation see Julia Lathrop, "The Development of the Probation System in a Large City," *Charities* 13 (1905): 344–51.

5. Instructions quoted in Carl Kelsey, "The Juvenile Court of Chicago and Its Work," *Annals of the American Academy of Political and Social Science* 17 (1901): 121–23. See also Lucy Friday, "The Work of the Probation Officer among Children," *Charities* 13 (1905): 357–61.

6. For quotation of such speeches in the Colorado legislature see Ben Lindsey, "Love and the Criminal Law," *Journal of Education* 70 (1909): 203–5.

7. Beitler, "The Juvenile Court in Philadelphia," 271.

8. By far, the federal Children's Bureau produced the most thorough assessments of the juvenile courts for the period 1900–1930. Especially useful are U.S. Department of Labor, CB, *Juvenile Courts at Work: Progress of the Juvenile Court Movement,* Publication 141 (Washington, D.C., 1925); U.S. Department of Labor, CB, *Courts in the United States Hearing Children's Cases,* Publication 65 (Washington, D.C., 1920); U.S. Department of Labor, CB, *Analysis and Tabular Summary of State Laws Relating to Jurisdiction in Children's Cases,* Chart Publication 17 (Washington, D.C., 1930); U.S. Department of Labor, CB, *List of References on Juvenile Courts and Probation in the United States and a Selected List of Foreign References,* Publication 124 (Washington, D.C., 1923). Note: the publication numbers given these documents by the U.S. Government Printing Office are cited in the Bibliography.

9. As late as 1920 only nineteen American cities had even 250,000 residents. Peter Bruck, "Telephone Books and Party Lines," *Reviews in American History* 14 (1986): 341.

10. Ben Lindsey, "The Boy and the Court," *Charities* 13 (1905): 350.

11. Ibid.

12. Steven Schlossman, *Love and the American Delinquent: The Theory and Practice of Progressive Juvenile Justice, 1825–1920* (Chicago, 1977), 190.

13. Anthony Platt, *The Child-Savers: The Invention of Delinquency* (Chicago, 1969), 177.

14. Mary Odem and Steven Schlossman, "Guardians of Virtue: The Juvenile Court and Female Delinquency in Early 20th-Century Los Angeles," *Crime and Delinquency* 37 (1991): 190.

15. Douglas Rendleman, "*Parens Patriae*: From Chancery to the Juvenile Court," *South Carolina Law Review* 23 (1971): 257.

16. Michael Grossberg is a rare exception. See his "Who Gets the Child? Custody, Guardianship, and the Rise of the Judicial Patriarchy in Nineteenth Century America," *Feminist Studies* 9 (1983): 235–60.

17. Steven Schlossman and Susan Turner, "Status Offenders, Criminal Offenders, and Children at Risk in Early Twentieth Century Juvenile Court," in Roberta Wollons, ed., *Children at Risk in America: History, Concepts, and Public Policy* (Albany, N.Y., 1993), 32–58; Schlossman and Odem, "Guardians of Virtue," 186–203; Mary Odem, "Single Mothers, Delinquent Daughters, and the Juvenile Court in Early Twentieth Century Los Angeles," *Journal of Social History* 25 (1991) 27–43; Michael Sedlak, "Youth Policy and Young Women, 1870–1972," *Social Service Review* 56 (1982): 449–65; Robert Mennel, *Thorns & Thistles: Juvenile Delinquents in the United States, 1825–1940* (Hanover, N.H., 1973); Joseph Hawes, *The Children's Rights Movement: A History of Advocacy and Protection* (Boston, 1991).

18. Schlossman, *Love and the American Delinquent,* 177.

19. Especially interesting are Schlossman and Odem, "Guardians of Virtue," 186–203; Odem, "Single Mothers, Delinquent Daughters." Lydia's tale is summarized in the latter, 34–35.

20. Michael Grossberg, "Who Gets the Child?" 235–60; J. Lawrence Schultz "The Cycle of Juvenile Court History," *Crime and Delinquency* 19 (1973): 457–76; Rendleman, "*Parens Patriae,*" 240–56; Sanford Fox, "Juvenile Justice Reform: An Historical Perspective," *Stanford Law Review* 22 (1970): 1186–1239.

21. See in addition to the citations in the previous note "The Uniform Juvenile Court Act: A Symposium on Juvenile Problems," *Indiana Law Journal* 43 (1968): 523–50.

22. Rendleman, "*Parens Patriae,*" 242–56.

23. For examples see Joseph Hawes, *Children in Urban Society: Juvenile Delinquency in Nineteenth Century America* (New York, 1971), 158–91; Susan Tiffin, *In Whose Best Interest? Child Welfare Reform in the Progressive Era* (Westport, Conn., 1982), 147–95; Margo Horn, *Before It's Too Late: The Child Guidance Movement in the United States, 1922–1945* (Philadelphia, 1989), 54–98.

24. Roscoe Pound, "Law in Books and Law in Action," *American Law Review* 44 (1910): 12–36. "The Ladies of Chicago" is a chapter title in Joseph Hawes, *Children in Urban Society,* 158–91.

25. In *The Transformation of American Law, 1870–1960: The Crisis of Legal Orthodoxy* (New York, 1992), the sequel to his Bancroft Prize–winning *The Transformation of American Law, 1780–1860* (New York, 1977), Morton Horwitz devotes enormous attention to the legacies of Progressive legal thought. Nonetheless, he never once mentions the connections, which clearly exist, between "sociological jurisprudence" and the emergence of the juvenile court.

26. A complete list of the members of the committee can be found in CF, Record Group, Legal Research Program (hereafter Legal), Box 8, Folder 113, RAC. Members included, besides those already mentioned in the text, Henry Bates, Dean of the University of Michigan Law School, Young Smith, Dean of the Columbia

University Law School, and Austin Scott, Story Professor of Law at Harvard Law School.

27. The phrase "classical legal thought" is Morton Horwitz's. Other scholars, like G. Edward White, prefer to call the structures of nineteenth-century legal thought "mechanical jurisprudence." For clear discussion of nineteenth-century thought and early attacks upon it see Morton Horwitz, *The Transformation of American Law, 1870–1960*, 9–109; G. Edward White, "From 'Sociological Jurisprudence' to 'Realism': Jurisprudence and Social Change in Early Twentieth Century America, *Virginia Law Review* 58 (1972): 1002–17; G. Edward White, "The Rise and Fall of Justice Holmes," *University of Chicago Law Review* 51 (1971): 75–80.

28. Among Roscoe Pound's most influential pieces were "Law in Books and Law in Action"; "Liberty of Contract," *Yale Law Journal* 18 (1909): 454–64; "The Scope and Purpose of Sociological Jurisprudence, Part I," *Harvard Law Review* 24 (1911): 591–619; "The Scope and Purpose of Sociological Jurisprudence, Part II," *Harvard Law Review* 25 (1912): 489–516.

29. See Typescript, "Review of the Legal Research Program" (undated), CF, Record Group, Legal, Box 3, Folder 33, RAC.

30. Memorandum, "Legal Research," 16 Sept. 1920, CF, Record Group, Legal, Box 3, Folder 33, RAC.

31. Typescript, "Research," 72, CF, Record Group, Legal, Box 3, Folder 33, RAC.

32. Barry Smith, "Report to Members of the Legal Research Committee," 30 Apr. 1929, CF, Record Group, Legal, Box 3, Folder 33, RAC.

33. "Plan for Legal Research," 1 Oct. 1920, CF, Record Group, Legal, Box 1, Folder 1 (emphasis in original), RAC.

34. Typscript File, "Carbons of Hastings Hart Materials Sent to Harrison, November 6, 1933: Juvenile Delinquency, Notes Dated: 9/18/29," RSF, Series 3, Box 38, Folder 315, RAC.

35. Memorandum, "Research in Law and Evidence: Program Proposals," 8 Dec. 1928, CF, Record Group, Legal, Box 8, Folder 113, RAC.

36. Horn, *Before It's Too Late*, 57–83, discusses the demonstration clinics, with a focus on the one in Philadelphia. Her emphasis, however, is not on their role within the structure of the juvenile courts, but rather on their seminal influence on the creation of the profession of child guidance. For discussion of the early planning of the clinics see "Report of the Director: Program for the Prevention of Delinquency," 16 Jan. 1922, CF, Record Group, Unprocessed Directors' Files (hereafter Directors), RAC.

37. "Confidential Director's Report: January 20, 1920," CF, Record Group, Directors, RAC.

38. "Report of the Director," 16 Jan. 1922, CF, Record Group, Directors, RAC.

39. For a report on the early years of the institute see "Confidential: Statement in Regard to the Institute for Juvenile Research," May 1924, Rosenwald, Box 21, Folder 10, UC.

40. Horn, *Before It's Too Late*, 54–56.

41. See financial data in "Program in Mental Hygiene and Child Guidance,"

June 1927, CF, Directors. See also "Revision of the Present Program for the Prevention of Juvenile Delinquency: Report of the Director," 15 Apr. 1926 (hereafter Revision), CF, Record Group, Directors, RAC.

42. William Healy, *The Individual Delinquent* (Boston, 1915), 15–16.

43. Horn, *Before It's Too Late,* 65–69; see also Revision, 10–17.

44. Graham Taylor, letter excerpt, 15 Dec. 1922, in "Report of the Director, Jan. 16, 1923," 9, CF, Record Group, Directors, RAC.

45. Barry Smith, undated memorandum (probably 1927), CF, Record Group, Directors, RAC.

46. Ibid.

47. Indeed, worries about whether publicly funded clinics would ever be "the right sort" emerged early. See "Report of the Director, January 16, 1923," 9, CF, Record Group, Directors, RAC.

48. "Publication Two of the Joint Committee on Methods of Preventing Delinquency" (New York, 1925) (hereafter *Three Problem Children*). Another Commonwealth Fund publication argued that "the [guidance] clinic may block its own way to usefulness by . . . concentrating effort on cases in which little benefit can possibly result" and suggested strongly that cases referred by juvenile courts often fit that category: "Some juvenile courts are especially prone to refer cases of low intelligence, or with other special handicaps." George Stevenson and Geddes Smith, *Child Guidance Clinics: A Quarter-Century of Development* (New York, 1934), 70–71.

49. Stevenson and Smith, *Child Guidance Clinics,* 50, 85. For the discussion below of the cases of Mildred, Sidney, and Kenneth, see pp. 34 ff., 63 ff., and 118 ff., respectively.

50. "Report #348: National Committee on Delinquency" (typed draft 2), CF, Record Group, Directors, RAC.

51. Report of the Director: "Program for Child Health, February 3, 1925," CF, Record Group, Directors, RAC. I am grateful to Ellis Hawley for recommending I examine Douglas Parks's dissertation, which provides detailed discussion of Hoover's relationship with the American Child Health Association. See Douglas Parks, "Expert Inquiry and Health Care Reform in New Era America" (Ph.D. diss., University of Iowa, 1994).

52. In 1929 the Commonwealth Fund collected and published papers delivered at several of its conferences. See Charles Hoffman, "The Juvenile Court, the Community, and the Child Guidance Clinic," in Graham Taylor, ed., *The Child Guidance Clinic and the Community* (New York, 1929), 48.

53. "The Present Program: Its Successes and Failures," 2–3, Revision, CF, Record Group, Directors, RAC.

54. Ibid., 4–10.

55. CB, *Juvenile Courts at Work,* 34,

56. Pound, "Law in Books and Law in Action," 12.

57. This editorial appears excerpted in "The Trend of Things," *Survey* 29 (1912): 590.

58. See Worth Tippy, "Transcript of Address at Memorial Service for Hastings Hart," Nov. 1932, RSF, Record Group 3, Box 381, Folder 314, RAC.

59. Chapter 2 discusses the Country Life Commission. A detailed summary of

the 1909 White House Conference can be found in "Hastings Hart, An Epoch in Child-Helping," RSF, Box 14, Folder 122B, RAC.

60. "Transcript of Remarks of Judge Julian Mack in Favor of HR Bill 24148," 27 Jan. 1909, in Papers of Edith and Grace Abbott (hereafter Abbott), Box 38, Folder 1, UC.

61. "Transcript of Remarks of Mr. Homer Folks in Favor of HR Bill 24148," 27 Jan. 1909, Abbott, Box 38, Folder 1, UC.

62. For the story of the final years of the campaign to establish a federal Children's Bureau see Walter Trattner, *Crusade for the Children: A History of the National Child Labor Committee and Child Labor Reform in America* (Chicago, 1970), 95–103.

63. See note 8.

64. The most important of these were Publications 65 and 141, full citations in note 8. For discussion of interactions between the Children's Bureau and the Russell Sage Foundation see RSF, Series 3, Box 38, Folder 314, RAC.

65. George Kirchwey, "Institutions for Juvenile Delinquents," *Clinic*, 331.

66. CB, *Juvenile Courts at Work*, 94.

67. Ibid., 94–98.

68. Ibid., 96.

69. This is a point emphasized by Schlossman and Turner, "Status Offenders, Criminal Offenders," 39–49. In this study the authors found that one-third of the girls brought to the Los Angeles Juvenile Court had syphilis. It should be noted that "Status Offenders, Criminal Offenders" focuses on the activities of the court during the 1930s. However, Schlossman and Turner's findings parallel those of Mary Odem for the year 1920 (Odem, "Single Mothers, Delinquent Daughters," 31–40).

70. CB, *Juvenile Courts at Work*, 36–47, 98–101.

71. Miriam Van Waters, "Juvenile Courts from the Child's Viewpoint," *Clinic*, 217–36.

72. CB, *Juvenile Courts at Work*, 24.

73. Ibid., 24–35; see also CB, *Courts in the United States Hearing Children's Cases*, 15–70.

74. "Sponsor Report: Budget of the State Board of Public Welfare, Appropriation #840," 28 June 1927, LSRM, Series 3, Subseries 7, Box 87, Folder 910, RAC.

75. "Memorandum of Interview: Sydnor Walker with Mrs. Jackson Davis," 16 June 1927, LSRM, Series 3, Subseries 7, Box 87, Folder 910, RAC.

76. Frank Bane to Sydnor Walker, 16 June 1927, LSRM, Series 3, Subseries 7, Box 87, Folder 910, RAC. It might be noted that Beardsley Ruml's letters to Bane were much more formal and emphasized the memorial's desire to keep its contributions quiet. Perhaps still smarting from the bad publicity attached to the GEB's supplements to Department of Agriculture salaries a decade earlier, the Rockefeller philanthropies in the 1920s all discouraged publicity whenever they cooperated with a public agency. Ruml in 1927, for instance, told Bane that "the Memorial would appreciate it if no public announcement were made of the gift (to the Department of Public Welfare), other than that which is made in a routine manner in your regular annual report." Beardsley Ruml to Frank Bane, 28 June 1927, LSRM, Series 3, Subseries 7, Box 87, Folder 910, RAC.

77. Sydnor Walker to Frank Bane, 10 Dec. 1928, LSRM, Series 3, Subseries 7, Box 87, Folder 910, RAC.

78. Sydnor Walker, "Confidential Memorandum: Trip to Virginia," LSRM, Series 3, Subseries 7, Box 87, Folder 910, RAC.

79. Ibid.

80. "Remarks of Lawrence Frank," typed transcript, Staff Meetings held in Hanover, New Hampshire, 24–27 Aug. 1927, LSRM, Series 2, Box 3, Folder 41A, RAC.

81. Hastings Hart to John Glenn, 18 Apr. 1929, RSF, Series 3, Box 38, Folder 314, RAC.

82. For typescript biographies of Hart see RSF, Series 2, Box 2, Folder 11, RAC.

83. Hastings Hart to John Glenn, 18 Apr. 1929, RSF, Series 3, Box 38, Folder 314, RAC. Before 1929 the vast majority of federal prisoners were boarded in state and county jails, under conditions Hart labeled "hopelessly unsatisfactory." See Hastings Hart, "United States Prisoners in County Jails: Report of the Committee of the American Prison Association on Lock-ups, Municipal and County Jails," Russell Sage Foundation Pamphlet Publication, 1926.

84. Edith Abbott, Typed transcript, Unpublished Biography of Grace Abbott (hereafter Biography), 28, Box 10, Folder 14, Abbott, UC.

85. Grace Abbott to Edith Abbott, Nov. 1930, Box 10, Folder 7, Abbott, UC. Barry Smith of the Commonwealth Fund shared Abbott's low opinion of Hoover. He was, according to Smith, "a man chiefly interested in spectacular work likely to secure wide publicity." "Report of the Director," 3 Feb. 1925, CF, Record Group, Directors, RAC.

86. Biography, 28–30, Abbott, UC; See Parks, "Expert Inquiry and Health Care Reform," for extensive discussion of Hoover's health policy reform agenda, as well as for a discussion of Wilbur's and Interior's proposed role in that agenda.

87. The heads of more than a dozen women's, labor, and reform organizations circulated a petition supporting the Children's Bureau. They either attended the 1930 Conference in person or sent representatives. Included among bureau supporters were American Association of University Women, Mary Wooley; American Federation of Teachers, Selman Borchardt; American Home Economics Association, Frances Swan; American Nurses Association, Clara Noyes; Council of Women for Home Missions, Sina Stanton; Young Women's Christian Association, Esther Danly; National Congress of Parents and Teachers, Florence Watkins: National Consumers' League, Florence Kelley; National Council of Jewish Women, Leah Pollock; National League of Women Voters, Marguerite Wells; and National Women's Trade Union League, Irma Hochstein. See Transcript, "Official Proceedings of the White House Conference on Child Health and Protection, November 19–22, 1930" (hereafter 1930 Conference), 34, in LSRM, Series 3, Subseries 5, Box 47, Folder 491, RAC.

88. Ibid., 35.

89. Ibid.

90. *New Republic,* 3 Dec. 1930, excerpt quoted in Biography, 73, Abbott, UC.

91. 1930 Conference, 19–20. For analysis of the impact of the decision by Congress not to renew the Sheppard-Towner Act and of the failure of supporters to

revive the program see Nancy Cott, *The Grounding of Modern Feminism* (New Haven, Conn., 1987), 98–113.

92. See excerpts collected by Edith Abbott in Biography, 73–80, Abbott, UC.

93. 1930 Conference, 4–5.

94. Ibid., 15–16.

95. See, for example, an assessment of the Virginia juvenile court system written at the onset of the Great Depression. Frank Hoffer, *Counties in Transition: A Study of County Private and Public Welfare Administration in Virginia* (Charlottesville, Va., 1929).

CHAPTER SIX—THE BUREAU OF SOCIAL HYGIENE: FROM ANTIPROSTITUTION TO SEX RESEARCH

1. Grace Abbott, "Case Work Responsibility of the Juvenile Courts," *Proceedings of the National Conference of Social Work* 5 (1929): 153.

2. Julian Mack, "Chancery Procedure in the Juvenile Court," in Addams, ed., *The Child, The Clinic, and the Court,* 319.

3. Accounts of the Progressive Era's response to prostitution include Mark Connelly, *The Response to Prostitution in the Progressive Era* (Chapel Hill, N.C., 1980); Ruth Rosen, *The Lost Sisterhood: Prostitution in America, 1900–1918* (Baltimore, 1982); Roy Lubove, "The Progressive and the Prostitute," *Historian* 24 (1962): 308–30; John Burnham, "The Progressive Revolution in American Attitudes towards Sex," *Journal of American History* 57 (1973): 885–908; Kenneth Yellis, "Prosperity's Child: Some Thoughts on the Flapper," *American Quarterly* 21 (1969): 44–64; Leslie Fishbein, "Harlot or Heroine: Changing Views of Prostitution, 1870–1920," *Historian* 43 (1980): 23–35; Judith Walkowitz, "The Politics of Prostitution," *Signs* 6 (1980): 123–35; Laura Hapke, "The Late Nineteenth Century American Streetwalker: Images and Realities," *Mid-America* 65 (1983): 155–62; Art Budros, "The Ethnic Vice Industry Revisited," *Ethnic and Racial Studies* 6 (1983): 438–56.

4. Connelly, *The Response to Prostitution,* 20–23.

5. Ibid., 114–35; Barbara Hobson's analysis of the politics of prostitution is not limited to the Progressive Era. Therefore she has much less to say about the specific time period this chapter analyzes than do the two major analysts here cited, Connelly and Rosen. However, her monograph is worth examining: *Uneasy Virtue: The Politics of Prostitution and the American Reform Tradition* (Chicago, 1987).

6. Rosen, *The Lost Sisterhood,* 48–49. Rosen describes here the ideas of anthropologist Mary Douglas on archetypal social responses to stress.

7. Ibid., 113–35; Walkowitz, "The Politics of Prostitution," 123–35; Fishbein, "Harlot or Heroine," 25–30; see also Joel Best, "Careers in Brothel Prostitution, St. Paul, 1865–1883," *Journal of Interdisciplinary History* 12 (1982): 597–619; David Pivar, "Sisterhood Lost/Sisterhood Regained," *Reviews in American History* 11 (1983): 243–47; Clare McKanna, "Hold Back the Tide: Vice Control in San Diego, 1870–1930," *Pacific Historian* 28 (1984): 54–64.

8. Connelly, *The Response to Prostitution,* 130.

9. Rosen, *The Lost Sisterhood,* 125.

10. Rosen quite rightly takes Connelly to task for basing his accounts of the

Rockefeller Grand Jury on contemporary newspaper reports, but she herself has used, not the archival report itself, but a three-page report about it that appeared in a 1910 issue of *McClure's Magazine*. None of the other historians cited shows evidence in footnotes of having used the actual lengthy report typescript either.

11. Connelly, *The Response to Prostitution*, 27.

12. Alta married prominent attorney Parmalee Prentice and lived the conventional life of a wealthy matron. Her sister Edith definitely did not. Even had Rockefeller Sr. not been a firm believer in primogeniture, it is doubtful that he would have trusted his third daughter with any truly significant portion of his vast wealth. Edith's marriage to Harold McCormick, however, made her rich twice over, in her status as wife as well as daughter, since McCormick was the principal heir to the International Harvester fortune. Edith Rockefeller McCormick defied family traditions—which allowed mansions, many servants, and every conceivable comfort, but not reckless extravagance. Edith's marriage was a continual spending spree, and she regularly toured Europe looking for yet more expensive acquisitions. For instance, she bought Napoleon's gold-rimmed china service for use in her Chicago residence. When she divorced McCormick in 1921, she became not just an embarrassment for the family, but, by Rockefeller standards, the worst scandal of all: a scarlet woman. As a divorcée, Edith openly had affairs with male secretaries and continued to spend lavishly. By the time of her death in 1932 she was a devoted follower of a European-based religious cult that believed in reincarnation. She announced to one and all that she was really the reincarnated bride of an Old Dynasty Egyptian pharaoh. Needless to say, Edith was not her father's favorite child. Since she preceded him in death, at least Senior had the comfort of knowing that she would not embarrass his memory further after his demise. For more information on Rockefeller Sr.'s daughters see Harr and Johnson, *The Rockefeller Century,*116–20; Peter Collier and David Horowitz, *The Rockefellers: An American Dynasty* (New York, 1976), 45–73.

13. For an account of the arrangements Rockefeller Sr. made before his death to dispose of his assets, see typescript, "Deposition of John D. Rockefeller Jr.," labeled by hand "Submitted by Mr. Debevoise in 1938, Information Never Used" (hereafter 1938 Deposition), Rockefeller Family Archives (hereafter Family), Record Group 2, John D. Rockefeller Jr., Personal Letterbook Three, 3–4, RAC.

14. John D. Rockefeller Jr. typescript, "Recollections of My Father," Aug. 1920, Family, Record Group 2, John D. Rockefeller Jr., Personal Letterbook Three, 11–12, RAC.

15. Harr and Johnson, *The Rockefeller Century,* 116–20.

16. 1938 Deposition, 3.

17. Harr and Johnson, *The Rockefeller Century,* 118

18. Transcript, Court of General Sessions, in and for the City and County of New York, "In the Matter of the Investigation as to the Alleged Existence in the City and County of New York of an Organized Traffic in Women for Immoral Purposes," Submitted to the Honorable Thomas O'Sullivan, Judge of the Court of General Sessions, 9 June 1910 (hereafter Rockefeller Grand Jury), Rockefeller Family Archives: Rockefeller Boards, the Bureau of Social Hygiene (hereafter Family: BSH), Record Group 2, Box 8, Folder 58, RAC. Quotation on p. 8.

19. One of the best contemporary accounts of the growth of brothel districts is

George Kneeland, *Commercialized Prostitution in New York* (New York, 1913). Knee-land periodically worked, between 1910 and 1920, as an investigator hired by John D. Rockefeller Jr., first working for the Rockefeller Grand Jury, and then for the BSH. Harr and Johnson note, "He may have gotten too close to his subject. He died of syphilis" (*The Rockefeller Century*, 577). See also Timothy Gilfoyle, "City of Eros: New York City, Prostitution and the Commercialization of Sex, 1790–1920" (Ph.D. diss., Columbia University, 1987); Craig Foster, "Tarnished Angels: Prostitution in Storyville, New Orleans, 1900–1910," *Louisiana History* 31 (1990): 387–97.

20. Usually the terms were interchangeable. Sometimes a "cadet" was a man who "sold" women to madams or others but maintained no long-term relationship with a prostitute or prostitutes; Rosen, *The Lost Sisterhood*, 76. For further discussion of the rising role of pimps and municipal attempts to control them see James Jones Jr., "Municipal Vice: The Management of Prostitution in Tennessee's Urban Experience," *Tennessee Historical Quarterly* 50 (1991): 33–41.

21. Rockefeller Grand Jury, 515.

22. Ibid., 520–21.

23. Marcus Braun to John D. Rockefeller Jr., 21 Apr. 1910, Family: BSH, Box 6, Folder 38, RAC.

24. Rockefeller Grand Jury, 14–15.

25. "Dismissal Statement of the Honorable William J. Gaynor to the Gentle-men of the Jury," 30 June 1910, Family: BSH, Box 8, Folder 57, RAC.

26. John D. Rockefeller Jr. to Paul Warburg, 26 Dec. 1912, Family: BSH, Box 7, Folder 43, RAC.

27. John D. Rockefeller Jr. to Clifford Barnes, 19 Dec. 1912, Family: BSH, Box 6, Folder 39, RAC.

28. John D. Rockefeller Jr. to James Reynolds, 11 July 1913, Family: BSH, Box 6, Folder 30, RAC.

29. R. G. Walters, "Merger of Social Hygiene Societies," *Survey* 31 (1914): 485.

30. For a complete roster of association officers and boards see typescript, "Officers and Committees of the American Social Hygiene Association," Abbott, Box 31, Folder 10, UC.

31. It should be noted that Jane Addams was an honorary president of the association. She did not exert any active leadership, however. For information about Davis's high profile among early-twentieth-century American women see Vern Bullough, "Katharine Bement Davis, Sex Research, and the Rockefeller Founda-tion," *Bulletin of the History of Medicine* 62 (1988): 74–89.

32. Scholars, at least, have rediscovered Davis. In addition to the above, see Fitzpatrick, *Endless Crusade;* Ellen Fitzpatrick, ed., *Katharine Bement Davis, Early Twentieth Century American Women, and the Study of Sex Behavior* (New York, 1987); Estelle Freedman, *Their Sisters' Keepers: Women's Prison Reform in America, 1830–1930* (Ann Arbor, Mich., 1981); Mary Jo Deegan, ed., *Women in Sociology* (Westport, Conn., 1991).

33. Katharine Bement Davis to John D. Rockefeller Jr., 9 Nov. 1911, Family: BSH, Box 6, Folder 30, RAC.

34. Ibid.

35. John D. Rockefeller Jr. to Nicholas Murray Butler, 19 Jan. 1912, Family, Record Group 2, Box 6, Folder 31, RAC. In her fine book *Endless Crusade,* Ellen Fitzpatrick quotes another letter sent by Rockefeller Jr. to Butler, with almost, but not exactly, identical wording (109). For Fitzpatrick's account of the Laboratory of Social Hygiene see *Endless Crusade,* 101–29. Estelle Freedman has also written, briefly, about the laboratory, but, unlike Fitzpatrick, she relies heavily for information on the prison's printed *Annual Reports,* rather than archival materials. Thus, her summary provides an overly positive, and unsatisfactory, overview (*Their Sisters' Keepers,* 117–21).

36. Statement for Immediate Release, John D. Rockefeller Jr., "The Origins, Work, and Plans of the Bureau of Social Hygiene" (hereafter "Statement"), 27 Jan. 1912, Family: BSH, Box 81, Folder 67, RAC.

37. Ida Tarbell, "What Shall We Do with the Young Prostitute?" Offprint from *American Magazine* (1912), 3, in Family: BSH, Box 9, Folder 76, RAC.

38. Ibid., 12.

39. Ibid., 13.

40. Ibid., 12, 14, 19, 22.

41. For a report on conditions at Bedford Hills after Moore's appointment see New York State Commission of Prisons, *Twentieth Annual Report* (New York, 1914), 112–20. See also Fitzpatrick, *Endless Crusade,* 120–27; Freedman, *Their Sisters' Keepers,* 141–42.

42. Katharine Bement Davis, "A Plan for the Conversion of the Laboratory of Social Hygiene at Bedford Hills into a State Clearing House for Women Convicted in the First, Second, Third, and Ninth Judicial Districts," Family: BSH, Box 6, Folder 31, RAC.

43. "Statement."

44. For information on John D. Rockefeller 3d and the Rockefeller Foundation's return to research into human reproduction and population planning see Harr and Johnson, *The Rockefeller Century,* 430–62; idem, *The Rockefeller Conscience.*

45. Bryan Strong, "Ideas of the Early Sex Education Movement in America: 1890–1920," *History of Education Quarterly* 12 (1972): 129–61.

46. Charles Eliot, Speech Transcript, "School Instruction in Sex Hygiene," Family, Record Group 2, Box 9, Folder 75, RAC.

47. John D. Rockefeller Jr. to James Reynolds, 11 July 1913, Family, Record Group 2, Box 6, Folder 30, RAC.

48. Copies of both of these pamphlets are in the RAC. John Gavin, *Some Inf'mation for Mother* (New York, American Social Hygiene Association, Publication #532), in RAC Pamphlet File, Box 8, Folder 101 (hereafter *Mother*); *Social Hygiene vs. the Sexual Plagues* (hereafter *Sexual Plagues*) exists as several reprinted versions. The copy reproduced and issued by the Indiana State Board of Health as its own publication can be found in Family: BSH, Box 9, Folder 76, RAC.

49. *Mother,* 1–16.

50. For contemporary descriptions of late-nineteenth- and early-twentieth-century medical techniques to treat syphilis and other venereal diseases see E. P. Hurd, "Syphilophobia and Spermatophobia," *Medical Age* 7 (1899): 244–46; Robert Bach-

man, "Venereal Prophylaxis, Past and Present," *Providence Medical Journal* 7 (1913): 231–44. The quotation from Frederick Hollick's *Venereal Diseases* appears in Gail Parsons, "Equal Treatment for All: American Medical Remedies for Male Sexual Problems, 1850–1900," *Journal of the History of Medicine and Allied Sciences* 32 (1977): 69.

51. For the state of late-nineteenth- and early-twentieth-century medical knowledge see Bullough, "Katharine Bement Davis, Sex Research, and the Rockefeller Foundation," 74–79; Wheatley, *The Politics of Philanthropy;* C. D. O'Malley, ed., *The History of Medical Education* (Berkeley, Calif., 1970); Elizabeth Fee, *Disease and Discovery: A History of the Johns Hopkins School of Hygiene and Public Health, 1916–1939* (Baltimore, 1987); Charles Rosenberg, "The Practice of Medicine in New York a Century Ago," *Bulletin of the History of Medicine* 41 (1967): 223–53; Parsons, "Equal Treatment for All."

52. *Sexual Plagues,* 9.

53. Ibid., 12.

54. Ibid.

55. Ibid., 15

56. See, for instance, David Pivar, *Purity Crusade: Sexual Morality and Social Control, 1868–1900* (Westport, Conn., 1973).

57. *Sexual Plagues,* 18.

58. Ibid., 14

59. Statistics about increasing rates of circumcisions done for stated goals of personal and public health can be found in the National Library of Medicine, Bethesda, Md.

60. Julia Richman to John D. Rockefeller Jr., 21 Mar. 1911, Family: BSH, Box 10, Folder 81, RAC.

61. Katharine Bement Davis to John D. Rockefeller Jr., 15 Mar. 1922, Family: BSH, Box 7, Folder 50, RAC.

62. Vern Bullough, "The Rockefellers and Sex Research," *Journal of Sex Research* 21 (1985): 113–25; Vern Bullough, "Katharine Bement Davis, Sex Research, and the Rockefeller Foundation," 74–89. In these articles Bullough focuses on the activities of the Committee for Research in Problems of Sex and does not emphasize the research work done directly by Katharine Bement Davis and others within the Bureau of Social Hygiene itself. He maintains that emphasis in his monograph, *Science in the Bedroom: A History of Sex Research* (New York, 1994).

63. "Report of the Executive Secretary of the Committee for Research on Sex Problems to the Bureau of Social Hygiene," 11 July 1922, Family: BSH, Box 7, Folder 50. The members of the committee were, in addition to Davis and Yerkes, W. B. Camnon, a professor of physiology at Harvard Medical School, E. G. Conklin, a biologist at Princeton, and T. W. Salmon, a psychiatrist at the College of Physicians and Surgeons of Columbia University.

64. The Committee on Maternal Health remains largely unstudied. For analyses see Merriley Borell, "Biologists and the Promotion of Birth Control Research: 1918–1938," *Journal of the History of Biology* 20 (1987): 51–87; James Reed, *The Birth Control Movement and American Society: From Private Vice to Public Virtue* (Princeton, 1984). Regrettably, scholars of the American birth control movement in the early

twentieth century continue to focus primarily on Margaret Sanger and the emergence of her Planned Parenthood Association. One of the best contemporary reviews of the Committee on Maternal Health's work is Robert Dickinson's own (with Lura Beam) *The Single Woman: A Medical Study in Sex Education* (Baltimore, 1934).

65. Robert Dickinson, "Transcript of Speech before Section of Obstetrical and Abdominal Surgeons," Annual Meeting of the American Medical Association, 27 May 1925 (hereafter Dickinson AMA Speech), Records of the Bureau of Social Hygiene (hereafter Bureau), Series 3, Subseries 2, Box 7, Folder 172, RAC.

66. "Review of the Committee on Maternal Health's Contraception Programs," typescript, Page "E," Bureau, Series 3, Subseries 2, Box 7, Folder 175, RAC.

67. Ibid.

68. Committee on Maternal Health, "Publications Issued, In Press, or In Preparation, January 1928," typescript with explanatory notes (hereafter CMH Publications), Bureau, Series 3, Subseries 2, Box 7, Folder 175, RAC.

69. "Review of the Committee on Maternal Health's Contraceptive Programs," typescript, Page "G," Bureau, Series 3, Subseries 2, Box 7, Folder 175, RAC.

70. For further information about members' political lobbying see Committee on Maternal Health, "Summary of Four Years' Service and Programs, January 1928," Bureau, Series 3, Subseries 2, Box 7, Folder 175, RAC.

71. Ibid. (Inserted page in above summary labeled "Researches.")

72. Dickinson AMA Speech.

73. See, for instance, Fitzpatrick, ed., *Katharine Bement Davis, Early Twentieth Century American Women, and the Study of Sex Behavior*; John D'Emilio and Estelle Freedman, *Intimate Matters: A History of Sexuality in America* (New York, 1988).

74. Representative articles are: Katharine Bement Davis, "Study of the Sex Life of Normal Married Women," *Journal of Social Hygiene* 9 (1923): 129–46; idem, "A Study of Certain Auto-Erotic Practices, Based on the Replies of 2,255 Women," *Mental Hygiene* 8 (1924): 668–723.

75. Katharine Bement Davis, *Factors in the Sex Life of Twenty-two Hundred Women* (New York, 1929), ix.

76. Ibid., x. Members of the committee included Mrs. Elmer Blair, General Federation of Women's Clubs; Martha Falconer, American Social Hygiene Association; Susan Kingsbury and Carola Woerishoffer, professors in the Department of Social Economy and Social Research at Bryn Mawr; psychiatrist Elizabeth McCall; Ellen Potter, head of the Division of Child Health, Pennsylvania State Department of Health; physicians Valeria Parker and Edith Swift; and psychologists Helen Wooley and Jessie Taft.

77. Ibid., xi. See also Davis, "A Study of Certain Auto-Erotic Practices," 668–715.

78. Davis, *Factors*, xiii.

79. Ibid., xvii.

80. Davis, "A Study of Certain Auto-Erotic Practices," 668–90.

81. *Sexual Plagues*, 38.

82. Davis, *Factors*, 26–27.

83. Ibid., xvii.

84. In 1972 Arno Press issued a reprint edition. Excerpts from the book appear also in Fitzpatrick, ed., *Katharine Bement Davis, Early Twentieth Century American Women, and the Study of Sex Behavior.*

85. The questionnaires no longer exist, at least so far as I have been able to discover. Who destroyed them and why remains a mystery.

86. Ellen Fitzpatrick tells this story in *Endless Crusade,* 203–6.

87. For information about its final years see Bureau, Series 1, Box 3, RAC.

88. "Statement."

89. Harr and Johnson, *The Rockefeller Century,* 460–66.

CHAPTER SEVEN—FOUNDATIONS, RECREATION,
AND THE PUBLIC'S MORAL HEALTH

1. Exhibit Nine, "When Bob Came Home," A Report of the Playground and Recreation Association, Dec. 1927, 3–5, LSRM, Series 3, Subseries 4, Box 16, Folder 175, RAC.

2. J. H. McCurdy to Rudolph Bertheau, 3 Feb. 1925, LSRM, Series 3, Subseries 4, Box 11, Folder 124, RAC.

3. Calvin Coolidge, "Statement of the President on Outdoor Recreation," 24 Apr. 1924, LSRM, Series 3, Subseries 4, Box 14, Folder 157, RAC.

4. The topic of early-twentieth-century reform and recreation policy is one largely neglected by scholars. The most interesting scholarship exists in article, not book, form. See, for instance, Don Kirschner, "The Perils of Pleasure: Commercial Recreation, Social Disorder, and Moral Reform in the Progressive Era," *American Studies* 21 (1980): 27–42; Carl Krog, " 'Organizing the Production of Leisure': Herbert Hoover and the Conservation Movement in the 1920s," *Wisconsin Magazine of History* 67 (1984): 199–218; Elisabeth I. Perry, "Recreation and Reform in the Progressive Era," *History of Education Quarterly* 24 (1984) 223–28. The best of several dissertations are Stephanie Wallach, "Luther Halsey Gulick and the Salvation of the American Adolescent" (Ph.D. diss., Columbia University, 1989); David Jones, "The Playground Association of America: A Thwarted Attempt at the Professionalization of Play Leaders" (Ph.D. diss., University of Oregon, 1989); Lawrence Finfer, "Leisure as Social Work in the Urban Community: The Progressive Recreation Movement, 1890–1920" (Ph.D. diss., Michigan State University, 1974). The best book on the subject is still Dominick Cavallo, *Muscles and Morals: Organized Playgrounds and Urban Reform, 1880–1920* (Philadelphia, 1981). Cavallo's focus is, however, relatively narrow. He is most interested in examining the connection between early-twentieth-century psychological theories of childhood development and the creation by reformers of a "playground movement" for children. Monographs describing the history of specific types of early-twentieth-century recreation that might with equal accuracy be called celebration do exist. The best example of this genre is David Glassberg's excellent *American Historical Pageantry: The Uses of Tradition in the Early Twentieth Century* (Chapel Hill, N.C., 1990).

5. Joseph Lee, "Play as an Antidote to Civilization," *The Playground* 5 (1911): 125.

6. Cavallo, *Muscles and Morals,* 18–20. For discussions of nineteenth-century

leisure and pleasure-taking see John Burnham, *Bad Habits: Drinking, Smoking, Taking Drugs, Gambling, Sexual Misbehavior and Swearing in American History* (New York, 1991); Paul Boyer, *Urban Masses and Moral Order in America: 1820–1920* (Cambridge, Mass., 1978); Benjamin Rader, *American Sports from the Age of Folk Games to the Age of Spectators* (Englewood Cliffs, N.J., 1983); Mark Peel, "On the Margins: Lodgers and Boarders in Boston: 1860–1900," *Journal of American History* 72 (1986): 813–34; Randy Roberts, "Baseball Myths and American Realities," *Reviews in American History* 10 (1982): 141–45; Steven Riess, "Professional Baseball and Social Mobility," *Journal of Interdisciplinary History* 11 (1980): 235–50; Dennis Brestensky, "Pastimes and Festive Customs in Early Mine Patches," *Pennsylvania Heritage* 8 (1982): 15–19.

7. For information on both Gulick and Lee see RSF, Series 2, Box 2, Folder 17, RAC. See also "Joseph Lee," *Dictionary of American Biography* 2 (New York, 1958), 374–75. Incidentally, Luther Gulick Sr. should not be confused with Luther Gulick Jr., his son. Scholars have made this error. Neither man used the senior or junior designation, but Luther Gulick Jr. was a political scientist who specialized in studies of government fiscal management. During the 1930s he advised Franklin Roosevelt's New Deal and sat on the President's Committee on Administrative Management. See Harold Orlans, "Academic Social Scientists and the Presidency: From Wilson to Nixon," *Minerva* 24 (1986): 172–204.

8. Joseph Lee, *Constructive and Preventive Philanthropy* (New York, 1902); Luther Gulick, *A Philosophy of Play* (New York, 1920). *A Philosophy of Play* provides the clearest overview of Gulick's justifications for organized recreation, but he was a prolific author. Other books include Luther Gulick, *The Dynamics of Manhood* (New York, 1917); *The Efficient Life* (New York, 1907); *Medical Inspection of Schools* (New York, 1917); *Morals and Morale* (New York, 1919); and *Physical Education by Muscular Exercise* (Philadelphia, 1904).

9. See descriptions included in "Dedication Ceremony Remarks for the Luther Halsey Gulick Playground, New York City," 3 Nov. 1933, RSF, Series 2, Box 2, Folder 17, RAC.

10. Dominick Cavallo exaggerates the intellectual differences between Lee and Gulick. Both saw a clear connection between direct physical activity and moral growth. Their importance was as able popularizers, not as advocates of a particular child development theory. See *Muscles and Morals*, 74–75.

11. Luther Gulick, *Mind and Work* (New York, 1909), 80.

12. Lee, *Constructive and Preventive Philanthropy*, 126.

13. Gulick, *A Philosophy of Play*, 238–39.

14. Lee, *Constructive and Preventive Philanthropy*, 123.

15. Gulick, *A Philosophy of Play*, 248–49.

16. "The Play Trust," *Survey* 29 (1913). The editorial ended with withering sarcasm: "Progressive members of the community should stop throwing stones at the canning industry and give their attention to the servant problem or something else that really needs improvement."

17. Charles Hughes, "Why We Want Playgrounds," 1 Oct. 1913 (Speech reprinted from Proceedings of the Second Annual Playground Congress), Playground and Recreation Association, New York, 1913.

18. Ibid.

19. Calvin Coolidge, "National Recreation Opportunities," *The Playground* 18 (1924): 194.

20. See Julia Lathrop, "Taking Play Seriously," *The Playground* 10 (1917): 357–58, for an example of such arguments made by play advocates. For information on corporate "welfare work" see Judith Sealander, *Grand Plans: Business Progressivism and Social Change in Ohio's Miami Valley, 1890–1929* (Lexington, Ky., 1988); Daniel Nelson, *Managers and Workers: Origins of the New Factory System in the United States, 1880–1920* (Madison, Wis., 1975); Stephen Meyer, *The Five-Dollar Day: Labor Management and Social Control in the Ford Motor Company, 1908–1921* (Albany, N.Y., 1981); Gerald Zahavi, "Negotiated Loyalty: Welfare Capitalism and the Shoeworkers of Endicott-Johnson, 1920–1940," *Journal of American History* 71 (1983): 602–20.

21. Joseph Fulk, *The Municipalization of Play and Recreation* (Lincoln, Nebr., 1922), 19.

22. Ibid., 22.

23. Howard Braucher, Executive Secretary of the Playground and Recreation Association, summarized the Russell Sage Foundation report in "Why I Believe That Community and Neighborhood Centers, Schools, and Parks Should Be under Government Direction and Support" (hereafter "Why I Believe"), *The Playground* 10 (1916): 88.

24. Fulk, *The Municipalization of Play,* 21.

25. Lee, "Play as an Antidote to Civilization," 119–26. See also Fulk, *The Municipalization of Play,* 21.

26. Joseph Lee, "Play as Medicine," *The Playground* 5 (1911): 290.

27. Lathrop, "Taking Play Seriously," 358.

28. Gulick, *A Philosophy of Play,* 84.

29. Ibid., 167.

30. Ibid., 89, 97.

31. Jane Addams, *Twenty Years at Hull House* (New York, 1910).

32. Gulick, *A Philosophy of Play,* 84. The book that outlined the principles of basketball is Luther Gulick and James Naismith, *Basketball* (New York, 1894).

33. See, for instance, Chester Marsh, "What a Superintendent of Recreation Needs to Know," *Recreation and the Playground* 18 (1924): 528–29; Ira Jayne, "The Budget," *The Playground* 11 (1917): 382–87.

34. Typescript, "Ten Years of the Playground and Recreation Association," LSRM, Series 3, Subseries 4, Box 17, Folder 182. *The Playground* became *Recreation and the Playground* in 1929, and then later just *Recreation*.

35. "Memorandum from Rudolph Bertheau and Kenneth Chorley to Beardsley Ruml," 12 Nov. 1926, LSRM, Series 3, Subseries 4, Box 17, Folder 178, RAC; George Vincent to Howard Braucher, 16 Jan. 1929, LSRM, Series 3, Subseries 4, Box 7, Folder 181, RAC. There is truly delicious irony in the fact that Beardsley Ruml headed the Laura Spelman Rockefeller Memorial during the decade when it was one of the nation's primary patrons of programs to expand publicly funded physical education and physical exercise. Ruml, fat, a connoisseur of fine wines and even better scotch, chain-smoked and loathed exercise. He could have been the only man in America with a precise definition of "indiscriminate" basketball. If it involved him, one minute was one minute too much. Should it be noted that despite a lifetime

of overeating, drinking, smoking, and carefully plotted sloth, Beardsley Ruml lived to a ripe old age?

36. Braucher, "Why I Believe," 92–93; emphasis in the original.

37. Clarence Perry, "Leadership in Neighborhood Centers," *Recreation and the Playground* 10 (1924): 463.

38. For information on wartime recreational planning for the military and on the Commission on Training Camp Activities see Raymond Fosdick, *Chronicle of a Generation: An Autobiography* (New York, 1958); Daryl Revoldt, "Raymond Fosdick: Reform, Internationalism, and the Rockefeller Foundation," (Ph.D. diss., University of Akron, 1982). Quotations cited here in Raymond Fosdick, "The Commission on Training Camp Activities," *Proceedings of the Academy of Political Science* 7 (1917–18): 168–70. For a discussion of connections made by the Army between physical fitness and moral readiness, see Nancy Bristow, *Making Men Moral: Social Engineering during the Great War* (New York, 1996). The best book on the impact of military mobilization on American domestic life during World War I is John Whiteclay Chambers, *To Raise an Army: The Draft Comes to Modern America* (New York, 1989). Recreation, however, is not Chambers's major emphasis. For that subject Fosdick's autobiographical accounts are more thorough. I am much influenced by and grateful to Ellis Hawley for the insights he has shared with me about the impact of wartime managerialism (including the management of recreation) on postwar developments.

39. Howard Braucher to Beardsley Ruml, 27 Oct. 1924, LSRM, Series 3, Subseries 4, Box 16, Folder 175, RAC.

40. Clarence Perry, Memorandum, "The Work of the Playground and Recreation Association," LSRM, Series 3, Subseries 4, Box 17, Folder 183, RAC. See also typescript, "Confidential Report on Selected Cities: 1922–1925," LSRM, Series 3, Subseries 4, Box 16, Folder 175, RAC.

41. Joseph Lee, "American Play Tradition and Our Relation to It," *The Playground* 7 (1913): 156.

42. In 1924, for instance, a ceramic sink manufacturer removed Troy, New York, from its list as it searched for a new factory location. The company owner felt that other finalists offered his workers better recreational opportunities. The city's newspaper editor, an ally of the field secretary assigned to Troy, quickly reprinted all the materials the latter sent him, and used the loss of the factory as a centerpiece for arguments about the need for Troy's city government to support planned recreation ("Confidential Report on Selected Cities").

43. Ibid.

44. "Report of Recreation," LSRM, Series 3, Subseries 4, Box 16, Folder 176, RAC.

45. Fulk, *The Municipalization of Play and Recreation,* 24–69.

46. Lee, *Constructive and Preventive Philanthropy,* 135.

47. David Waldstreicher has argued that the parade has been a crucial element in the formation of Americans' notions of unity and nationhood from the very beginning. As he says, "Whatever social grounding and local reality American nationalism actually possessed lay not in any truly lasting political or ideological consensus among its followers, but in its practices: in the gathering of people at celebratory events"; "Rites of Rebellion, Rites of Assent: Celebrations, Print Culture, and

the Origins of American Nationalism," *Journal of American History* 82 (1995): 61. For examinations of the parade's importance in America see Susan Davis, *Parades and Power: Street Theater in Nineteenth Century Philadelphia* (Philadelphia, 1986); Mary Ryan, *Women in Public: Between Banners and Ballots* (Baltimore, 1990); Mary Ryan, "The American Parade: Representations of the Nineteenth Century Social Order," in *The New Cultural History*, ed. Lynn Hunt (Berkeley, Calif., 1989), 131–53; John Budnar, *Remaking America: Public Memory, Commemoration, and Patriotism in the Twentieth Century* (Cambridge, Mass., 1976).

48. Luther Gulick, "Popular Recreation and Public Morality," *Annals of the American Academy of Political and Social Science* 34 (July 1909): 36.

49. Hazel MacKaye, "Outdoor Plays and Pageants," *The Independent* 66 (1910): 1227–34.

50. Hartley Alexander, *The Pageant of Lincoln* (Lincoln, Nebr., 1915); Constance D'Arcy MacKaye, *The Pageant of Schenectady* (Schenectady, N.Y., 1912). I owe my discovery of these works to David Glassberg's insightful article, "History and the Public: Legacies of the Progressive Era," *Journal of American History* 73 (1987): 957–80. See also his "Restoring a 'Forgotten Childhood': American Play and the Progressive Era's Elizabethan Past," *American Quarterly* 32 (1980): 351–68; and most important, his monograph, *American Historical Pageantry*. Glassberg examines many aspects of the early-twentieth-century historical pageant beyond the scope of this chapter, which focuses on its place within a new kind of public recreation policy. For example, his thoughts about pageantry's role in the Country Life Movement, in mobilization for World War I, and in the creation of American folk identity are well worth reading.

51. For contemporary discussions of the Westchester Pageant see Mary Fanton Roberts, "The Value of Outdoor Plays to America," *Craftsman* 16 (1909): 491–505; Frances Bjorkman, "A Nation Learning to Play," *World's Work* 18 (1909): 12038–45.

52. Glassberg, "History and the Public Legacies of the Progressive Era," 975–78. The emphasis in this chapter on the passivity imposed at historic recreations is mine, not Glassberg's. The subject, were it raised within the text, would take this chapter too far afield, but links between the early-twentieth-century pageant and the growth of the community theater movement certainly exist and await fuller exploration by other historians. This topic, like so many others, demands a synthesis of social history and political history that does not now really exist. All historians of the early-twentieth-century theater should be required to read at least one book about the city manager movement. All historians of American politics should be told to read at least one book that explains clearly why Mark Twain's Duke and Dauphin were so sure they could make money presenting "Shakespeare" in backwoods Arkansas.

53. Roberts, "The Value of Outdoor Plays to America," 491.

54. Michael Davis, *The Exploitation of Pleasure* (Russell Sage Foundation Pamphlet 84, 1910), 44, in RSF Pamphlet File, RAC.

55. For a history of the American Physical Education Association see "Memorandum from J. H. McCurdy to Beardsley Ruml," 31 Oct. 1923, LSRM, Series 3, Subseries 4, Box 11, Folder 124, RAC. For further information about the reception given the Army's announcement of so many physically defective recruits see John Whiteclay Chambers, *To Raise an Army: The Draft Comes to Modern America* (New York, 1989); David Kennedy, *Over Here: The First World War and American Society*

(New York, 1980); Neil Wynn, *From Progressivism to Prosperity: World War I and American Society* (New York, 1986); Steven Pope, "An Army of Athletes: Playing Fields, Battlefields and the American Military Sporting Experience, 1890–1920," *Journal of Military History* 4 (1995): 35–56.

56. "Minutes of the Motor Ability Committee," 18 Dec. 1924, LSRM, Series 3, Subseries 4, Box 11, Folder 124, RAC.

57. Ibid.

58. "Motor Ability Tests," Report of the American Physical Education Association, Nov. 1924, 1–6, in LSRM, Series 3, Subseries 4, Box 11, Folder 124, RAC.

59. Ibid., 5.

60. Lillian Schoedler, "Report of the Executive Secretary, Women's Division: Given at the Annual Meeting of the Amateur Athletic Federation," 29 Dec. 1924, 5, LSRM, Series 3, Subseries 4, Box 14, Folder 156, RAC.

61. Ibid.

62. J. F. Rogers, *Athletics for Women,* Education Pamphlet 4, Apr. 1924, Bureau of Education, Department of the Interior, Washington, D.C.

63. Ibid., 3. It might be noted here that the first in-depth biography of Babe Didrikson has only recently been published. Susan Cayleff, *Babe: The Life and Legend of Babe Didrikson Zaharias* (Urbana, Ill., 1995).

64. Herbert Hoover to Chauncey Hamlin, 4 Dec. 1926, Rosenwald, Box 26, Folder 27, UC.

65. "Extract from the Minutes of the 24th Meeting of the Executive Committee," 8 May 1929, LSRM, Series 3, Subseries 4, Box 14, Folder 160, RAC.

66. "The President's Conference on Outdoor Recreation" (Released for Morning Papers: 5 May 1924), LSRM, Series 3, Subseries 4, Box 14, Folder 157, RAC. For scholarly discussion of the history of environmentalism in the early twentieth century see Samuel Hays, *Conservation and the Gospel of Efficiency: The Progressive Conservation Movement, 1890–1920* (Cambridge, Mass., 1959); Donald Swain, *Federal Conservation Policy, 1921–33* (Berkeley, Calif., 1963); Roderick Nash, ed., *The American Environment; Readings in the History of Conservation* (Reading, Pa., 1968); James Penick, *Progressive Politics and Conservation: The Ballinger-Pinchot Affair* (Chicago, 1968); Ashley Schiff, *Fire and Water: Scientific Heresy in the Forest Service* (Cambridge, Mass., 1962); Michael Cohen, *The History of the Sierra Club, 1892–1970* (New York, 1988); Stephen Fox, *John Muir and His Legacy: The American Conservation Movement* (Boston, 1981); Donald Worster, ed., *The Ends of the Earth: Perspectives on Modern Environmental History* (Cambridge, 1988).

67. Chauncey Hamlin to Beardsley Ruml, 12 July 1924, LSRM, Series 3, Subseries 4, Box 14, Folder 157, RAC.

68. The subscribing organizations included the Amateur Trapshooting Association, American Association for the Advancement of Science, American Association of Museums, American Automobile Association, American Bison Society, American Fisheries Society, American Forestry Association, American Game Protective Association, American Institute of Architects, American Institute of Park Executives, American Ornithologists' Union, American Physical Education Association, American Scenic and Historic Preservation Society, American Society of Landscape Architects, American Society of Mammalogists, Appalachian Mountain Club, Asso-

ciated Mountaineering Clubs of America, Audubon Society, Boone and Crockett Club, Boy Scouts of America, Camp Fire Girls of America, Catholic Boys' Brigade of America, Chamber of Commerce of the United States, Ecological Society of America, Federated Societies on Planning and Parks, General Federation of Women's Clubs, Girl Scouts of America, Inkowa Clubs of America, Izaak Walton League, National Collegiate Athletic Association, National Geographic Society, National Highways Association, National Parks Association, New York Zoological Society, Playground and Recreation Association of America, Roosevelt Wild Life Experiment Station, Save the Redwoods League, Sierra Club, Society of American Foresters, and Wild Flower Preservation Society. The list can be found in Rosenwald, Box 27, Folder 26, UC.

69. The committee structure was as follows: Committee on Birds, Committee on Child Needs in Outdoor Recreation, Committee on Citizenship Value in Outdoor Recreation, Committee on Closer Correlation of Work Units of Government Organizations, Committee on Correlation of Agencies Other Than Federal, Committee on Education Programs and Outdoor Recreation, Committee on Federal Land Policies, Committee on Financial Encouragement of Outdoor Recreation, Committee on Fish, Committee on Game and Fur-Bearing Animals, Committee on International Agreements, Committee on Municipal Parks and Forests, Committee on Plants and Flowers, Committee on Pollution of Waterways, Committee on Resolutions, Committee on State and County Parks and Forests, Committee on Surveys of Recreation Resources, and Committee to Effect Permanent Organization. This list can be found in "National Conference on Outdoor Recreation," Bulletin to Invited Organizations, 10 May 1924, LSRM, Series 3, Subseries 4, Box 14, Folder 157, RAC. It should be noted that Lee Hanmer or other members of the Russell Sage Foundation's Department of Recreation chaired five of these committees.

70. Robert S. Yard, "Information for Members," 20 June 1928, LSRM, Series 3, Subseries 4, Box 14, Folder 160, RAC.

71. "Minutes of the Third Meeting of the Joint Committees on Recreational Survey and Federal Lands," 29 May 1925, LSRM, Series 3, Subseries 4, Box 15, Folder 163, RAC.

72. "Discussion of Wilderness Areas: A Report to the Executive Committee," 13 June 1927 (hereafter June 1927 Report), 5, LSRM, Series 3, Subseries 4, Box 14, Folder 159, RAC.

73. Typescript, "Program of Objectives and Projects," LSRM, Series 3, Subseries 4, Box 14, Folder 157, RAC.

74. Calvin Coolidge, "Statement on the National Conference on Outdoor Recreation," LSRM, Series 3, Subseries 4, Box 14, Folder 157, RAC.

75. In later negotiations, the status of the proposed Shenandoah National Park was changed, and much of the area originally designated as a national park site became a United States Forest. June 1927 Report, 1–2.

76. Calvin Coolidge, "Statement on the National Conference on Outdoor Recreation."

77. Henry Curtis, *Play and Recreation for the Open Country* (New York, 1914), 252.

78. Ibid., 250–51.

CONCLUSION—THE FOUNDATION COMES OF AGE

1. George Soule, "The American Drift," *New Republic* 73 (1933): 231.

2. The President's Research Committee on Social Trends, *Recent Social Trends in the United States* (New York, 1933) (hereafter *Social Trends*), xiii.

3. Senate Bill 6888, 2 Mar. 1910, 61st Congress, 2d Session, 1–2.

4. The most detailed account of the federal dissolution case is still to be found in Allan Nevins, *Study in Power: John D. Rockefeller, Industrialist and Philanthropist* (New York, 1953), vol. 2, ch. 36. For a more objective, though much briefer, account see Ralph Andeano, "Competitive Structures of the American Petroleum Industry, 1880–1911," in *Oil's First Century,* ed. Ralph Hidy (Cambridge, Mass., 1960).

5. Starr Murphy, Confidential memorandum, "Should We Seek a Charter from Congress or from the Legislature of New York?" Rockefeller Family Archives, Rockefeller Boards: Rockefeller Foundation (hereafter Family: RF), Box 24, Folder 250, RAC.

6. Ibid.

7. Ibid.

8. For a discussion of the place of Standard Oil within American industry see Alfred Chandler, *The Visible Hand: The Managerial Revolution in American Business* (Cambridge, Mass., 1977), 287–381; for information on reactions to Senior see Collier and Horowitz, *The Rockefellers: An American Dynasty,* 44–60.

9. Records of the Rockefeller Foundation (hereafter RF), Record Group 3, Series 900, Box 18, Folder 131, Stenographic transcript, "Testimony of Jerome Greene Given before United States Commission on Industrial Relations, February 2, 1915" (hereafter Greene, Commission), RAC.

10. Typescript, "Source Book for a History of the Rockefeller Foundation: typed notes, 1954" (hereafter Source Book), 18r, RF, Record Group 3, Series 00, Box 7, RAC.

11. *New York Times,* 2 Mar. 1910.

12. For a complete transcript of the committee hearings see Senate Report 405, 16 Mar. 1910, 61st Congress, 2d Session.

13. *Los Angeles Record* editorial quoted in Source Book, 23.

14. See extensive sample of quotations from newspapers around the country in ibid., 23–26.

15. Ibid., 25.

16. For full details of the proposed amendments to the charter bill see Senate Report 1258, 62d Congress, 3d Session.

17. For an account of the value of each of the "Standards" see John McLean and Robert Haight, *The Growth of Integrated Oil Companies* (Boston, 1984), 30–190; Chandler, *The Visible Hand,* 350–60.

18. Frederick Gates to John D. Rockefeller Sr., 19 May 1911, Family: RF, Box 24, Folder 244, RAC.

19. Source Book, 41.

20. *Congressional Record,* House of Representatives, 62d Congress, 2d Session, 15 Apr. 1912, 4815–27.

21. Jerome Greene to A. J. Peters, 8 Jan. 1913, quoted in Source Book, 58f.

22. Ibid., 57h–58g.

23. For discussion of the Los Angeles bombing see Graham Adams, *Age of Industrial Violence, 1910–1915,* 1–25; Sidney Fine, *"Without Blare of Trumpets": Walter Drew, The National Erectors' Association, and the Open Shop Movement, 1903–57* (Ann Arbor, Mich., 1995), 81–129; Herbert Shapiro, "Lincoln Steffens and the McNamara Case: A Progressive Response to Class Conflict," *American Journal of Economics and Sociology* 38 (1981): 399–410.

24. Jerome Greene to A. W. Freeman, 5 Mar. 1913, quoted in Source Book, 58m.

25. Jerome Greene to John D. Rockefeller Jr., 9 Mar. 1940, quoted in Source Book, 58r.

26. Ibid., 58r.

27. A. W. Green to Julius Rosenwald, 28 June 1926, Rosenwald, Box 32, Folder 8, UC.

28. John D. Rockefeller Jr. to Jerome Greene, 14 July 1913, RF, Record Group 3, Series 900, Box 21, Folder 159, RAC.

29. Ibid.

30. Frank Walsh, "Are the Great Foundations Perilous?" *The Independent* 83 (1915): 262–63.

31. "Larger Bearings of the McNamara Case: Testimony of John Glenn," *Survey* 27 (1911): 1423. Details of Rosenwald's support can be found in Paul Kellogg, "The Constructive Work before the Industrial Relations Commission," *Survey* 30 (1913): 371–89.

32. Scholars have paid relatively little attention to the Commission on Industrial Relations. Thomas Kochan discusses it briefly in his *Transformation of American Industrial Relations* (New York, 1986), as does Clarence Wunderlin, *Visions of a New Industrial Order: Social Science and Labor Theory in America's Progressive Era* (New York, 1992). The standard work remains Graham Adams's disorganized and unsatisfying *Age of Industrial Violence.* The Walsh Commission, it should be noted, was only one of several national conferences or commissions that studied industrial relations between 1913 and 1920. To date, historians have paid more attention to President Wilson's Industrial Conferences of 1919 and 1920.

33. For a discussion of the potential role Brandeis might have played see Confidential memorandum, "Hearings on the Federal Industrial Relations Commission: Louis Brandeis," RSF, Record Group 4B1, Series 3, Box 33, Folder 260, RAC.

34. Adams, *Age of Industrial Violence,* 54–57; see also Walter Lippman, "The Greatest Question," *Everybody's Magazine* 31 (1914): 502–12.

35. Commission activities are summarized in Commission on Industrial Relations, *Report and Testimony, Serial Set 6929–6939,* Senate Documents: 19–29, 64th Congress, 1st Session.

36. For scholarly discussion of the impact of Ludlow see Adams, *Age of Industrial Violence,* 146–77; Gitelman, *Legacy of the Ludlow Massacre,* 1–40. The best contemporary assessment can be found in U.S. Congress, *Report of the Colorado Coal Commission on the Labor Difficulties in the Coal Fields of Colorado during the Years 1914 and 1915* (Washington, D.C., 1915).

37. Gitelman, *Legacy of the Ludlow Massacre,* 40–71.

38. Basil Manly to John Glenn, 22 Dec. 1914, RSF, Record Group 4B1, Series 3, Box 33, Folder 260, RAC.

39. Burton Hendrick, *Life of Andrew Carnegie* (New York, 1932), 356–64.

40. Clarence Perry to John Glenn, "Comments on Afternoon Hearing of January 29, 1915," RSF, Record Group 4B1, Series 3, Box 33, Folder 260, RAC.

41. Franz Schneider to John Glenn, "Confidential Report on Hearings of the Industrial Relations Commission, Thursday Morning, January 21, 1915" (hereafter Schneider Report), RSF, Record Group 4B1, Series 3, Box 33, Folder 260, RAC.

42. Ibid.; see also Edna Bryner to John Glenn, "Confidential Report on Morning and Afternoon Sessions, January 28, 1915," RSF, Record Group 4B1, Series 3, Box 33, Folder 260, RAC.

43. Ibid.

44. "Transcript of Testimony of John D. Rockefeller Sr., Given before the United States Commission on Industrial Relations, New York City, February 5, 1915," 404–13, RF, Record Group 3, Series 900, Box 18, Folder 131, RAC.

45. "Transcript of Testimony of John D. Rockefeller Jr., in Connection with the Rockefeller Foundation, Given before the United States Commission on Industrial Relations" (hereafter Junior, Commission), 26 Jan. 1915, 12–13, RF, Record Group 3, Series 900, Box 18, Folder 131, RAC. Walsh never tried to hide his hatred of the Rockefellers. They and their associates, in turn, returned the compliment. The Rockefeller public relations agent, Ivy Lee, for instance, circulated reports that Walsh had stolen tens of thousands of dollars from legal clients, tampered with sealed evidence, and was a fraud, a supposed friend of the little man who was, in reality, a rich lawyer who "lived in an imposing residence with a magnificent yard." F. T. Hamilton to Ivy Lee, 26 Mar. 1915, RF, Record Group 3, Series 900, Box 21, Folder 156, RAC.

46. Junior, Commission, 26 Jan. 1915, 28–29.

47. Ibid., 27 Jan. 1915, 83–85.

48. Greene, Commission, 250–51.

49. Ibid., 250.

50. Schneider Report.

51. For discussion of the disintegration of the commission as it concluded its work see Adams, *Age of Industrial Violence*, 210–28; see also Edward Fitzpatrick, *McCarthy of Wisconsin* (New York, 1944).

52. "Larger Bearings of the McNamara Case: Testimony of Lincoln Steffens," *Survey* 27 (1911): 1436.

53. *Final Report of the United States Commission on Industrial Relations; Report of Basil Manly; Report of John Commons, with Supplemental Statements by Commissioners Walsh, Lennon, O'Connell, Garretson, Weinstock and Ballard,* Senate Document 19, Serial Set: 6929 (Washington, D.C., 1916), 30–31. The Manly Report listed, in addition, three other important causes of unrest: unemployment, legal injustice, and denial of the right of labor to form effective organizations, 31.

54. Ibid., 34–40, 116–26.

55. Ibid., 120–26; quotation on 269.

56. Ibid., 220.

57. Ibid., 170–73.

58. Ibid., 242–44.

59. Carl Sandburg, "The Two Mr. Rockefellers—and Mr. Walsh," *International Socialist Review* 16 (1915): 22.

60. For examples of press coverage see "Clippings Files on Social Trends," Papers of Charles Merriam (hereafter Merriam), Series 6, Box 267, Folder 16, UC.

61. President's Research Committee, *Social Trends,* lxxvii.

62. This is a point made by Barry Karl, one of the very few historians to have paid any attention to the Hoover Research Committee. Karl, however, overemphasizes the origins of the committee in Hoover's faith in expertise and progressive social science and underestimates the role of the commission as part of the president's political agenda. See Barry Karl, "Presidential Planning and Social Science: Mr. Hoover's Experts," *Perspectives in American History* 3 (1969): 347–413; idem, *Charles E. Merriam and the Study of Politics* (Chicago, 1974), 201–25.

63. French Strother to William Ogburn, 4 Sept. 1930, Papers of William Ogburn (hereafter Ogburn), Box 7, Folder 4, UC.

64. Hoover did write a foreword to the Research Committee's final report, but it was remarkably brief and glum, consisting of only a few sentences. The soon-to-be-lame-duck president wrote in October 1932, "Since the task assigned to the Committee was to inquire into changing trends, the result is emphasis on instability, rather than stability in our social structure" (President's Research Committee, *Social Trends,* v).

65. French Strother to George Vincent, 28 Oct. 1929, Ogburn, Box 7, Folder 4, UC. As part of its major reorganization in 1928–29 the Rockefeller philanthropies merged the Spelman Memorial with the Rockefeller Foundation. However, at the same time that consolidation took place, the foundation created an entity that was eventually liquidated, called the Spelman Fund, with a principal fund of $10 million to carry on programs that did not seem to fit well within the foundation's new Division of Social Science. Many historians have confused the Spelman Memorial with the Spelman Fund, but they were indeed quite different philanthropic organizations. During the 1930s Charles Merriam helped to guide the Spelman Fund toward a focus on questions of functional operations of government. For further information on the Spelman Fund's history see Raymond Fosdick, *The Story of the Rockefeller Foundation* (New York, 1952), 203–5.

66. William Ogburn to Edmund Day, 5 Sept. 1929, Ogburn, Box 3, Folder 12, UC. In his answer to Ogburn, Day agreed: "I hardly need add that I share your disappointment that it does not seem wise to be in on that dinner at the White House." Edmund Day to William Ogburn, 18 Sept. 1929, ibid. It should be noted that Charles Merriam had long enjoyed a role as a prominent go-between, facilitating contact between Rockefeller philanthropies and academe. He would continue his close contact with the Rockefeller Foundation through the 1930s and 1940s. See Karl, *Charles Merriam,* 201–71.

67. William Ogburn to Beardsley Ruml, 22 Mar. 1930, Ogburn, Box 3, Folder 17, UC; see also Shelby Harrison to George Beal (Comptroller of the Rockefeller Foundation), 3 Jan. 1930, Ogburn, Box 4, Folder 2, UC.

68. Mark Sullivan, "Hoover's First Year," 8 *Herald Tribune Magazine,* 2 Mar. 1930.

69. Will Rogers, letter to the editor, *New York Times,* 21 Dec. 1929.

70. William Ogburn to Edmund Day, 5 Sept. 1929, Ogburn, Box 3, Folder 12, UC.

71. Alva Johnston, "Mr. Hoover's Commissions," *New York Herald Tribune,* 23 Dec. 1929.

72. Herbert Hoover to Howard Odum, 7 Jan. 1930, Ogburn, Box 7, Folder 15, UC.

73. Howard Odum to Wesley Mitchell, 10 Jan. 1930, ibid.

74. French Strother to Wesley Mitchell, 2 Feb. 1930, Ogburn, Box 7, Folder 25, UC.

75. William Ogburn to Shelby Harrison, 5 Sept. 1929, Ogburn, Box 4, Folder 2, UC.

76. Charles Merriam, "Minutes of Conference of President's Committee on Social Trends, March 14, 1931," 72, Ogburn, Box 1, Folder 16, UC.

77. William Ogburn to French Strother, 10 Nov. 1932, Ogburn, Box 7, Folder 4, UC.

78. President's Research Committee, *Social Trends,* quotation on xv; see also 1–45, 90–122, 661–700, 857–912.

79. Ibid., xxviii.

80. Howard Odum, typescript draft, "Social Scientists in Government, 1931," Ogburn, Box 15, Folder 17, UC.

81. Sydnor Walker, "Progress Report #231, December 31, 1931," Merriam, Box 259, Folder 22, UC. See also President's Research Committee, *Social Trends,* 1204–17.

82. President's Research Committee, *Social Trends,* 1204.

83. Ibid., lxi.

BIBLIOGRAPHY

MANUSCRIPT AND ARCHIVAL COLLECTIONS

THE ARCHIVES OF THE UNIVERSITY OF CHICAGO, CHICAGO, ILL.

Organizational Records

Records of the Chicago School of Civics and Philanthropy; Records of the Julius Rosenwald Fund; Records of the School of Social Service Administration, University of Chicago; Records of the Social Science Research Committee, University of Chicago

Personal Papers

Papers of Edith and Grace Abbott; Papers of Sophonisba Breckinridge; Papers of Ernest Burgess; Papers of Charles Judd; Papers of Charles Merriam; Papers of William Ogburn; Papers of Bessie Louise Pierce; Papers of Julius Rosenwald; Papers of Beardsley Ruml; Papers of Louis Wirth; Papers of Quincy Wright

ARCHIVES OF THE UNIVERSITY OF ILLINOIS AT CHICAGO, CHICAGO, ILL.

Records of the Juvenile Protective Association

BEREA COLLEGE ARCHIVES, BEREA, KY.

Correspondence Files, Berea College; Papers of William Frost

LABOR MANAGEMENT DOCUMENTATION CENTER, CORNELL UNIVERSITY, ITHACA, N.Y.

Records of the American Association for Labor Legislation

NATIONAL ARCHIVES AND RECORD ADMINISTRATION, WASHINGTON, D.C.

Records of the Children's Bureau; Records of the Commission on Industrial Relations; Records of the National War Labor Board; Records of the Secretaries of Labor, U.S. Department of Labor; Records of the Women's Bureau

THE NATIONAL LIBRARY OF MEDICINE, BETHESDA, MD.

The Milton Senn Oral History Interviews in Child Development and Child Guidance

THE ROCKEFELLER ARCHIVE CENTER, TARRYTOWN, N.Y.

Organizational Records

Records of the Bureau of Social Hygiene; Records of the Commonwealth Fund; Records of the General Education Board; Records of the Health Research Fund; Records of the International Education Board; Records of the Laura Spelman Rockefeller Memorial; Records of the Rockefeller Brothers' Fund; Records of the Rockefeller Foundation; Records of the Rockefeller Sanitary Commission for the Eradication of Hookworm Disease; Records of the Russell Sage Foundation

Personal Papers

Papers of Nelson Aldrich; Papers of Wallace Buttrick; Papers of Lawrence Dunham; Papers of Simon Flexner; Papers of Raymond Fosdick; Papers of Frederick Gates; Papers of Leonard Outhwaite; Papers of Wickliffe Rose; Papers of George Vincent

Rockefeller Family Archives

General Files; Offices of the Messrs. Rockefeller; Papers of John D. Rockefeller, Senior; Papers of John D. Rockefeller, Junior; Papers of William Rockefeller

SOCIAL WELFARE HISTORY ARCHIVES CENTER, UNIVERSITY OF MINNESOTA, MINNEAPOLIS, MINN.

Records of the Playground Association of America, Executive Committee

SOPHIA SMITH COLLECTION, SMITH COLLEGE

Records of the Young Women's Christian Association

University of Cincinnati Library, Cincinnati, Ohio

Papers of James R. and John J. McNamara

University of Michigan Library, Ann Arbor (Microfilm copies)

Papers of Theodore Roosevelt; Papers of William Howard Taft; Papers of Woodrow Wilson

Unpublished Materials

Agahi, Hossein. "Farmer Assessment of the Dairy Initiative: The Demonstration Farm Program in Minnesota." Ph.D. diss., University of Minnesota, 1993.

Anderson, Paul Gerard. "The Good to Be Done: A History of the Juvenile Protective Association of Chicago, 1898–1976." Ph.D. diss., University of Chicago, 1988.

Bartoo, Jean H. "Major Legal Aspects of Sex Education in the Public Schools of the United States of America." Ph.D. diss., Kent State University, 1972.

Bell, Lacey Dell. "A Study of the Policies Governing Interscholastic Athletic Programs for Girls in American Public Secondary Schools." Ed.D. Diss., New York University, 1959.

Bourgeois, Mary Audrey. "A Study of the Preparation for the Role of Parent-as-Educator in Selected Catholic Women's Colleges." Ph.D. diss., Catholic University of America, 1961.

Buford, Jacqueline Joyce. "Education of the Lost, the Left, and the Homeless: Chicago Public Education of Truants, Incorrigibles, and Delinquents from 1899 to 1990." Ph.D. diss., Loyola University of Chicago, 1993.

Corrigan, Gary Joseph. "The Resurgence of Vocationalism in American Education." Ph.D. diss., University of Toledo, 1977.

Cross, Stephen John. "Designs for Living: Lawrence Frank and the Progressive Legacy in American Social Science." Ph.D. diss., Johns Hopkins University, 1994.

Drew, John Clayton. "Child Labor and Child Welfare: The Origins and Uneven Development of the American Welfare State." Ph.D. diss., Cornell University, 1987.

Finfer, Lawrence. "Leisure as Social Work in the Urban Community: The Progressive Recreation Movement, 1890–1920." Ph.D. diss., Michigan State University, 1974.

Flanzer, Sally Manesberg. "Education for Parents about Nonparental Child Care: Published Child-Rearing Advice for Parents, 1926–1989." Ph.D. diss., Catholic University of America, 1990.

Gilfoyle, Timothy. "City of Eros: New York City, Prostitution and the Commercialization of Sex, 1790–1920." Ph.D. diss., Columbia University, 1987.

Goldmeier, Harold. "An Evaluation of the Parent Education Program of the United

Synagogue of America in Three New England Area Sites." Ed.D. diss., Harvard University, 1975.

Goodwin, Joanne Lorraine. "Gender, Politics, and Welfare Reform: Mothers' Pensions in Chicago, 1900–1930." Ph.D. diss., University of Michigan, 1991.

Grittner, Frederick Karl. "White Slavery: Myth, Ideology, and American Law." Ph.D. diss., University of Minnesota, 1986.

Hamilton, Linda Kay Parker. "A Survey of Professional Preparation in the Area of Physical Education for Public School Elementary Teachers and Physical Education Specialists in Geographic Areas Served by the American Alliance for Health, Physical Education, Recreation, and Dance." Ph.D. diss., Peabody College for Teachers of Vanderbilt University, 1981.

Heffron, John Marcher. "Science, Southernness, and Vocationalism: Rockefeller's 'Comprehensive System' and the Reorganization of Secondary School Science Education, 1900–1920." Ph.D. diss., University of Rochester, 1988.

Heyman, Richard. "The Role of the Carnegie Corporation in African Education." Ed.D. diss., Teachers College, Columbia University, 1970.

Jones, David. "The Playground Association of America: A Thwarted Attempt at the Professionalization of Play Leaders." Ph.D. diss., University of Oregon, 1989.

Kean, Carol Judy. "The Origins of Vocational Education in the Milwaukee Public Schools, 1870–1917: A Case Study in Curricular Change (Wisconsin)." Ph.D. diss., University of Wisconsin–Madison, 1983.

Lindenmeyer, Kriste. "A Right to Childhood: A History of the U.S. Children's Bureau, 1912–38." Ph.D. diss., University of Cincinnati, 1991.

Moore, Libba Gage. "Mothers' Pensions: The Origins of the Relationship between Women and the Welfare State." Ph.D. diss., University of Massachusetts–Amherst, 1986.

Nelson-Rowe, Shan. "Markets, Politics, and Professions: The Rise of Vocationalism in American Education." Ph.D. diss., State University of New York at Stony Brook, 1988.

Parks, Douglas. "Expert Inquiry and Health Care Reform in New Era America." Ph.D. diss., University of Iowa, 1994.

Revoldt, Daryl. "Raymond Fosdick: Reform, Internationalism, and the Rockefeller Foundation." Ph.D. diss., University of Akron, 1982.

Rosen, Robyn Lisa. "Federal Responsibility or Government Tyranny? The Reproductive Reform Impulse and the Welfare State, 1917–1940." Ph.D. diss., State University of New York at Binghamton, 1992.

Rowe, Joyce Louse. "The 'Working Poor': Single Mothers and the State, 1911–1950." Ph.D. diss., Ohio State University, 1993.

Saunders, Dawn Marie. "Class, Gender, and Generation: Mothers' Aid in Massachusetts and the Political Economy of Welfare." Ph.D. diss., University of Massachusetts, 1994.

Thomas, Gillian Rosemary Clare. "State Maintenance for Women during the First

World War: The Case of Separation Allowances and Pensions." Ph.D. diss., University of Sussex, 1989.

Tweton, Donald. "The Attitudes and Policies of the Theodore Roosevelt Administration toward American Agriculture." Ph.D. diss., University of Oklahoma, 1964.

Van de Pol, Ann Frances. "From Mothers' Pensions to ADC: The Origins of the Aid to Dependent Children Program." Ph.D. diss., University of California at Berkeley, 1983.

Wallach, Stephanie. "Luther Halsey Gulick and the Salvation of the American Adolescent." Ph.D. diss., Columbia University, 1989.

Weiner, Lynn Y. "From the Working Girl to the Working Mother: The Debate over Women, Work, and Morality in the United States, 1820–1980." Ph.D. diss., Boston University, 1981.

Weiss, Nancy. "Save the Children: A History of the Children's Bureau, 1903–1918." Ph.D. diss., University of California at Los Angeles, 1974.

White, Kevin Francis. "The Flapper's Boyfriend: The Revolution in Morals and the Emergence of Modern American Male Sexuality, 1910–1930." Ph.D. diss., Ohio State University, 1990.

Wollons, Roberta Lynn. "Educating Mothers: Sidonie Matsner Gruenberg and the Child Study Association of America, 1881–1929." Ph.D. diss., University of Chicago, 1983.

PRIMARY SOURCES

BOOKS

Abbott, Edith. *The Child and the State, II.* Chicago, 1938.

——. *Public Assistance: American Principles and Policies.* Chicago, 1940.

Addams, Jane. *Twenty Years at Hull House.* New York, 1910.

Addams, Jane, ed. *The Child, the Clinic, and the Court.* New York, 1925.

Alexander, Hartley. *The Pageant of Lincoln.* Lincoln, Nebr., 1915.

Andrews, F. Emerson. *Foundation Watcher.* Lancaster, Pa., 1973.

Anthony, Katharine. *Mothers Who Must Earn.* New York, 1914.

Ayres, Leonard P. *Seven Great Foundations.* New York, 1911.

Brandt, Lilian. *How Much Shall I Give?* New York, 1921.

Brasol, B. L. *The Elements of Crime: Psycho-Social Interpretation.* New York, 1931.

Breckinridge, Sophonisba. *Family Welfare Work in the Metropolitan Community: Selected Case Records.* Chicago, 1924.

——. *Women in the Twentieth Century.* New York, 1933.

Brunner, Edmund de Schweinitz. *Rural Social Trends.* New York, 1933.

Bullock, Edna. *Selected Articles on Mothers' Pensions.* New York, 1915.

Burtt, H. E. *Legal Psychology.* New York, 1931.

Butler, Amos. *Proceedings of the National Conference of Charities and Correction.* Fort Wayne, Ind., 1915.

Campbell, John. *The Southern Highlander and His Homeland.* New York, 1921.

Cantor, N. F. *Crime, Criminals and Criminal Justice.* New York, 1932.

Carnegie, Andrew. *An American Four-in-Hand in Britain.* New York, 1883.

———. *Andrew Carnegie Centenary, 1835–1935.* New York, 1935.

———. *The Autobiography of Andrew Carnegie.* Garden City, N.Y., 1909.

———. *The Gospel of Wealth and Other Timely Essays.* Edited by Edward Kirkland. Cambridge, Mass., 1962.

———. *Manual of the Public Benefactions of Andrew Carnegie.* New York, 1919.

Carstens, C. C. *Public Pensions to Widows with Children: A Study of Their Administration in Several American Cities.* New York, 1913.

Chambers, M. M. *Charters of Philanthropies: A Study of Selected Trust Instruments: Charters, By-Laws, and Court Decisions.* New York, 1948.

Coffman, Harold C. *American Foundations: A Study of Their Role in the Child Welfare Movement.* New York, 1936.

Coon, Horace. *Money to Burn: What the Great American Philanthropic Foundations Do with Their Money.* New York, 1938.

Curtis, Henry. *Education through Play.* New York, 1915.

———. *Play and Recreation for the Open Country.* New York, 1914.

D'Arcy MacKaye, Constance. *The Pageant of Schenectady.* Schenectady, N.Y., 1912.

Davis, Katharine Bement. *Factors in the Sex Life of Twenty-two Hundred Women.* New York, 1929.

Devine, Edward T. *The Principles of Relief.* New York, 1904.

Dickinson, Robert, and Lura Beam. *The Single Woman: A Medical Study in Sex Education.* Baltimore, 1934.

Dillard, James H., ed. *Twenty-Year Report of the Phelps Stokes Fund, 1911–1931.* New York, 1932.

Douglas, Paul. *Real Wages in the United States: 1890–1926.* New York, 1930.

Elliott, Edward C., and M. M. Chambers. *Charters of Philanthropies: A Study of the Charters of Twenty-Nine American Philanthropic Foundations.* New York, 1935.

Embree, Edwin R. *Julius Rosenwald Fund: Review of Two Decades, 1917–1936.* Chicago, 1936.

Embree, Edwin R., and Julia Waxman. *Investment in People: The Story of the Julius Rosenwald Fund.* New York, 1949.

Faris, Ellsworth, Ferris Laune, and Arthur J. Todd, eds. *Intelligent Philanthropy.* Chicago, 1930.

Flexner, Abraham. *The American College: A Criticism.* New York, 1908.

———. *Do Americans Really Value Education?* Cambridge, Mass., 1927.

———. *Henry S. Pritchett: A Biography.* New York, 1943.

———. *I Remember.* New York, 1940.

Flexner, Abraham, and Esther S. Bailey. *Funds and Foundations: Their Policies Past and Present.* New York, 1952.

Fosdick, Raymond B. *Adventure in Giving: The Story of the General Education Board, A Foundation Established by John D. Rockefeller.* New York, 1962.

———. *Chronicle of a Generation: An Autobiography.* New York, 1958.

———. *John D. Rockefeller: A Portrait.* New York, 1956.

———. *John D. Rockefeller, Jr.* New York, 1956.

———. *Letters on the League of Nations.* Princeton, N.J., 1966.

———. *The Old Savage in the New Civilization.* Garden City, N.Y., 1928.

———. *A Philosophy for a Foundation: On the Fiftieth Anniversary of the Rockefeller Foundation, 1913–1963.* New York, 1963.

———. *The Story of the Rockefeller Foundation.* New York, 1952.

Fulk, Joseph. *The Municipalization of Play and Recreation.* University Place, Nebr., 1922.

Gates, Frederick. *Chapters in My Life.* New York, 1977.

The General Education Board: An Account of Its Activities, 1902–1914. New York, General Education Board, 1930.

Gillin, John Lewis. *Poverty and Dependency: Their Relief and Prevention.* New York, 1937.

Glenn, John M., Lillian Brandt, and F. Emerson Andrews. *Russell Sage Foundation, 1907–1946.* New York, 1947.

Green, John J., ed. *American Civilization Today: A Summary of Recent Social Trends.* New York, 1934.

Gulick, Luther. *The Dynamics of Manhood.* New York, 1917.

———. *The Efficient Life.* New York, 1907.

———. *The Healthful Art of Dancing.* New York, 1911.

———. *Medical Inspection of Schools.* New York, 1917.

———. *Mind and Work.* New York, 1908.

———. *Morals and Morale.* New York, 1919.

———. *A Philosophy of Play.* New York, 1920.

———. *Physical Education by Muscular Exercise.* Philadelphia, 1904.

Gulick, Luther, and James Naismith, *Basketball.* New York, 1894.

Hall, Fred, and Elisabeth Brooke. *American Marriage Laws in Their Social Aspects.* New York, 1919.

Hall, G. Stanley. *Life Confessions of a Psychologist.* New York, 1923.

Hart, Hastings H. *Endowments: How to Leave Wisely $25,000 to $1,000,000.* Chicago, 1921.

Haynes, F. E. *Criminology.* New York, 1930.

Healy, William. *The Individual Delinquent.* Boston, 1915.

Hillquit, Morris. *The Double Edge of Labor's Sword.* New York, 1971.

Hollis, Ernest V. *Philanthropic Foundations and Higher Education.* New York, 1938.

Huntley, Kate. *Financial Trends in Organized Social Work in New York City.* New York, 1935.

Judd, Charles Hubbard. *Problems of Education in the United States.* New York, 1933.

Keppel, Frederick P. *The Arts in American Life.* New York, 1933.

———. *The Foundation: Its Place in American Life.* New York, 1930.

———. *Philanthropy and Learning, with Other Papers.* New York, 1936.

King, Willford Isbell. *Trends in Philanthropy.* New York, 1928.

Kneeland, George. *Commercialized Prostitution in New York.* New York, 1913.

Laski, Harold J. *Dangers of Obedience.* New York, 1930.

Lasser, J. K. *How Tax Laws Make Giving to Charity Easy.* New York, 1948.

Lee, Herbert C. *The Investment History of Carnegie Corporation of New York.* New York, 1943.

Lee, Joseph. *Constructive and Preventive Philanthropy.* New York, 1902.

———. *Play in Education.* New York, 1915.

Leland, Arthur, and Lorna Leland, eds. *Playground Technique and Playcraft.* New York, 1910.

Lester, Robert M. *Forty Years of Carnegie Giving: A Summary of the Benefactions of Andrew Carnegie and the Works of the Philanthropic Trusts Which He Created.* New York, 1941.

Lindeman, Edward C. *Wealth and Culture: A Study of One Hundred Foundations and Community Trusts and Their Operations during the Decade 1921–1930.* New York, 1936.

Mack, Julian. *Legal Problems Involved in the Establishment of the Juvenile Court.* New York, 1912.

May, Geoffrey. *Marriage Laws and Decisions in the United States.* New York, 1929.

McKelvey, Blake. *American Prisons.* Chicago, 1936.

McKenzie, Roderick Duncan. *The Metropolitan Community.* New York, 1933.

Melendy, Mary Ries. *Modern Eugenics for Men and Women: A Complete Medical Guide to a Thorough Understanding of the Principles of Health and Sex Relations.* New York, 1931.

Moley, R. *Our Criminal Courts.* New York, 1930.

Patch, Buel W. *Tax-Exempt Foundations.* Washington, D.C., 1949.

Pifer, Alan. *Philanthropy in an Age of Transition: The Essays of Alan Pifer.* New York, 1984.

———. *Speaking Out: Reflections on Thirty Years of Foundation Work.* Washington, D.C., 1984.

President's Research Committee on Social Trends. *Recent Social Trends in the United States: Report of the President's Research Committee on Social Trends.* New York, 1933.

Rainwater, Clarence. *The Play Movement in the United States.* Chicago, 1922.

Report of the Commission on Country Life with an Introduction by Theodore Roosevelt. Chapel Hill, N.C., 1944.

Richmond, Mary. *The Good Neighbor in the Modern City.* Philadelphia, 1908.

——. *The Long View.* New York, 1930.

Richmond, Mary, and Fred Hall. *Child Marriages.* New York, 1925.

——. *Marriage and the State.* New York, 1929.

——. *Medical Certification for Marriage.* New York, 1925.

——. *A Study of Nine Hundred and Eighty-five Widows Known to Certain Charity Organization Societies.* New York, 1913.

Rockefeller, John D. *Random Reminiscences of Men and Events.* New York, 1909.

Rubin, Herman Harold. *Eugenics and Sex Harmony: The Sexes, Their Relations and Problems, including Recent Fascinating Medical Discoveries, Prevention of Disease, and Special Advice for Common Disorders.* New York, 1942.

Savage, Howard J. *The First Twenty-Five Years: The Story of a Foundation.* Battle Creek, Mich., 1955.

——. *Fruit of an Impulse: Forty-Five Years of the Carnegie Foundation, 1905–1950.* New York, 1953.

Schneider, David M., and Albert Deutsch. *The History of Public Welfare in New York State, 1867–1940.* Chicago, 1941.

Sears, Jesse Brundage. *Philanthropy in the History of American Higher Education.* Washington, D.C., 1922.

Sen, P. K. *From Punishment to Prevention.* New York, 1932.

Shaw, C. R. *Delinquency Areas.* Chicago, 1929.

Slingerland, William, ed. *A Child Welfare Symposium.* New York, 1915.

Smith, James G. *Development of Trust Companies in the United States.* New York, 1928.

Steiner, Jesse Frederick. *Americans at Play: Recent Trends in Recreation and Leisure Time Activities.* New York, 1933.

Stevenson, George, and Geddes Smith. *Child Guidance Clinics: A Quarter-Century of Development.* New York, 1934.

Sydenstricker, Edgar. *Health and Environment.* New York, 1933.

Tarbell, Ida. *The History of the Standard Oil Company.* New York, 1904.

Taylor, Graham, ed. *The Child Guidance Clinic and the Community.* New York, 1929.

Thom, Douglas. *Everyday Problems of the Everyday Child.* New York, 1927.

Thompson, Warren Simpson. *Population Trends in the United States.* New York, 1933.

Thorndike, Edward L. *Education: A First Book.* New York, 1912.

——. *Educational Psychology.* New York, 1913.

——. *Notes on Child Study.* New York, 1901.

Van Waters, Miriam. *Parent Education.* Minneapolis, 1927.

——. *Parents on Probation.* New York, 1927.

Watson, John. *Behaviorism.* New York, 1925.

——. *Psychological Care of Infant and Child.* New York, 1928.

Weidensall, Jean. *The Mentality of the Criminal Woman.* Baltimore, 1916.

White, Leonard Dupee. *Trends in Public Administration.* New York, 1933.

Willey, Malcolm Macdonald. *Communication Agencies and Social Life.* New York, 1933.

Wilson, Robert N. *The American Boy and the Social Evil, from a Physician's Standpoint.* Philadelphia, 1905.

Wood, Struthers, & Company. *Trusteeship of American Endowments.* New York, 1932.

Woofter, Thomas Jackson. *Races and Ethnic Groups in American Life.* New York, 1933.

Woolston, H. B. *Prostitution in the United States.* New York, 1921.

Zenner, Philip. *Education in Sexual Physiology and Hygiene.* Cincinnati, 1913.

JOURNAL ARTICLES

Abbott, Grace. "Case Work Responsibility of the Juvenile Courts." *Proceedings of the National Conference of Social Work* 5 (1929): 153–57.

Adams, George. "Mothers' Pensions." *Ohio Bulletin of Charities and Correction* 21 (1915): 18–22.

Almy, Frederick. "Public Pensions for Widows." *Child* 5 (1912): 51–54.

American, Sadie. "The Movement for Small Playgrounds." *American Journal of Sociology* 4 (1898): 159–70.

———. "The Movement for Vacation Schools." *American Journal of Sociology* 4 (1898): 309–25.

Bachman, Robert. "Venereal Prophylaxis, Past and Present." *Providence Medical Journal* 7 (1913): 231–44.

Bailey, Liberty Hyde. "Rural Development in Relation to Social Welfare." *Proceedings of National Conference of Social Work* (1908): 83–91.

Beane, James. "A Survey of Three Hundred Delinquent Girls." *Journal for Juvenile Research* 15 (1931): 198–208.

Beitler, Abraham. "The Juvenile Court in Philadelphia." *Annals of the American Academy of Political and Social Sciences* 21 (1902): 271–88.

Belden, Evelina. "The Boys Court of Chicago: A Record of Six Months' Work." *American Journal of Sociology* 20 (1915): 731–44.

Bjorkman, Frances. "The Children's Court in American City Life." *Monthly Review of Reviews* 33 (1906): 306–8.

———. "A Nation Learning to Play." *World's Work* (1909): 1238–45.

Bradstreet, Howard. "Does the Influence of the Playground Extend to the Neighborhood?" *The Playground* 2 (1908): 17–18.

Braucher, Howard. "The Social Worker and the Playground Association of America." *Proceedings of the National Conference of Charities and Corrections* (1910): 219–22.

———. "Why I Believe That Community and Neighborhood Centers, Schools, and Parks Should Be under Government Direction and Control." *The Playground* 10 (1916): 83–96.

Brickwedel, F. J. "Accumulations under Trusts in Perpetuity for Philanthropic or Educational Purposes." *Trust Companies* 10 (1929): 837–42.

Cannon, Cornelia J. "Philanthropic Doubts." *Atlantic Monthly* 127 (1921): 291–300.

Carnegie, Andrew. "The Best Fields for Philanthropy." *North American Review* 149 (1889): 682–98.

——. "The Country Life Commission: How Much Did It Accomplish?" *Country Gentleman* 74 (1909): 231–35.

——. "Wealth." *North American Review* 148 (1889): 653–64.

Coolidge, Calvin. "National Recreation Opportunities." *The Playground* 18 (1924): 194.

Davis, Ada. "The Evolution of the Institution of Mothers' Pensions in the United States." *American Journal of Sociology* 35 (1930): 573–87.

Davis, Katharine Bement. "A Study of Certain Auto-Erotic Practices, Based on the Replies of 2,255 Women." *Mental Hygiene* 8 (1924): 668–723.

——. "Study of the Sex Life of Normal Married Women." *Journal of Social Hygiene* 9 (1923): 129–46.

Deland, Margaret. "The Change in the Feminine Ideal." *Atlantic Monthly* 105 (1910): 290–91.

Devine, Edward. "How Fundamental Is the Play Movement?" *The Playground* 8 (1915): 422–23.

——. "Pensions for Mothers." *Survey* 30 (1913): 457–60.

——. "State Funds to Mothers." *Survey* 29 (1913): 747–48.

Dorr, Rheta Childe. "Reclaiming the Wayward Girl." *Hampton's Magazine* 26 (1911): 67–68.

Edmonds, T. J., and Maurice Hexter. "State Pensions to Mothers in Hamilton County." *Survey* 33 (1914): 289–90.

Eliot, Charles W. "The New Education: Its Organization." *Atlantic Monthly* 23 (1869): 203–20.

Embree, Edwin. "The Business of Giving Money Away." *Harper's Monthly* 161 (1930): 320–32.

——. "Education for Negroes: Divided We Fall." *American Scholar* 5 (1936): 312–22.

——. "How the Negro Schools Have Advanced under the Rosenwald Fund." *The Nation's Schools* 1 (1928): 37–44.

"The Farm Commission." *Independent* 63 (1908): 1012–14.

Flexner, Abraham. "Is Social Work a Profession?" *Proceedings of the National Conference of Charities and Corrections* 42 (1915): 576–90.

——. "Private Fortunes and the Public Future." *Atlantic Monthly* 156 (1935): 215–24.

Fosdick, Raymond. "The Commission on Training Camp Activities." *Proceedings of the Academy of Political Science* 7 (1917–18): 819–26.

Friday, Lucy. "The Work of the Probation Officer among Children." *Charities* 13 (1905): 357–61.

Furley, Paul. "The Juvenile Court Movement." *Thought* 6 (1931): 207–27.

Gilman, Charlotte Perkins. "Paid Motherhood." *Independent* 61 (1907): 75–78.

Gladden, Washington. "Mr. Rockefeller as a Truth-Teller." *Independent* 58 (1905): 1290–91.

Glenn, John M. "Foundations in the Twentieth Century." *The Councillor* 12 (1938): 1–7.

Gompers, Samuel. "Sycophancy and Callousness." *American Federationist* 22 (1915): 514–15.

Gratton, C. Hartley. "Beardsley Ruml and His Ideas." *Harper's Magazine* 204 (1952): 78–86.

Gulick, Luther. "Municipal Aspects of Health and Recreation." *Life and Health* 25 (1910): 544–46.

——. "The Playground." *The Playground* 1 (1907): 7–8.

——. "Popular Recreation and Public Morality." *Annals of the American Academy of Political and Social Science* 34 (July 1909): 33–42.

——. "Rhythm and Education." *American Physical Education Review* 10 (1905): 164–69.

——. "Team Games and Civil Loyalty." *School Review* 14 (1906): 676–78.

Hall, G. Stanley. "Child Study: The Basis of Exact Education." *Forum* 16 (1893): 429–41.

——. "The Contents of Children's Minds." *Princeton Review* 11 (1883): 249–71.

Hall, Winfield. "The Relation of Education in Sex to Race Betterment." *Journal of Social Hygiene* 1 (1914): 67–80.

Hard, William. "Motherless Children of Living Mothers." *Delineator* 81 (1913): 19–20.

Harrison, Shelby M. "Being Neighbor to the Whole Country." *World Outlook* 14 (1919): 21–22, 31.

Hayes, Ralph. "Dead Hands and Frozen Funds." *North American Review* 227 (1929): 607–14.

Heller, Harriet. "The Playground as a Phase of Social Reform." *American Physical Education Review* 13 (1908): 498–505.

"Henry Neil: Pension Agent." *Survey* 29 (1913): 590.

"The Henry Neil League for Mothers' Pensions." *Survey* 29 (1913): 849.

Hollis, Ernest V. "Evolution of the Philanthropic Foundation." *Educational Record* (1939): 575–88.

Hurd, E. P. "Syphilophobia and Spermatophobia." *Medical Age* 7 (1899): 244–46.

Jayne, Ira. "The Budget." *The Playground* 11 (1917): 382–87.

Judd, Charles. "A Method of Securing National Educational Standards." *Educational Record* 19 (1928): 81–95.

Kellogg, Paul. "The Constructive Work before the Industrial Relations Commission." *Survey* 30 (1913): 371–89.

Kelsey, Carl. "The Juvenile Court of Chicago and Its Work." *Annals of the American Academy of Political and Social Science* 17 (1901): 121–23.

Kemmerer, Edwin Walter. "Endowments in Jeopardy." *Atlantic Monthly* 159 (1937): 729–39.

Knapp, Seaman. "Farmers' Cooperative Demonstration Work and Its Results." *Proceedings of the Ninth Conference for Education in the South*. Richmond, Va., 1906.

"Larger Bearings of the McNamara Case: Testimony of John Glenn." *Survey* 27 (1911): 1423.

"Larger Bearings of the McNamara Case: Testimony of Lincoln Steffens." *Survey* 27 (1911): 1434–36.

Lathrop, Julia. "The Development of the Probation System in a Large City." *Charities* 13 (1905): 344–51.

———. "Taking Play Seriously." *The Playground* 10 (1917): 356–63.

Laughlin, Clara. "Girls Who Go Wrong." *Pearsons' Magazine* 23 (1910): 377–87.

Lee, Joseph. "American Play Tradition and Our Relation to It." *The Playground* 7 (1913): 148–59.

———. "Democracy and the Illiteracy Test." *Survey* 35 (January 1918): 497–99.

———. "Play and Congestion." *Charities and the Commons* 20 (1908): 43–48.

———. "Play as a School of the Citizen." *Charities and the Commons* 18 (1907): 486–91.

———. "Play as an Antidote to Civilization." *The Playground* 5 (1911): 110–26.

———. "Play as Medicine." *The Playground* 5 (1911): 289–302.

———. "Work and Citizenship." *Survey* 30 (1913): 611.

Lenroot, Katharine. "The Evolution of the Juvenile Court." *Annals of the American Academy of Political and Social Science* 105 (1923): 213–22.

Lindsey, Ben. "The Boy and the Court." *Charities* 13 (1905): 350–57.

———. "Love and the Criminal Law." *Journal of Education* 70 (1909): 203–5.

Lippman, Walter. "The Greatest Question." *Everybody's Magazine* 31 (1914): 502–12.

MacKaye, Hazel. "Outdoor Plays and Pageants, A Sketch of the Movement in America." *Independent* 66 (1910): 1227–34.

Marks, Jeanette. "The Curse of Narcotism in America: A Reveille." *American Journal of Public Health* 5 (1915): 314–22.

Marsh, Chester. "What a Superintendent of Recreation Needs to Know." *Recreation and the Playground* 18 (1924): 528–29.

"Mary Richmond: Tribute." *Family* 9 (1929): 320–21.

McAdoo, W. "Causes and Mechanisms of Prevalent Crimes." *Scientific Monthly* 24 (1927): 415–20.

Merriam, Charles. "Political Research." *American Political Science Review* 16 (1922): 315–21.

Miner, Maud. "Two Weeks in the Night Court." *Survey* 22 (1909): 229–34.

Mitchell, Wesley C. "Statistics and Government." *Journal of the American Statistical Association* 16 (March 1919): 223–36.

Orbison, T. J. "Drug Addiction and Its Relationship to Crime." *Juvenile Delinquent* 10 (1926): 525–31.

Paddon, Mary. "A Study of Fifty Feeble-Minded Prostitutes." *Journal of Delinquency* (1918): 1–11.

Perry, Clarence. "Leadership in Neighborhood Centers." *Recreation and the Playground* 10 (1924): 462–70.

Pound, Roscoe. "Law in Books and Law in Action." *American Law Review* 44 (1910): 12–36.

———. "Liberty of Contract." *Yale Law Journal* 18 (1909): 454–64.

———. "The Scope and Purpose of Sociological Jurisprudence, Part I." *Harvard Law Review* 24 (1911): 591–619.

———. "The Scope and Purpose of Sociological Jurisprudence, Part II." *Harvard Law Review* 25 (1912): 489–516.

Pritchett, Henry S. "Should the Carnegie Foundation Be Suppressed?" *North American Review* 201 (1915): 554–56.

———. "The Use and Abuse of Endowments." *Atlantic Monthly* 144 (October 1929): 517–24.

Remson, Jane. "Russell Sage, Yankee." *New England Quarterly* 11 (1938): 4–28.

Richmond, Mary. "Motherhood and Pensions." *Survey* 29 (1 March 1913): 774–80.

Riis, Jacob. "Playgrounds in Washington and Elsewhere." *Charities and the Commons* 20 (1908): 101–4.

Roberts, Mary Fanton. "The Civic Theatre." *Craftsman* 21 (1914): 140–41.

———. "The Value of Outdoor Plays in America." *Craftsman* 16 (1909): 491–506.

Robertson, G. "State's Duty to Fatherless Children." *Child Welfare Magazine* 6 (1912): 160–70.

Robinson, Charles. "Educational Value of Public Recreation Facilities." *Annals of the American Academy of Political and Social Science* 35 (1910): 134–40.

Root, Elihu. "Experiments in Government and the Essentials of the Constitution." *North American Review* 198 (1913): 1–17.

Rosenwald, Julius. "Principles of Public Giving." *Atlantic Monthly* 143 (1929): 599–606.

———. "Trends Away from Perpetuities." *Atlantic Monthly* 145 (1930): 741–49.

Ruml, Beardsley. "Pulling Together for Social Services." *Social Service Review* 4 (1930): 1–10.

Sandburg, Carl. "The Two Mr. Rockefellers and Mr. Walsh." *International Socialist Review* 16 (1915): 22–28.

Sheffield, Ada. "Administration of the Mothers' Aid Law in Massachusetts." *Survey* 31 (1914): 645–47.

Soule, George. "The American Drift." *New Republic* (1933): 231–35.

Stevens, David Harrison. "Life and Work of Trevor Arnett." *Phylon* 16 (1955): 127–40.

Tait, W. D. "Crime and Its Causes." *Journal of Abnormal and Social Psychology* 21 (1926): 234–39.

"Ten Years of Mothers' Pensions." *Survey* 49 (1923): 634–36.

Thom, Douglas. "Habit Clinics for Children of Pre-School Age." *American Journal of Psychiatry* 79 (1922–23): 31–38.

Thompson, Warren. "The Eugenics Bugaboo." *American Mercury* 19 (1930): 33–37.

"The Play Trust." *Survey* 29 (1913).

"The Trend of Things." *Survey* 29 (1912): 590.

Walsh, Frank. "Are the Great Foundations Perilous?" *The Independent* 83 (1915): 262–63.

Walters, R. G. "Merger of Social Hygiene Societies." *Survey* 31 (1914): 485–86.

——. "Mr. Rockefeller's War on the Social Evil." *Literary Digest* 46 (1913): 283–84.

——. "Sex in Education." *Arena* 24 (1900): 206–14.

——. "The Social Evil." *Outlook* 101 (1912): 245–48.

"Wildfire Spread of Widows' Pensions: Its Start, Its Meaning, and Its Cost." *Everybody's Magazine* 32 (1915): 780.

Woodson, Carter G. "Progress in Negro Status and Race Relations, 1911–1946: The Thirty-Five Year Report of the Phelps-Stokes Fund." *Journal of Negro History* 34 (1949): 368–69.

Woolston, F.G. "Russell Sage Foundation." *Educational Review* (1922): 275–85.

Youcha, Geraldine. "The Needy Mother and the Neglected Child." *Outlook* 104 (1917): 280–83.

——. "Resolutions Adopted by Second International Congress on Child Welfare, National Congress of Mothers." *Child Welfare Magazine* 5 (1911): 193–96.

Young, James C. "The Dead Hand in Philanthropy." *Current History* (1926): 837–42.

Zinnser, Hans. "The Perils of Magnanimity: A Problem in American Education." *Atlantic Monthly* 139 (1927): 246–50.

SECONDARY SOURCES

BOOKS

Abramowitz, Mimi. *Regulating the Lives of Women: Social Welfare Policy from Colonial Times to the Present.* Boston, 1988.

Abrams, Richard M. *The Issue of Federal Regulation in the Progressive Era.* Chicago, 1963.

Acheson, Roy. *Wickliffe Rose of the Rockefeller Foundation: 1862–1914, the Formative Years.* Cambridge, 1992.

Adams, Graham. *The Age of Industrial Violence, 1910–1915: The Activities and Findings of the U.S. Commission on Industrial Relations.* New York, 1966.

Alchon, Guy. *The Invisible Hand of Planning: Capitalism, Social Science, and the State in the 1920's.* Princeton, N.J., 1985.

Anderson, James D. *The Education of Blacks in the South, 1860–1935.* Chapel Hill, N.C., 1988.

Arnove, Robert F., ed. *Philanthropy and Cultural Imperialism: The Foundations at Home and Abroad.* Boston, 1980.

Ashby, Leroy. *Saving the Waifs: Reformers and Dependent Children.* Philadelphia, 1984.

Bailey, Joseph. *Seaman Knapp: Schoolmaster of American Agriculture.* New York, 1945.

Baker, George, ed. *A Handbook of the Community College in America: Its History, Mission and Management.* Westport, Conn., 1994.

Barber, William. *From New Era to New Deal: Herbert Hoover, the Economists, and American Economic Policy.* New York, 1985.

Bell, Winifred. *Aid to Dependent Children.* New York, 1965.

Benjamin, Gerald, ed. *Private Philanthropy and Public Elementary and Secondary Education: Proceedings of the Rockefeller Archive Center Conference.* Tarrytown, N.Y., 1980.

Berliner, Howard S. *A System of Scientific Medicine: Philanthropic Foundations in the Flexner Era.* New York, 1985.

Berman, Edward H. *The Influence of the Carnegie, Ford, and Rockefeller Foundations on American Foreign Policy: The Ideology of Philanthropy.* Albany, N.Y., 1983.

Blackford, Mansel. *The Politics of Business in California.* Columbus, Ohio, 1977.

Bowers, William. *The County Life Movement in America: 1900–1920.* Port Washington, N.Y., 1974.

Boyer, Paul. *Urban Masses and Moral Order in America, 1820–1920.* Cambridge, Mass., 1978.

Brandes, Stuart D. *American Welfare Capitalism, 1880–1940.* Chicago, 1970.

Bremner, Robert. *American Philanthropy.* Chicago, 1988.

Bremner, Robert, Gary Reichard, and Richard Hopkins. *American Choices: Social Dilemmas and Public Policy.* Columbus, Ohio, 1986.

Brenzel, Barbara. *Daughters of the State: A Social Portrait of the First Reform School for Girls in North America.* Cambridge, Mass., 1984.

Bristow, Nancy. *Making Men Moral: Social Engineering during the Great War.* New York, 1996.

Brown, Dorothy M. *Setting a Course: American Women in the 1920's.* Boston, 1987.

Brown, E. Richard. *Rockefeller Medicine Men: Medicine and Capitalism in America.* Berkeley, Calif., 1979.

Brown, Jerold, and Patrick Reagan, eds. *Voluntarism, Planning, and the State: The American Planning Experience, 1914–1946.* Westport, Conn., 1988.

Brownell, Blaine A. *Bosses and Reformers: Urban Politics in America, 1880–1920.* Boston, 1973.

Budnar, John. *Remaking America: Public Memory, Commemoration, and Patriotism in the Twentieth Century.* Cambridge, Mass., 1976.

Bullough, Vern. *Science in the Bedroom: A History of Sex Research.* New York, 1994.

Bulmer, Martin, Kevin Bales, and Kathryn Kish Sklar, eds. *The Social Survey in Historical Perspective, 1880–1940.* Cambridge, 1991.

Burnham, John. *Bad Habits: Drinking, Smoking, Taking Drugs, Gambling, Sexual Misbehavior and Swearing in American History.* New York, 1991.

Callahan, Raymond E. *Education and the Cult of Efficiency.* Chicago, 1962.

Campbell, Barbara Kuhn. *The "Liberated" Woman of 1914: Prominent Women in the Progressive Era.* Ann Arbor, Mich., 1977.

Cashman, Sean Dennis. *America in the Age of Titans: The Progressive Era and World War I*. New York, 1988.

Cavallo, Dominick. *Muscles and Morals: Organized Playgrounds and Urban Reform, 1880–1920*. Philadelphia, 1981.

Cayleff, Susan. *Babe: The Life and Legend of Babe Didrikson Zaharias*. Urbana, Ill., 1995.

Chambers, Clarke A. *Paul U. Kellogg and the Survey: Voices for Social Welfare and Social Justice*. Minneapolis, 1971.

———. *Seedtime for Reform: American Social Service and Social Action, 1918–1933*. Westport, Conn., 1980.

Chambers, John Whiteclay. *To Raise an Army: The Draft Comes to Modern America*. New York, 1989.

———. *The Tyranny of Change: America in the Progressive Era, 1900–1917*. New York, 1980.

Chandler, Alfred. *The Visible Hand: The Managerial Revolution in American Business*. Cambridge, Mass., 1977.

Chandler, Alfred, and Richard Tedlow, eds. *The Coming of Managerial Capitalism: A Casebook on the History of American Economic Institutions*. Homewood, Ill., 1985.

Chickering, A. L., ed. *The Politics of Planning*. San Francisco, 1976.

Cohen, Michael. *The History of the Sierra Club, 1892–1970*. New York, 1988.

Colburn, David R., and George E. Pozzetta, eds. *Reform and Reformers in the Progressive Era*. Westport, Conn., 1983.

Collier, Peter, and David Horowitz. *The Rockefellers: An American Dynasty*. New York, 1976.

Collins, Robert M. *The Business Reponse to Keynes, 1929–1964*. New York, 1981.

Connelly, Mark Thomas. *The Response to Prostitution in the Progressive Era*. Chapel Hill, N.C., 1980.

Conner, Valerie Jean. *The National War Labor Board: Stability, Social Justice, and the Voluntary State*. Chapel Hill, N.C., 1983.

Coon, Horace. *Money to Burn: Great American Foundations and Their Money*. New Brunswick, N.J., 1990.

Costin, Lela. *Two Sisters for Social Justice*. Urbana, Ill., 1983.

Cravens, Hamilton. *The Triumph of Evolution: American Scientists and the Heredity-Environment Controversy*. Philadelphia, 1978.

Critchlow, Donald. *The Brookings Institution: Expertise and the Public Interest in a Democratic Society*. De Kalb, Ill., 1985.

Critchlow, Donald, and Ellis Hawley, eds. *Federal Social Policy: The Historical Dimension*. Philadelphia, 1988.

Curti, Merle, and Roderick Nash. *Philanthropy in the Shaping of American Higher Education*. New Brunswick, N.J., 1965.

Danbom, David. *Born in the Country: A History of Rural America*. Baltimore, 1995.

———. *The Resisted Revolution: Urban America and the Industrialization of Agriculture, 1900–1930*. Ames, Iowa, 1979.

Davidson, Alastair. *Antonio Gramsci: The Man and His Ideas.* Sydney, 1968.

Davis, Susan. *Parades and Power: Street Theater in Nineteenth Century Philadelphia.* Philadelphia, 1986.

Deegan, Mary J. *Jane Addams and the Men of the Chicago School: 1892–1918.* New Brunswick, N.J., 1988.

———. *Women in Sociology.* Westport, Conn., 1991.

Degler, Carl. *In Search of Human Nature: The Decline and Revival of Darwinism in American Social Thought.* New York, 1991.

D'Emilio, John, and Estelle Freedman. *Intimate Matters: A History of Sexuality in America.* New York, 1988.

Derthick, Martha. *Policymaking for Social Security.* Washington, D.C., 1979.

Dittmer, John. *Black Georgia in the Progressive Era, 1900–1920.* Urbana, Ill., 1977.

Ebner, Michael, and Eugene M. Tobin, eds. *The Age of Urban Reform: New Perspectives on the Progressive Era.* Port Washington, N.Y., 1977.

Edgar, Richard E. *Urban Power and Social Welfare: Corporate Influence in an American City.* Beverly Hills, Calif., 1970.

Ettling, John. *The Germ of Laziness: Rockefeller Philanthropy and Public Health in the New South.* Cambridge, Mass., 1981.

Fee, Elizabeth. *Disease and Discovery: A History of the Johns Hopkins School of Hygiene and Public Health, 1916–1939.* Baltimore, 1987.

Fine, Sidney. *"Without Blare of Trumpets": Walter Drew, the National Erectors' Association, and the Open Shop Movement, 1903–1957.* Ann Arbor, Mich., 1995.

Fisher, Donald. *Fundamental Development of the Social Sciences: Rockefeller Philanthropy and the United States Social Science Research Council.* Ann Arbor, Mich., 1993.

Fitzpatrick, Edward. *McCarthy of Wisconsin.* New York, 1944.

Fitzpatrick, Ellen. *Endless Crusade: Women Social Scientists and Progressive Reform in America, 1830–1930.* New York, 1990.

Fitzpatrick, Ellen, ed. *Katharine Bement Davis, Early Twentieth Century American Women, and the Study of Sex Behavior.* New York, 1987.

Flamming, Douglas. *Creating the Modern South: Millhands and Managers in Dalton, Georgia, 1884–1984.* Chapel Hill, N.C., 1992.

Fligstein, Neil. *Going North: Migration of Blacks and Whites from the South, 1900–1950.* New York, 1981.

Forcey, Charles. *The Crossroads of Liberalism: Croly, Weyl, Lippman, and the Progressive Era.* New York, 1961.

Fox, Daniel. *Engines of Culture: Philanthropy and Art Museums.* Madison, Wis., 1963.

———. *Health Policies, Health Politics: The Experience of Britain and America, 1911–1965.* Princeton, N.J., 1986.

Fox, Kenneth. *Better City Government: Innovation in American Urban Politics.* Philadelphia, 1977.

Fox, Stephen. *John Muir and His Legacy: The American Conservation Movement.* Boston, 1981.

Freedman, Estelle B. *Maternal Justice: Miriam Van Waters and the Female Reform Tradition*. Chicago, 1996.

———. *Their Sisters' Keepers: Women's Prison Reform in America, 1830–1930*. Ann Arbor, Mich., 1981.

Freyer, Tony Allan. *Forums of Order: The Federal Courts and Business in American History*. Greenwich, Conn., 1979.

Furner, Mary O. *Advocacy and Objectivity: A Crisis in the Professionalization of American Social Science, 1865–1905*. Lexington, Ky., 1975.

Gaylin, Willord, ed. *Doing Good: The Limits of Benevolence*. New York, 1978.

Geiger, Roger L. *To Advance Knowledge: The Growth of American Research Universities, 1900–1940*. New York, 1986.

Gies, D. L., J. S. Ott, and J. M. Shafritz. *The Nonprofit Organization: Essential Readings*. Pacific Grove, Calif., 1990.

Gilbert, Neil, and Harry Specht. *Dimensions of Social Welfare Policy*. Englewood Cliffs, N.J., 1986.

Gitelman, Howard M. *Legacy of the Ludlow Massacre: A Chapter in American Industrial Relations*. Philadelphia, 1988.

Glassberg, David. *American Historical Pageantry: The Uses of Tradition in the Early Twentieth Century*. Chapel Hill, N.C., 1990.

Glazer, Penina, and Miriam Slater. *Unequal Colleagues: The Entrance of Women into the Professions*. New Brunswick, N.J., 1987.

Goggin, Jacqueline. *Carter G. Woodson: A Life in Black History*. Baton Rouge, La., 1993.

Goodenow, Ronald, and Arthur White, eds. *Education and the Rise of the New South*. Boston, 1981.

Gordon, Clark, and Michael Dear. *State Apparatus, Structures, and the Language of Legitimacy*. London, 1984.

Gordon, Linda, ed. *Women, the State, and Welfare*. Madison, Wis., 1990.

Gordon, Lynn D. *Gender and Higher Education in the Progressive Era*. New Haven, Conn., 1990.

Gottlieb, Peter. *Making Their Own Way: Southern Blacks' Migration to Pittsburgh, 1916–1930*. Urbana, Ill., 1987.

Grant, H. Roger. *Insurance Reform: Consumer Action in the Progressive Era*. Ames, Iowa, 1979.

Gruber, Carol S. *Mars and Minerva: World War I and the Uses of Higher Learning in America*. Baton Rouge, La., 1975.

Haan, Norma, Robert N. Bellah, Paul Rainbow, and William M. Sullivan, eds. *Social Science as Moral Inquiry*. New York, 1983.

Haber, Samuel. *Efficiency and Uplift: Scientific Management in the Progressive Era, 1890–1920*. Chicago, 1964.

Hammack, David. *The Russell Sage Foundation: A Guide to the Microfiche Collection*. Frederick, Md., 1988.

Hammack, David, and Dennis Young, eds. *Nonprofit Organizations in a Market Economy.* San Francisco, 1993.

Harr, John Ensor, and Peter J. Johnson. *The Rockefeller Century: Three Generations of America's Greatest Family.* New York, 1988.

——. *The Rockefeller Conscience: An American Family in Public and in Private.* New York, 1991.

Harvey, A. McGehee, and Susan Abrams. *"For the Welfare of Mankind": The Commonwealth Fund and American Medicine.* Baltimore, 1986.

Haskell, Thomas L. *The Authority of Experts: Studies in History and Theory.* Bloomington, Ind., 1984.

——. *The Emergence of Professional Social Science: The American Social Science Association and the Nineteenth Century Crisis of Authority.* Urbana, Ill., 1977.

Haskins, Ron, and Diane Adams, eds. *Parent Education and Public Policy.* Norwood, N.J., 1983.

Haveman, Robert, ed. *A Decade of Federal Antipoverty Programs: Achievements, Failures and Lessons.* New York, 1977.

Hawes, Joseph. *Children in Urban Society: Juvenile Delinquency in Nineteenth Century America.* New York, 1971.

——. *The Children's Rights Movement: A History of Advocacy and Protection.* Boston, 1991.

Hawes, Joseph, and Ray Hiner, eds. *American Childhood: A Research Guide.* Westport, Conn., 1985.

Hays, Samuel. *Conservation and the Gospel of Efficiency: The Progressive Conservation Movement, 1890–1920.* Cambridge, Mass., 1959.

Hendrick, Burton. *The Life of Andrew Carnegie.* Garden City, N.Y., 1932.

Hidy, Ralph, ed. *Oil's First Century.* Cambridge, Mass., 1960.

Hobson, Barbara. *Uneasy Virtue: The Politics of Prostitution and the American Reform Tradition.* Chicago, 1987.

Hodgkinson, Virginia Ann, and Richard W. Lyman, eds. *The Future of the Nonprofit Sector: Challenges, Changes and Policy Considerations.* San Francisco, 1989.

Holl, Jack M. *Juvenile Reform in the Progressive Era: William R. George and the Junior Republic Movement.* Ithaca, 1973.

Horn, Margo. *Before It's Too Late: The Child Guidance Movement in the United States.* Philadelphia, 1989.

Horwitz, Morton. *The Transformation of American Law, 1870–1960: The Crisis of Legal Orthodoxy.* New York, 1992.

Huggins, Nathan Irwin. *Protestants against Poverty: Boston's Charities, 1870–1900.* Westport, Conn., 1971.

Hunt, Lynn, ed. *The New Cultural History.* Berkeley, Calif., 1989.

Israel, Jerry, ed. *Building the Organizational Society: Essays on Associational Activities in Modern America, 1921–1923.* New York, 1972.

Jacoby, Stanford M. *Employing Bureaucracy: Managers, Unions, and the Transformation of Work in American Industry, 1900–1945.* New York, 1985.

James, Thomas, and Henry Levin, eds. *Comparing Public and Private Schools: Institutions and Organizations.* New York, 1987.

Janowitz, Morris. *Social Control of the Welfare State.* New York, 1976.

Jenkins, J. Craig. *Between Private and Public.* New Haven, Conn., 1987.

Jordan, John. *Machine-Age Ideology: Social Engineering and American Liberalism, 1911–1939.* Chapel Hill, N.C., 1994.

Kadushin, Alfred. *Child Welfare Services.* New York, 1967.

Karl, Barry D. *Charles E. Merriam and the Study of Politics.* Chicago, 1974.

———. *Donors, Trustees, Staffs: A Historical View, 1890–1930.* Pocantico Hills, N.Y., 1977.

Katz, Michael B. *In the Shadow of the Poorhouse: A Social History of Welfare in America.* New York, 1986.

———. *Poverty and Policy in American History.* New York, 1983.

Keller, Morton. *Regulating a New Economy: Public Policy and Economic Change in America.* New York, 1990.

Kennedy, David. *Over Here: The First World War and American Society.* New York, 1980.

Kilpatrick, Dee, and Robert Roberts, eds. *Child Caring, Social Policy, and the Institution.* Chicago, 1973.

Kirby, Jack Temple. *Rural Worlds Lost: The American South, 1920–1960.* Baton Rouge, La., 1987.

Kloppenberg, James. *Uncertain Victory: Social Democracy and Progressivism in European and American Thought.* New York, 1986.

Kochan, Thomas. *Transformation of American Industrial Relations.* New York, 1986.

Koven, Seth, and Sonya Michel, eds. *Mothers of a New World: Maternalist Politics and the Origins of Welfare States.* New York, 1993.

Kuznets, Simon. *Long Term Changes in the National Income of the United States since 1870. Income and Wealth,* series 2. Baltimore, 1952.

Ladd-Taylor, Mary Madeleine. *Mother-Work, Ideology, Public Policy and the Mothers' Movement, 1890–1930.* Ann Arbor, Mich., 1987.

Ladd-Taylor, Mary Madeleine, ed. *Raising a Baby the Government Way: Mothers' Letters to the Children's Bureau, 1915–1932.* New Brunswick, N.J., 1986.

Lagemann, Ellen Condliffe. *A Generation of Women: Education in the Lives of Women Progressive Reformers.* Cambridge, Mass., 1979.

———. *The Politics of Knowledge: The Carnegie Corporation, Philanthropy, and Public Policy.* Middletown, Conn., 1989.

———. *Private Power for the Public Good: A History of the Carnegie Foundation for the Advancement of Teaching.* Middletown, Conn., 1983.

Lankford, John. *Congress and the Foundations in the Twentieth Century.* River Falls, Wis., 1964.

Larson, Magali Sarfatti. *The Rise of Professionalism: A Sociological Analysis.* Berkeley, Calif., 1977.

Leiby, James. *A History of Social Welfare and Social Work in the United States.* New York, 1978.

Levy, Daniel C., ed. *Private Education: Studies in Choice and Public Policy.* New York, 1986.

Lindblom, Charles E., and David K. Cohen. *Usable Knowledge: Social Science and Social Problem Solving.* New Haven, Conn., 1979.

Link, William. *A Hard Country and a Lonely Place: Schooling, Society, and Reform in Rural Virginia, 1870–1920.* Chapel Hill, N.C., 1986.

———. *The Paradox of Southern Progressivism.* Chapel Hill, N.C., 1992.

Lubove, Roy. *The Professional Altruist: The Emergence of Social Work as a Career, 1880–1930.* New York, 1969.

———. *The Progressive and the Slums: Tenement House Reforms in New York City, 1890–1917.* Westport, Conn., 1974.

Lustig, R. Jeffrey. *Corporate Liberalism: The Origins of Modern American Political Theory, 1890–1920.* Berkeley, Calif., 1982.

McCarthy, Kathleen D. *Noblesse Oblige: Charity and Cultural Philanthropy in Chicago, 1849–1929.* Chicago, 1982.

McClymer, John F. *War and Welfare: Social Engineering in America, 1890–1925.* Westport, Conn., 1980.

McCraw, Thomas K., ed. *Regulation in Perspective: Historical Essays.* Cambridge, Mass., 1981.

McLean, John, and Robert Haight. *The Growth of Integrated Oil Companies.* Boston, 1984.

Melosh, Barbara. *The Physician's Hand: Work Culture and Conflict in American Nursing.* Philadelphia, 1982.

Mennel, Robert. *Thorns & Thistles: Juvenile Delinquents in the United States, 1825–1940.* Hanover, N.H., 1973.

Meyer, Donald. *The Protestant Search for Political Realism, 1919–1941.* Middletown, Conn., 1988.

Meyer, Stephen. *The Five-Dollar Day: Labor Management and Social Control in the Ford Motor Company, 1908–1921.* Albany, N.Y., 1981.

Miller, Robert Moats. *Harry Emerson Fosdick: Preacher, Pastor, Prophet.* New York, 1985.

Mock, James Chrisman, and Arthur McLure. *Education for Work: The Historical Evolution of Vocational and Distributive Education in America.* Charlotte, N.C., 1985.

Mullan, Fitzhugh. *Plagues and Politics: The Story of the United States Public Health Service.* New York, 1989.

Nash, Roderick, ed. *The American Environment: Readings in the History of Conservation.* Reading, Pa., 1968.

Nelson, Daniel. *Frederick W. Taylor and the Rise of Scientific Management.* Madison, Wis., 1980.

——. *Managers and Workers: Origins of the New Factory System in the United States, 1880–1920*. Madison, Wis., 1975.

Nevins, Allan. *Study in Power: John D. Rockefeller, Industrialist and Philanthropist*. New York, 1953.

Nielson, Waldemar. *The Golden Donors: A New Anatomy of the Great Foundations*. New York, 1985.

Noble, David F. *America by Design: Science, Technology and the Rise of Corporate Capitalism*. New York, 1977.

O'Connell, Brian. *America's Voluntary Spirit*. New York, 1983.

Odendahl, Teresa, ed. *America's Wealthy and the Future of Foundations*. New York, 1987.

Odendahl, Teresa. *Charity Begins at Home: Generosity and Self-Interest among the Philanthropic Elite*. New York, 1990.

Oleson, Alexandra, and John Vess, eds. *The Organization of Knowledge in Modern America*. Baltimore, 1979.

O'Malley, C. D., ed. *The History of Medical Education*. Berkeley, Calif., 1970.

O'Neill, Michael. *The Third America: The Emergence of the Nonprofit Sector in the United States*. San Francisco, 1989.

O'Neill, William L. *Divorce in the Progressive Era*. New Haven, Conn., 1967.

Ownby, Ted. *Subduing Satan: Religion, Recreation, and Manhood in the Rural South, 1865–1920*. Chapel Hill, N.C., 1990.

Parker, Franklin. *George Peabody: A Biography*. Nashville, Tenn., 1971.

Patterson, James. *America's Struggle against Poverty, 1900–1985*. Cambridge, Mass., 1986.

Pechman, Joseph. *How Taxes Affect Economic Behavior*. Washington, D.C., 1981.

Penick, James. *Progressive Politics and Conservation: The Ballinger-Pinchot Affair*. Chicago, 1968.

Phillips, David Graham. *Contemporaries: Portraits in the Progressive Era*. Westport, Conn., 1981.

Pivar, David. *Purity Crusade: Sexual Morality and Social Control, 1868–1900*. Westport, Conn., 1973.

Platt, Anthony. *The Child Savers: The Invention of Delinquency*. Chicago, 1969.

Quandt, Jean. *From the Small Town to the Community: The Social Thought of Progressive Intellectuals*. New Brunswick, N.J., 1970.

Rabinowitz, Alan. *Social Change and Philanthropy in America*. New York, 1990.

Rader, Benjamin. *American Sports from the Age of Folk Games to the Age of Spectators*. Englewood Cliffs, N.J., 1983.

Reed, James. *The Birth Control Movement and American Society: From Private Vice to Public Virtue*. Princeton, 1984.

Reese, William J. *Power and Promise of School Reform: Grassroots Movements during the Progressive Era*. Boston, 1986.

Rice, Bradley. *Progressive Cities: Commission Government in America, 1901–1920*. Austin, Tex., 1977.

Richardson, Teresa T. *Century of the Child: Children's Policy and the Mental Hygiene Movement in the United States and Canada*. Albany, N.Y., 1989.

Rosen, Ruth. *The Lost Sisterhood: Prostitution in America, 1900–1918*. Baltimore, 1982.

Rosenberg, Charles E. *No Other Gods: On Science and American Social Thought*. Baltimore, 1976.

Ross, Dorothy. *G. Stanley Hall: The Psychologist and Prophet*. Chicago, 1972.

Rothman, David J. *Conscience and Convenience: The Asylum and Its Alternatives in Progressive America*. Boston, 1980.

Rubin, Paul H. *Business Firms and the Common Law: The Evolution of Efficient Rules*. New York, 1983.

Ryan, Mary. *Women in Public: Between Banners and Ballots*. Baltimore, 1990.

Ryerson, Ellen. *The Best-Laid Plans: America's Juvenile Court Experiment*. New York, 1978.

Salzman, Jac, ed. *Philanthropy and American Society: Selected Papers*. New York, 1987.

Schachter, Hindy Lauer. *Frederick Taylor and the Public Administration Community*. Albany, N.Y., 1989.

Schiff, Ashley. *Fire and Water: Scientific Heresy in the Forest Service*. Cambridge, Mass., 1962.

Schlossman, Steven L. *The Chicago Area Project Revisited*. Santa Monica, Calif., 1983.

——. *Delinquency Prevention in South Chicago*. Santa Monica, Calif., 1984.

——. *Love and the American Delinquent: The Theory and Practice of "Progressive" Juvenile Justice, 1825–1920*. Chicago, 1977.

——. *Studies in the History of Early Twentieth Century Delinquency*. Santa Monica, Calif., 1983.

——. *Who Will Teach?* Santa Monica, Calif., 1986.

Schneider, Dorothy. *American Women in the Progressive Era, 1900–1920*. New York, 1993.

Sealander, Judith. *As Minority Becomes Majority: Federal Reaction to the Phenomenon of Women in the Work Force*. Westport, Conn., 1983.

——. *Grand Plans: Business Progressivism and Social Change in Ohio's Miami Valley, 1890–1929*. Lexington, Ky., 1988.

Segal, Howard P. *Technological Utopianism in American Culture*. Chicago, 1985.

Senn, Milton J. E. *Insights on the Child Development Movement in the United States*. Chicago, 1975.

Silva, Edward, and Sheila Slaughter. *Serving Power: The Making of the Academic Social Science Expert*. Westport, Conn., 1984.

Sklar, Kathryn Kish. *Doing the Nation's Work: Florence Kelly and Women's Political Culture, 1860–1930*. New Haven, Conn., 1992.

Sklar, Martin J. *The United States as a Developing Country: Studies in U.S. History in the Progressive Era and the 1920's.* Cambridge, Mass., 1992.

Skocpol, Theda. *Protecting Soldiers and Mothers: The Political Origins of Social Policy in the United States.* Cambridge, Mass., 1992.

Skowronek, Stephen. *Building a New American State: The Expansion of National Administrative Capacities.* New York, 1982.

Smith, James. *The Idea Brokers: Think Tanks and the Rise of the New Policy Elite.* New York, 1991.

Solomon, Barbara Miller. *In the Company of Educated Women: A History of Higher Education in America.* New Haven, Conn., 1985.

Stanfield, John H. *Philanthropy and Jim Crow in American Social Science.* Westport, Conn., 1985.

Starr, Paul. *The Social Transformation of American Medicine.* New York, 1982.

Swain, Donald. *Federal Conservation Policy, 1921–33.* Berkeley, Calif., 1963.

Swain, Martha. *Ellen S. Woodward: New Deal Advocate for Women.* Jackson, Miss., 1995.

Thorne, Barrie, and Marilyn Yalom, eds. *Rethinking the Family: Some Feminist Questions.* New York, 1982.

Tiffin, Susan. *In Whose Best Interest? Child Welfare Reform in the Progressive Era.* Westport, Conn., 1982.

Tilly, Louise A., and Patricia Gurin, eds. *Women, Politics, and Change.* New York, 1990.

Titmuss, Richard M. *Social Policy: An Introduction.* New York, 1975.

Tobey, Ronald C. *The American Ideology of National Science, 1919–1930.* Pittsburgh, 1971.

Tobin, Gary A., ed. *Social Planning and Human Service Delivery in the Voluntary Sector.* Westport, Conn., 1985.

Trattner, Walter I. *Crusade for the Children: A History of the National Child Labor Committee and Child Labor Reform in America.* Chicago, 1970.

———. *From Poor Law to Welfare State: A History of Social Welfare in America.* New York, 1984.

———. *Homer Folks: Pioneer in Social Welfare.* New York, 1968.

Trattner, Walter I., ed. *Social Welfare or Social Control? Some Historical Reflections on "Regulating the Poor."* Knoxville, Tenn., 1983.

Vaughan, George. *The Community College in America: A Short History.* Washington, D.C., 1985.

Van Til, Jon. *Critical Issues in American Philanthropy.* San Francisco, 1990.

Vicinus, Martha. *Independent Women: Work and Community for Single Women, 1850–1920.* Chicago, 1985.

Wall, Joseph Frazier. *Andrew Carnegie.* New York, 1970.

Ward, David, and Oliver Zunz, eds. *The Landscape of Modernity: Essays on New York City, 1900–1940.* New York, 1992.

Ware, Susan. *Beyond Suffrage: Women and the New Deal.* Cambridge, Mass., 1981.

———. *Partner and I: Molly Dewson, Feminism, and New Deal Politics.* New Haven, Conn., 1987.

Warner, Hoyt Landon. *Reforming American Life in the Progressive Era.* New York, 1971.

Weidenthal, Maurice. *Who Cares about the Inner City? The Community College's Response to Urban America.* Washington, D.C., 1988.

Wheatley, Steven C. *The Politics of Philanthropy: Abraham Flexner and Medical Education.* Madison, Wis., 1988.

Whitaker, Ben. *The Foundations: An Anatomy of Philanthropic Bodies.* London, 1979.

White, G. Edward. *The American Judicial Tradition: Profiles of Leading American Judges.* New York, 1976.

Wilensky, Norman M. *Conservatives in the Progressive Era: The Taft Republicans of 1912.* Gainesville, Fla., 1965.

Wilson, Daniel. *Science, Community, and the Transformation of American Philosophy, 1860–1930.* Chicago, 1990.

Wolch, Jennifer. *The Shadow State: Government and Voluntary Sector in Transition.* New York, 1990.

Wollons, Roberta, ed. *Children at Risk in America: History, Concepts, and Public Policy.* Albany, N.Y., 1993.

Wood, Donna J. *Strategic Uses of Public Policy: Business and Government in the Progressive Era.* Boston, 1986.

Wood, Stephen B. *Constitutional Politics in the Progressive Era: Child Labor and the Law.* Chicago, 1968.

Worster, Donald, ed. *The Ends of the Earth: Perspectives on Modern Environmental History.* Cambridge, 1988.

Wunderlin, Clarence. *Visions of a New Industrial Order: Social Science and Labor Theory in America's Progressive Era.* New York, 1992.

Wynn, Neil. *From Progressivism to Prosperity: World War I and American Society.* New York, 1986.

Youcha, Geraldine. *Minding the Children: A History of Child Care in America.* New York, 1994.

Zietz, Dorothy. *Child Welfare: Service and Perspective.* New York, 1969.

Zunz, Olivier. *Making America Corporate.* Chicago, 1990.

Journal Articles

Adams, David W. "Philanthropists, Progressives, and Southern Black Education." *History of Education Quarterly* 23 (1983): 99–111.

Ahmad, Salma. "American Foundations and the Development of the Social Sciences between the Wars: Comment on the Debate between Martin Bulmer and Donald Fisher." *Sociology* 23 (1991): 511–20.

Anderson, James D. "Northern Foundations and the Shaping of Southern Black Rural Education, 1902–1935." *History of Education Quarterly* 18 (1978): 371–96.

Becker, Dorothy. "Exit Lady Bountiful: The Volunteer and the Professional Social Workers." *Social Service Review* 34 (1964): 57–72.

Belles, A. Gilbert. "The NAACP, the Urban League, and the Julius Rosenwald Fund." *Crisis* 86 (1979): 97–106.

Best, Gary Dean. "President Wilson's Second Industrial Conference." *Labor History* 16 (1975): 505–20.

Best, Joel. "Careers in Brothel Prostitution: St. Paul, 1865–1883." *Journal of Interdisciplinary History* 12 (1982): 597–619.

——. "Keeping the Peace in St. Paul: Crime, Vice, and Police Work, 1869–1874." *Minnesota History* 47 (1981): 240–48.

Borell, Merriley. "Biologists and the Promotion of Birth Control Research, 1918–1938." *Journal of the History of Biology* 20 (1987): 51–87.

Brestensky, Dennis. "Pastimes and Festive Customs in Early Mine Patches." *Pennsylvania Heritage* 8 (1982): 15–19.

Brown, Carol. "Sexism and the Russell Sage Foundation." *Signs* 1 (1972): 25–44.

Brown, E. Richard. "Public Health in Imperialism: Early Rockefeller Programs at Home and Abroad." *American Journal of Public Health* 66 (1976): 897–903.

Bruck, Peter. "Telephone Books and Party Lines." *Reviews in American History* 14 (1986): 341–43.

Budros, Art. "The Ethnic Vice Industry Revisited." *Ethnic and Racial Studies* 6 (1983): 438–56.

Bullough, Vern. "Katharine Bement Davis, Sex Research and the Rockefeller Foundation." *Bulletin of the History of Medicine* 62 (1988): 74–89.

——. "The Rockefellers and Sex Research." *Journal of Sex Research* 21 (1985): 113–25.

Bulmer, Martin. "The Early Institutional Establishment of Social Science Research: The Local Research Committee at the University of Chicago, 1923–1930." *Minerva* 18 (1980): 51–110.

——. "Philanthropic Foundations and the Development of the Social Sciences in the Early Twentieth Century: A Reply to Donald Fisher." *Sociology* 18 (1984): 572–84.

——. "Support for Sociology in the 1920's: The Laura Spelman Rockefeller Memorial and the Beginnings of Modern, Large-Scale Sociological Research in the University." *American Sociologist* 17 (November 1982): 185–92.

Bulmer, Martin, and Joan Bulmer. "Philanthropy and Social Science in the 1920's: Beardsley Ruml and the Laura Spelman Rockefeller Memorial, 1922–1929." *Minerva* 19 (1981): 347–407.

Burnham, John. "The Progressive Revolution in American Attitudes towards Sex." *Journal of American History* 57 (1973): 885–908.

Butler, Anne M. "Military Myopia: Prostitution on the Frontier." *Prologue* 13 (1981): 233–50.

Carp, E. Wayne. "Professional Social Workers, Adoption, and the Problem of Illegitimacy: 1915–1945." *Journal of Policy History* 6 (1994): 161–84.

Chambers, Clarke A. "Toward a Redefinition of Welfare History." *Journal of American History* 73 (1986): 407–33.

———. "Women in the Creation of the Profession of Social Work." *Social Service Review* 60 (1986): 1–33.

Cloward, Richard. "Foundations and Professions: The Organization Defense of Autonomy." *Administrative Science Quarterly* 6 (1961): 167–84.

Coats, A. W. "The American Economic Association, 1904–1929." *American Economic Review* 54 (1964): 261–85.

Coben, Stanley. "Foundation Officials and Fellowships: Innovation in the Patronage of Science." *Minerva* 14 (1976): 279–306.

Cravens, Hamilton. "The Wandering I.Q.: American Culture and Mental Testing." *Human Development* 28 (1985): 113–30.

Curti, Merle, Judith Green, and Roderick Nash. "Anatomy of Giving: Millionaires in the Late 19th Century." *American Quarterly* 15 (1963): 416–35.

Doherty, William T., Jr. "The Nineteenth Century Businessman and Religion." *North Dakota Quarterly* 46 (1978): 4–18.

Domhoff, G. William. "State and the Ruling Class in Corporate America." *Insurgent Sociologist* 4 (1974): 3–16.

Eisen, George. "Sport, Recreation and Gender: Jewish Immigrant Women in Turn-of-the-Century America (1880–1920)." *Journal of Sport History* 18 (1991): 103–20.

Ellsworth, Clayton. "Theodore Roosevelt's Country Life Commission." *Agricultural History* 34 (1960): 155–72.

Fell, James E., Jr. "Rockefeller's Right-Hand Man: Frederick T. Gates and the Northwestern Mining Investments." *Business History Review* 52 (1978): 537–61.

Fishbein, Leslie. "Harlot or Heroine: Changing Views of Prostitution, 1870–1920." *Historian* 43 (1980): 23–35.

Fisher, Donald. "Boundary Work: Toward a Model of the Relation of Power/Knowledge." *Knowledge* 10 (1988): 156–76.

———. "Philanthropic Foundations and the Social Sciences: A Response to Martin Bulmer." *Sociology* 18 (1984): 580–89.

———. "The Role of Philanthropic Foundations in the Reproduction and Production of Hegemony: Rockefeller Foundation and the Social Sciences." *Sociology* 17 (1983): 206–23.

Foster, Craig. "Tarnished Angels: Prostitution in Storyville, New Orleans, 1900–1910." *Louisiana History* 31 (1990): 387–97.

Fox, Daniel M. "Abraham Flexner's Unpublished Report: Foundations and Medical Education, 1909–1928." *Bulletin of the History of Medicine* 54 (1980): 475–96.

Fox, Sanford. "Juvenile Justice Reform: An Historical Perspective." *Stanford Law Review* 22 (1970): 1186–1239.

Freyer, Tony A. "The Federal Courts, Localism and the National Economy, 1865–1900." *Business History Review* 53 (1979): 343–63.

Gaddis, John Lewis. "The Corporatist Synthesis." *Diplomatic History* 10 (1986): 357–62.

Galambos, Louis. "Technology, Political Economy, and Professionalization: Central Themes of the Organizational Synthesis." *Business History Review* 57 (1983): 471–93.

Gardner, John W. "Abraham Flexner, Pioneer in Educational Reform." *Science* 131 (1960): 594–95.

Gettleman, Marvin E. "Philanthropy and Social Control in Late Nineteenth Century America: Some Hypotheses and Data on the Rise of Social Work." *Societas* 5 (1975): 49–59.

Glassberg, David. "History and the Public: Legacies of the Progressive Era." *Journal of American History* (1987): 957–80.

———. "Restoring a 'Forgotten Childhood': American Play and the Progressive Era's Elizabethan Past." *American Quarterly* 32 (1980): 351–68.

Gordon, Linda. "Single Mothers and Child Neglect." *American Quarterly* 37 (1985): 173–92.

Gronbjerg, Kirsten A. "Patterns of Institutional Relations in the Welfare State." *Journal of Voluntary Action Research* 16 (1987): 64–80.

———. "Private Welfare: Its Future in the Welfare State." *American Behavioral Scientist* 26 (1983): 773–93.

Grossberg, Michael. "Who Gets the Child?: Custody, Guardianship, and the Rise of the Judicial Patriarchy in Nineteenth Century America." *Feminist Studies* 9 (1983): 235–60.

Grossman, David. "American Foundations and Support of Economic Research, 1913–1929." *Minerva* 20 (1982): 59–82.

Haag, Pamela Susan. "Commerce in Souls: Vice, Virtue, and Women's Wage Work in Baltimore, 1900–1915." *Maryland Historical Magazine* 86 (1991): 292–308.

Hammack, David. "Private Organizations, Public Purposes: Nonprofits and Their Archives." *Journal of American History* 76 (1989): 181–91.

Hapke, Laura. "The Late Nineteenth Century American Streetwalker: Images and Realities." *Mid-America* 65 (1983): 155–62.

Harvey, Charles E. "John D. Rockefeller, Jr. and the Social Sciences." *Journal of the History of Sociology* 2 (1982): 1–31.

———. "Robert S. Lynd, John D. Rockefeller, Jr., and Middletown." *Indiana Magazine of History* 70 (1983): 330–54.

Harvie, Robert A., and Larry V. Bishop. "Police Reform in Montana, 1890–1918." *Montana* 33 (1983): 46–59.

Hijiha, James A. "Four Ways of Looking at a Philanthropist: A Study of Robert Weeks DeForest." *Proceedings of the American Philosophical Society* 124 (1980): 404–18.

Himmelberg, Robert F. "Business, Antitrust Policy, and the Industrial Board of the Department of Commerce, 1919." *Business History Review* 42 (1968): 1–23.

Hogan, Michael. "Corporatism: A Positive Appraisal." *Diplomatic History* 10 (1986): 363–72.

Howard, Christopher. "Sowing the Seeds of 'Welfare': The Transformation of Mothers' Pension, 1900–1940." *Journal of Policy History* 4 (1992): 188–227.

Humphrey, David C. "Prostitution and Public Policy in Austin, Texas, 1870–1915." *Southwestern Historical Quarterly* 86 (1983): 473–516.

Jambor, Harold. "Theodore Dreiser, the *Delineator,* and Dependent Children." *Social Service Review* 32 (1958): 33–35.

Jones, James, Jr. "Municipal Vice: The Management of Prostitution in Tennessee's Urban Experience." *Tennessee Historical Quarterly* 50 (1991): 33–41; 50, no. 2: 110–22.

Jordan, John. "To Educate Public Opinion: John D. Rockefeller, Jr. and the Origins of Social Scientific Fact-Finding." *New England Quarterly* 64 (1991): 292–97.

Karl, Barry D. "Philanthropy, Policy Planning and the Bureaucratization of the Democratic Ideal." *Daedalus* 105 (1976): 129–50.

——. "Presidential Planning and Social Science: Mr. Hoover's Experts." *Perspectives in American History* 3 (1969): 347–413.

Karl, Barry D., and Stanley N. Katz. "The American Private Philanthropic Foundation and the Public Sphere, 1890–1930." *Minerva* 19 (1981): 236–70.

——. "Foundations and Ruling Class Elites." *Daedalus* 116 (1987): 1–40.

——. "Philanthropy and the Social Sciences." *Proceedings of the American Philosophical Society* 129 (1985): 14–19.

Kevles, Daniel. "Foundations, Universities, and Trends in Support for the Physical and Biological Sciences." *Daedalus* 121 (1992): 195–235.

Kirschner, Don. "The Perils of Pleasure: Commercial Recreation, Social Disorder, and Moral Reform in the Progressive Era." *American Studies* 21 (1980): 27–42.

Kohler, Robert E. "A Policy for the Advancement of Science: The Rockefeller Foundation, 1924–1929." *Minerva* 16 (1978): 480–515.

——. "Science and Philanthropy: Wickliffe Rose and the International Education Board." *Minerva* 23 (1985): 75–95.

——. "Science, Foundations, and American Universities in the 1920's." *Osiris* 3 (1987): 135–64.

Koven, Seth, and Sonya Michel. "Womanly Duties: Maternalist Politics and the Origins of the Welfare State in France, Germany, Great Britain, and the United States, 1880–1920." *American Historical Review* 95 (1990): 1076–1114.

Kraines, Oscar. "Brandeis' Philosophy of Scientific Management." *Western Political Quarterly* 13 (1960): 191–201.

Krantz, David, and David Allen. "The Rise and Fall of McDougall's Instinct Doctrine." *Journal of the History of the Behavioral Sciences* 9 (1973): 66–76.

Krog, Carl E. "'Organizing the Production of Leisure': Herbert Hoover and the

Conservation Movement in the 1920s." *Wisconsin Magazine of History* 67 (1984): 199–218.

Kusmer, Kenneth L. "The Functions of Organized Charity in the Progressive Era: Chicago as a Case Study." *Journal of American History* 60 (1973): 657–78.

Lagemann, Ellen Condliffe. "The Politics of Knowledge: The Carnegie Corporations and the Formulation of Public Policy." *History of Education Quarterly* 27 (1987): 205–20.

Lane, James B. "Jacob A. Riis and Scientific Philanthropy during the Progressive Era." *Social Service Review* 47 (1973): 32–48.

Leff, Mark. "Consensus for Reform: The Mothers'-Pension Movement in the Progressive Era." *Social Service Review* 47 (1973): 397–417.

Leiby, James. "Moral Foundations of Social Welfare and Social Work: A Historical View." *Social Work* 30 (1985): 323–30.

Levy, Daniel C. "Private Versus Public Financing of Higher Education: U.S. Policy in Comparative Perspective." *Higher Education* 2 (1982): 607–28.

Link, William. "Privies, Progressivism, and Public Schools: Health Reform and Education in the Rural South, 1909–1920." *Journal of Southern History* 54 (1988): 623–42.

Lipset, Seymour, and Everett Ladd. "The Politics of American Sociologists." *American Journal of Sociology* 78 (1972): 67–104.

Lomax, Elizabeth. "The Laura Spelman Rockefeller Memorial: Some of Its Contributions to Early Research in Child Development." *Journal of the History of Behavioral Sciences* 13 (1977): 283–93.

Lorini, Alessandra. "The Progressives' Rhetoric on National Recreation: The Play Movement in New York City (1880–1917)." *Storia Nordamericana* 1 (1984): 34–71.

Lubove, Roy. "The Progressive and the Prostitute." *Historian* 24 (1962): 308–30.

Lynch, Edmund C. "Walter Dill Scott: Pioneer Industrial Psychologist." *Business History Review* 42 (1968): 149–70.

Madison, James H. "John D. Rockefeller's General Education Board and the Rural School Problem in the Midwest, 1900–1930." *History of Education Quarterly* 24 (1984): 181–200.

Maier, Charles S. "Between Taylorism and Technocracy: European Ideologies and the Vision of Industrial Productivity in the 1920's." *Journal of Contemporary History* 5 (1970): 27–61.

May, Margaret. "Innocence and Experience: The Evolution of the Concept of Juvenile Delinquency in the Mid–Nineteenth Century." *Victorian Studies* 17 (1973): 7–29.

McCurdy, Charles W. "American Law and the Marketing Structure of the Large Corporation, 1875–1890." *Journal of Economic History* 38 (1978): 631–49.

McKanna, Clare. "Hold Back the Tide: Vice Control in San Diego, 1870–1930." *Pacific Historian* 28 (1984): 54–64.

Meiksins, Peter F. "Scientific Management and Class Relations." *Theory and Society* 13 (1984): 177–209.

Miner, Curtis. "The 'Deserted Parthenon': Class, Culture and the Carnegie Library of Homestead, 1898–1937." *Pennsylvania History* 57 (1990): 107–35.

Minton, Henry L. "The Iowa Child Welfare Research Station and the 1940 Debate on Intelligence: Carrying on the Legacy of a Concerned Mother." *Journal of the History of the Behavioral Sciences* 20 (1984): 160–76.

Muncey, Robyn. "Gender and Professionalization in the Origins of the U.S. Welfare State: The Careers of Sophonisba Breckinridge and Edith Abbott." *Journal of Policy History* 2 (1990): 290–315.

Murphy, Mary. "The Private Lives of Public Women: Prostitution in Butte, Montana, 1878–1917." *Frontiers* 7 (1984): 30–35.

Nye, Russel B. "Eight Ways of Looking at an Amusement Park." *Journal of Popular Culture* 15 (1981): 63–75.

Odem, Mary. "Single Mothers, Delinquent Daughters, and the Juvenile Court in Early 20th-Century Los Angeles." *Journal of Social History* 25 (1991): 27–43.

Odem, Mary, and Steven Schlossman. "Guardians of Virtue: The Juvenile Court and Female Delinquency in Early 20th-Century Los Angeles." *Crime and Delinquency* 37 (1991): 186–203.

O'Keefe, Deborah. "Annals of Social Work: They Were Called 'Friendly Visitors' and They Indeed Visited, but Could They Really Be Considered Friendly?" *American History* 36 (1985): 100–123.

Orlans, Harold. "Academic Social Scientists and the Presidency: From Wilson to Nixon." *Minerva* 24 (1986): 172–204.

Orloff, Ann. "Gender in Early U.S. Social Policy." *Journal of Policy History* 3 (1991): 249–82.

Pantich, Leo. "Recent Theorizations and Corporatism: Reflections on a Growth Industry." *British Journal of Sociology* 31 (1980): 159–87.

Parker, Jacqueline K., and Edward M. Carpenter. "Julia Lathrop and the Children's Bureau: The Emergence of an Institution." *Social Service Review* 55 (1981): 60–77.

Parsons, Gail. "Equal Treatment for All: American Medical Remedies for Male Sexual Problems, 1850–1900." *Journal of the History of Medicine and Allied Sciences* 32 (1977): 55–71.

Peel, Mark. "On the Margins: Lodgers and Boarders in Boston: 1860–1900." *Journal of American History* 72 (1986): 813–34.

Peeps, J. M. Stephen. "Northern Philanthropy and the Emergence of Black Higher Education: Do-Gooders, Compromisers, or Co-Conspirators?" *Journal of Negro Education* 50 (1981): 251–69.

Peri, Arnold. "Herbert Hoover and the Continuity of American Public Policy." *Public Policy* 20 (1972): 525–44.

Perry, Elisabeth I. "Recreation and Reform in the Progressive Era." *History of Education Quarterly* 24 (1984): 223–28.

Pittman-Munke, Peggy. "Mary E. Richmond: The Philadelphia Years." *Social Casework* 63 (1986): 160–66.

Pivar, David J. "Sisterhood Lost/Sisterhood Regained." *Reviews in American History* 11 (1983): 243–47.

Pope, Steven. "An Army of Athletes: Playing Fields, Battlefields and the American Military Sporting Experience, 1890–1920." *Journal of Military History* 4 (1995): 35–56.

Quadagno, Jill. "Two Models of Welfare State Development: Reply to Skocpol and Amenta." *American Sociological Review* 50 (August 1985): 575–78.

———. "Welfare Capitalism and the Social Security Act of 1935." *American Sociological Review* 49 (1984): 632–47.

Rendleman, Douglas. "*Parens Patriae:* From Chancery to the Juvenile Court." *South Carolina Law Review* 23 (1971): 205–58.

Riess, Steven. "Professional Baseball and Social Mobility." *Journal of Interdisciplinary History* 11 (1980): 235–50.

Roberts, Randy. "Baseball Myths and American Realities." *Reviews in American History* 10 (1982): 141–45.

Robinson, Marshall. "Private Foundations and Social Science Research." *Society* 21 (1984): 76–80.

Rogers, Martha. "The Bronx Parks System: A Faded Design." *Landscape* 27 (1983): 13–21.

Ruggles, Steven. "The Transformation of the American Family Structure." *American Historical Review* 99 (1994): 103–28.

Samuelson, Franz. "Organizing for the Kingdoms of Behavior: Academic Battles and Organizational Policies in the Twenties." *Journal of the History of the Behavioral Sciences* 21 (1985): 33–47.

Sandos, James. "Prostitution and Drugs: The United States Army on the Mexican-American Border, 1916–1917." *Pacific Historical Review* 49 (1980): 621–45.

Sarvasy, Wendy. "Beyond the 'Difference versus Equality' Policy Debates: Post-suffrage Feminism, Citizenship, and the Quest for a Feminist Welfare State." *Signs* 17 (1992): 329–62.

Schlossman, Steven. "Before Home Start: Notes toward a History of Parent Education in America, 1897–1929." *Harvard Educational Review* 46 (1976): 436–67.

———. "Philanthropy and the Gospel of Child Development." *History of Education Quarterly* 21 (1981): 275–99.

Schultz, J. Lawrence. "The Cycle of Juvenile Court History." *Crime and Delinquency* 19 (1973): 456–76.

Seagle, William. "The Twilight of the Mann Act." *American Bar Association Journal* 55 (1969): 641–47.

Sedlak, Michael. "Young Women and the City: Adolescent Deviance and the Transformation of Educational Policy." *History of Education Quarterly* 23 (1983): 1–28.

——. "Youth Policy and Young Women, 1870–1972." *Social Service Review* 56 (1982): 449–65.

Shapiro, Herbert. "Lincoln Steffens and the McNamara Case: A Progressive Response to Class Conflict." *American Journal of Economics and Sociology* 38 (1981): 399–410.

Shaw, Jean. "The Story of the U.S. Public Health Service in Two Centuries." *Medical World News* 30 (1989): 34–40.

Shumsky, Neil Larry, and Larry M. Springer. "San Francisco's Zone of Prostitution, 1880–1934." *Journal of Historical Geography* 7 (1981): 71–89.

Skidmore, P. G. "Reforming Women." *Canadian Review of American Studies* 14 (1983): 437–46.

Sklar, Kathryn. "A Call for Comparisons." *American Historical Review* 95 (1990): 1009–14.

Skocpol, Theda, and John Ikenberg. "The Political Formation of the American Welfare State in Historical and Comparative Perspective." *Comparative Social Research* 6 (1983): 87–148.

Smythe, Donald. "Venereal Disease: The AEF's Experience." *Prologue: The Journal of the National Archives* 9 (1977): 65–74.

Stanfield, John H. "The Cracked Back Door: Foundations and Black Social Scientists between the Wars." *American Sociologist* 17 (1982): 193–204.

Stapleton, Darwin. "Plumbing the Past: Foundation Archives Are Becoming an Invaluable Resource." *Foundation News* 1 (1987): 67–68.

Strong, Bryan. "Ideas of the Early Sex Education Movement in America: 1890–1920." *History of Education Quarterly* 12 (1972): 129–61.

Taylor, Peter. "Denied the Power to Choose the Good: Sexuality and Mental Defect in American Medical Practice, 1850–1920." *Journal of Social History* 10 (1976): 472–82.

Terrell, Karen A. "Exposure of Prostitution in Western Massachusetts: 1911." *Historical Journal of Massachusetts* 8 (1980): 3–11.

Thompson, Dennis F. "Public-Private Policy: An Introduction." *Policy Studies Journal* 11 (1983): 419–26.

Trattner, Walter I. "Private Charity in America: 1700–1900." *Current History* 65 (July 1973): 25–28, 40.

"The Uniform Juvenile Court Act: A Symposium on Juvenile Problems." *Indiana Law Journal* 43 (1968): 523–50.

Urban, Wayne. "Organized Teachers and Educational Reform during the Progressive Era: 1890–1920." *History of Education Quarterly* 16 (1976): 35–52.

Useem, Michael. "Government Influence on the Social Science Paradigm." *Sociological Quarterly* 17 (1976): 146–61.

Vandepol, Ann. "Dependent Children, Child Custody, and the Mothers' Pensions:

The Transformation of State-Family Relations in the Early 20th Century."
Social Problems 29 (1982): 221–25.

Veysey, Lawrence. "What's a Professional? Who Cares?" *Reviews in American History* 3 (1975): 419–23.

Waldstreicher, David. "Rites of Rebellion, Rites of Assent: Celebrations, Print Culture, and the Origins of American Nationalism." *Journal of American History* 82 (1995): 37–61.

Walkowitz, Daniel. "The Making of a Feminine Professional Identity: Social Workers in the 1920's." *American Historical Review* 95 (1990): 1051–75.

Walkowitz, Judith R. "The Politics of Prostitution." *Signs* 6 (1980): 123–35.

Walters, R. G. "Sexual Matters as Historical Problems: A Framework of Analysis." *Societas: A Review of Social History* 6 (1976): 157–75.

Weigley, Emma. "It Might Have Been Euthenics: The Lake Placid Conference and the Home Economics Movement." *American Quarterly* 26 (1974): 79–96.

Westfall, Barry W. "The William Rainey Harper/John D. Rockefeller Correspondence: Religion and Economic Control at the University of Chicago, 1889–1905." *Vitae Scholasticae* 4 (1985): 109–23.

White, G. Edward. "From 'Sociological Jurisprudence' to 'Realism': Jurisprudence and Social Change in Early Twentieth Century America." *Virginia Law Review* 58 (1972): 1002–17.

——. "The Rise and Fall of Justice Holmes." *University of Chicago Law Review* 51 (1971): 75–80.

Woods, Wilma M. "The Role of Federal Dollars and the Economics of Recreation in the Development of Idaho's State Parks, 1908–1965." *Idaho Yesterdays* 34 (1991): 15–21.

Wunsch, James. "The Social Evil Ordinance." *American Heritage* 33 (1982): 50–55.

Yellis, Kenneth. "Prosperity's Child: Some Thoughts on the Flapper." *American Quarterly* 21 (1969): 44–64.

Zahavi, Gerald. "Negotiated Loyalty: Welfare Capitalism and the Shoeworkers of Endicott-Johnson, 1920–1940." *Journal of American History* 71 (1983): 602–20.

UNITED STATES GOVERNMENT DOCUMENTS

CONGRESS

House of Representatives

Committee on the District of Columbia. Comabell, P. P. *Report Favoring S. 5287, to Parole Juvenile Offenders.* House Report 960. Washington, D.C., 1910.

——. *Juvenile Court and Removing Disabilities Resting upon Children Who Have Been Convicted of Crime in Juvenile Court, Hearing on H. 8348, Amending Act Relative to Juvenile Court in District of Columbia, and H. 9803, for Removing of Disabili-*

ties Resting upon Children Who Have Been Convicted of Crime in Juvenile Court. Y4.D63/1:J98. Washington, D.C., 1916.

——. *Home Care for Dependent Children: Report to Accompany H. 7669 to Provide Home Care for Dependent Children and to Establish Mothers' Aid Board for Administering Provisions of Act.* House Report 124. Washington, D.C., 1926.

Committee on Education. *Federal Aid for Physical Education, Hearing on H. 12652, for Promotion of Physical Education in United States through Cooperation with States in Preparation and Payment of Supervisors and Teachers of Physical Education, Including Medical Examiners and School Nurses, to Appropriate Money and Regulate Its Expenditure, and for Other Purposes.* Y4.Ed8/2:P56. Washington, D.C., 1921.

——. Hughes, D. M. *Report Amending S. J. R. 5 for Appointment of Commission to Consider Need and Report Plan for National Aid to Vocational Education.* House Report 75. Washington, D.C., 1913.

——. *Laws Relating to Vocational Education: Public Law No. 347, 64th Congress; Public Law No. 64, 178, 279, 65th Congress.* Y1.2:V85/920. Washington, D.C., 1920.

——. *Laws Relating to Vocational Education: Public Law No. 95, 63d Congress; Public Law No. 347, 64th Congress; Public Law No. 64, 178, 279, 65th Congress; Public Law No. 11, 52, and 236, 66th Congress.* Y1.2:V85/921. Washington, D.C., 1920.

——. *Laws Relating to Vocational Education: Public Law No. 347, 64th Congress; Public Law No. 64, 65th Congress; Public Law No. 178, 65th Congress; Public Law No. 279, 65th Congress; Public Law No. 11, 66th Congress; Public Law No. 52, 66th Congress; Public Law No. 236, 66th Congress; Public Law No. 47, 67th Congress; Public Law No. 172, 67th Congress.* Y1.2:V85/922. Washington, D.C., 1922.

——. Lewis, Elmer A. *Laws Relating to Vocational Education and Agricultural Extension Work.* Y1.2:V85/5. Washington, D.C., 1930.

——. Smith, Hoke, and Carroll S. Page. *Hearings on S. J. R. 5 for Appointment of Commission to Consider Need and Report Plan for National Aid to Vocational Education.* Y4.Ed8/2:V85. Washington, D.C., 1913.

Committee on the Judiciary. Houston, W. C. *Report Amending H. 21594, to Appoint Commission to Consider and Report upon Treatment of Juvenile and First Offenders, with Best System of Detention of Federal Prisoners.* House Report 919. Washington, D.C., 1912.

——. *Transfer of Interdepartmental Social Hygiene Board, Hearing on H. 11490 to Enlarge Powers and Duties of Department of Justice in Relation to Repression of Prostitution for Protection of the Armed Forces.* Y4.J89/1:In8/4. Washington, D.C., 1922.

Senate

Committee on Agriculture and Forestry. *Report of Subcommittee on S. 3, to Cooperate with States in Encouraging Instruction in Agriculture, Trades, and Industries, and Home*

Economics in Secondary Schools, in Maintaining Instruction in These Vocational Subjects in State Normal Schools and in Maintaining Extension Departments in State Colleges of Agriculture and Mechanic Arts. Y4.Ag8/2:Ed8/3. Washington, D.C., 1912.

Committee on the District of Columbia. Dean, I. A. *Letter to Senator Hoke Smith, Submitting Suggestions with Reference to Application of Educational Training in America to Rural Schools.* Senate Document 8. Washington, D.C., 1919.

———. Gamble, R. J. *Report Amending S. 5443, to Create Juvenile Court in District.* Senate Report 3812. Washington, D.C., 1905.

———. Gamble, R. J. *Report Favoring S. 51, to Create Juvenile Court in District.* Senate Report 18. Washington, D.C., 1905.

———. Gamble, R. J. *Report Favoring S. 8518 Empowering Juvenile Court of District to Issue Execution on Forfeited Recognizances.* Senate Report 920. Washington, D.C., 1909.

———. *Mothers' Aid in District of Columbia, Hearings before Subcommittee, 69th Congress, First Session, on S. 120, Bills to Establish a Board of Mothers' Assistance in Aid of Destitute Mothers and to Provide Home Care for Dependent Children in District of Columbia.* Y4.D63/2:M85. Washington, D.C., 1926.

Committee on Education and Labor. *Federal Aid for Physical Education, Hearing on S. 3950, for Promotion of Physical Education in United States through Cooperation with States in Preparation and Payment of Supervisors and Teachers of Physical Education, Including Medical Examiners and School Nurses, to Appropriate Money and Regulate Its Expenditure and for Other Purposes.* Y4.Ed8/3:P56. Washington, D.C., 1920.

———. *Report to Accompany S. 703 to Provide for Promotion of Vocational Education, to Provide for Cooperation with States in Promotion of Such Education in Agriculture, Trades, Industries, and Home Economics, to Provide for Cooperation with States in Preparation of Teachers of Vocational Subjects.* House Report 181. Washington, D.C., 1916.

———. Smith, Hoke, *Report Favoring S. J. R. 5, for Appointment of Commission to Consider Need and Report Plan for National Aid to Vocational Education.* Senate Report 54. Washington, D.C., 1913.

Committee on the Judiciary. *Laws Relating to Vocational Education, Public Law No. 347, 64th Congress; Public Law No. 64, 178, 279, 65th Congress; Public Law No. 11, 21, 52, 73, 155, 236, 246, 264, 384, 389, 66th Congress; Public Law No. 18, 67th Congress.* Y1.3:V85. Washington, D.C., 1921.

———. *Enlarging Powers and Duties of Department of Justice in Relation to Protection of Armed Forces of United States, Report to Accompany S. 3544: To Enlarge Powers and Duties of Department of Justice in Relation to Repression of Prostitution for Protection of Armed Forces.* Senate Report 1032. Washington, D.C., 1923.

Smith, Hoke. *Vocational Education Conference Report on S. 703, to Provide for Promotion of Vocational Education, to Provide for Cooperation with States in Promotion of Such*

Education in Agriculture and Trades and Industries, to Provide for Cooperation with States in Preparation of Teachers of Vocational Subjects, and to Appropriate Money and Regulate Its Expenditure. Senate Document 711. Washington, D.C., 1917.

DEPARTMENTS

Department of Agriculture

Bureau of Plant Industry. *Field Instructions for Farmers' Cooperative Demonstration Work in Western Texas and Oklahoma.* A19.2:F22/11. Washington, D.C., 1910.

Knapp, S. A. "The Farmers' Cooperative Demonstration Work." *The Yearbook of the Department of Agriculture for 1909.* A1.10:909. Washington, D.C., 1910.

——. Knapp, Seaman. "The Mission of Cooperative Demonstration Work in the South." Department of Agriculture, Office of the Secretary, Circular 33. Washington, D.C., 1910.

True, Alfred. "A History of Agricultural Education in the United States: 1785– 1925." Miscellaneous Publication 36: Department of Agriculture, Washington, D.C., 1929.

Department of Commerce

Bureau of the Census. *Prisoners and Juvenile Delinquents, General Tables.* C3.3:121. Washington, D.C., 1913, 1914.

Bureau of Immigration and Naturalization. *Further Response to Resolution, Information Concerning Repression of Trade in White Women.* Senate Document 214. Washington, D.C., 1910.

Bureau of Labor. *Juvenile Delinquency and Its Relation to Employment.* Senate Document 645. Washington, D.C., 1911.

Department of the Interior

Bureau of Education. *Agricultural Instruction in Secondary Schools: Papers Read at Third Annual Meeting of American Association for Advancement of Agricultural Teaching, Atlanta, Ga.* I16.3:913/14. Washington, D.C., 1913.

——. *Athletic Badge Tests for Boys and Girls; Prepared for Bureau of Education by the Playground and Recreation Association of America.* I16.40:2. Washington, D.C., 1923.

——. Barrows, H. P. *Development of Agricultural Instruction in Secondary Schools.* I16.3:919/85. Washington, D.C., 1920.

——. Bawden, William T. *Progress in Vocational Education.* I16.1/1a:V85/2. Washington, D.C., 1914.

——. Bawden, William T. *Vocational Education.* I16.1/1a:V85/4. Washington, D.C., 1915.

——. Bawden, William T. *Progress in Vocational Education.* I16.1/1a:1/85/3. Washington, D.C., 1915.

——. Bawden, William T. *Vocational Education.* I16.1/1a:V85/5. Washington, D.C., 1916.

——. Bawden, William T. *Vocational Education.* I16.3:919/25. Washington, D.C., 1919.

——. Bawden, William T. *Examples of Good Teaching in Industrial Education.* I16.33:6. Washington, D.C., 1920.

——. Cobb, Walther F., and Dorothy Hutchinson. *Suggestion for Physical Education Program for Small Secondary Schools Arranged with Special Consideration of Problems in Physical Education Which Face Local School Officials Where There Is No Director of Physical Education.* I16.40:3. Washington, D.C., 1923.

——. Edson, Newell W. *States of Sex Education in High Schools, Prepared in Cooperation with Public Health Service.* I16.3:922/14. Washington, D.C., 1922.

——. Evans, Henry R. *Bibliography of Industrial, Vocational, and Trade Education.* I16.3:913/22. Washington, D.C., 1913.

——. *Foundations of Family Life: Reading Course for Parents.* I16.12:33. Washington, D.C., 1929.

——. Gruenger, Benjamin C. *High Schools and Sex Education, Manual of Suggestions on Education Related to Sex.* Washington, D.C., 1922.

——. Hartwell, Edward Mussey. *Physical Training.* I16.1/1a:p56/1. Washington, D.C., 1899.

——. Hartwell, Edward Mussey. *Physical Training.* I16.1:903. Washington, D.C., 1905.

——. Hutchinson, Dorothy. *Preparation of School Grounds for Play Fields and Athletic Events.* I16.40:1. Washington, D.C., 1923.

——. Jarvis, Chester D. *Training of Vocational Teachers for Secondary Schools, What Land-Grant Colleges Are Doing to Prepare Them.* I16.3:917/38. Washington, D.C., 1917.

——. Jenks, F. B. *Review of Agricultural Education.* I16/2.1/1a:Ag8/25. Washington, D.C., 1912.

——. *List of References on Vocational Education.* I16.10/2:V85/2. Washington, D.C., 1914.

——. Lombard, Ellen C. *Parent Education, 1926–28: Advance Sheets from Biennial Survey of Education in United States.* I16.3:929/15. Washington, D.C., 1929.

——. O'Leary, Iris Prouty. *Cooking in Vocational School as Training for Home Making.* I16.3:915/1. Washington, D.C., 1915.

——. *Papers Presented at Organization Meeting of Vocational Guidance Association.* I16.3:914/14. Washington, D.C., 1914.

——. *Physical Education in Secondary Schools, Report of Commission on Reorganization of Secondary Education Appointed by National Education Association.* I16.3:917/45. Washington, D.C., 1917.

——. *Professional Schools.* E8–678/2. Washington, D.C., 1912.

——. *Reading Course for Parents Prepared in Home Education Division.* I16.12:3. Washington, D.C., 1920.

——. *Reading Course for Parents Prepared in Home Education Division.* I16.12:3/9. Washington, D.C., 1924.

——. Ready, Marie M. *Physical Education in American Colleges and Universities.* I16.3:927/14. Washington, D.C., 1927.

——. Ready, Marie M. *Physical Education in City Public Schools.* I161.40:10. Washington, D.C., 1929.

——. *Report of Commissioner about Physical Training.* House Document 5. Washington, D.C., 1903.

——. *Report of Progress of Subcommittee on College Instruction in Agriculture.* I16.17:21. Washington, D.C., 1920.

——. Rogers, James Frederick. *Problems in Physical Education, Report of Conference of State Directors of Physical Education Held in New York City.* I16.40:5. Washington, D.C., 1925.

——. *State Industrial Schools.* I16.1/1a:st2/19. Washington, D.C., 1913.

——. Storey, Thomas A., and Willard S. Small. *Recent State Legislation for Physical Education.* I16.40:2. Washington, D.C., 1923.

——. *Twenty Good Books for Parents.* I16.12:21/4. Washington, D.C., 1924.

——. Whitcomb, Emeline S. *Typical Child Care and Parenthood Education in Home Economics Departments.* I16.3:927/17. Washington, D.C., 1927.

Department of Justice

Bureau of Investigation. Hoke, Effie. *Nos. 381, 588, 602 and 603 in Supreme Court, 1912, Cases Involving Constitutionality of White Slave Traffic Act.* J1.13:H689. Washington, D.C., 1913.

——. *Supplement to Annual Report of Attorney General, Fiscal Year 1914, Embodying First Report of Committee Appointed by Attorney General to Study Need for Legislation Affecting Children in District of Columbia, Including Drafts of New Juvenile Court Laws.* J1.1:914. Washington, D.C., 1915.

——. *White Slave Traffic Act.* J1.14/2:w58. Washington, D.C., 1910.

Department of Labor

Chidren's Bureau. Abbott, Edith, and Sophonisba Breckinridge. *Administration of Aid-to-Mothers Law in Illinois.* L5.13:7. Washington, D.C., 1921.

——. *Analysis and Tabular Summary of State Laws Relating to Jurisdiction in Children's Cases.* Chart Publication 17. Washington, D.C., 1930.

——. Bailey, William. *Children before Courts in Connecticut.* L5.7:6. Washington, D.C., 1918.

——. Bloodgood, Ruth. *Defective and Delinquent Classes: Federal Courts and the Delinquent Child, Study of Methods of Dealing with Children Who Have Violated Federal Laws*. L5.20:103. Washington, D.C., 1922.

——. Bogue, Mary. *Administration of Mothers' Aid in Ten Localities, with Special Reference to Health, Housing, Education, and Recreation*. L5.20:184. Washington, D.C., 1928.

——. Breckinridge, Sophonisba, and Helen Jeter. *Summary of Juvenile Court Legislation in United States*. L5.13:5. Washington, D.C., 1920.

——. Channing, Alice. *Alcoholism among Parents of Juvenile Delinquents: Study of Group of Delinquent Children Referred to Judge Foundation of Boston*. L5.2:A11. Washington, D.C., 1927.

——. Chute, Charles. *Probation in Children's Courts*. L5.7:11. Washington, D.C., 1921.

——. Claghorn, Kate Holladay. *Juvenile Delinquency in Rural New York*. L5.7:4. Washington, D.C., 1918.

——. *Community Care of Dependent, Delinquent, and Handicapped Children*. L5.22:7. Washington, D.C., 1926.

——. *Conference on Mothers' Pensions: Proceedings of Conference on Mothers' Pensions, Held under Auspices of Mothers Pensions Committee Family Division of National Conference of Social Work, and Children's Bureau, Providence, R.I.* L5.20:109. Washington, D.C., 1922.

——. Deardorff, Neva. *Extent of Child Dependency and Delinquency in 7 Pennsylvania Counties*. L5.2:C43/5. Washington, D.C., 1926.

——. Echman, Lutu. *Laws Relating to Mothers' Pension in United States Passed 1920–23*. L5.2:M85/2. Washington, D.C., 1924.

——. Echman, Lutu. *Tabular Summary of State Laws Relating to Public Aid to Children in Their Own Homes, in Effect Jan. 1, 1925, and Text of Laws of Certain States*. L5.21:3:2. Washington, D.C., 1925.

——. Flexner, Bernard, and Lenden Oppenheimer. *Legal Aspects of the Juvenile Court*. L5.20:99. Washington, D.C., 1922.

——. *From School to Work, What a State and Community Should Do to Protect Young Workers*. L5.22:6. Washington, D.C., 1926.

——. *From School to Work: Least a State and Community Should Do to Protect Young Workers*. L5.22/6/2. Washington, D.C., 1928.

——. Healy, William. *Practical Value of Scientific Study of Juvenile Delinquents*. L5.2:D37. Washington, D.C., 1922.

——. Jeter, Helen. *Chicago Juvenile Court*. L5.20:104. Washington, D.C., 1922.

——. *Juvenile Court Standards, Report of Committee Appointed by Children's Bureau, August, 1921, to Formulate Juvenile-Court Standards, Adopted by Conference Held under Auspices of Children's Bureau and National Probation Association*. L5.20:121. Washington, D.C., 1923.

——. *Juvenile Court Standards, Report of Committee Appointed by Children's Bureau, August 1921, Draft for Discussion at General Meeting Held under Auspices of Na-*

tional Probation Association and Children's Bureau. L5.2:J98. Washington, D.C., 1923.

———. *Juvenile Court Statistics, Tentative Plan for Uniform Reporting of Statistics of Delinquency, and Neglect*. L5.20:159. Washington, D.C., 1926.

———. *Juvenile Court Statistics, 1927, Based on Information Supplied by 42 Courts*. L5.20:195. Washington, D.C., 1929.

———. *Juvenile Court Statistics, 1928, Based on Information Supplied by 65 Courts, Second Annual Report*. L5.20:200. Washington, D.C., 1930.

———. Lenroot, Katharine F., and Emma O. Lundberg. *The Juvenile Court at Work, Study of Organization and Methods of Ten Courts*. L5.20:141. Washington, D.C., 1925.

———. Lundberg, Emma O. *Public Aid to Mothers with Dependent Children, Extent and Fundamental Principles*. Washington, D.C., 1926.

———. Rochester, Anna. *Juvenile Delinquency in Certain Countries at War, A Brief Review of Available Foreign Sources*. L5.20:39. Washington, D.C., 1918.

———. Thompson, Laura A. *Laws Relating to Mothers' Pensions in United States, Denmark, and New Zealand*. L5.20:7. Washington, D.C., 1914.

Women's Bureau. *Mothers' Pension Laws in United States*. L13.5:10. Washington, D.C., 1919.

———. *Mothers' Pensions Laws*. L13.6:6. Baltimore: A. Hoen, 1921.

Department of State

International Prison Commission. Barrows, Samuel J. *Children's Courts in United States, Their Origin, Development, and Results: Reports Prepared for Commission*. House Document 701. Washington, D.C., 1905.

Response to Resolution Concerning Repression of Trade in White Women. S1.6:909. Washington, D.C., 1909.

Department of the Treasury

Public Health Service. *The Case against Red Light Districts*. T27.20:54. Washington, D.C., 1920.

———. Ellis, Grace F. *High School Course in Physiology in Which Facts of Sex Are Taught*. T27.20:50. Washington, D.C., 1919.

———. *High Schools and Sex Education, Manual of Suggestions on Education Related to Sex*. T27.2:se9/1. Washington, D.C., 1922.

———. *Kentucky Conference of Educators: Subject: Sex Education in High School, Louisville, Ky., Dec. 1919*. T27.25:919/12. Washington, D.C., 1919.

———. *Need for Sex Instruction for Parents and Their Children*. T27.20:38/1. Washington, D.C., 1919.

———. *Need for Sex Education for Parents and Children.* T27.20:72. Washington, D.C., 1923.

———. *Northern Ohio Conference of Educators: Subject, Sex Education in High School, Cleveland, Ohio, Dec. 1919.* T27.25:919/10. Washington, D.C., 1919.

———. *Parents' Part in Providing Sex Instruction.* T27.20:32. Washington, D.C., 1919.

———. *Problems of Sex Education in Schools, with Selected Readings for Educators: Books on Sex Education.* T27.20:7/1. Washington, D.C., 1918.

———. *Psychiatric Studies of Delinquents.* T27.6/a:598. Washington, D.C., 1920.

———. *Sex Education in the Home.* T27.20:61. Washington, D.C., 1920.

———. *Sex Education in the Home.* T27.20:61/2. Washington, D.C., 1922.

———. *Sex Instruction: You and Your Boy.* T27.20:71. Washington, D.C., 1922.

———. *Symposium for Educators, Approach to Sex Education in High School, Preparation of Teachers to Use Sex for Character Education, Progress in Sex Education, Sex Education as Factor in Mental Hygiene, Role of Home and School in Sex Education.* T27.20:86. Washington, D.C., 1927.

———. *What Representative Citizens Think about Prostitution.* T27.20:66. Washington, D.C., 1921.

Treasurer of the United States. Andrews, Benjamin R. *Education for the Home.* I16.3:914/37. Washington, D.C., 1915.

———. *Report of Commission on National Aid to Vocational Education.* House Document 1004. Washington, D.C., 1914.

Department of War

Training Camp Activities Commission (1917–1918). Johnson, Bascom. *Next Steps, Program of Activities against Prostitution and Venereal Diseases for Communities Which Have Closed Their Red Light Districts.* W85.2:P94. Washington, D.C., 1918.

———. *Standard Forms of Laws for Repression of Prostitution, Control of Venereal Diseases, Establishment and Management of Reformatories for Women and Girls, and Suggestions for Laws Relating to Feeble-Minded Persons.* W85.2:L44. Washington, D.C., 1919.

MISCELLANEOUS

District of Columbia

2nd Annual Report of Juvenile Court, with Accompanying Papers. Senate Document 540. Washington, D.C., 1908.

4th Annual Report of Juvenile Court. Senate Document 683. Washington, D.C., 1910.

5th Annual Report of Juvenile Court. Senate Document 109. Washington, D.C., 1911.

6th Annual Report of Juvenile Court. House Document 913. Washington, D.C., 1912.

7th Annual Report of Juvenile Court. Senate Document 125. Washington, D.C., 1913.

Juvenile Court, and Removing Disabilities Resting upon Children Who Have Been Convicted of Crime in Juvenile Court, Hearing on H. 8348, Amending Act Relative to Juvenile Court in District of Columbia, and H. 9803, for Removing of Disabilities Resting upon Children Who Have Been Convicted of Crime in Juvenile Court. Y4.D63/1:J98. Washington, D.C., 1916.

Reports of Clerk and Chief Probation Officer of Juvenile Court, District of Columbia, for Two Years Ended June 30, 1917. House Document 1265. Washington, D.C., 1918.

Federal Board for Vocational Education

4th Annual Report of Federal Board for Vocational Education. VE1.1:920. Washington, D.C., 1920.

6th Annual Report of Federal Board for Vocational Education. VE1.1:922. Washington, D.C., 1922.

7th Annual Report of United States Employees' Compensation Commission. EC1.1:923. Washington, D.C., 1923.

8th Annual Report of Federal Board for Vocational Education. VE1.1:924. Washington, D.C., 1924.

10th Annual Report to Congress of Federal Board for Vocational Education, 1926. VE1.1:926. Washington, D.C., 1926.

Allen, Charles R., and Michael J. Kane. *Foremen Training Courses: 1. Foremen Training and Vocational Education Act, 2. Suggestive Schedule for 82 Foreman Meetings, 3. Need for Foreman Training, Some Past Difficulties, 4. Planning and Initiation of Foreman Training Courses, 5. Conducting Foreman Training Courses.* VE1.3:36 pt. 1. Washington, D.C., 1920.

Allen, Charles R., and C. F. Klinefelter. *Training of Foremen Conference Leaders: Suggestions as to Methods to be Followed and Types of Subject Matter Recommended by Committee of Experienced Conference Leaders.* VE1.3:125. Washington, D.C., 1927.

Bigelow, Zella E. *Survey of Needs in Field of Vocational Home Economics Education.* VE1.5:2/9. Washington, D.C., 1919.

Billington, R. V. *Employment Training in Civilian Vocational Rehabilitation: Definition, Characteristics, and Possibilities of Employment Training as Means of Effecting Rehabilitation of the Physically Disabled.* VE1.3:110. Washington, D.C., 1926.

Burdick, Anna Labor. *Trade and Industrial Education for Girls and Women: Pt. 1: Economic and Social Aspects of Vocational Education for Girls and Women, Pt. 2: Ways and Means of Establishing and Operating Program.* VE1.3:58. Washington, D.C., 1920.

Carris, Lewis H. *Trade and Industrial Education, Organization and Administration.* VE1.3:17. Washington, D.C., 1918.

Champan, Paul W. *Promoting Vocational Education in Agriculture, Guiding Principles in*

Planning Community Program of Promotional Work. VE1.3:97. Washington, D.C., 1925.

Charges against Federal Board for Vocational Education, Hearings. Y4.Ed8/2V85/7, vol. 1, parts 1–2. Washington, D.C., 1920.

Crandall, W. G. *Training of Teachers for Agriculture Evening Class Work: Statement of Experiences, Working Facilities, Operative Practice, and Procedure Relative to One Phase of Teacher Training.* VE1.3:120. Washington, D.C., 1928.

Elaton, Theodore H. *Principles in Making Vocational Courses of Study in Agriculture in High School: Objectives, Procedure, and Criteria to be Observed in Formulating Agricultural Part of Vocational Curriculum in High School.* VE1.3:98. Washington, D.C., 1925.

Franks, Edward T. *Waste in Human Energy and Cost of Untrained Youth.* VE1.2:In8. Washington, D.C., 1928.

Gifts to Vocational Education Board: Letter Transmitting Report of All Gifts and Donations Offered and Accepted by Board. Senate Document 244. Washington, D.C., 1920.

Humell, W. G. *Training of Teachers of Vocational Agriculture.* VE1.3:27. Washington, D.C., 1919.

Jacobs, Charles L. *Bibliography on Vocational Guidance, Selected List of Vocational Guidance References for Teachers.* VE1.3:66. Washington, D.C., 1921.

Lane, C. H. *Place of Vocational Agriculture in Present Agricultural Situation.* VE1.11:3. Washington, D.C., 1926.

Lathrop, Frank W. *Principles Underlying Distribution of Aid to Vocational Education in Agriculture, Bases of Apportioning Aid to Local Communities and Limiting Provisions under Which Aid Is Granted.* VE1.3.84. Washington, D.C., 1923.

Maltby, Robert D. *Supervised Practice in Agriculture, Including Home Projects, Aims and Values of Such Practice and Responsibilities of Pupils, Teachers, State Administrators, and Local Boards of Education.* VE1.3:112. Washington, D.C., 1926.

Myers, Charles Everett, *Effectiveness of Vocational Education in Agriculture, Study of Value of Vocational Instruction in Agriculture in Secondary Schools as Indicated by Occupational Distinction of Former Students.* VE1.3:82. Washington, D.C., 1923.

Plant and Equipment for Vocational Classes in Home Economics Intended for Use of Those Responsible for Determining Plant and Equipment for Vocational Schools and Classes. VE1.3:124. Washington, D.C., 1927.

Policies of Federal Board for Vocational Education, Approved Dec. 17, 1925, Rulings Relating to (1) Qualifications of Teacher Trainers, (2) Use of Federal Teacher-Training Funds for Salaries of Qualified Local Supervisors of Home Economics Education. VE1.2:p75/2. Washington, D.C., 1925.

Some Problems in State Supervision: State Supervision and Teacher Training, Professional Improvement of Teachers in Service. VE1.3:20. Washington, D.C., 1918.

Student Teaching in Agriculture, Training through Observation and Student Teaching in Land-Grant Colleges. VE1.3:100. Washington, D.C., 1925.

Supervised Practice in Agriculture, Aims and Values of Such Practice and Responsibilities of

Pupils, Teachers, State Administrators, and Local Boards of Education. VE1.3:83. Washington, D.C., 1923.

Supplemental Estimate of Appropriation, Federal Board for Vocational Education, Supplemental Estimate of Appropriation Required for Vocational Rehabilitation for Current Fiscal Year. House Document 631. Washington, D.C., 1920.

To Amend Act for Promotion of Vocational Education in Respect to Board Created Thereby, Hearings on H. 11724. Y4.Ed8/2:V85/5–2. Washington, D.C., 1920.

Training for Leadership in Trade and Industrial Education, Report of National Committee on Advanced Courses in Vocational Education; 1. Report of Committee on Training for Leadership in Vocational Education; 2. Report of Committee on Training for Leadership in Field of Trade and Industrial Education. VE1.3:114. Washington, D.C., 1927.

Training Administrators of Vocational Education, Report of National Committee on Advanced Courses in Vocational Education. VE1.3:141. Washington, D.C., 1930.

Interdepartmental Social Hygiene Board

United States Interdepartmental Social Hygiene Board, *General Analysis of Answers Given in 15,010 Case Records of Women and Girls Who Came to Attention of Field Workers of Interdepartmental Social Hygiene Board, and of Its Predecessors: War Department and Navy Department Commissions on Training-Camp Activities.* Y3.in8/2a:W842. Washington, D.C., 1921.

U.S. Commission on Industrial Relations

Final Report of the United States Commission on Industrial Relations; Report of Basil Manly; Report of John Commons, with Supplemental Statements by Commissioners Walsh, Lennon, O'Connell, Garretson, Weinstock and Ballard. Senate Document 19, Serial Set 6939. Washington, D.C., 1916.

State physical fitness legislation, 209
State physical fitness standards, 207–8
Steffens, Lincoln, 232
Stiles, Charles Wardell, 57–58, 62, 67
Stolz, Herbert, 89, 91–93, 97
Strother, French, 237, 240
Suitable home doctrine, 107, 126–27
Survey, 109, 113, 117, 225; criticism of "play
    trust," 192–93; and sex education, 177

Taft, William Howard, 218–19, 221, 225
Tarbell, Ida, 56, 219; *History of the Standard
    Oil Company,* 56; and Laboratory of Social
    Hygiene at Bedford Hills, 172–73
Tax Act of 1935, 5
Taylor, Graham, 141–42
Teachers' Insurance and Annuity Association
    of America, 19
Thom, Douglas, 87
Thymol, 62–63
Tuskegee Institute, 68, 69
Tuthill, Richard, 137

United Mine Workers of America, 227
University of Chicago, 82, 85, 122, 123,
    170

Van Kleeck, Mary, 25, 39
Van Waters, Miriam, 83–84, 90–91, 128; as
    referee of Los Angeles Juvenile Court,
    128, 150; reputation and influence, 150
Venereal disease: early-twentieth-century
    treatment of, 149–50, 178–81; and mar-
    riage law reform, 119–20
Villiard, Oswald Garrison, 73
Vincent, George, 3, 237
Vocational education, 42; and Country Life
    Commission, 41–43; and education for

rural South, 45–57; and farm demonstra-
    tions, 43–57; and philanthropy, 45–57,
    67–76; and "rural crisis," 41–43, 76–78;
    and U.S. Department of Agriculture, 45–
    57

Walker, Sydnor, 93, 238, 241–42; and juve-
    nile courts, 152–53
Walsh, Frank, 224, 225–26; and Colorado
    Fuel and Iron Company, 228; and hearings
    of the Commission on Industrial Rela-
    tions, 228–32
Walsh Commission. *See* Commission on In-
    dustrial Relations
Warburg, Paul, 168
Watson, John, 82, 83, 87; and behaviorism,
    83–88, 91–94
Welch, William, 169, 176, 179
Welfare reform, and Russell Sage Founda-
    tion, 117–27
White House Conference on Child Health
    and Protection (1930), 129, 130, 154–58
"White Slave" Grand Jury, 163–68, 189
Wilbur, Ray Lyman, 155
Wilson, James, 47
Wilson, Woodrow, 52, 225, 236
Women's Bureau (U.S.), 122, 267
Woodson, Carter, 71–72
World War I: and cost of living escalation,
    114; and impact on public policy of U.S.
    Army standards for fitness, 209–10; im-
    pact on Report of Commission on Indus-
    trial Relations, 234; and postwar "farm
    depression," 77; and Rockefeller Founda-
    tion's aid to Commission on Training
    Camp Activities, 200

Yerkes, Robert, 182

Library of Congress Cataloging-in-Publication Data

Sealander, Judith.
Private wealth and public life : foundation philanthropy and the reshaping of American
social policy from the Progressive Era to the New Deal / Judith Sealander.
    p.   cm.
  Includes bibliographical references and index.
  ISBN 0-8018-5460-1 (alk. paper)
   1. Endowments—United States—History—20th century.   2. United States—Social
policy.   I. Title.
HV91.S3   1997
361.7'0973—dc20   96-41649
                                                   CIP